The Quest for Redemption

Comparative Cultural Studies

Ari Ofengenden, Series Editor

The series examines how cultural practices, especially contemporary creative media, both shape and themselves are shaped by current global developments such as the digitization of culture, virtual reality, global interconnectedness, increased people flows, transhumanism, environmental degradation, and new forms of subjectivities. We aim to publish manuscripts that cross disciplines and national borders in order to provide deep insights into these issues.

The Quest for Redemption: Central European Jewish Thought in Joseph Roth's Works

By Rares G. Piloiu

Purdue University Press
West Lafayette, Indiana

The saint lives in the world. He does not reject it.
—Max Brod, *Paganism, Christianity, Judaism: A Confession of Faith*

Cataloging-in-Publication Data is on file at the Library of Congress.

Paperback ISBN: 978-1-55753-830-7
ePub ISBN: 978-1-61249-550-7
ePDF ISBN: 978-1-61249-549-1

Cover image: ©Yvette Depaepe

Contents

Avant-Propos

The argument for writing a study on Joseph Roth has first of all a personal motivation. I was born and raised in Eastern Europe, and my family roots reach into the multicultural world of the former Habsburg Empire, a world that constitutes the background for much of Roth's work. Spending holidays with my mother's side of the family in Transylvania, I grew accustomed to hearing a mélange of languages, including Romanian, Hungarian, and German, imperceptibly melting into each other as the need required in a harmonious coexistence of what later I understood to be the specificity of *Mitteleuropa*. I would not want to idealize this notion, whose historical avatars carry an ambiguous legacy, but I do want to draw on my personal interest for it, an interest stimulated in part by personal experience and in part by literary experience. Crossing the Carpathians each summer and winter had something ritualistic and purifying about it, and this was not simply due to the sacred nature of the religious holidays that marked my childhood visits into Transylvania or to the warmth of our family's reunions. There was something objective about it that I could feel while still on the train, a type of permanence embedded in the mild rolling hills of the countryside, in the almost dull reappearance of similar towns and villages densely built around ancient church steeples, and in the obstinately slow rhythm in which everything seemed to move. For me, as for a Hans Castorp of another era and geographical location, crossing the Carpathians from the flatlands was like moving from an ugly and omnipresent history (it was, after all, Nicolae Ceausescu's 1980s Romania) to a place outside of history, a magical realm under the rule of eternity. There, more powerful than history, tradition left its indelible mark on everything. Later in life as I read Roth's novels of Austrian inspiration of the 1930s, I could almost immediately relate to his fascination with the permanence of the Habsburg world at a time when history had started to show its hideous and inhumane face. His recollection of the smells, sounds, and sights that repeated themselves in a dizzying kaleidoscope everywhere one went awoke in me similar feelings of familiarity and reassurance. If cultures have a spirit of their own that defies politics, history, and territorial partitions, as the Hungarian Jewish writer György Konrád claims, then the spirit of Central Europe that Roth depicted in his writings was definitely the same one that marked some of my strongest childhood memories.

The image of Central Europe that emerges from the works of other authors who influenced me, such as Ingeborg Bachmann, Milan Kundera, and Peter Esterházy, is also, as I later learned, influenced significantly by Roth's fiction. The indebtedness of many modern Central European writers (and not only European if one takes into consideration the admissions of Nadine Gordimer and J. M. Coetzee) to Roth's nostalgic depiction of imperial Austria reinforced my curiosity about Roth, especially the fact that his work took on a distinct political meaning in the 1970s and 1980s. In the years succeeding the defeat of the Prague Spring of 1968, the phrase "Central European literature" represented an intellectual protest against a grim historical reality dictated by the stern partition of Europe between West and East. At the same time, the tragedy of Central Europe, which Kundera decried in his famous 1984 article, started to be associated with the tragedy of Central European Jews, of which the Austrian Joseph Roth was one. Kundera, but also Konrád, saw in the Central European Jewish cultural model the embodiment of everything Central Europe stood for: tolerance, tradition, moderation, and respect for culture and education. Reviving the memory of that Jewish world, a world vanished in the tumult of a murderous and impatient history, became synonymous with restoring the memory of that part of Europe that was too easily wiped out in the conflict between the western and the eastern parts of the continent. In the politically charged atmosphere of the 1980s, Central Europe even represented for some an alternative to the political divisions between East and West, the culture of peace and denuclearization, and the end of ideologies. I later realized that assigning Central Europe a quasi-utopian role, mediating between the spirit of the West (technology) and that of the East (ideology), was not a new trope. Roth had also depicted Habsburg Austria as well as the traditional life of Central European Jewry in utopian colors in order to create an alternative to what during the 1920s and 1930s appeared to be the irreconcilable forces confronting each other in Europe: on the one hand the bourgeois individualist model and on the other hand the fascist and communist collectivist one. Like many Jewish intellectuals of his time, Roth was interested in articulating an idea of redemption that allowed the Jewish identity and the modern human condition in general to reconcile themselves with a tragic history and even to sow the seeds of a future emancipation.

The search for redemption carried out by an entire generation of Central European Jewish intellectuals who came of age in the first quarter of the twentieth century represents one of the major paradigms within which modern Jewish intellectual history manifested itself. This search testifies to not only the historical difficulties encountered by European Jews at the time of a crucial moment in their history but also the synthetic power of their political imagination, their central locality within the German culture, and their revaluation of the Judaic religious heritage that their parents' generation had almost forgotten. Roth dedicated his energy and literary imagination to developing this idea of redemption. In more than fifteen novels and countless journal articles, essays, and short stories he addresses some of the thorniest problems encountered by the modern individual, from political disillusionment to moral paralysis and from social estrangement to historical dissolution. For Roth, as for many members of his generation, the solution to even the most mundane problems lies in a profoundly moral, quasi-religious relation with the world, which he tries to reconstruct piece by piece starting from the negative consciousness of the redemptive dimension of human existence to its positive, unequivocal affirmation. His social, religious-existentialist, and historical novels reassert in one form or another the necessity for a reunification of *Weltgeschichte* and *Heilsgeschichte*, making redemption part of everyday existence and imparting to history the hope of spiritual deliverance. By revisiting the Chasidic tradition, Roth unites the apparently contradictory notions of tradition and innovation, faith and reason, salvation and history. It is through this synthesis made possible by the idea of redemption that one can comprehend Roth's many paradoxes, including the coexistence of socialism and conservatism, of his radical individualism and collective traditionalism and of his anarchism and stoicism, which represent so many puzzles for numerous interpreters who often speak of Roth's "contradictions," "paradoxes," and "ambivalence."

This study is a revised, updated, and extended version of my doctoral thesis, written at the State University of New York at Buffalo in 2006. I am indebted to Professors Henry Sussman, Rodolphe Gasché, and Georg Iggers for their helpful guidance and continued encouragement. I also want to thank OhioLink for offering access to an unparalleled wealth of bibliographic sources and Otterbein University for its continued support of my research. This study is dedicated to my family for their love and devoted support.

Introduction

The Judaic Dimension of Redemption in Roth's Work and a Brief Review of the Relevant Secondary Literature

While much is known about Roth's complex relationship with the Jewish identity and with Judaism, little is known about his connection with the intellectual universe of the Central European Jews who came of age in the first decades of the twentieth century and who, although raised in assimilated middle-class families, grew increasingly disenchanted with the secular, rationalist, and individualist project of assimilation adopted by the Jews in the nineteenth century. Unlike their parents, these intellectuals returned to traditional—particularly Eastern—Judaic spirituality in order to find solutions to the deadlocks of not only modern Jewish identity but also modern subjectivity in general. The generation's reawakened interest in Judaism and Jewish issues even led Martin Buber to talk of a "Jewish Renaissance" in the first half of the twentieth century, as Paul Mendes-Flohr points out (*German Jews* 57). Although a heterogeneous group politically and intellectually, "their thinking took shape around the Jewish (Kabbalistic) idea of *tikkun*, a polysemic term for *redemption* (*Erlösung*), restoration, reparation, reformation and the recovery of lost harmony" (Löwy 2). Michael Löwy refers to this generation as a "generation of dreamers and utopians" that includes figures as diverse as Gustav Landauer, Franz Kafka, Gershom Scholem, Georg Lukács, Martin Buber, Walter Benjamin, Franz Rosenzweig, Ernst Toller, Ernst Bloch, Max Brod, and Leo Löwenthal. The present study articulates the nexus between Joseph Roth's work and this generation's preoccupation with the idea of redemption in order to demonstrate that Roth's constant search for the restoration of a unified identity—individual or collective, Jewish or universal—is indebted to a rediscovered Judaic and, more specifically, Chasidic notion of redemption.

Placing Roth within a group of theoretical thinkers that included mostly philosophers but also theologians, sociologists, and literary critics is a bit problematic because of his avowed contempt for theory, especially for speculative thinking in the tradition of German idealist philosophy. Roth, the self-styled "practical" intellectual for whom writing was allegedly nothing more than a trade, preferred the company of like-minded people, including journalists, novelists, and historians. He avoided the theorists, intentionally overlooked their books, and in general did not appear to have too much time for lengthy speculations. In his busy, productive life Roth preferred the "Latin" clarity, the simple style, and the short and penetrating insight, so different from the German *Dichtung* tradition, and saw himself, in his critics' words, as a "one-off in German literature," as he declared in a 1927 letter to his French translator Félix Bertaux (*Joseph Roth: A Life* 105). Yet, Roth's fiction and nonfiction alike use the guise of simplicity in order to arrive at a lofty, spiritual purpose. This purpose, rarely asserted as such, is hinted at throughout Roth's entire work as the centerpiece around which revolve his social critique, his political convictions, his moral intuitions, and his meditations on history. It is the idea of redemption, which also attracted, albeit in a profoundly philosophical-speculative way, the other members of his generation. This intragenerational affinity for spiritual renovation, for a return to the religious roots of historical existence, and for the unification of the self and the world justifies Roth's treatment alongside the other theorists of the idea of redemption.

This notion of redemption presents itself in Roth's work as a solution to the profound crisis in which modernity—understood in a political, moral, and philosophical sense—plunged both the individual and society. Redemption promises the recovery of a long-forgotten meaningfulness by reuniting the religious and historical dimensions of existence, both in a private and communal sense. By revisiting the Judaic idea of salvation as a mystical conjunction of divine miraculous intervention and individual effort, Roth offers a counterbalance to the excessive reliance on human reason in defining the role of the individual in the modern world. At the same time, his view of redemption does not simply mark a return to the premodern ethos of collective religious traditions. It creates instead an original and unconventional way of thinking about restoring the lost unity with the world by imagining the inherited, collective traditions as a living organism that keeps itself open to the spontaneity of individual variations. In a world torn apart by the individualism of the liberal-bourgeois traditions and by the collectivism of the rising tide of ethic and social populisms, as the European world was in the interwar years, the political dimension of redemption sought to arrive at an almost impossible synthesis of individual and collective as well as particular and universal identities. It is probably for this reason that although first formulated in the Central European intra-Jewish debates about the projects of assimilation and nation building, the idea of redemption acquires in Roth's work a universal character, reinforced by the belief that the historical experience of the Jews was not singular and instead was prototypical for the entirety of humankind.

Whether couched in the political concept of Utopia or considered in its moral-religious dimension, this particular idea of redemption is not the same as the Judaic idea of redemption and combines both religious and secular elements. Unlike traditional messianic thinking, it is not apocalyptical; that is, it does not promote a notion of redemption based on the obliteration of creation and the birth of an entirely new Kingdom of God. Instead, it is incorporated into creation in a manner that preserves its transcendent character but infuses it into history. In this manner, its secular, political, and moral aspects become an integral part of the redemptive process in which the humans play an active role. It is this notion of salvation in history and not outside of it that attracted both Roth and many of his contemporaries to the Chasidic idea of redemption and to Eastern Judaic spirituality in general. On the other hand, making redemption a historical event in which the individuals participate does not mean that salvation is a rational, planned, and guaranteed project. In that, it is different from what Northrop Frye calls a "rational" Utopia, one in which the mechanisms of salvation are rationally transparent, predictable, and clear.[1] To the contrary, its occurrence is sudden and unpredictable. It is primarily an event in the logic of the transcendent realm; its arrival is transformative because the world of history and creation is delivered through it from its corrupt condition. Thus, the religious, mystical character of redemption is preserved. The individual, however much involved in the fashioning of one's own salvation in history, cannot rely on morality and reason alone. He must resort to an attitude of religious beseeching of the Kingdom, to a hopeful expectation that it will come. The notion of redemption thus developed is simultaneously active and expectant: it motivates the individual to act in order to bring forth a promise made but not guaranteed.

Hence, the condition of possibility for redemption is the simultaneity of history and Utopia, of the real and the ideal. This unity, however, is dynamic and is relative to the individual ability to bring it into existence; in other words, it depends on the individual ability to transcend both the narrow confines of historical, rational existence and the chiliastic passion of the antihistorical eschaton. There is no possibility of redemption without the individual who takes up this task under the commandment of a yearning for renovation that is inscribed in the very creation as the desire to improve, to seek betterment. Inspired by this view of salvation in the here and now, Roth and his contemporaries emphasize the importance of the present moment in assuming the redemptive condition. The present is crucial in linking up the inherited past and the desired future into a whole that uplifts historical existence to the transcendent realm, while also preserving its concrete, mundane form. As a result of this fusion, an exchange takes place between that which was inherited and that which is desired: we are not simply the passive receivers of a given past, just as we are not totally autonomous in regard to shaping our future however we want. Instead, we have the moral ability to infuse a redemptive expectation into what we inherit from the past while also informing our future expectation with the genetic makeup of the inherited past, so to speak. Thus for Roth, the order of redemption allows for a shift in understanding both the past and the future: instead of a passively inherited past and an actively desired future, it proposes a "desired" past shaped by the moral demand for redemption and an "inherited" future influenced by the legacy of the past.

Therefore, history acquires a unique status in the tradition of early twentieth-century Central European Jewish thinking, including in Roth's own writing. This is because the concept of redemption places at its center the surpassing of the opposition between the restorative and prospective character of salvation, by virtue of which future deliverance is relative to a restitution of the past mediated through the values of the present. History, understood as the repository of the valuable tradition that needs to be actualized in the utopian hope for salvation, represents for Roth no longer a strictly descriptive science of irreversible events. Instead, it becomes intricately knit into the normative selection and modeling that the present requires in order to answer the demands expressed by its hope for future redemption. By not extricating salvation from history (as traditional utopians and mystics but also historians, albeit for the opposite reasons, have done) and instead making it into a principle of historical development thanks to its capacity to mobilize the individual toward the attainment of the promised renewal, redemption becomes for Roth synonymous with the temporal meaningfulness of human existence.

Roth's quest for redemption is also a quest for a synthetic principle capable of harmonizing contradictory notions, such as history and Utopia, past and future, action and expectation, certainty and possibility. The space in which redemption unfolds, at the intersection of conceptually opposing terms, requires an unconventional understanding of notions such as individual and collective identity, or society and history. It is a particularity of Roth's own writing that certain realities take on both a historical, real but also figurative, allegorical sense. His use of certain literary loci, such as the East European Jew, Austria, or Germany, is often allegorical, symbolizing higher notions, such as salvation, memory, or damnation, but at the same time denotative, explicating historically concrete social and political situations. This bifocal perspective on reality can only be explained circularly: in building the conditions of possibility for surmounting the opposition between reality and imagination, Roth's logic of redemption treats them already as the same thing. Because of its totalizing character, the idea of redemption has no moment of inception: it was always already there, acting retrospectively. One has to take a leap of faith in order to see it. It is probably for this reason that many critics have such a hard time placing Roth's literary world in a temporal or narrative category: it is simultaneously "no longer" and "not yet," actual and possible, historical and utopian, real and fictional.

Although the notion of redemption developed by Roth's generation has not been addressed in a unitary fashion in the Roth scholarship, there are studies that touch on separate aspects of this problem. In her 1984 *Von der Würde des Unscheinbaren: Sinnerfahrung bei Joseph Roth* (*On the Grandeur of the Inconspicuous: The Experience of Meaning in Joseph Roth's Work*), Esther Steinmann demonstrates the connection between Roth's religious imagination and the Chasidic religious experience, an experience characterized by an ambiguous combination of conservative tradition and messianic expectation, but she relegates this aspect to Roth's theological affinities with Judaism and not to a larger movement of Judaic renaissance rooted in the notion of renovation and redemption. Two decades later in 2004, Almuth Hammer analyzed in her study *Erwählung erinnern: Literatur als Medium jüdischen Selbstverständnisses* (*Remembering Divine Election: Literature as a Medium of Jewish Self-Identity*) the issue of Roth's generation's return to Judaic traditions, pointing out that this return should be interpreted not as an embrace of the actual Judaic traditions but instead as an interpretation of tradition in the context of modernity ("im Kontext der Moderne") (208).[2] However, Hammer fails to provide a detailed explanation of this process with convincing evidence drawn from Roth's work itself, instead devoting most of her study to an analysis of the abstract dialectical relationship between modernity and tradition.

Although Roth's messianic imagination and his interest in a religious reformulation of the idea of Utopia have been mentioned, albeit in passing, by some critics, such as Markus May and Bernd Oei, not all believe that Roth's fiction points to a better world, a Utopia to be found either in fiction or at the end of all times. Wolfgang Müller-Funk, for instance, argues that for Roth "Messianismus . . . eher fremd war" 'Messianism was rather alien' (*Joseph Roth* 195). Instead, Roth appears to these critics as a disenchanted, skeptical, and antiutopian writer for whom no other world is possible except in death or, ironically, in fiction, as Blanke, Hüppauf, and Butler argue. There are also interpreters who place Roth's messianism in the context of his hostility toward the historical present and toward modernity in order to demonstrate that for Roth redemption is possible only through the negation of reality, "die Erlösung aus dem Exil der Geschichte" 'the redemption from the exile of history' (Sebald 91). The drive toward permanence, toward tradition, is understood by these interpreters as a push outside history and into the past. Even when redemption is anticipated as something yet to happen, it is often seen as a restoration of an old order, of a golden age, a "backward-looking Utopia" (*rückwärts gewandte Utopie*), as Martha Wörschnig, drawing on Ernst Bloch or possibly on a 1930 Stefan Zweig review of Roth's novel *Hiob* (*Job*), memorably put it (90). However, what these critics fail to account for is Roth's persistent interest in the future-oriented correction of the state of the modern world through a "here and now" solution. The pull of the mythical past is counterbalanced by a counterforce in the opposite direction, toward the future, the present acting like the fulcrum. As the present study demonstrates, this present is the time of redemption. Not only Roth but also other thinkers of his generation, such as Rosenzweig, Benjamin, Bloch, and Buber, have been equally captivated by the power of the present to offer solutions, echoing thus—in a secular fashion—the Chasidic idea of redemption as an event of everyday existence. It should be noted that Fritz Hackert is nonetheless one of the first critics to mention, although briefly, the tight connection between Roth's religious imagination and his penchant toward fabulous writing and Chasidism.

Probably the critic who stands most closely to the present study is Claudio Magris, whose monograph *Lontano da dove*, widely available in its German translation as *Weit von wo* (*Away from Where*), elaborates most convincingly Roth's connection with the Chasidic world and with Martin Buber's philosophy. Magris emphasizes Roth's constant dialogue with a Chasidic storytelling and mystical tradition, one that is fundamentally skeptical about history but also about the possibility of a final, firm absolution from history. In this respect, Magris argues, Roth comes close to Yiddish literature, which finds a refuge from history in tradition, in the world of the shtetl, albeit a fictional refuge. For Roth, the function of literature is to create a space in which both the organic connection with the traditional world and the fulfillment of the individual desire to exist in history coexist harmoniously, a space of ambivalence that opens up the realm of possibilities beyond the constraints of place and time. Roth's predilection for the parable, for a form of storytelling that transcends the coordinates of the fictional chronotope, stems, Magris contends, from his affinity with the Chasidic tale, whose role is to transfigure reality into the realm of the possible (267).

In Magris's view, Roth's indebtedness to Chasidism resides in his "geschichtsfeindliche, religiöse Individualismus" 'antihistorical religious individualism' (287). In this sense, even Roth's emphasis on classicism and nobility are an expression of a typical Jewish rejection of history, which is always seen as a history of decay and of exile. This explains why the position outside of history, the melancholy contemplation, comes naturally to Roth, who consciously chooses "der Standpunkt 'außerhalb'" 'the "external" point of view' or "der Standpunkt der Metageschichte des 'Golus', des jüdischen Exils" 'the metahistorical point of view of the "Golus," of the Jewish exile' (91). From this position, the flow of history appears as a narrative of decay and defeat, similar to Benjamin's view. Magris points out, however, that Roth does not either share or oppose Benjamin's messianic impulse in his evaluation of history. If Utopia appears anywhere, it is in the form of the "Utopie einer Vergangenheit" 'Utopia of a past' that cannot replace the present anymore of a "Mythos des Nicht-mehr-Möglichen" 'Myth of the no-longer-possible' (20).

On the other hand, Magris demonstrates how important life in the present and the joys of simple existence are for Roth, as if to counterbalance the drive outside of history into myth. This attitude finds its expression in the Chasidic pietas: "Freude anstatt des erlösenden Leids, Demut statt der titanischen Utopie" 'Joy instead expiatory suffering, humility instead of titanic Utopia' (179). Magris emphasizes the fact that Roth rejects the apocalyptical Messiah of the hereafter and embraces the "here and now" of everyday life in the destinies of the common people such as Mendel Singer of *Hiob*, who was a "simple man." The redemptive act, Magris argues, is in the catharsis of storytelling itself, which unites the storyteller and the audience, as the Chasidic tradition suggests (180). He insists that Roth manages to achieve in the realm of literature the apparently impossible synthesis between the escape from the misery of history and the return to history as the inevitable condition of everyday humanity.

And yet for Magris, Roth's search for redemption rests solely in the realm of literature. It is a fictional construct that is unavoidably bound to the melancholy of the absence of reality, a literary strategy to survive the disaster of history. However, given how complexly intertwined Roth's notions of literature and reality are, it is hard to circumscribe Roth's world entirely to the realm of the imagination. For him, the fictional world is real to the same extent that all reality is just a fictional projection. His own empirical self-staging (*Selbstinszenierung*) bears testimony to the fact that he made a conscious effort to treat his created world as real, to bring it down to earth. For this reason, the idea of redemption needs to be considered in its capacity to reconcile these contradictions and provide a solution to the conflict between reality and fiction upon which Magris's argument is predicated. By understanding that the idea of redemption as "restoration, reparation, reformation and the recovery of lost harmony," as Löwy puts it (2), encompasses the entirety of life, possible and real, it becomes apparent that its aim is to surmount the conflicts between history and Utopia, object and subject, past and future. From the point of view of redemption, the conventional opposition between fiction and reality has no meaning, being simply the result of a corrupt, fallen consciousness in need of renovation.

Naturally, this does not mean that this idea of redemption always has a direct application in real life, although many of its proponents would argue differently. Especially in the field of politics, the idea of a "recovery of lost harmony" raises many questions about its ability to find a concrete expression but also to avoid any ideological contagions with the ideologies of radical renovation of human nature that shaped the fate of the twentieth century. For this reason, the present study often points out that some of Roth's ideas indeed reside in the realm of the literary imagination. And yet, there is an immediate impact of the idea of redemption on reality and an appeal to the individual to alter one's relationship with the world. The crucial point of the philosophy of redemption discussed here is the reenthronement of the individual moral mind in history. Whether we are talking about Utopia, salvation, justice, or memory, the thinkers analyzed here emphasize the importance of reuniting the individual with the world, of obtaining that "encounter," that authentic relationship of which Buber speaks in *I and Thou*. And since any such deeper connection involves the "responsibility of an I for a You" (Buber, *I and Thou* 66), it follows that the individual must cease to delegate the responsibility for the world to ready-made, mechanistic categories of reason, politics, and religion and assume the moral responsibility for the world. Maybe this appeal to moral responsibility for the world is the practical message couched in the idea of redemption. Viewed in this light, Roth's work can be interpreted as a guide to a better world, as a call to responsibility and moral wakefulness in a modern era of individual disengagement from tradition and from the "countenance of the You" (Buber, *I and Thou* 92).

It is the purpose of the present study to demonstrate that Roth's idea of redemption is part of a larger generational effort to articulate a notion of redemption that can resolve the contradictions of modern consciousness and bring about an eon of harmony in all realms of life: political, epistemological, moral-religious, and psychological. It is also characteristic of the members of this generation that they found inspiration for this idea of redemption in the Judaic, especially Chasidic, concept of religious salvation as a messianism of everyday existence. By using this notion of salvation, these thinkers are able to pose the possibility of a Utopia of the here and the now, to redeem history but also to let it continue, to find a middle way between the messianic end of history and the unavoidably historical dimension of human existence. In this sense, the present work demonstrates precisely how this synthesis takes shape in Roth's work and how it relates to similar concepts formulated by other thinkers: Utopia, hope, redemption, this-worldly miracle.

Roth's Ambivalence, Its Critical Reception, and Some Observations of Methodological Nature

Writing a critical study devoted to Joseph Roth's work is, from the very beginning, an uphill battle. It is as if the work itself resists any attempts at clear-cut categorizations and conceptualizations, in spite of the fact that it remains accessible to a wide readership. As literary critic Marcel Reich-Ranicki once humorously remarked, "Ob er [Roth] es wollte oder nicht: Er hat es seinen Lesern immer leicht- und seinen Interpreten oft schwergemacht" 'Whether he [Roth] intended it or not, he always made it easy for his readers and hard for his critics' ("Die besten Romane von Joseph Roth"). A possible explanation for this interpretative difficulty might reside with Roth's own hostility toward literary criticism and theory in general, although he himself penned many literary reviews in the German-language press of the interwar years. As Soma Morgenstern recalls in his book of memoirs *Joseph Roths Flucht und Ende: Erinnerungen* (*Joseph Roth's Flight and End: Memoirs*), Roth was from very early on dismissive of Lukács's *Theory of the Novel*, of which he said he could read only two pages, and of Walter Benjamin and Ernst Bloch's philosophy, which to him seemed too "German" (80). How Roth conceived of literature is somewhat difficult to gauge, but based on a 1935 letter to his friend and compatriot Stefan Zweig, one might argue that writing was for Roth a very practical undertaking: "Writing is a terrestrial thing, and, from a 'metaphysical' vantage point, is in no way different from shoemaking" (*Joseph Roth: A Life* 433). As for reading literature, Roth did not make a secret out the fact that he did not see much point in it, especially for a writer. According to Géza von Cziffra's memoir *Der heilige Trinker: Erinnerungen an Joseph Roth* (*The Holy Drinker: Memories of Joseph Roth*), when asked about his literary tastes, Roth often quoted Karl Kraus's aphorism "Ein Dichter, der liest, ist wie ein Kellner, der ißt" 'a writer who reads is like a waiter who eats' (105).

And yet Roth consumed literature, reviewed it in the press of the time (he lived on the income from his journalism most of his adult life), and had clear opinions about what he liked and disliked. His admiration for French literature is well known, as exemplified by his opinion of Marcel Proust: "Bei Marcel Proust ist mir der Knopf aufgegangen" 'I had a revelation with Marcel Proust' (Morgenstern 103), while his dislike of German literature is also well documented. An illustration of this is provided by Morgenstern himself, who recalls in his memoir the details of the encounter between Roth and another great Austrian writer, Robert Musil. When Musil expressed admiration for the novel *Hiob* and for the authenticity of the main character, Mendel Singer, Roth replied caustically that this might be impressive for a "*goy*" such as Musil, not a Jew such as himself. As for his opinion of Musil, Roth quickly dismissed him as a "German" writer, too abstract and convoluted. How can the contradiction between Roth the practical writer who—allegedly—did not read other writers and Roth the corrosive and opinionated critic be explained? And how can we explain the fact that even Roth's harsh judgments changed depending on mood or context, as Morgenstern remembers: "Roth [ist] der einzige Schriftsteller . . . der jedem Gespräch über Literatur ausweicht, aber gern über Schriftsteller spricht und von einem zum andern Mal vergißt, wie er sie einschätzt" 'Roth [is] the only writer . . . who avoids any talk about literature but likes to talk about writers and forgets his opinion of them from one time to another' (81)? Critics have provided various, often conflicting explanations, but that is not uncommon for anyone undertaking an interpretation of Roth's work. These are just several instances of what many commentators have called Roth's structural "inconsistency" or "ambivalence," which is why any attempt at a systematical analysis of his work is bound to a partial, often relative validity. It is also the case with the present study. As Wendelin Schmidt-Dengler beautifully concludes in his analysis of Roth's reception in the literary history and with an allusion to Roth's study *Juden auf Wanderschaft* (*The Wandering Jews*), "Roths Werk ist in keinem Kapitel daheim; es ist auf der Wanderschaft" 'Roth's work does not reside in any chapter; it is on the move' (Schmidt-Dengler 32). But the difficulty of obtaining a unitary picture of Roth's work is not necessarily an inconvenience. The fact that it "resists interpretation" ("sich der Greifbarkeit entzieht") can be seen as a source of continued creativity and fresh explanations, "always compelling to new interpretations" ("immer zu neuer Formulierung zwingt" (Schmidt-Dengler 32).

The lack of critical consensus is augmented in Roth's case by the author's sinuous intellectual and historical trajectory and by his own ambiguous self-positioning in multiple contexts. The question "who was the real Joseph Roth?" is often and justifiably asked by a critical audience accustomed to modern, clear-cut, and unequivocal national, political, and religious identities, an audience for whom hybrid or context-bound identities are highly uncommon. Was Roth the Galician Jew, the German socialist, the Austrian legitimist, or the Catholic thinker? But this ambiguity cannot be said to be the result of temporal distance alone. To his contemporaries Roth was a puzzle as well, as demonstrated by the famous episode of Roth's funeral when, as David Bronsen explains in his seminal *Joseph Roth: Eine Biographie* (*Joseph Roth: A Biography*), Roth's friends gathered to pay their final respects: the monarchists and the communists, the Jews and the Catholics, each one claiming Roth as one of their own (602). There is plenty of evidence that Roth was aware of this ambiguity and that he even intentionally cultivated it. Whether he did it for artistic effect or indeed as the result of a form of self-understanding that transcended the traditional categories of the self is another matter of debate among the critics. Roth's own 1926 self-description as "a Frenchman from the East, a Humanist, a rationalist with religion, a Catholic with a Jewish intelligence, an actual revolutionary" bears testimony to the multiple facets of his identity, an identity that simultaneously puzzles and stimulates the imagination (*Joseph Roth: A Life* 88).

Still, this ambiguity might have been more easily bypassed by literary criticism had it been simply a question of personal identity and not so interlocked with Roth's literary work. But Roth stands out through the original (and almost postmodern) interweaving of private life, social persona, and auctorial self, as Peter Wilhelm Jansen points out: "Bei kaum einem anderen Romancier dieses Jahrhunderts sind Leben und Werk so eng mit einander verflochten, so dicht verzahnt" 'There is no other [twentieth-]century novelist for whom life and work are so closely intertwined, so tightly interlocked' ("Weltbezug und Erzählhaltung" 21). Moreover, the complex interconnections between Roth's fiction, journalism, and essayistic nonfiction make it doubly difficult to draw conclusions about realities that inhabit multiple, often shifting registers. First of all, as Reinhard Baumgart observes, "fast alles, was er geschrieben hat, ob Reisebericht, Polemik oder erzählende Prosa, bleibt immer durchsichtig auf den, der schreibt" 'the author [Roth] remains visible in almost everything he wrote, whether travel report, polemic, or narrative prose' ("Drei Ansichten" 330). There is an intentional presence of Roth's personal voice in almost everything he writes, and the reason for this is that he sees literature in a very practical sense, as a tool used by the author to touch, to entertain, but also to awaken the moral instincts of the reader. Not only does Roth's personal voice speak often in his fiction, breaking down the barriers between author and narrator, but this voice itself is also somehow "fictionalized," staged, so that the author himself becomes in a way another character. According to Thomas Bauer, Roth selects which auctorial voice he makes present in his fiction depending on which self-identification he chooses: "Wenn man Roth liest, liest man, wie er sich in das, was er schreibt, einmischt und welches Konzept von Persönlichkeit er einmischt" 'In reading Roth, one reads how he interferes with what he writes and what concept of personality he mixes in' (445).

In addition to allowing his personal voice and biographical details to transpire in his fiction, Roth also "fictionalizes" his own life to the point where reality becomes hardly distinguishable from story. In this sense, Steinmann is right to argue that "Roth [sah] auch sein eigenes Leben als Legende, in dem Dichtung und Wahrheit, Fiktion und Wirklichkeit ununterscheidbar ineinanderflossen" 'Roth saw his own life as a legend as well, in which literature and truth, fiction and reality undistinguishably coalesced' (". . . ein Mann von Ehre" 59). As his biographer David Bronsen points out, Roth's own autobiographical accounts were a mix of fiction and reality in the sense that Roth always tried to create partially fictive narratives around his life, origins, and family. He tried to cast himself as a character in his own life, so to speak, which explains why some aspects of his biography are not clear to this day. There exist several accounts, sometimes contradictory, that testify to the author's mythomaniacal tendencies (*Joseph Roth: Eine Biographie* 487). As Hermann Linden writes,

> Joseph Roth trug im Leben viele Masken. Gerne erschien er als Realist, als Skeptiker, ja sogar als arroganter Zyniker. Auch sahen wir ihn, der zuerst ganz links stand, später rechts, sahen ihn, als Monarchisten, vorübergehend sogar im Banne des Katholizismus, als Demütigen, Traditionsgläubigen, und am Ende seines Lebens sehen wir ihn wieder in der Maske des Anfangs. ("Tage mit Joseph Roth" 103)

> Joseph Roth wore many masks in life. He liked to act as a realist, as a skeptic, even as an arrogant cynic. We also saw him first quite on the left, then on the right, then as monarchist, temporarily even under the spell of Catholicism, wearing the mask of humility and traditionalism, and at the end of his life we see him once again wearing the mask of the beginning.

While many agree that Roth wore many masks, the question about the justification of his masquerading still remains a matter of dispute. Is it, as Katharina Ochse points out, the expression of Roth's own ambiguous dealing with his identity as a Jew living in an anti-Semitic environment? Or is it an instance of creativity that stretches beyond the literary realm, as is suggested through Jansen's idea of "autofiction" (*Autofiktion*), according to which Roth creates a fictional universe that he subsequently assumes to be real? Jansen explains this process as a form of fictional identity constitution that bears in turn upon the constitution of fiction itself, since "die Erfüllung des Ich . . . nicht tatsächlich sein kann und nur möglich ist im Fiktiven" 'the fulfillment of the ego . . . cannot happen in reality and is possible only in the fictional world' ("Der autofiktive Ezähler" 372). For Wolfgang Müller-Funk, the existence of a circularity between Roth's biography and his fiction brings evidence to his work being autoreferential ("selbstbezüglich") rather than mimetic ("mimetisch") (*Joseph Roth* 30). As a result of this autoreferentiality, there is no clear distinction between fictional and nonfictional reality, which explains why for Roth literary concepts such as documentary writing and fictional writing (*Dichtung*) have no meaning. By rejecting the categories of literary theory, the distinctions between author and narrator, between objective reality and created reality, Roth reaffirms in the 1929 article "Es lebe der Dichter!" ("Long live the writer!") the pragmatic nature of literature: "Es gibt kein 'Gesetz,' keine 'Norm,' keine 'Regel.' Es gibt nur schlechte Autoren und gute" 'There is no "law," no "norm," no "rule." There are only bad and good authors' (*Werke* 3: 46).

The implications of Roth's original conception of fictional and empirical reality are also felt in the circularity of his fictional and nonfictional writing. If all observation of reality is already fictionalized, then all fiction bears in it a close connection with observable reality; it is, so to speak, documentary, argues Roth in "Es lebe der Dichter!": "Auch 'erfinden' heißt 'beobachten', gesteigertes 'Finden'. Es lebe der Dichter! Er ist immer 'dokumentarisch'!" 'Also "to invent" means "to observe," augmented "discovery." Long live the writer! He is always "documentary"!' (*Werke* 3: 46). As a result Roth takes great liberties with his journalistic, essayistic, and fictional writing, which he understands as a unitary endeavor or, in Jürgen Heizmann's words, as "das *eine, einzige* Buch, das seinen gesamten Kosmos enthält" 'the *one, the only* book, that contains his entire cosmos' (*Joseph Roth* 11). Ideas, characters, themes, situations, and sometimes entire sentences appear to migrate from nonfiction to fiction and then back into nonfiction but half fictionalized (Ochse 11). Words that belong to the reporter Roth appear in the mouths of his characters in the novels. As Reinhard Baumgart points out, "der Aggregatzustand 'Fiktion' lässt sich von dem Aggregatzustand 'Feuilleton' oder 'Reportage' in Roths Prosa durchaus nicht klar unterscheiden" 'in Roth's prose, the state of aggregation "fiction" is in no way clearly distinguishable from the state of aggregation "feuilleton" or "reportage"' (*Auferstehung* 44). The vast continuity in Austrian themes, characters, and issues among Roth's fictional works has even prompted Herman Kesten to refer to a veritable "*comédie autrichienne*" (101) similar to Balzac's *comédie humaine*. And yet in spite of these commonalities, Roth does not create a consistent whole, a fictional-documentary world without fissure. The characters may share the same names and the situations may seem identical from one work to another, but often a closer inspection reveals inconsistencies that question the very assumption of continuity or sameness. Roth frequently undermines realities that he himself creates, continuously challenging the reader's preconceived notions of identity, temporality, and causality. As Scheible observes, "der Konstruktion seiner 'comédie humaine' vermeidet Roth Erstarrung durch Eindeutigkeit" 'in the construction of his "comédie humaine," Roth avoids the immobility brought by unambiguousness' (*Joseph Roth: Mit einem Essay* 86).

Roth's ambivalent notion of identity is structural to his writing, for which reason his work does not lend itself very easily to categorizations or interpretations that employ the standard categories of the narrative discourse or genre theory. Categories such as author, narrator, and character, person and persona, or reality and fiction are ambiguously merged and constantly undermined, forcing the interpreter into constantly new territories. The novels lead to the feuilletons, the feuilletons to the biography, and the biography to letters and journalism and finally back to the novels. As Irmgard Wirtz notes, since the opposition between reality and fiction is not a point of departure in the interpretation of Roth's work, one should adopt a dialogical model of explanation, one that sees all the distinctive elements in a dialogue and relationship of mutual influence. She finds this approach particularly useful in the analysis of the relationship between Roth's early reports and his late historical fiction (118). The present study engages with Roth's work in a similar fashion. It makes use of various elements of his writings, including his novels, short stories, correspondence, reportage, polemics, reviews, and newspaper commentaries, in order to shed a new light on his fictional work. In doing this, it treats these elements as part of a literary whole that is, however, unstable and in constant need of contextual interpretation. This instability accounts for the methodological liberties that this study takes in the holistic treatment of Roth's fiction, nonfiction, and correspondence.

The present study is structured into five chapters: the first chapter, devoted to Roth's pivotal preoccupation with the idea of redemption in the context of a wider generational return to Judaism among the secular Jewish intellectuals of his time and focused mainly on his nonfictional writings; the second chapter, focused on the major early novels written before *Job* (*Perlefter*, written in 1929, is not treated here);[3] the third chapter, devoted to Roth's fiction of direct religious inspiration; the fourth chapter, which explores Roth's fiction of historical inspiration; and the fifth chapter, dealing with the particular case of the novel *The Tale of the 1002nd Night*. The idea of redemption is analyzed through its negative manifestations in the early novels; in its positive, explicit form in the late ones; and in its ironic form in the novel *The Tale of the 1002nd Night*. This study does not follow the stylistic convention of using the gender-neutral pronominal construction "he/she" for the simple reason that it may get in the way of comprehending an often abstract and difficult content. As a nonnative English speaker, I consider the use of the generic pronoun "he" less awkward, with the mention that the choice of "he" is purely conventional, being interchangeable with "she." For the most important sources in German I used existing translations when available, whereas for the sources of secondary importance and for those for which no translation is available I used my own translation.

Notes

1. "In such utopias the guide explains the structure of the society and thereby the significance of the behavior being observed. Hence, the behavior of society is presented as rationally motivated" (Frye, "Varieties" 323–47).
2. Unless otherwise noted, the translations from the original foreign language belong to the author.
3. *Perlefter* is not only unfinished but is also reconstructed from Roth's *Nachlass*. As Rosenfeld points out, the novel, first published in 1978, was reconstructed like a jigsaw puzzle from various fragments. For this reason, it lacks unity and reads more like an exercise in the technique of the literary portrait. Although Rosenfeld dismisses it as a "lusterless book" (*Understanding* 37), the portraits of the two main protagonists, Perlefter and Bidak, are wonderfully chiseled and can easily fit into any of Roth's major works.

Chapter 1

The Promise of Redemption and the Meaning of History: A Central European Jewish Synthesis

In order to understand the particular ethos of Roth's literary—fictional and nonfictional—thinking, it is important to situate him within a historical-biographical context. More important than the narrow, personal context of his intellectual and artistic development is the wider context of which Roth was part. Hailing from the then preponderantly Jewish small town of Brody, in eastern Galicia on the outskirts of Austria-Hungary, Roth grew up in a Jewish middle-class family, raised by his mother's side of the family. His father's exact origins and the circumstances of his separation from the rest of the family have been the subject of some speculation due in large part to Roth's own conflicting accounts (Sternburg 27). However, Roth's most important biographer, David Bronsen, maintains that Roth's father was a salesman who was forced to leave his family by an early onset of mental illness (*Joseph Roth: Eine Biographie* 42). His father's absence as well as the almost fated return later in Roth's life of mental illness through the person of his wife, Friedl, would affect Roth deeply and leave a mark on his literary work as well. Although he sometimes claimed to have had an underprivileged childhood, his biographers argue, relying on evidence of family accounts and pictures, that his mother ensured him a relatively sheltered life and offered him the educational opportunities that most middle-class Jewish children of the time enjoyed (Bronsen, *Joseph Roth: Eine Biographie* 57–58). In school the young Roth studied in German and was introduced to Hebrew, but at home he spoke Yiddish and German. Although his mother's side of the family was fairly assimilated, he was exposed early on to Orthodox Judaism through his maternal grandfather and had a connection to Chasidism through his father's side of the family. Later in life, Roth's declared affinity with this Eastern Jewish world would define his identity as a writer.

After graduating from high school in 1913, Roth began his studies at the University of Lemberg (Lviv), in the provincial capital, where he was exposed to the political conflicts dominating the Austrian world in the years preceding the outbreak of World War I. Lemberg at the time was one of the most important centers of Jewish urban life in Eastern Europe, but the city was also claimed by the other two major ethnic groups of the region, the Poles and the Ukrainians. Its ethnic diversity would later in 1924 make Roth characterize Lemberg as a "colorful speck" in Eastern Europe and a "kleine Filiale der großen Welt" 'small branch office of the wide world' (*Werke* 2: 286–87). The burgeoning nationalist movement increased the competition among these groups and polarized them in their attitude toward the central authority of the Austrian state. Separatists clashed with loyalists, and Roman Catholics clashed with Greek Catholics and the Jews (Bronsen, *Joseph Roth: Eine Biographie* 113). Within the Jewish community itself there were various groups competing for hegemony, including assimilated German-speaking representatives of the Haskalah tradition, Zionist nationalists, and also Orthodox and Chasidic Jews who had recently moved into the city from the eastern borderlands. Roth, who identified himself with the German culture at this point, was privy to all these clashes and even attended the 11th Zionist Congress in Vienna in 1913, although later in his career he would criticize the Zionist movement in extremely harsh terms. In 1914 Roth began his studies at the University of Vienna in the German department. The period between his arrival in Vienna and his departure in 1916 for the Eastern Front during World War I is a period of material struggles but also of great intellectual stimulation for the small-town young writer, who experienced the cosmopolitan atmosphere of Vienna even during a time of war mobilization (Bronsen, *Joseph Roth: Eine Biographie* 149).

Roth's image at the time was, in the eyes of his contemporaries, that of a person seeking assimilation into the German culture and Western society in general. David Bronsen reproduces in his Roth biography the words of Heinz Kindermann, a former assistant from the University of Vienna who remembers the young student Roth as an alacritous speaker of educated *Hochdeutsch*: "Unser Deutsch hatte einen wienerischen Klang, Roth dagegen sprach ein betontes Hochdeutsch" 'Our German had a Viennese ring to it, whereas Roth, to the contrary, spoke an emphatic High German' (*Joseph Roth: Eine Biographie* 133). Similarly, in Józef Wittlin's memories of the Viennese student Joseph Roth, the latter appears as a "Gigerl," a Viennese dandy from the middle-class stratum of the imperial administration, and not as a provincial Jew (18). Soma Morgenstern remembers Roth during the time in the same manner: "Er war damals sehr elegant gekleidet, fast stutzerhaft. Sein blondes Haar war in der Mitte gescheitelt, und er trug zum Erstaunen der kleinen Gruppe ein Monokel" 'He was very elegantly dressed back then, almost dandified. His blond hair was parted in the middle and, to the astonishment of our small group, he wore a monocle' (8). According to Morgenstern, Roth suffered occasionally from "Assimilitis" during that period, a term coined, ironically, by Roth himself (31). Roth's affected manners, his Germanic gesticulation and dandy elegance, so different from his later self-styled image as a modest Austrian Jew, a "Catholic with a Jewish intelligence," already sketch the portrait of a masquerader, as Linden characterizes him ("Tage mit Joseph Roth" 103). If Roth uses the mask of assimilation, even though in a somewhat caricatured fashion, to gain acceptance in cosmopolitan Vienna during his youth, he later employs the mask of the "authentic Eastern Jew" who rejects the artifice and foppishness of the West in order to profile himself against the assimilated German Jews.

Roth's relationship with his Jewish identity becomes more and more complex over time. If early on he displays only occasional concern for the Jewish dilemmas of his age, such as Jewish nationalism or assimilation, modernization or traditionalism, these topics begin to gain in importance throughout the 1920s, in parallel with his increasing critique of modern civilization. But even if Roth sees himself as an assimilated Jew, solidly anchored in the German language, culture, and traditions at the turn of the 1920s, he is still very much aware of the pervasive anti-Semitism dominating Central and Eastern Europe. Joining Alfred Polgar's Viennese newspaper *Der Neue Tag* (*The New Day*) at the end of the war, Roth begins to travel extensively throughout Europe and to document the life of the people in the aftermath of the war. In 1919 he reflects on the situation of the Jews in the disputed borderlands between Austria and Hungary and in Hungary proper, where the civil war was raging. He is deeply moved by the resilience of the Austrian Jews of Burgenland, who kept their traditions for centuries and were also accepted by the Gentiles, whose prejudice extended "only" to the Budapest Jews ("Die Juden von Deutsch-Kreuz und die Schweh-Khilles," *Werke* 1: 115). In Hungary, on the other hand, the generalized anti-Semitism, augmented by fear of the communist revolution, appalls him. "'Noch nie ist mit dem Namen Christi schändlicherer Mißbrauch getrieben worden als jetzt in Ungarn" 'Never before has the name of Christ been more shamefully misused as in Hungary now,' writes Roth in "Die Lage in Westungarn" ("The Situation in Western Hungary") (*Werke* 1: 136). On this occasion, he articulates a distinction between the medieval "naive" anti-Semitism of the Inquisition and the modern, racially substantiated, and politically manipulated anti-Semitism, a distinction that would later allow him to reconcile his admiration for Catholic Austria and his contempt for the National Socialists. But not only East European anti-Semitism, with its pogroms and collective violence, horrifies Roth. He begins relatively early to condemn German anti-Semitism as well, which he perceives to be more insidious although less violent. In articles such as "Deutschösterreich 1930" ("German Austria 1930") of 1919 and "Die reaktionären Akademiker" ("The Reactionary Academics") of 1920, he lampoons the nationalists (*Deutschnationalen*) in both their uneducated and academic varieties. The 1922 assassination of Weimar Republic foreign minister Walther Rathenau by a group of anti-Semitic German nationalists makes it clearer than ever for Roth that there is no hope for the Jews to be accepted in Germany. In the 1923 article "Vergebliche Ruhrpropaganda" ("Pointless Ruhr Propaganda"), Roth declares somberly that he feels no compassion with the plight of a defeated Germany, whose response to the French postwar occupation "bereitet Pogrome auf Juden vor" 'prepares pogroms of the Jews' (*Werke* 1: 978). Almost prophetically, he declares in the same article that the young German Weimar Republic is headed not toward the democratic "black-red-gold" but instead toward the despotic "schwarzweißrote und das Hakenkreuz" 'black-white-red and the Swastika' (979).

After Roth resettles in Berlin in 1920 and begins his collaboration with various German newspapers, such as *Neue Berliner Zeitung* (*New Berlin Gazette*), *Freie Deutsche Bühne* (*Free German Stage*), and *Berliner Börsen-Courier* (*Berlin Stock Exchange Courier*), his interest in the East European Jews starts to grow, bearing testimony to his changing attitude toward his own identity. His encounters with the Jews are telling of the compassion he feels for their stories of deracination and flight from war, poverty and prejudice. In the typical style of the feuilleton, with humor, empathy, and melancholy, Roth paints little vignettes of his encounters with various emblematic individuals and situations. If in 1919 he relates the story of a Jew who made it all the way to America but failed professionally and had to return to Vienna, destitute and forced to beg in order to make a living ("Interviews mit Strassentypen"), in 1920 he revisits the theme of the migrating Jews in an article titled "Flüchtlinge aus dem Osten" ("Refugees from the East"). In this article, Roth depicts the situation of the East European Jews migrating westward in search of a home but temporarily stuck in Berlin. He decries their wretched lot: impoverished, feared and hated by the local Germans, with loneliness as their only friend, they hope naively for a future that might only turn out to be illusory. Roth's increasing skepticism of Western, mostly American, technological society begins to play a role in his evaluation of the Jewish migration question and anticipates his later belief that Jews should avoid assimilation in the Western societies. Another article from 1920, titled "Der Tempel Salomonis in Berlin" ("Solomon's Temple in Berlin"), symbolically relates the case of a Polish Jew in Berlin who spent nine years building a miniature replica of Solomon's Temple out of cardboard. The Orthodox Jew's faith and almost childish desire to restore the glory of the destroyed Jerusalem Temple contrast in Roth's article with the indifference of a world that has lost its belief in a final redemption.

As the question of Jewish identity in a modernizing world becomes more and more central to Roth, leading eventually to his rejection of assimilation and professed belief in the necessity of a spiritual form of deliverance from the vagaries of history, it becomes important to situate him more clearly within a generation of Central European Jewish intellectuals who came of age during the first two decades of the twentieth century and struggled with the same questions, arriving, albeit by different ways, to similar conclusions. The common experience of this generation is that the project of assimilation, undertaken under the auspices of the Enlightenment in the nineteenth century, failed. Roth's own turn away from his German cultural identity, his growing awareness of the pervasiveness of anti-Semitism within the heart of the modern societies, and his subsequent search for a redemptive figure in the allegorized image of the Eastern Jew testify to his membership in this generation of disillusioned young Jewish intellectuals. But how did this generation, which was raised in assimilated homes and enjoyed a liberal education in the spirit of the German *Bildungsideal*, arrive at such a radical conclusion, and why did this generation seek drastic, revolutionary solutions to their predicament? To answer this question we need to go back a generation, at the end of the nineteenth century.

The Crisis of Jewish Assimilation in Central Europe: A Brief Historical Sketch

By the end of the nineteenth century, the life of the Central European Jewish intelligentsia started to undergo a massive transformation caused by at least three factors: the rise in anti-Semitism throughout Europe, where the Dreyfus Affair was just the culmination and confirmation of an increasing institutional and social anti-Semitism; the failure of the assimilation project undertaken in the aftermath of Jewish emancipation in Germany and Austria-Hungary in the second half of the nineteenth century; and the growing influence of neo-Romantic and antirationalist philosophies in the German-speaking world. As Michael Löwy explains in his study *Redemption and Utopia: Jewish Libertarian Thought in Central Europe*, the existence of a considerable socially uprooted Jewish intelligentsia in Central Europe at the turn of the last century was itself a testimony to the difficulties that the Jews were encountering in their process of assimilation in these modernizing states. Consisting primarily of the children of the average-educated yet well-off bourgeois strata of the large metropolitan areas of the region, this intelligentsia boasted a generation of intellectuals whose sole possibility of surmounting de facto social discriminations rested on securing positions of status achievable through an exceptional education and a high standard of qualification.[1]

Prisoners of a costly yet often impractical professional training (with a strong component in the humanities, which Hannah Arendt viewed as the generation's reanimation of the traditional Jewish contempt for practical pursuits and esteem for gratuitous learning),[2] the members of this intelligentsia experienced more agonizingly than the previous generation the reality of social alienation. That the promise of assimilation that still motivated the older generation of the Jewish bourgeoisie proved to be a failure soon became a matter-of-course reality for the young generation, who recognized, in Arendt's words, "how ambiguous [was] the freedom which emancipation has ensured, and how treacherous the promise of equality which assimilation held out" (*Jew as Pariah* 68). What this generation found very difficult to come to terms with was what they perceived to be the conformism and self-deception of their parents' generation, a generation still caught up in the equalitarian fantasies promised by a secular and humanist tradition with roots in Enlightenment, for whom the German language and culture guaranteed both political acceptance and assimilation into a distinguished European culture with exemplary exponents such as Goethe and Schiller.[3]

The "Jewish question" as a problem of identity and assimilation, which Arendt defines as a strictly Central European affair, made some adopt a more trenchant position in matters of social and cultural integration of the Jews. While pressing for the unambiguous acknowledgment of the anti-Semitic environment in which they lived, these young intellectuals also demanded a straightforward clarification of positions that would put an end to the harmful self-deception that one could be socially accepted *as a Jew* with secular and *national* loyalties. The author and publicist Moritz Goldstein made this position very clear in 1912: "Dir eben, trotz deines europäischen Gebarens und Aussehens, verzeiht man den Juden nicht. . . . [M]ögen wir uns immerhin ganz deutsch fühlen, die andern fühlen uns ganz undeutsch" 'Precisely to you, in spite of your European demeanor and appearance, they cannot forgive your Jewishness. . . . [N]o matter how German we may feel, the others feel us very un-German.' As for the Jews who refused to see this, "wir werden sie zwingen, sich als Juden zu bekennen oder sich taufen zu lassen" 'we shall force them to own up to their Jewishness or to get baptized' (Goldstein 286–87). Even Stefan Zweig, in his nostalgic and sympathetic attitude toward the liberal-bourgeois generation of his parents, admitted that the Austrian Jews' fiction of assimilation was based on the denial of reality: "little did they think in their touching liberalism and optimism that each succeeding day that dawns outside our window can smash our life" (27). For this young generation, the sobering reality of anti-Semitism signaled the end of the Enlightenment promise of assimilation: "Alle Hoffnungen, die mit liberalen und aufklärerischen Ideen der Gleichberechtigung in Verbindung gestanden waren, schienen zu zerbrechen, die Lebenskonzepte von Anpassung und Partizipation gefährdet" 'All the hopes that were connected with the liberal and Enlightenment ideas of equal rights appeared to shatter, and the principles of assimilation and participation endangered' (Lichtblau 39).

For the critics of assimilation, not only was the prospect of being assimilated as an ethnic Jew in a nation-state an illusion, but so was the idea that assimilation would be possible if the Jewish identity was seen as a purely religious one, similar to Christianity. They argued that those Jews who claimed that there was no such thing as a Jewish "people," only religious Jewish minorities within the German, Czech, or Hungarian nations, were mistakenly playing into the hands of those anti-Semites who denied the Jews their rights as both individuals and a collectivity. Max Brod attacked this tendency among the Jewish assimilationists in a 1920 article titled "Unsere Assimilanten," in which he argued that the liberal promise of assimilation was a ruse meant to treat the Jews as second-class citizens: "'Die Juden sind kein Volk' hört der Assimilant heraus und möchte dem 'Liberalen' vor Entzücken um den Hals fallen. . . . Da kriegt er den Tritt in den Hinteren" '"The Jews are not a people" hears out the supporter of assimilation and, enraptured, would like to fling his arms around the neck of the "liberals." . . . And he gets a kick in the rear' (*Im Kampf* 83). Almuth Hammer argues that this attempt to "confessionalize the Jews" according to a Christian model misunderstood or intentionally neglected the simultaneously ethnic and religious nature of Jewish identity. As a result, many Jews rejected the assimilationist idea that one can be only religiously a Jew as an attack on the Jewish identity itself (26).

The liberal-bourgeois environment of the Central European Jewish middle strata—with their highly respected values of education, assimilation, and patriotism, cultivating a rationalist approach to Judaism, an approach that gradually became a ritual purged of the archaic, Oriental, and mystical elements—collided head-on with the disillusioned sobriety of the young intelligentsia. A conflict that might have been only generational soon became an open confrontation concerning the very values and culture of the Central European Jews (Mosès 146). Leo Löwenthal described his generation's rejection of the bourgeois culture of the previous generations in an unequivocal manner: "My family household, as it were, was the symbol of everything I did not want—shoddy liberalism, shoddy *Aufklärung*, and double standards" (qtd. in Löwy 33). The same self-deceptive mentality—oblivious of the actual social and cultural disparities, paradoxically optimistic and insecure about the prospect of assimilation, cleansed of the traditional Jewish heritage and eager to adopt a fabricated identity—angered Franz Kafka, who called it a "petty, dirty, sly mentality" (qtd. in Arendt, "Introduction" 34). Similarly, Franz Rosenzweig, in search of a genuine "Jewish sphere" of life in German society, could not help decrying in a 1918 open letter to the famous German Jewish philosopher Hermann Cohen the assimilationist educational policies that had led to the abandonment of the distinctly Jewish character of Jewish public life during the previous three generations (*Zeit ists* 4). Not only had these policies estranged the Jews from their authentic relationship with their Judaic heritage, he argued, but they also failed in that the individual promise of emancipation was never fully achieved.

In his influential 1930 study of the unique psychological phenomenon known as "Jewish self-hatred" (*Der jüdische Selbsthaß*), Theodor Lessing denounced the self-deceptive Jewish pride over assimilation in Western societies. This assimilation came, he argued, at the price of Jewish spirituality, which was exchanged for an oppressive and inauthentic bourgeois respectability:

> Man pflegt überall zu preisen, was der Jude durch seinen Eintritt in die europäische Kultur und was Europa durch die Juden gewonnen habe. Aber man sieht es nicht oder man sagt es nur leise, um welchen Preis die Juden zu Europas Bürgern geworden sind: Durch den Verrat an den Gesichten ihrer Hoffnung. Durch das Opfer ihrer zeitlosen Träume. Heute wird das Volk nicht mehr von frommen Weisen gelenkt, sondern von Rechtsanwälten und Großbankiers organisiert. (55)

> People everywhere routinely praise what the Jew has gained by his entry into the European culture and what Europe has gained through the Jews. But nobody sees or whispers only at what price the Jews became European citizens: by betraying the visions of their hope. By sacrificing their timeless dreams. Today the Jewish people is no longer guided by pious wise men, but organized by lawyers and bankers.

The spirit of revolt against the bourgeois mentality made itself felt even in the case of very assimilated Jews, such as the Austrian writer Hugo von Hofmannsthal, himself the descendant of a long line of mixed Jewish-Catholic families. As Hermann Broch explains, Hofmannsthal's aristocratic rejection of the bourgeois culture of his family, his marriage to a Jewish woman (albeit one converted to Catholicism) for the first time in three generations, and his paradoxical literary "conservative" modernism were the expression of his confrontation with the reality of anti-Semitism and with the failure of assimilation that his ancestors had pursued through honorable careers, religious conversions, and even the acquisition of a nobility title (expressed in the "von" particle of the family name).[4] Hofmannsthal's literary inclination toward inaccessible, moral characters communicates a sense of estrangement and anxiety in the face of the modern mass society of the early twentieth century, a society driven by the passions of collective politics of national and ideological inspiration. The aristocracy of the value-creating art, Broch argues, allowed the isolated Jewish conscience to secure a place for itself in a disintegrating and vacuous world.

Stéphane Mosès pays particular attention to the intergenerational aspect of the revolt of the young Jewish intellectuals. It was not just a revolt against discrimination and isolation but also one against the fathers' and grandfathers' generations and their values. If Hofmannsthal affirmed a Jewish identity that his ancestors tried to dissolve, so did Kafka and, before him, Sigmund Freud, who revolted against their fathers' assimilation and estrangement from the Judaic traditions (Mosès 147). The typical assimilation story stretched over three generations, Mosès explains, with the grandfather leaving the shtetl for the big city, the father becoming secularized and sometimes even changing the last name to make the son's integration even easier, and the son rejecting all their assimilation efforts, in spite of the opportunities that they laid out for him. The sons' reawakened interest in Judaism, in Eastern Jewish spirituality, often at the cost of their parents' outrage, became commonplace at the time. Not only Kafka but also Gershom Scholem was attracted by the traditional East European Jewish world, this in spite of his parents' contempt for the "backwardness" of that world: "Je mehr wir in unseren eigenen assimilierten Familien auf Ablehnung ostjüdischer Art und Verachtung für alles, was Ostjuden und ihre Lebenswelt anging, stießen . . . , desto stärker zog uns gerade dieses Wesen an" 'the more repudiation of the Eastern Jewish type and contempt for everything that concerned the Eastern Jews and their environment we came across in our own assimilated families . . . , the more attractive this universe became to us' (Scholem qtd. in Kiefer 74).

Joseph Roth's case is somewhat atypical in this context because he represents, in a way, all of these three generations merged in a single person. If as an adolescent Roth left the Galician shtetl seeking acceptance and opportunity in Vienna, as a young adult he assimilated to the dress, language, and values of the German-speaking world and even claimed a German origin (Bronsen, *Joseph Roth: Eine Biographie* 32), only to return as a mature man to his Eastern Jewish roots, rejecting the Western world and the assimilationist ideals, although still maintaining an open admiration for Catholicism and the Austrian monarchy. It would be hard to speak in Roth's case of a revolt against father figures, since his own life was marked by the absence of such a figure and by the desire to obtain one, albeit figuratively, through the ideas of order and tradition. Sternburg even argues that Roth was a "father seeker" (*Vatersucher*) his whole life (29). Whether his rejection of assimilation was motivated, as Bronsen argues, by a certain form of self-hatred or disappointment with his own assimilation is still debatable (*Joseph Roth: Eine Biographie* 153). However, regardless of Roth's psychological motivations, it is evident that his opposition to the assimilationist model grew steadily throughout the 1920s and peaked during the 1930s. His articles and correspondence make progressively more references to several Jewish types that embody, in his opinion, the corrupt idea of assimilation: the successfully assimilated "Westerner," mostly in its American variety, the German nationalist Jew, the social democrat, and the Zionist. These types are contrasted with a different kind of Jewish identity: the East European poor, religious, humble, and stoic Jew who refuses assimilation to the Western world. Even in his first novels, Roth features East European Jews who either reject assimilation in the West or cannot find their place in it, such as Benjamin Lenz of *The Spider's Web* (1923) and Gabriel Dan of *Hotel Savoy* (1924).

But the issue of assimilation is for the first time treated in detail in Roth's 1927 study *The Wandering Jews*. In this study he analyzes the situation of the European Jews at the time, from the remote Russian shtetls to the modern Western urban centers of Western Europe and North America. Roth analyzes the deception of the Jews in their social contract with the Western world. While the Jews imagined that they would assimilate into an enlightened, liberal, and cultured society whose values they learned and cherished from early childhood, modern European society in fact regressed to a quasi-barbaric stage, abandoned its once defining tolerance and liberalism, and was governed by racial fear, suspicion, and hatred: "To the Eastern Jew, Germany, for example, remains the land of Goethe and Schiller, of the German poets, with whom every keen Jewish youth is far more conversant than our own swastika'd secondary school pupils" (*Wandering Jews* 6). Instead of receiving recognition and acceptance for their effort to assimilate, the Jews were rejected more than ever. Roth strikes here a similar note to Moritz Goldstein, who in his famous 1912 article "Deutsch-jüdischer Parnass" ("German-Jewish Parnassus") decries the same contrast between the exemplary cultural assimilation of the Jews and the Germans' refusal to grant them equal status: "die Aufgaben der Deutschen haben die Juden zu ihrer eignen Aufgabe gemacht. . . . *Wir Juden verwalten den geistigen Besitz eines Volkes, das uns die Berechtigung und die Fähigkeit dazu abspricht*" 'the Jews have made the Germans' mission into their own mission. . . . *We Jews manage the intellectual wealth of a nation that denies us the authority and the ability to do so*' (283). And yet, the more the failure of assimilation became visible, Roth argues, and the more unequivocal the rejection and hatred showed by the European societies, the less inclined the European Jews were to acknowledge the hopelessness of their situation and the irredeemable nature of European modern barbarity: "It is hard to avoid such a fate. And so, instead of running away from it, many decide to do the opposite" (*Wandering Jews* 8). Searching for ways to satisfy the whims of a political and cultural establishment that simultaneously accused the Jews of "cosmopolitanism" and "nationalism," of "separation" and "zealous integration," of "atheism" and "religious fanaticism," the European Jews turned the deceptive promise of assimilation into a mechanism of self-deception and endless justification of their humiliation: "They wander into deception, and the worst kind of deception at that—self-deception," writes Roth in the preface of the 1937 edition of *The Wandering Jews* (129).[5]

The self-deception of the Jews seeking assimilation was the more painful, Roth writes, the less interested they became in the political issues of their day or in their own traditions. Displaying an Olympian contempt for the rising tide of populist anti-Semitism and for the widening gap between the professed principles of European culture and their actual application, many Jews took refuge in the world of the arts, which in the classical German tradition was considered to provide a better reflection of reality than reality itself, because its truth was unadulterated by the mundane logic of politics.[6] Self-appointed guardians of the European cultural heritage, the assimilated Jews engaged in an activity of lofty cultural production and promotion that ensured the survival of the old European ideals of high culture at a time when the continent was swept by the vulgarity of modern mass politics. This type of activity, sometimes carried out without a critical distance, bound the Jews to a European world of artificial values that replaced their own authentic relationship with Judaism, contends Roth in his 1933 article "The Auto-da-Fé of the Mind": "They felt entitled to take out a lease on 'German civilization' . . . undiscriminating as they had become, *novarum rerum cupidissimi*, to admire every version of corruption in literature, in the visual arts, in the theater, because they had forgotten Jehovah" (*What I Saw* 211).

Roth's indictment of the Jews' infatuation with the German *Bildungsideal* and the idea of *Kulturnation* at the expense of their own identity is typical for the entire generation of Jewish intellectuals who, "caught between the [dying] Empire and the emerging nations" (Rupnik 254), witnessed the betrayal of both the old liberal promise of assimilation and the new promise of national recognition. Searching for a genuine Jewish identity, they turned against the principles of Enlightenment that until then had constituted the formal gateway through which the integration of the Jews was considered possible.[7] Roth's admonition to the European Jews to return to Yahweh is consistent with the intragenerational call to rediscover the essence of Judaism, its authentic core. It is true that Leo Baeck had already taken up the task of envisioning an "essence" of Judaism in his 1905 book *The Essence of Judaism* (*Das Wesen des Judentums*), but he approached the issue in the spirit of the nineteenth-century idea of Judaism as a religion of reason, under the influence of Hermann Cohen's ideas. Baeck's second edition, in 1922, captures, however, the change of heart taking place within the Jewish intellectual world in the first two decades of the twentieth century. In it, Baeck focuses more on the irrational, mystical elements in Judaism and especially on its messianism (Brenner 43). This shift is revealing for the transformation of the idea of Jewish identity that is at the heart of Roth's *The Wandering Jews* and foregrounds the necessity of abandoning the rational lure of the Enlightenment and of returning to the roots of Judaism, to its ancient, Oriental wisdom. When at the beginning of the twentieth century Hermann Cohen conceived of Judaism as a religion of reason, he had done so in an attempt to diminish the messianic and mystical undertones of the Talmudic tradition and to present the rabbinic teaching of the laws in neo-Kantian key, as a moral imperative. This conception of Judaism was seen as a prerequisite for assimilation and as the Jewish counterpart to the Protestant civil religion dominant in Germany at the time. Just like Protestantism, it emphasized the values of education, progress, and reform and supported a social model based on the rule of law and the politics of German nationalism and *Staatsräson*. But the principles of progress and rationality, upon which Cohen's concept of "ethical monotheism" was based, appeared to the young Jewish intellectuals as unfounded and inauthentic, the emblems of a capitulation in front of the national-bourgeois ideology of reason, individualism, and state authority.

The young intelligentsia rejected the enlightened liberalism of Cohen's philosophy because, they argued, it annihilated the cathartic spirit of messianism and utopianism inherent in Judaism and subordinated the freedom of the spirit to the control of the state. Between 1916 and 1917 Martin Buber conducted a passionate polemic with Cohen in which Buber formulated more clearly his personal political ideas. In opposition to Cohen's view of the state as the creator and guarantor of the nation, Buber viewed the modern state as an institutional constraint on the freedom of the national sprit and a genuine destroyer of communities. While Cohen considered that the Jewish identity in Germany could only legitimately manifest itself within the framework of the German state, Buber rejected any subordination of the spiritual identity of the Jews to an abstract construct such as the state, profiling himself as an advocate of the creative forces of religiosity and community: "Cohen, der die Religion durch die Ethik kontrolliert, deren Quintessenz die Idee des Staates ist, will, ob es ihm auch nicht bewußt wird, den Geist unter den Staat beugen; ich will den Staat unter den Geist beugen" 'Cohen, who controls religion through ethics, whose quintessence is the idea of the state, wants, whether he realizes that or not, to subordinate the spirit to the state; I want to subordinate the state to the spirit' ("Zion" 429).

Cohen's student Franz Rosenzweig, who was following the polemic between Cohen and Buber from the Balkan front, also attacked his teacher's German nationalism as well as his moralist, reformed view of Judaism, which in Rosenzweig's opinion "betrayed the messianic idea" (qtd. in Löwy 59). Max Brod also reiterated the importance of the spiritual, mystical elements in Judaism, elements that had been illegitimately suppressed in favor of the individualist, rationalist, and moral ones. In his 1921 polemical-philosophical study *Paganism, Christianity, Judaism*, he argues that moral freedom is important as are good works, but the key ingredient is the miraculous divine intervention, or grace, that elevated the works to a redeemed status: "In the index we look in vain for the word 'grace' (Hessed). This is typical of a liberal and rationalistic concept of Judaism, and it is about time to correct that" (33). For Brod, the role of modern Judaism is to recover the mystical aspect of salvation and couple it with the preoccupation for individual moral action in history, thus reestablishing the connection with the ancient Judaic traditions. In a similar fashion for Gershom Scholem, Cohen's overemphasis on morality transformed the Judaic idea of redemption into a rational Utopia, stripping it of its sudden, messianic, and "restorative" character (*Messianic Idea* 26).

In *The Wandering Jews*, Roth provides a similar critique of the crisis of the modern Jewish identity. He considers the roots of the calamitous situation of the Jews in Europe as reaching back to the beginnings of modernity, to Protestantism, bourgeois liberalism, secularism, and nationalism. He criticizes modernity for its Protestant cult of individual faith, its abandonment of tradition, its glorification of rationality and technology, and its separation between church and state, with the subsequent replacement of the divine will (embodied by the monarch) with the will of nature (embodied by the nation). The Jews were, Roth insists, the first and exemplary victims of this process that logically culminates in the twentieth century with its self-dissolution: the principle of reason, personified in the modern individual, reached its final stage, a process to which Theodor Adorno and Max Horkeimer referred to as "the self-destruction of the Enlightenment" in their book *Dialectic of Enlightenment*. The prelude to the catastrophe and to the tragic destiny of the European Jews (a destiny that Roth documents until the year of his death, 1939) started earlier, Roth argues, but nobody listened. It started when the Jews accepted fighting and dying for other nations; when they accepted the oath of allegiance to an earthly principle, such as the nation or individualism; when they gave up their connection with the Eastern Jewish world; and when they purified their religious heritage of the messianic faith and became "Jewish Protestants": "They assimilated. They no longer pray in synagogues and prayerhouses, but in boring temples where the worship is as mechanical as it is in the better class of Protestant church" (*Wandering Jews* 21–22).

For Roth's generation, the crisis of the modern Jewish identity was no longer exclusively a crisis of political and social nature, as it had been for the previous generations. It was, in the first place, a crisis of spiritual nature. Buber's argument that the modern Jews had to redefine their identity away from the forms imposed on them by the nation-states and by the rationalist legacy of the Enlightenment and seek their true essence in a rediscovered Judaic tradition resonated throughout the entire generation. Roth himself echoes this idea in *The Wandering Jews*. His interest in the spiritual renovation of the world in general was already given form in his 1920 article "Die Auferstehung des Geistes" ("The Resurrection of the Spirit"), in which he decries the secularization and rationalization of the world and heralds its salvation through a spiritual renovation. During his travels to southern France in 1925 and the Soviet Union in 1926, Roth reaffirms his belief that technological progress was not a solution for the modern individual, who had to seek a deeper identity in some form of spiritual coherence with the world and with tradition. In *The Wandering Jews*, Roth questions the very process of modernization to which the Jews were eagerly subjecting themselves in the hope that they would escape poverty, discrimination, and violence. The price for this escape, Roth argues, is their spiritual impoverishment: "They gave themselves up. They lost themselves. They shed their aura of sad beauty. Instead a dust-gray layer of suffering without meaning and anxiety without tragedy settled on their stooped backs" (*Wandering Jews* 14). By becoming mere citizens, proletarians, social democrats, and Zionists, the Jews gave away their unique spiritual identity and mission, Roth argues. The Jews have, he continues, a higher mission than to fit into the neat boxes cut out for them by Western modern rationality, and this mission is collective and spiritual.

Not surprisingly, other members of the generation shared the same belief. In the 1916 article "Das Mittel des Geistes" ("The Agency of the Spirit"), Arnold Zweig discarded the economic and political paths of action in the Jewish struggle for emancipation, arguing instead that the Jews should use their natural affinity for the work of the spirit to achieve their true potential. For Franz Rosenzweig too, the individual achievements of the Jews, albeit materially significant, were damaging the spiritual coherence and strength of the Jewish community. The legalistic path to individual emancipation that the Enlightenment had opened had failed, he concluded: "Wir haben gelernt, dass mit der paragraphierten Berechtigung der Einzelnen wenig gewonnen ist" 'We have learned that little has been gained through the codified entitlement of the individuals' (*Zeit ists* 27). Hence, the spirit of the community had to assert itself in order to make the Jewish collectivity internally coherent and externally visible but not in the way in which the conservative political milieus wanted it, as a politically uniform mass. The Jews had to go beyond their ethnic-political self-identification and aspire to spiritual unity based on the precepts of Judaic religious teaching, Rosenzweig argued: "Nicht die Judenschaft zwar, wie die Reaktionäre der Mitte des nineteenthen Jahrhunderts wollten, gilt es organisch zu verkörpern, aber das Judentum. Nicht judenschaftliche, sondern jüdischgeistige Organisationen gilt es zu schaffen" 'It is not the Jewish community, as the reactionaries of the middle of the nineteenth century wanted, that we are called to organically embody, but Judaism. It is not necessary to create Jewish community organizations, but Jewish spiritual ones' (27). His argumentation, representative for the entire generation of which he was part and that he partly influenced, moved the emphasis in the public conversation about Jewish identity from the individual and secular to the collective and the religious-spiritual.[8]

The Jewish Renaissance and the "Turn to the East"

The rejection of the Western Jewish assimilationist model was, at the same time, accompanied by the creative revaluation of the Eastern Judaic heritage. The burdensome legacy that the parents' and grandparents' generations had tried to repress or even forget was now rediscovered, albeit in a modified "Westernized" form by the children's generation, who took pride in it and even endowed it with a transformative, ennobling function. As Hannah Arendt points out, "a genuine enthusiasm for this last phase of Jewish mysticism spread through the younger generation who generally were quite unconcerned with the intellectual life of their Eastern brethren, but felt themselves surprisingly close to this spiritual world and mentality" (*Jew as Pariah* 103). Martin Buber, the emblematic figure of this "turn to the East," had a seminal role in spreading the interest in the world of East European Jews, especially for the Chasidim. His translations of Chasidic folklore beginning with 1906 had the effect of an earthquake throughout this entire generation of young Central European Jewish thinkers. From Georg Lukács to Gershom Scholem and Gustav Landauer, from Ernst Bloch and Franz Kafka to Erich Fromm and Walter Benjamin, the publication of the Chasidic tales and of the legend of the Baal-Shem appeared not only as a testimony of an unadulterated spiritual tradition filled with a clear sense of authenticity but also as an alternative to the simplified, alienating, and "disenchanted" (to use Max Weber's word) modern world.

In a 1910 review of Buber's *Legend of the Baal-Shem*, Gustav Landauer saluted the renewed interest in Jewish folklore, which would elevate the prestige of Jewish mythology to the level enjoyed by more established national mythologies, such as the Greek, Chinese, and German. For Landauer, himself a political anarchist in search of more authentic forms of community than those offered by the modern national and bureaucratic states, the revival of Jewish mysticism heralded a turn toward a more spiritual type of collectivity. According to Landauer, Buber's Chasidic tales had the power to awaken in the young Jews an awareness "daß das Judentum nicht eine äußere Zufälligkeit, sondern eine unverlierbare innere Eigenschaft ist, deren Gleichheit eine Zahl Individuen zu einer Gemeinsamkeit verbindet" 'that Judaism is not an external coincidence, but an enduring inner property whose similarity binds together a number of individuals into a community' (Landauer, *Werkausgabe* 3: 158). In Landauer's view, the Oriental wisdom of the Chasidic legends brought with it a return to a communitarian ethos that the European Jews had lost in the modern era by re-creating the original, unmediated, and meaningful relationship of the individual with the cosmos. Moreover, the community to which Jewish mysticism would give shape constituted for Landauer a solution not only for the Jews but also for humanity as a whole, being a symbol of a wider renaissance of the human spirit and of its return from the exile of civilization and rationality. In a similar fashion, Erich Fromm in his 1922 dissertation *Das jüdische Gesetz: Ein Beitrag zur Soziologie des Diaspora-Judentums (Jewish Law: A Contribution to the Study of Diaspora Judaism)* singles out Chasidism as the only type of Judaic movement that genuinely represents the Jewish spirit, in opposition to Reform Judaism, which was corrupted by the Protestant spirit of capitalism (Akrap 176).

Chasidism also offered a Jewish counterpart to the popular traditions so much admired by the German Romantics, who found in them the basis on which to wage their critique of the modern world. After all, Buber's generation was strongly influenced by Romanticism and by the German philosophy and sociology of the turn of the twentieth century, which were marked by a pronounced antipositivist and utopian spirit.[9] Nietzsche's critique of modernity and Franz von Baader's cosmological and mystical systems (and through him, those of Jakob Böhme) inspired their skepticism of rationality and their interest in spirituality.[10] Wilhelm Dilthey's philosophy of life, Heinrich Rickert's neo-Kantian philosophy of values, and Max Weber's critical sociology also exerted a considerable influence on younger Jewish thinkers such as Lukács and Bloch, whose early systems articulated a philosophy of culture and history that was originally centered on the idea of modern alienation through abandonment of traditional forms of solidarity.[11] The poet Stefan George's antibourgeois modernism influenced, directly or through mediators (such as the sociologist Georg Simmel), the early thinking of a Scholem and Bloch. Other sociologists of the time, such as Ferdinand Tönnies and Werner Sombart, inspired Buber's religious communitarianism and Karl Mannheim's sociological utopianism through their writings about the annihilating effect of rationality and modernity on the communitarian traditional spirit (Löwy 49; Loader 103). Through their critique of Enlightenment rationality, modern institutions, individualism, and bourgeois values, these thinkers offered the Central European Jewish intelligentsia the means to deepen an already growing disenchantment with the promise of assimilation and to justify, from a philosophical point of view, a revaluation of Eastern Judaism.[12]

Not only Buber's books but also the influx of East European Jews after World War I increased the exposure of the assimilated Central European Jews to Chasidic spirituality and contributed to what Steven Aschheim called the "cult of the *Ostjuden*" (qtd. in Horrocks, "The Construction" 128). In a 1920 article titled "Busstag" ("Day of Repentance"), Max Brod describes the life-changing episode of his encounter with a group of Chasidic refugees at the grave of the influential eighteenth-century rabbi Yechezkel Landau in his native Prague: "Und Scham erfaßt mich, wie ich hier neben meinen östlichen Brüdern stehe. . . . Aus der Ferne, von Galizien mußten Flüchtlinge kommen, um mich an die Größe eines Juden, der in meiner Heimatstadt gewirkt hat, zu erinnern" 'And shame engulfs me, as I stand here beside my eastern brothers. . . . From the distance, from Galicia, refugees had to come to remind me of the greatness of a Jew who had been active in my hometown' (*Im Kampf* 101). The Chasids' sense of spiritual belonging sets them apart from their "modern" Western brethren: "Dieses durchaus erlebte, hingebungsvolle Vertrauen, diese volkstümliche Unterordnung unter den Geist, unter die geistige Größe und Führerschaft . . . : wo findet man das noch auf Gottes weiter Erde, außer bei Juden, freilich bei den 'modernen' Juden schon in wesentlich geringerem Maße als bei den chassidischen" 'This thoroughly lived, devoted confidence, this popular subordination to the spirit, to spiritual greatness and leadership . . . : where is this still to be found on God's earth, except with the Jews, certainly with the "modern" Jews to a much lesser degree than with the Chassidic' (101–2). The redemptive power of this mystical form of faith seemed to provide answers that the rational, reformed, Western-style Judaic faith could not.

Additionally, the Yiddish theater played an important role in the cultural contacts between Eastern and Western Jews, contributing to the latter's increased fascination with Chasidism. According to Giuliano Baioni, Franz Kafka's encounter with a Yiddish theater company from Lemberg (Lviv) in 1911 represented a life-changing experience for the Prague author (in Magris, *Weit von wo* 23). The first Yiddish theater companies were already touring internationally around the turn of the twentieth century, but they got a boost after the Bolshevik Revolution of 1917 as a result of the Bolshevik cultural policies that encouraged the Yiddish language and popular culture, although often to the expense of Hebrew and religious traditions. During his 1926 visit to Moscow, Joseph Roth attended a performance of the Moscow Yiddish Theater, which he found exotic and ecstatic. The mixture of Chasidic storytelling and acting made the Eastern Jews appear as "Juden von höherer Temperatur, jüdischere Juden. . . . Es war eine Art dionysischer Juden" 'Jews of higher temperature, more Jewish Jews. . . . A kind of Dionysian Jews' (*Werke* 2: 679). Similarly, the historian Rudolph Heilbrunn's 1927 review of a theatrical performance in Frankfurt am Main by the Moscow-based Habimah Company tells of the fascination exerted by Chasidism over the Frankfurt Jews:

> Die tiefste künstlerische Erschütterung aber, die mir aus jenen Tagen geblieben ist, ging von einem Theater aus, von dessen Existenz Westeuropa fast noch weniger Kenntnis haben mochte, als von den russischen Experimenten, der hebräischen Truppe Habima. Die chassidischen Tänze offenbarten eine

> unbekannte Welt voller Geheimnis und Glauben, Inbrunst und Ekstase, in der schwermutsvolle Musik eine bedrückte und erniedrigte Existenz erlöste und verklärte. (qtd. in Heuberger and Krohn 154–55)
>
> But the deepest artistic shock that has stayed with me from those days came from a theater company of whose existence Western Europe may almost have less knowledge than of the Russian [artistic] experiments, the Hebrew company Habima. The Chasidic dances revealed an unknown world full of mystery and faith, fervor and ecstasy, in which melancholy music liberated and transfigured a depressed and degraded existence.

According to Katharina Ochse, the Eastern Jews fueled the imagination of many assimilated Western Jews, who invested them with the redemptive power to transform society in a socialist-revolutionary (Arnold Zweig), religious (Sammy Gronemann), or even Nietzsche-inspired "Oriental-Dionysian" direction (Martin Buber) (Ochse 126). Gustav Landauer's 1916 article "Ostjuden und Deutsches Reich" ("Eastern Jews and the German Empire") epitomizes the idea of the messianic role of the Eastern Jews, who could give hope and comfort to all of humanity through their free and authentic natures ("Ostjuden" 439).

The fascination with the Orient in general was not exclusively a Jewish phenomenon in Central Europe at the time and had its roots in the West European discovery of Eastern spirituality, history, and languages during the eighteenth and nineteenth centuries. If the Romantics opened the way for the Western intellectual curiosity about the Orient at the turn of the nineteenth century and neo-Romantic philosophers such as Schopenhauer and Nietzsche furthered it in the following decades, it was the linguists, folklorists, historians of religion, and musicologists who provided at the turn of the twentieth century the academic rigor necessary to turn a mere fascination into an actual science. At the same time, the Orient became fashionable especially among the educated classes, who showed a particular interest in what they perceived to be the defining characteristic of the East, its mysticism. Paul Mendes-Flohr argues that even Martin Buber, a student of the Romantic and neo-Romantic intellectual traditions, used the fascination with the Orient to shape his own version of mystical Chasidism (*Divided Passions* 90). For Joseph Roth, the Galician Jew seeking assimilation during his youth, the "turn to the East" that he encountered in Vienna and Berlin appeared superficial and ridiculous, nothing more than an empty form of cultural affectation that he often mocked in his early articles. For example, "Ukrainomanie" ("Ucrainomania") of 1920 ridicules the historically and culturally ignorant attraction to anything Ukrainian in Berlin at the time. Likewise, "Rabindranath Tagore" of 1921 derides the snobbery of the Berlin Tagore-mania, and "Theosophische Laienpredigt" ("Theosophical Lay Sermon") of 1923 mocks the superficial spirituality of the Europeans avid for exotic esotericism. And yet Roth, although a lucid observer and corrosive critic, always aware of the finest distinctions and nuances, conversant in the history and culture of Eastern and Western Europe, also indulged in cultural stereotyping, especially in his middle and late career. However, he did it in a highly unconventional and always nonideological, open-ended fashion that allowed for a revolving door between objective and metaphorical reality. The fact that gradually throughout the 1920s Roth started to use the image of the Eastern Jew as a signifier for his moral and religious thinking might have to do with both his shifting attitude toward his own Jewish identity and the fact that as an East European Jew living in a Central and West European world that stigmatized the Oriental Jews in particular, he felt that he could use the image of the outsider as a vehicle toward a new kind of "insideness."

The Wandering Jews paints the classical portrait of the East European Jew in Roth's works: poor, simple, pious, sometimes misguided or victim of one's own weaknesses but always ready to repent and to return to what is essential—the love of God and the expectation of redemption. This messianic passion sets him apart from his Western counterpart, Roth argues, and gives him the power to withstand the onslaught of history, of change, and of the pressure of all passing earthly authorities (*Werke* 2: 842). Particularly the Chasidim, Roth argues, with their love of music, their "ecstatic" prayers that entreat the Messiah's arrival in the here and now (850), their joy of life and God alike, and their religious devotion experienced as "carnal excess" (848) testify to the transformative, redemptive power of belief. Roth does not fail to point out how the Chasidic religious experience is not so different from that of Himalayan shamans or Indian fakirs, although it does not enjoy the same interest among West Europeans (843). This analogy does not necessarily "exoticize" the Chasidim, as Andreas Kilcher argues (287), but to the contrary allows Roth to demonstrate the superficiality and prejudice of the European Orientalist fads, fascinated with the mysticism of the Far East but completely unable to recognize it among the neighboring East European Jews. *The Wandering Jews* is not only an ethnographic report written for a German-speaking, mostly non-Jewish audience but is also a stern warning against the dangers of assimilation. The process of modernization, a process with roots in secular humanism and the Enlightenment, in brief, in the West, has begun to affect the Eastern part of the continent, Roth argues, replacing the traditional religious worldview of the Jews with the belief that progress can solve all their problems. As a result, they mistakenly seek assimilation in the West and idealize a world that does not deserve it (*Werke* 2: 828). In a similar fashion to Buber's criticism of Hermann Cohen, in *The Wandering Jews* Roth contrasts the foundations of Western culture, of which rationality and nationalism are an integral component, to the idea of spirituality, on which the very justification of Jewish existence rests:

> And the name for all this is Western civilization ["westliche Kultur"]. Whoever has it is entitled to despise his cousin who, authentic and uncontaminated, comes from the East. Such an Eastern Jew has within himself more humanity and more divinity than all the preachers can come up with in all the theological colleges of Western Europe. With luck the cousin will have the fortitude not to lapse into assimilation. (22–23)

In the preface to the 1937 edition of *The Wandering Jews*, Roth repeatedly refers to this modernization process as a "superstitious belief in progress" (122) and a form of "idolatry" (123). In fact, the prosperity and happiness promised by the West are only apparent, as apparent are the poverty and misery of the East. Instead, Roth argues, the Jews should appreciate the "quality of the people" in the East, their simplicity, responsible equally for "holy men and murderers," the generosity of the land, the sad greatness of the songs, and the passionate nature of the Slavic soul (6).[13] And yet, after indulging to some length in the clichéd pastoralizing of Eastern Europe, Roth takes distance from the Orientalist stereotype of the East European Jew as a *Wunderrabbi* and of the East European Christian as a peasant. Such a misperception of the East rivals the opposite one of the West, he argues, that imagines that every Western Jew is a successful banker and that Western society as a whole is a paradise of prosperity and rights (13). This presence of ethnic stereotyping alongside its intentional dismantling has constituted a source of puzzlement for the critics. Sarah Bailey argues that although Roth "takes up a form of Orientalizing rhetoric in *Juden auf Wanderschaft*," it is difficult to associate it with a form of Western "colonizing" discourse because Roth's perspective ambiguously crosses the cultural line separating the Western Jews and the Eastern Jews (para. 11).

Edward Timms identifies in Roth's fascination with the Eastern Jews a common trend among the assimilated Jewish authors of the time, such as Arnold Zweig or Kafka, but wonders if this idealization is not a stereotypical response, albeit in the opposite direction, to the slandering stereotypes spread by anti-Semites hostile to the migration of the Eastern Jews to the West (25).

Whether Roth reinforces certain stereotypes about the Jews or, to the contrary, undermines them through recourse to ambiguous first-person testimony (Gelber, "*Juden auf Wanderschaft*") or through reductio ad absurdum (Horrocks, "The Representation") is relative to the point of view of the reader. Thus, the stereotype of the excessively cerebral artificial Jew, incapable of emotion, is undermined by another stereotype, that of the sensuous rustic Oriental Jew and the other way around.[14] In *The Wandering Jews*, the narrator's technique of the "revolving door" between cliché and authenticity offers Roth the liberty to reinterpret familiar stereotypes in order to paint an allegorical portrait of the Jew as a figure of redemption. Thus, he never descends into pure folkloric idealizations and instead walks the fine line between reportage and essay, or between objective reporting and subjective, cultural interpretation (Scheichl 18). That Roth never saw a contradiction in this ambiguous juxtaposition of objective observation and subjective interpretation is made clear by a 1925 letter to his publisher, Benno Reifenberg, in which he states that "I should like to write a whole 'subjective' book, in other words something completely objective" (*Joseph Roth: A Life* 53).

The rediscovered interest in the Jewish identity that characterized Roth's generation should not be seen, however, exclusively as an attempt to break away from the liberal traditions of the previous generations or as a collective rejection of the Western intellectual heritage and enthusiastic embrace of the Eastern Judaic traditions. As Michael Brenner demonstrates in his study *The Renaissance of Jewish Culture in Weimar Germany*, the reinvigoration of Jewish public life in the beginning of the twentieth century took on many forms. Although we can speak, with Martin Buber, of a "Jewish renaissance" in the sense of an awakened sense of pride in the unique origins, history, and essence of Jewish life in Central Europe at the time, it would be a mistake to subsume the entirety of Jewish public life to the idea of asserting a Jewish identity separate from the national identities of Central Europe:

> Those who were part of such a Jewish sphere had multiple identities and lived in a variety of worlds: the same writers drew inspiration from German myths and Hasidic tales, the same educators were active in the adult education movements of the German *Volkshochschule* and the Jewish *Lehrhaus*, the same painters depicted German soldiers and East European Jews. (Brenner 2)

George Mosse makes a similar argument when he contends that the rediscovery of the Jewish identity in the wake of the failed assimilation project of the late nineteenth century did not necessarily lead to a cultural separation of all the young Jewish intellectuals from the heritage of the Enlightenment. Figures such as Emil Ludwig, the popular biographer, and Stefan Zweig, the equally popular Austrian writer and, incidentally, a close friend of Joseph Roth, kept their allegiance to the classical German *Bildungsideal*, to universal values and cosmopolitanism, and refused a "retreat behind bars" (Mosse 27). Even in the case of those Jewish intellectuals who contested the liberal-bourgeois traditions of the nineteenth century, there existed various forms of asserting their Jewish identity. As Sidney Rosenfeld remarks in his book on Joseph Roth, the political responses to their identity dilemma offered by this generation of Central European Jewish intellectuals ranged "from socialist and communist universalism to Jewish nationalism in the form of Zionism" (*Understanding* 91). Some saw themselves either as an integral part of the European nations, as in the case of social democratic and socialist Jews, or as a part of an international movement, as in the case of the communist ones, while others pursued a nation-building program, such as the Zionists; a revolutionary Utopia, such as the anarcho-libertarians; or even a return to traditional Judaism without concern for modern political or national identities (Friedländer 41). Some simply defied classifications and moved across categories, creating new syntheses and original forms of self-identification. This is the case for Roth too.

The present study focuses, however, on that group of thinkers for whom the "Jewish renaissance" meant the affirmation of the Jewish identity through the rejection of the Enlightenment rationalist traditions, of the Hegelian teleological philosophy of the state and of history, and of liberal-bourgeois individualism and contractualism while at the same time reviving the religious-mystical traditions of Judaism, especially Eastern Judaism. Their interest in these religious traditions stemmed not from a strictly theological interest but instead from the belief that they held the key to questions of political and moral relevance for the secular Jews and for the modern individuals in general. As Elke Dubbels argues, these thinkers stand outside of the religious traditions of Judaism but return from their position of exteriority ("Jenseits der Tradition") to specific aspects of this tradition in order to construct a philosophy of the modern spirit ("eine Philosophie der Moderne") (2). As Roth's case demonstrates, the aspect he values the most in the Judaic tradition is the ability to joyfully assert the belief in the redemption of all existence in spite of any historical difficulty or personal challenge. For Roth, this messianic passion carries an existential meaning in that it is able to offer a moral and political solution to all the Jews and even Gentiles who lost their sense of spiritual direction through their capitulation in front of modern existence. The messianic promise is something so deeply embedded in the life of traditional Judaism that it manages to uplift existence even in its most mundane form and prepare it for the imminent arrival of the Kingdom of God. This was, at least, the lesson that East European and especially Chasidic Judaism appeared to teach. This perspective on the world as if it were hovering on the brink of redemption and even as holding redemption in its very kernel, connecting this world to the next, is the common thread running through the thinking of the figures analyzed in this chapter. Paul Mendes-Flohr summarizes their idea of redemption with what he terms "the Judaic principle": "the eschatological conception of the future as an alternative reality to all possible social configurations to be conjured up by an unredeemed world, and thus as a source of hope and critique of the imperfect here and now" (*Divided Passions* 16).

The Messianic Promise and the Idea of Redemption

The appeal of the notion of radical renovation and reformation, which, according to Löwy, attracted these tinkers to the "Jewish (Kabbalistic) idea of *tikkun*, a polysemic term for *redemption* (*Erlösung*)," was enhanced by the prevailing cultural pessimism of the time and by the belief that the modern world as a whole was lying in spiritual ruins (2). Since none of the rational, Cartesian and Hegelian, liberal, and positivist theories of the state, history, and individual consciousness could provide a satisfactory answer, the solution had to lie in prerational or even irrational modes of liberation that had the potential to redeem existence in its entirety. Judaic messianism fit this role through its ability to short-circuit the logic of the teleological and progressive theories about human development and rational reform. It could bring about the end of the old world and the sudden outbreak of the new at any moment and through this redeem the world either by restoring an old harmony or by inaugurating a brand-new eon. But by reviving the messianic idea, these thinkers arrived, with or without intent, at the core of old theological debates within Judaism about the role of the individual in God's salvation plan. If the Messiah's arrival was sudden and unanticipated, what was the responsibility of the individual living in history? If the individual acquired an esoteric knowledge about the messianic moment, would he then not be able to hurry its arrival? And if so, how would the idea of unpredictability and mystery of the divine mind be impacted? At the same time, if the arrival of the Kingdom denied the old world, would that mean that the world that God created was corrupt and in need of repair? Or was the arrival of the Kingdom the restoration of an ancient Golden Age rather than the outburst of a brand-new one, and if so, would that not mean that it was possible to know in advance what God's plan was? Hence, messianism was interpreted by each one slightly differently, either as an aspirational horizon that forever retreats or as a hope immanent to all creation, as in Bloch's case; as the moral engine motivating human action, as in the case of Buber and Brod; or as a revolutionary latency within history itself, as in Benjamin's case. How did Roth view the role of messianism? It is the argument of the present study that for Roth, the Messiah's arrival is not apocalyptical but instead is a mundane act of volition that engages human beings and God alike in redeeming all aspects of existence, individual and collective, private and historical.

In his book *In the Shadow of Catastrophe: German Intellectuals between Apocalypse and Enlightenment,* Anson Rabinbach articulates a typology of messianisms in order to discuss the early twentieth-century varieties of messianism in the German-speaking world. He distinguishes four types of messianism that (1) restore a golden age, (2) redeem the world through a revolutionary utopian event, (3) inaugurate a brand-new eon by bringing about the destruction of the world, and (4) descend into pessimism due to the incongruity between human action and God's salvation plan (32). However, Rabinbach does not acknowledge the existence of a mitigated kind of messianism, one that in Scholem's words "neutralizes" the apocalyptical nature of conventional Judaic messianism. Hence, for Rabinbach the focus is on the interrelated (and Gnostic) aspects of esoteric knowledge and political extremism in the messianic philosophy of this generation: "Esoteric knowledge and political extremism are the two poles of the political ethics of messianism" (34). While it is true that political radicalism and "revolutionary gnosis" (Boldyrev 2) partially characterized some of these thinkers' philosophy, making them receptive to the mystique of irrational violence, so did the idea of a moral and "antipolitical" renovation of the world that prophesied not destruction but instead joyful affirmation and unification. For Roth, for example, the idea of redemption and renovation does not imply the violent denial of existence but rather, as in the Chasidic tradition, implies affirmation through spiritual transfiguration, as Scholem argues (*Messianic Idea* 195). Influenced by the Chasidic conviction that the Messiah's presence makes itself manifest in history, not outside of it, Roth rejects a redemption accessible only to the initiated. Instead, as Buber argues, the mundane, democratic nature of the relationship between God and man in Chasidism is the very opposite of the Gnostic doctrine of initiation: "Hasidism guards against the tendency to break down the distinction between the living God and his human partner by praising the simple person rather than enshrining the 'knower'" (Oppenheim 115). The mood of this type of messianism is not pessimistic, as Rabinbach suggests; it is optimistic, affirming and creating, welcoming the world and its otherworldly counterpart in the same gesture. Or, in Buber's words,

> the world in which you live, just as it is and not otherwise, affords you that association with God, which will redeem you and whatever divine aspect of the world you have been entrusted with. . . . All the contradictions with which the world distresses you are only that you may discover their intrinsic significance, and all the contrary trends tormenting you within yourself, only wait to be exorcised by your word. All innate sorrow wants only to flow into the fervor of your joy. (Buber, "Introduction" 4)

It could be argued that the typology of messianisms proposed by Chrisoph Schulte comes closer to recognizing this type of messianic thinking than does Rabinbach's. Schulte argues that there are five type of messianism in the Judaic tradition: (1) the messianism of the present time ("präsentischer Messianismus"), (2) the messianism of the future time ("futurischer Messianismum"), (3) apocalyptical messianism, (4) disappointed messianism, and (5) skeptical messianism. While the messianism of the future time and the apocalyptical one are fairly self-explanatory—the Messiah will come in the future only, at the end of time, and his arrival will happen only after the complete destruction of the world, respectively—disappointed messianism purports a type of messianism in which the Messiah has failed in his direct redemptive action although his mission is fulfilled indirectly, through the consequences of his failure. Skeptical messianism, on the other hand, exemplifies the case of those thinkers who, like Maimonides, rationalized the Messiah's arrival and linked it to a series of conditions that would prove his authenticity as a Messiah. Finally, the messianism of the present time assumes that the Messiah is already here, in the present, and that the only point of contention is the recognition of his legitimacy. Schulte associates this type of messianism with the monarchic tradition of the House of David, but it might be argued that the idea of the historic Messiah, of the redemption in the here and now, could be seen as a kind of messianism of the present time.

The idea of redemption developed by this generation of Jewish intellectuals is certainly complex, and no typology can do it justice if for the reason that many of those who used it were themselves highly antisystematic, atypical, and indeed sometimes self-contradictory thinkers. Some tended more toward apocalyptical and revolutionary thinking, while others entertained a more reform-oriented, liberal approach; some were highly political, while others rejected any form of political affiliation, limiting their thinking to the sphere of philosophical ideas; some foregrounded individual ethics, while others favored the collective ethos; finally, some drew more intently on Jewish sources, while others attempted original Jewish-Christian syntheses. Rabinbach himself acknowledges that there are different ways of grouping them together depending on what one searches (31). For Löwy, whose study is tellingly subtitled "Jewish Libertarian Thought in Central Europe," the criterion is the libertarian tendencies dividing along religious and secular lines; for Mosès, the criterion is the common preoccupation with the crisis of historicism and the prospect of conceiving of history as a time of "possibles" (12). Paul Mendes-Flohr foregrounds the political dimension of redemption, particularly in its Marxist embodiment ("To Brush History"). Elke Dubbels exploits the rhetorical dimension of messianism as a discourse aimed at reforming the philosophy of language, politics, and history. In Ivan Boldyrev's recent study *Ernst Bloch and His Contemporaries*, the intellectual landscape of the generation includes revolutionary Gnosticism, Judaic messianism, and expressionist experimentalism. Rabinbach himself favors the apocalypticist and anarchist component of this generation's messianic tendencies: "Whether theoretical or actual, the politics of Jewish messianism is in the final analysis apocalyptic" (30).

The present study places at its center the idea of redemption as an everyday, historical experience that at the same time is infused with the sparks of a transcendent salvation. That this very idea of redemption has been associated with the Chasidic belief that God lives through an everyday dialogue with the individual is due in large part to Buber's own interpretation of Chasidism as "intercourse with God in the lived everyday, the accepting and dedicating of what is happening here and now" (Buber, "Replies" 736). This does not mean, however, that his interpretation of Chasidism was uncritically accepted by all the representatives of his generation. Gershom Scholem's own historical interpretation of Chasidism is probably the best-known example of an alternative interpretation to Buber's (for more on the difference between them, see Oppenheim). Yet Buber's influence among the entire generation and his popularization of Chasidic spirituality and folklore have played a huge role in shaping the interest in and outlook on Eastern Judaic spirituality among the Central European Jewish intellectuals of the early twentieth century. Buber's own arguably Romantic interpretation of Chasidism echoes throughout the writings of many of the representatives of this generation. The present study looks at how this particular idea of redemption offers a renewed conception of morality, identity, and history and contends that its core concepts were used by many representatives of this generation, although in slightly different, sometimes divergent ways. It is not the purpose of this work to analyze the individual ways in which they reconciled the idea of redemption with their own philosophical convictions, political ideas, and intellectual affinities. Instead, this work will focus on those common elements that underpin a philosophy of redemption within history, such as what Roth envisioned in his literary universe.

For Roth as well as for the other members of his generation, the Judaic principle of redemption deserved attention not only because it held the key to the Jewish identity question but also because it could be applied to non-Jewish situations, from the crisis of modern consciousness to the social and political crises of the modern state and to the epistemological problems plaguing modern thinking in general. Their position at the interface of the Jewish and non-Jewish worlds allowed the representatives of this generation to make this conceptual transfer from the sphere of religious Judaic thinking to philosophy, sociology, history, and political theory. The Jews occupy a special position in their narrative of decay and restoration, because as Roth writes in the 1938 article "Das Passahfest" ("Feast of Passover"), they have already experienced the ruinous destiny of the world before anyone else but have also hoped for salvation before anyone else (*Werke* 3: 805). Hence, their misfortune is inseparable from that of the Christians, as he declares in the preface to the 1937 edition of *The Wandering Jews* (133). Theodor Lessing, in his 1930 book on the pathology of Jewish self-hatred, makes a similar argument: the Jews have a leading role in the coming social revolution due to their early exposure to the suffering produced by modernity. Like an organism that has already experienced an infection, they possess the "antibodies" that will help the other nations of the world overcome their predicament, although in this "purely spiritual mission" to help the others they may run the risk of losing their own specificity (235). The same idea is expressed by Martin Buber, whose 1933 contribution to the *Almanach des Schocken Verlags* (*Almanac of the Schocken Publishing House*), tellingly titled "Der Jüdische Mensch von heute" ("Today's Jewish Person"), argues that modernity has singled out the Jews as a test case for humanity as a whole. Will the individual resist the destructive forces of modernity, or will he break down? The answer to this question rests, Buber argues, on the outcome of the Jewish response to the challenge of modernity (Ausserhofer 286).

Already in 1905 in his seminal study *Das Wesen des Judentums* (*The Essence of Judaism*), Leo Baeck argued that the hope for redemption is the same for Jews and non-Jews and that the same truth is revealed by God to both: "Die Hoffnung für die Menschheit ist die Hoffnung für Israel. Das Wort Gottes an die Menschheit ist kein anderes als das Wort Gottes an sein Volk" 'The hope for humanity is the hope for Israel. The Word of God to mankind is no other than the Word of God to His people' (66). The same argument is employed by Gustav Landauer in his 1913 essay "Sind das Ketzergedanken?" ("Are These Heretical Thoughts?"). Landauer argues that the Jews are a source of comfort and hope for all the other nations because their messianic expectation for an end of exile offers the leading example for all humanity's return from spiritual exile. Thus, the Jews have the mission of being a Messiah for the nations (Landauer, *Werkausgabe* 3: 173). In his 1921 *Star of Redemption*, Franz Rosenzweig offers a similar dramatic expression of his belief that Jewish suffering has a universal expiatory function:

> Israel intercedes with him [God] in behalf of the sinning peoples of the world and he afflicts Israel with disease so that those other peoples may be healed. Both stand before God: Israel, his servant, and the kings of the peoples; and the strands of suffering and guilt, of love and judgment, of sin and atonement, are so intrinsically twined that human hands cannot untangle them. (307)

Also published in 1921, Max Brod's *Paganism, Christianity, Judaism* offers a correction of the mistaken perception that Judaism is a religion that promises redemption to the Jews alone. The Judaic form of redemption does not limit redemption to the members of a particular religious group, Brod argues, nor does it require adherence to a set of core beliefs. To the contrary, "Judaism has always taught that the righteous of other nations have a place in the world to come" (74). For him, the shift in emphasis from one's own companions in faith alone to humanity as a whole is the true essence of Judaism. In recalling the words of Ben Azzai "'Man' refers to all men as a unit and in equality, as it says further on, they were created 'in the image of God,'" Brod argues that Judaism's view of redemption can provide everyone with answers to the dilemmas of historical and religious existence (189).

How can this notion of a common destiny that the Jews share with the other nations be reconciled with the opposite thinking that also dominated this generation, the one that argued for a distinctly Jewish solution to the problems encountered by the Jews? Were not assimilation and identification with the other nations a barrier in the way of arriving at a true, genuine form of cultural and spiritual identification with the ancestral Jewish heritage? One answer, although not entirely free of contradictions, was that the Jewish search for a true essence was not motivated by the desire to assert an identity in opposition to that imposed on them by the societies in which they lived but instead was motivated by the need to restore a coherent and meaningful spiritual relationship with the world. The issue was not that assimilation and incorporation into the cultural logic of modernity had to be rejected because they were required from and, at the same time, denied to the Jews by the Gentiles but instead because the mental mold in which these forms were created was corrupt and in dire need of renovation. The Jewish search for redemption was thus a search for a wider redemption, one from which the Gentiles could also profit. George Mosse emphasizes this universal aspect of the generation's thinking, although he acknowledges that their starting point was a narrow, ethnic definition of identity: "the *Volk* was only a stepping-stone toward a common humanity" (36). Mosse shows that although Buber and his generation, including Scholem, Bloch, and others, were fascinated by a parochial, folkish definition of Jewish identity, they were also looking "beyond Judaism." Similarly, Roth's argument, expressed in a 1925 letter to Benno Reifenberg (*Joseph Roth: A Life* 50) and reiterated in *The Wandering Jews*, that Jews betray their true self when they start working for non-Jewish causes seems to suggest that the messianic mission of the Jews becomes universal only after it is assumed on an ethnic level. In brief, the Jews cannot assume a leading role for the rest of the world as long as they are not, in the first place, Jews in a traditional religious sense. This paradoxical conceptualization of the relationship between particular and universal is typical for the generation's ability to use the concept of redemption as a kind of totalizing trope that can reconcile all logical contradictions.

The Secular and Religious Facets of Redemption

The redemptive promise held by Judaism in the form of a hope for all of humankind took on two major forms among the members of Roth's generation, a rational-secular and a mystical-religious one.[15] Naturally this classification is imperfect, given the fact that religious elements intermingled with secular ones in their philosophy, creating new syntheses that challenged the traditional distinction between religious and secular thinking. But in a more heuristic sense, similar to the Weberian *Idealtypen*, a distinction could be made between the use of the notion of redemption as a social-political project that would radically renovate the relationship between individual and society and its use as a moral-religious project that would repair the relationship between individual and God. In the former case, the notion of redemption is rationalized and instrumentalized as a political idea, while in the latter it is relegated to the realm of the miraculous manifestation of the divine within history. The most typical example of rationalization of redemption is the idea of Utopia, popular among many representatives of the generation, such as Bloch, Buber, and Mannheim. It is much harder to find one single exemplary expression of the second type of conception of redemption, the mystical-religious one, but Rosenzweig's redemptive ontology, Brod's moral salvationism, and Benjamin's historical eschatology are edifying examples. Roth's own use of the idea of redemption falls between the two categories, containing elements that highlight the moral-political, secular, and social dimension of a possible Utopia but also elements that demonstrate the mystical-religious and moral-individual character of salvation. His political writings, social commentaries, and historical interpretations often fall within the realm of the rational-utopian, while his religious-moral novels enact the idea of redemption as a miraculous event. This does not mean, however, that moral-religious elements do not surface in the political-historical writings or social-utopian elements in the religious ones. To the contrary, the two dimensions are deeply interrelated because they are expressions of the underlying philosophy of redemption that permeates Roth's entire work.

The critics have acknowledged the importance of utopianism in understanding Roth's fiction, but their standard response has been to assign his Utopia to the realm of nostalgia or of the escapist imagination. Beginning with Stefan Zweig's 1930 assertion that Roth is "der Apologet einer rückwärts gewendeten Utopie" 'the apologist of a backward-facing Utopia' (qtd. in Oei 88), continuing with Magris's 1971 belief that Roth builds a "utopia of a past time" and a "Mythos des Nicht-mehr-Möglichen" 'myth of the no-longer-possible' (*Weit von wo* 20), and culminating with Wörschnig's influential 1974 characterization of Roth's fictional universe as a "rückwärts gewandte Utopie" 'backward-looking Utopia' (90), the critics have constantly emphasized the antihistorical and melancholy aspect of Roth's version of Utopia. This interpretation fits in well with the perspective favored by other critics, namely that Roth's work is profoundly antiutopian (Hüppauf 33; Müller-Funk, *Joseph Roth* 195) because it does not favor an optimistic view of the future and does not posit the certainty of salvation for a world that seems to be condemned to await deliverance in perpetuity. Whether they accept the presence of Utopia in Roth's works or reject it is only secondarily relevant. What matters is that for both groups of critics, Roth does not offer a solution for the future, like all utopians do, but at most he builds his Utopia retrospectively, as a place and a time out of reach. According to Wirtz, Roth's historical mood is "disillusioned" (214); for Henze, Roth's depictions of the East European shtetl are utopian only in retrospect, as an "Arcadian place" (147); and for Magris, Roth's Utopias are not "titanic" but instead are "humble" and metaphorical (*Weit von wo* 179).

Nonetheless, these critics fail to acknowledge the unconventional nature of Utopia that one encounters in Roth's work, one that can be understood in conjunction with the thinking of Utopia that his contemporaries also promoted. Their interest in Utopia resulted, as we have seen, from their rediscovery of the Judaic notion of redemption but also from their opposition to scientific Marxism and sociological rationalism, two currents that had pushed the theory of Utopia, popular in the mid-nineteenth century, to the margins of the political discourse, dismissing it as romantic fantasy. The notion of Utopia that these Jewish thinkers developed differed, however, from the traditional forms of Utopia: it aimed at a new synthesis between the mystical expectation of the Kingdom of God and the rational understanding of the world. Moreover, for them, Utopia could only have meaning if it happened in history, while in turn history needed Utopia to advance in a meaningful manner. This understanding of Utopia differed significantly from its previous incarnations because traditionally, history and Utopia had been opposed to each other. Utopia had been generally seen as a cessation of all change, in the form of either a completion of an ideal teleological principle (rational or religious) or a return to an original state of perfection (a mythological golden age). Thomas Molnar argues that conventionally, Utopias attempt to arrest the linear conception of time or return to a cyclical time of the myth (16). The City of God and the Island of Utopia illustrate the idea of Utopia outside of history and contingency, frozen in a form of inorganic permanence. Analyzing the imaginary design of the utopian city, from the early religious Utopias to the social Utopias of the nineteenth century, Raymond Ruyer similarly argues that the emphasis on order and symmetry is an indication of the deductive, antihistorical, and antivital character of Utopia (43). According to Lutz Niethammer, the modern positivist Utopias have all opposed history, which they defined as a chaotic series of unrelated events. In opposition to the disharmony and purposelessness of the historical development of humanity, these Utopias of reason claimed to be able to ensure permanent peace and prosperity in a posthistorical period (17).

The Jewish philosophers of Utopia turned this tradition upside down, arguing instead for a codependency between history and Utopia, a living "concrete" form of Utopia, and an aspirational, transcendent view of history. The same reciprocity between history and Utopia defines Roth's own thinking about Utopia. As we shall further see, the interconnection between history and Utopia leads to a distortion of the idea of temporality itself in that all of history—past, present, and future—becomes permeated with the possibility of redemption. Thus, all time becomes concentrated into a single moment, the moment when Utopia enters history and redeems it in its entirety, yet this moment is eternally present as a potential. As Stéphane Mosès puts it in his study on Rosenzweig, Benjamin, and Scholem, what characterizes this vision of history is the "passage from a time of necessity to a time of possibles" (12). In this sense, Roth's Utopia is only apparently backward-looking. In fact, it unites the past with the present and the future in an attempt to redeem history in its entirety and give hope to the future generations. Not incidentally, Roth stresses the Jewish ability to hope in *The Wandering Jews*, to provide the world with faith in the eventual redemption of history. For this reason, Steinmann argues that Roth does not limit himself to creating nostalgic images of a world that no longer exists, but by using Dorothee Sölle's notion of sense-creation in literature, she argues that he engages in the utopian creation of new possibilities (*Von der Würde* 2).

The other facet of Roth's use of the idea of redemption, the mystical-religious one, has been acknowledged by the critics as well and often placed in the context of his interest in Judaism. His preoccupation with the problem of salvation and with the major questions of sin, atonement, and miracle have occasioned a variety of interpretations that focused principally on the messianic element in Roth's writing. Markus May points out that the narrative of sin, decline, punishment, return from exile, and redemption that is at the heart of much of Roth's fiction reenacts the messianic narrative in Judaism and indicates a similar interest in messianism to Bloch and Benjamin (252). Likewise, Almuth Hammer argues that the Judaic messianic motif appears in Roth's preoccupation with the end of exile through a metaphorical return to a spiritual home (199). For Thorsten Juergens, Roth's imagination is apocalyptic and messianic but mostly in the social sense of an expectation of the destruction of the social order and the outbreak of a new redeemed order. Juergens's interpretation places Roth at the intersection between Benjamin's historical apocalypticism and Bloch's principle of hope as a secular substitute for redemption, yet a redemption delayed in eternity (117). Magris frames the discussion about Roth's religious thinking within the wider context of Chasidism and is the first critic to analyze this relationship in detail and demonstrate that Roth promotes a view of salvation similar to Buber's, one inspired by Chasidism in which life and redemption coexist, as do history and Utopia, although for Magris the medium of the story is the only place where this synthesis can take place (*Weit von Wo* 129).

But most of these critics consider Roth's moral-religious writings as a reinterpretation of the ancient Judaic tension between redemption and history and posit the possibility for individual or collective salvation only through an escape from history and reality, hence their focus on the apocalyptical end of history as a sign of messianic deliverance. Blanke illustrates this idea when he refers to Roth's eschatological understanding of history and refuge in myth (31), as does Sebald when he points out Roth's search for a redemption from the exile of history (91). Few critics consider Roth's religious writings as an expression of a thinking about redemption in history, not outside of it, as a transformative mechanism that can repair the relationship between individual, God, and the universe in this world. Steinmann acknowledges Roth's distinctive place in the landscape of Judaic religious thinking, apart from both the enlightened Haskalah and the more mystical forms of apocalyptical messianism (*Von der Würde* 23). Instead, she argues, Roth works with a life-affirming idea of salvation of Chasidic inspiration that merges the past and the present with the promised future into a sacred eternal time that defies the temptation to escape history and to find refuge in either the past or an idealized time to come. Mehrens interprets Roth's religious writings as an illustration of a "divine mandate" of literature to recast the moral and redemptive content of the religious laws in narrative format and thus to revive them (359). Mehrens thus endows Roth's moral-religious literature with the ability to enact a redemptive promise in actuality and not in fiction alone, as Magris argued. It is the present study's contention that far from being a prophet of the apocalypse and of the end of history or a melancholy chronicler of the impossibility of Utopia, Roth uses the idea of redemption in order to transform rather than deny and to heal the relationship between the individual and society, God, and history. It is true, on the other hand, that Roth has not always been able to articulate the idea of redemption in these terms, resorting therefore to the apocalyptical antihistorical imagination, particularly in his early literary phase. This early phase is, however, an attempt to formulate the idea of renovation "in the negative" and is part of a wider search for an affirmative notion of redemption that will become explicit in his late career.

The idea of redemption analyzed here, whether in its secular-rational or its mystical-religious from, manifests itself in three separate but interrelated dimensions: the moral-individual, the collective-traditional, and the historical. After nineteenth-century philosophy and political theory had assigned the guiding role in shaping history to the state or even to the autonomous idea of reason, as in Hegel's case, Roth's generation reassigned it to the individual. All the members of this generation emphasized the importance of individual responsibility for the fate of the world and the necessity of defining the individual moral conscience in relation to some regulatory principles and values. However, postulating the simultaneous existence of moral freedom and normative constraints was not entirely free of contradictions. How could a system of norms and values be imposed on a free conscience without sacrificing its freedom? The solution they provided came in the form of the idea of redemption: instead of functioning like an immutable law, outside of history, the salvationist idea in Judaism enters into a dialogue with the historical individual, changing itself according to individual circumstances that in turn become changed by its presence. Hence, the morally free individual engages in a mutually transforming relationship with the regulatory norms so that while the purpose of redeeming the world remains permanent, it does not impose an already-made notion of salvation on the individual. For this reason, their idea of redemption is always associated with that of possibility, a possibility that requires a constant striving for the promised salvation. This striving is often rendered by the notion of hope, which encapsulates the dual nature of redemption: promised by God and desired by humans.[16]

The notion of redemption also remodeled the relationship between individual and community. The revaluation of the Judaic religious thinking offered a solution to the deadlock to which Enlightenment rationality and its supreme expression, the modern state, had brought the individual by constraining him to choose between the tyranny of collectivity and estrangement. This impossible choice facing the modern individual corresponded historically to the hopelessness of the Jewish political situation in Central Europe in the beginning of the twentieth century, a situation resulting from the incapacity of choosing between a vanishing bourgeois individualism and an emerging ethnic nationalism. The return to messianic Judaism represented an alternative to these two choices, an attempt to reconcile the irreconcilable conflicts within the modern society and offer a liberating alternative. The role of redemption in society was to offer a more meaningful identification of the individual with the community and with tradition, thus avoiding both the alienation brought by modern social fragmentation and the collective "mass loneliness" of which Buber spoke in his *Paths in Utopia* (14). Redemption as expectation represented above all a type of yearning that was simultaneously individual and collective: it summoned the individual to a position of moral responsibility for all of humankind. It gave meaning to the collective destiny of humanity while preserving the autonomy of the person. This higher synthesis overcame, in the opinion of many representatives of this generation, the exclusionary logic inherent to the nation-state and opened the way for theorizing the idea of identity, individual and collective, in nonconventional, plastic ways. This explains why for Roth the idea of identity is so malleable and often apparently contradictory.

A consequence of putting the individual in charge of the unfolding of history is the rethinking of history beyond the rationalist paradigm inaugurated by nineteenth-century historicism. Instead of considering history a closed chapter, an object to be known but not experienced, these thinkers proposed a view of history as a living organism, one that communicates across time with individuals and expects from them a moral investment in its unfolding. In order to prepare the ground for the possibility of redemption, one has to be simultaneously contemplating the past and entreating the future. Not coincidentally, these thinkers drew on the Judaic conception of history because of its messianic ability to unite the past and the future. There are no historical laws, they argued; there is our moral agency that decides in the present moment how history will be shaped, and by shaping history they did not mean only the things to come but also the past things, which are still present through their consequences and await the deliverance promised to all historical creation. The revaluation of the Judaic religious heritage, especially of Chasidism, was motivated by the desire to demonstrate that salvation does not have to be opposed to historical existence. To the contrary, salvation is possible only in history, regardless of how corrupt history actually is, by enlisting the moral agency of the individuals. Instead of waiting for the Messiah's arrival at the end of time, the Chasidic emphasis on salvation in the here and now gives the messianic redemption a historic, human dimension, reflected by the notion of individual salvation, or *devekut* (Idel, *Old Worlds* 214–16). Utopia takes on the same character. From a "major utopia," intended by the classical utopists as a vision that offers definitive solutions and grand plans of happiness, it becomes a "minor utopia," as Agnes Heller would say (57). In fact, through the emphasis on individual responsibility for the redemption of the world, Utopia becomes a form of messianic expectation, neither a guaranteed salvation nor an indefinite goal. Roth's reflections on the nature of individual and collective identity, tradition, and history illustrate these three dimensions of his redemptive philosophy.

The Moral-Individual Dimension of Redemption

If in *The Wandering Jews* Roth distances himself from the assimilated Jewish identity, favoring instead the East European, unassimilated, traditional identity, he also stops short of idealizing the latter. The "revolving door" between fictionalization and observation allows him to escape the unproblematic idealization of the East European Jews and often to present their situation with realism: "Here Jews live in dirty streets and collapsing houses. Their Christian neighbor threatens them. The local squire beats them. The official has them locked up" (*Wandering Jews* 6). Moreover, although he opposes Jewish assimilation in the West because the benefits of such an assimilation come at the price of a loss of Jewish spirituality, Roth considers the migration of the Jews from the East as being justified. In the 1934 article "Der Segen des ewigen Juden" ("The Blessing of the Eternal Jew") he remarks, "Wie aufrichtig waren die Juden des Zaren und die polnischen Juden, als sie flohen!" 'How sincere were the Jews of the Czar and the Polish Jews when they fled!' (*Werke* 3: 531). Such a contradiction between, on the one hand, his admiration for the ancestral world of the East European Jews and the criticism of assimilation in the West and, on the other hand, his honest acknowledgment of the brutal oppression of the Jews in Eastern Europe and his approval of their migration can be explained by the fact that Roth redefines the concepts of identity and belonging at a metahistorical and spiritual level, a level where the contradictions of historical existence are resolved. He uses actual historical situations, ethnic groups, or countries to construct some allegorical, "polemical and didactic" situations, as David Horrocks points out ("The Construction" 128), that act in turn back on their original context as realities of a higher order. This metamorphosis of reality into a higher spiritual kind of reality that has the ability to overcome all contradictions and conflicts is achieved through the use of the redemptive imagination, which restores the harmonious unity of reality. Roth does not seek unrealistic, idealized solutions for the Jews but offers instead a way to harmonize historical contingency and spiritual essence by redeeming history as history. Thus, if the traditional messianic promise in Judaism prophesied the actual end of history and suffering, for Roth redemption does not mean the end of human history and suffering but rather their transfiguration into a spiritual register that does not render them any less real. Only thus can one understand why Roth is able to see redemption at work even in a state of historical transience and misery, such as the migration of the Jews and life in the East European shtetl.

The true state of redemption, which Roth figuratively identifies with the Chasidic belief in salvation as an everyday condition, as an embrace of "here and now" but also of "beyond," does not cancel out history and instead redeems it: "Das Ostjudentum und der Osten erscheinen . . . nicht als Rückzugsort, nicht als 'Verneinung der Gegenwart', sondern vielmehr als Tor zur Nachmoderne" 'Eastern Judaism and the East do not appear as a retreat, or as a "denial of the present," but rather as a gateway to postmodernity' (Ochse 126–27). The fact that the Jews can accept a condition of restless migration and give up their roots as if these roots did not exist (an idea for which Roth received some harsh criticism from fellow German Jewish émigrés in 1934)[17] does not contradict the basic interdiction to renounce one's traditions and to seek assimilation, Roth argues. It is precisely because the Jews are loyal to their own traditions and to their own "spiritual" country, so to speak, that they try to maintain them under any circumstances, including those of exile and suffering: "Sie verleugnen nicht ihre Herkunft, aber sie unterdrücken auch nicht berechtigte Gefühle—was uns noch schimpflicher erscheint als die Verleugnung der Heimat" 'They do not deny their origin, but they do not suppress justified feelings either, which [would seem] to us even more disgraceful than the denial of the homeland,' he continues in the same article, "Der Segen des ewigen Juden" (*Werke* 3: 531). Redemption appears therefore as a way of living virtuously within history, not outside of it, and as a middle way between the immobilism of abstract constructs and the transience of historical change.

Those Jews who stubbornly venerate abstract ideas, Roth suggests, and uncritically cling to the notion of a permanent Jewish character and ritualistic Judaism look very much like the assimilated Jews who much too eagerly embrace the historical notions of individualism, progress, and nationalism. Whoever rejects history for the sake of a fetishized ideal forgets to live in the present and thus falls into the same trap as those who fetishize present history and forget about their connection with the redemptive "beyond": "Es gibt . . . nur eine bedingungslose Liebe: die zu Gott" 'There is only one unconditional love: that to God,' he writes in the 1934 article "Die Juden und die Nibelungen" 'The Jews and the Nibelungs' (*Werke* 3: 523). The true love of God is a principle that unites the historical, physical existence with the transcendental one, providing the mechanism that, in Roth's view, makes historical existence holy and gives an actual sense to divine law. Suggestively, it is only among the Chasidim that Roth encounters this authentic fusion of life and sacredness in what Idel calls "'worship in corporeality'—'*avodah be-gashmiyyut*'—worshiping God by whatever form of activity" (*Old Worlds* 216): "It moved me deeply to see a whole people that didn't separate physical cravings from spiritual joys but united them, consecrating its sensual pleasures to its God, making the book that contained its strictest laws into a beloved" (*Wandering Jews* 40).[18]

Viewed in this light, Roth's lamenting of the tragic "homelessness" of the European Jews does not refer to the loss of a particular geographic country. Wolfgang Müller-Funk identifies this country with the "Geborgenheit" or "feeling of security" offered by community and tradition (*Joseph Roth* 137), but Roth means by "country" a lot more than that, namely the home of the higher truth of redemption. This kind of belonging is an unconventional, dynamic concept, one that postulates the existence of a country even when on the move and that of a home when homeless. Remaining in their country and migrating are not mutually exclusive concepts for the European Jews; to the contrary, in a situation in which staying anywhere means being a stranger everywhere, to be at home is to be on the road. This historical condition of the Jews reflects their existential condition, Roth argues, that of being here but living with the anticipation of future salvation. Only by abandoning the clichés of our thinking, Roth continues, can we understand how one can be both at home and a refugee and why it is more relevant to know not where we come from but rather where we go: "And what matters to the wanderer is his destination, not his point of departure" (*Wandering Jews* 124). This connection with history, with the future, with the moral autonomy of the individual who decides where the homeland is located is reflected in Müller-Funk's witty remark that Roth's notion of home "nicht mehr um Herkunft, sondern eher um Hinkunft geht" 'no longer refers to origin, but to future' (*Joseph Roth* 195). This explains why, for Roth, the image of the wanderer, of the exile, and the immigrant carries with it the disruptive potential of redemption and is therefore assigned a central role in his entire work.

By emphasizing the importance of an authentic spiritual Jewish identity but at the same time rejecting its frozen, rigid forms, predicated on a fetishism of history, society, state, or even religion and tradition, Roth argues that there is no prescribed solution to the crisis of modern identity, whether Jewish or not. The idea of redemption in history that he promotes encourages instead a constantly renewed notion of identity that manages to respond to both the contingencies of history and the metaphysical immutability of deliverance. Hence, the state of migration becomes the only authentic manner of "being at home" and is "a moral imperative not just for Jews, but for all mankind" (Lazaroms, *The Grace of Misery* 169). The existential condition of the Jews, to live in history while continually expecting the Messiah's arrival, conveys in Roth's opinion this idea of salvation lived in constant historical deferment and readjustment:

> Der Messias läßt lange auf sich warten, man muß sich als Volk an die Nationalen Formen der anderen assimilieren. Und die gewaltige Tragik der Juden liegt [darin], daß sie vorläufig nur *eine* Rettung sehn. . . . Sie waren über die Welt verstreut worden, um Gottes Namen zu verbreiten. Sie haben indessen Gott selbst vergessen und müssen sich nun wieder in eine geographisch beschränkte Nationalität zurückziehen. In dieser "Heimkehr" der Juden liegt vielleicht noch mehr Tragik als in ihrer Zerstreuung. ("Der Segen des ewigen Juden," *Werke* 3: 531)

> The Messiah is a long time coming; one must assimilate as a nation to the national forms of the others. And the great tragedy of the Jews lies in the fact

> that, for the time being, they only see *one* salvation. . . . They had been scattered across the world to spread God's name. Meanwhile, they have forgotten God himself and now must return to a geographically delimited national form. In this "return" of the Jews, there may be more tragedy than in their dispersion.

The responsibility for ending the exile of the Jews falls directly with the Messiah, but his delay is also part of the narrative of redemption, Roth argues. For this reason, the historical condition of exile is not opposed to redemption but instead is an integral part of it, a step toward its completion. This particular religious view brings Roth yet again close to the religious ethos of Chasidism, where redemption takes place not away from but instead in exile, which amounts to "the destruction of exile by its spiritualization" (Scholem, *The Messianic Idea* 195). Finding easy solutions to this profound existential question unavoidably leads to moral devastation and spiritual ruin. In *The Antichrist*, a 1934 nonfictional novel, Roth argues that humanity's greatest temptation in modernity is to find comfortable, rational, and permanent solutions to its problems. The Antichrist lures humans into believing that they know God or that they are gods themselves, when in reality they only worship illusions. These illusions prevent them from knowing that the real goal of their search lies ahead of them and is the beacon that points the way toward the promised redemption. Humanity's condition is therefore also the unending search, the allegorical homelessness, that Roth turns from a curse into the prerequisite of redemption: "Our home is still indefinitely far away. But by no means do we go towards it. We halt by the wayside. We remain in the desert and imagine that we have reached our eternal home" (*Antichrist* 44).

The Jewish identity that Roth defines in a more theoretical-historical fashion in his middle and late career reshapes the idea of identity in general in a disruptive and radical manner, "zwischen Deplatzierung und kultureller Gebundenheit" 'between displacement and cultural attachment' (Hartmann 16). Their unique connection with God gives the Jews a mandate not only to reshape the modern Jewish identity, an identity torn between the temptation of assimilation and the resistance of tradition, but also to call into question the modern concepts of belonging, nation, territory, and state. It should not come as a surprise, then, why Roth rejected these modes of identification for the Jews, whether they came in the form of liberalism, socialism, Zionism, or even excessive traditionalism. Although interested in Zionism as a teenager and avowing his socialist beliefs in his youth, when he signed many of his early articles under the self-explanatory pseudonym "Der rote Joseph" (Red Joseph), Roth disavowed both Zionism and socialism during his middle and late career even if with some ambiguities, as Klaus Zelewitz argues ("Zur Dialektik"). Zionism represents, as Roth points out in the 1929 article "Wailing Wall," "the reversion to a primal, long since outmoded, form of national existence" (*What I Saw* 49) and a form of idolatry of history and territory that is alien to the Jews, who have already adopted a redeemed, "nomadic" identity.[19] After all, everything the Jews stand for, Roth argues in *The Wandering Jews*, is the very opposite of the idea of a Jewish *Vaterland*: "Given all the millennial grief of the Jews, they still had one consolation: the fact that they *didn't* have such a fatherland" (19). The Zionists' idolatry of territory and their ethnocentric view of the world pushed them in the ideological vicinity of the Nazis, argues Roth in an emotional letter to Stefan Zweig from 1935: "A Zionist is a National Socialist, a National Socialist is a Zionist" (*Joseph Roth: A Life* 414). Similarly, when the Jews succumb to the socialist temptation they are no longer Jews, Roth confesses in a 1925 letter to Benno Reifenberg, "because they have taken up the cudgels for some foreign proletariat" (59). Instead of remaining true to their religious messianic calling, they believe in social salvation and the proletarian struggle for equality, which is a messianic simulacrum resulting too from the idolatry of history and human reason.

The same nonconventional idea of identity, an identity shaped by the relationship with God, is present in Rosenzweig's *Star of Redemption*. Rosenzweig sees in the Jewish existence—much like Roth—the exemplary striving of humanity for living in history under the sign of the promise of redemption. The specific attribute of Jewish existence in the early twentieth century, that of living in exile, is seen by Rosenzweig as a unique ability to find roots within oneself and not outside, in a specific place. The Gentiles' reliance on a geographic location as a condition for their existence as a national group appears to Rosenzweig as a frozen attachment to a place that limits the group's ability to experience true historical change, that is to say, the unpredictable arrival of a redemption that is not conditioned in space or time: "we were the only ones who separated what lived within us from all community with what is dead. For while the earth nourishes, it also binds" (299). Instead of separating themselves from themselves by putting earth in between, the Jews turned to their own blood community, to the succession of generations as the guarantee of communal existence. Instead of separating the past from the future ("one sinking back, the other coming on"), they brought the two together in the "infinite Now": "the son is born so that he may bear witness to his father's father" (298). Finally, instead of binding themselves to a national history without beginning and without end (without final redemption), for the nation lives forever in its imaginary state-endorsed form, the Jews elevated the provisional character of existence in exile (and by extension in history) until the arrival of the Messiah to the principle that governs the day-to-day life of the community.

Rosenzweig's belief that for the Jews redemption is possible in exile, within history and not outside of it, echoes Roth's and Scholem's interpretation of the Chasidic idea of redemption: salvation does not require the end of *galut* but does require its spiritual transfiguration. Being a people (a political community) is not something that can be delegated to an outside entity that defines, regulates, and gives a definitive form to it, such as the state and the territory. Such a delegation demotivates the individual and the community and removes them from any obligation to others, such as the obligation embedded in the divine commandment to love. The Jews, however, live in history without such external guarantees, so they actively accept the aspiration for redemption, expressed as yearning for the Promised Land, as part of who they are: "the will to be a people dares not cling to any mechanical means; the will can realize its end only through the people itself" (*Star* 300). By relegating the promise of redemption to a constantly changing, wandering community, Rosenzweig reverses the meaning of belonging. In accepting the provisional nature of existence in exile, the Jews find an authentic form of rooting, while the peoples who settle for statehood and territory actually become uprooted: "We do not root in earth and so we are eternal wanderers, but deeply rooted in our own body and blood. And it is this rooting in ourselves, and in nothing but ourselves, that vouchsafes eternity" (305).

The rooting in oneself, in one's own essence, and not in easy, ready-made solutions is the redemptive condition that allows for historical change, transformation, and even assimilation, as Roth surprisingly contends, but also for maintaining a living bond with tradition and with the spiritual and transcendent purpose of all existence. Roth seems to suggest that only by turning toward oneself in this sense could assimilation take place without assimilating the spiritual core of one's identity. He claims that the individual has the power to rise above external constraints and to decide where home is and what one's identity is as long as this decision is not arbitrary but instead is grounded in the recognition of a spiritual purpose. This voluntary aspect of belonging is at the heart of his moral understanding of the world. Echoing Leo Baeck's idea that the Jews' messianic fervor produces their moral view of the world, Roth suggests that doing the right thing, improving the world, demonstrates that God's work is also done through us: "*wherever there is good, there is my home*," he writes in *The Antichrist*. "Above all, we are Children of God, and God alone is our home" (*Antichrist* 163). The world, the home, and our identity are all within our power. Making a home is more important than simply having one because it requires individual action and moral commitment, which explains why Klaus Bohnen considers the idea of home the central trope of Roth's literary universe, the "*Fixpunkt*" that balances all contradictions (58). Rather than subjecting ourselves to external conditioning, Roth suggests in *The Antichrist* that we need to take charge of our destiny and tear the veil of illusions. This power is given to us by our creator: "He has given us legs and feet not only so that we may be at home in all His countries, but also that we may leave a home where evil is perpetrated" (*Antichrist* 163–64). The conjunction of God's will and individual will is illustrative for the idea that we are accountable for the way in which redemption is made part of our everyday existence. The moral responsibility toward the world falls upon each individual and demands that one should not resign to the whims of history or seek refuge from them.

The idea that the world is redeemed through the joint labor of individual conscience and divine will is common to other thinkers of Roth's generation. Just like him, they drew on the Judaic notions of responsibility, morality, and love in order to show the importance of the moral involvement of the individual. In his *Paganism, Christianity, Judaism*, Max Brod argues that in order to have a redemptive character, morality needs to be free and mandated at the same time. Generosity alone, kindness in itself, oblivious of the redemptive direction given by God, scatters over creation without achieving a genuine unification with God in the sense of the Judaic notion of *tikkun*. On the other hand, acting morally out of fear or interest alone does not ensure salvation: there has to be also a natural desire to act morally. For Brod, probably influenced by the Weberian idea of "ethics of conviction," the morality preached by Christianity, that of the love that transcends all commandments, is characteristic of the former type. The latter, however, is typical of secular morality, which Brod associates with modern Paganism. Judaism, on the other hand, is a religion that strives to achieve a fusion between nature and duty, to fulfill the law with joy, as an act that brings pleasure in itself. Brod's belief that the divine law has to be fulfilled with earthly joy in order to unleash the redemptive moment reflects his fondness of the Chasidic emphasis on joyful religious fervor, a fondness shared also by Buber and Roth. These moments of intersection between prescribed law and natural predisposition are the true moments of divine grace, when what we do on Earth achieves a different, transcendent meaning.

For Brod, the transformative moment when human morality and divine law meet is a mystery that requires active expectation or a form of hopeful entreating of divine mercy. It is true, he argues, that the ecstatic moment of redemption in history is achievable only through miraculous divine intervention, through the sudden penetration of the historical plane of existence by eternity, and that any human effort alone does not guarantee it, but this should not demotivate the individual: "solitariness and waiting, hoping for grace, without actively interfering, is self-derision, and activity without waiting in humility is empty noise" (*Paganism* 78). Therefore, Brod argues, in Judaism the moral responsibility toward the world carries a redemptive meaning; it is the gateway through which God's grace is imparted upon the world and the embryonic cord, so to speak, between creation and redemption, between man and God. One must try, regardless of the odds, to redeem the world—this is the only acceptable alternative for the morally free individual. Only thus can one keep the ground prepared for the unexpected divine act of mercy. This emphasis on responsible action brings Brod closer to Rosenzweig's belief that "insofar as he [man] acts responsibly, the goal of his actions can only be redemption or the kingdom of God. Here, in the essence of concrete responsibility, which is always a worldly action, man experiences the love of God, which directs him and which gives content to responsibility" (Casper 106).

Brod also addresses the use of human reason in solving the problems faced by individuals. According to him, secular modernity claims that all human problems can be solved through reason and its offshoots, including science, technology, and politics. Brod argues that by relying exclusively on reason, secular modernity acknowledges only the ignoble misfortune (*unedles Unglück*). Christianity, on the other hand, acknowledges only the noble misfortune (*edles Unglück*). There is nothing in the misfortune that humankind encounters that can be solved by human reason, Christianity argues, and the hope for salvation comes from God alone, not from human action. Judaism, on the other hand, recognizes both the noble and the ignoble misfortune (26). According to Brod, Judaism offers the prospect of a transcendent salvation but also urges human action, the application of the laws, and the moral involvement with one's condition. The improvement of the world through good works is a fundamental dimension of Judaism, but so is the miraculous intervention of God as a redeemer of creation. The idea that reason in itself is not the root of the spiritual crisis of modernity but instead is its separation from the sphere of religion is an idea also shared by Roth. In *The Antichrist*, Roth points out that reason was first given to humans by God as an act of divine mercy, but when they started relying exclusively on it to deal with all life's questions, this reason became destructive. Hence, Roth contends, rational action has its role in solving humanity's problems, but this role must be limited by the recourse to religious faith: "Was . . . ist die irdische, die menschliche Vernunft, wenn sie sich nicht als Tochter der sittlichen, der himmlischen bekennt?" 'What . . . is the earthly, the human reason, if it does not see itself as the daughter of the moral, the heavenly reason?' (untitled article from 1937 published by Klaus Westermann under the title "Der Monarch verhindert den Diktator," *Werke* 3: 765). For Roth as for Brod, rational action plays an important role in improving the world because it is the human counterpart to the divine plan of salvation.

The fusion of moral-rational work and divine miracle that Brod sees at work only in Judaism is discussed by Roth, who is interested in a broader Judeo-Christian synthesis, in conjunction with Christian theology.[20] In his 1936 lecture "Glauben und Fortschritt" ("Faith and Progress"), the mature Roth resorts to Thomas Aquinas's conception of reason to convey the same idea: reason has been given to humans to promote the work of God, that is, love and not progress. Morality and reason are united at the roots: "Es ist, wie wir wissen, ein immanent Gutes im Menschen vorhanden. Es ist, wie wir ferner gesehen haben, nicht möglich daß diese Gute ausgeführt werde ohne Vernunft" 'There exists, as we know, intrinsic good in the human being. It is not possible, as we have further seen, that this good is done without reason' (*Werke* 3: 703). When reason is employed in the right way, it produces divine effects in the world and opens up the way for miracles. But, Roth argues, modern humans have ceased to use reason the way it was intended, as an instrument of the divine effort to redeem existence, and are no longer capable of hoping or of perceiving the miracle of God's work (704). Instead, their actions, even when they are moral, lack the spark of redemption, and their faith, even when deep, lacks the anchoring in reason and morality.

The moral imperative in Judaism is also emphasized by Ernst Bloch in his 1918 *The Spirit of Utopia*. Bloch seeks to free human conscience from the autonomous principle of reason, which, according to Hegel, defines moral action in light of the necessary identity between the real and the ideal, or between the "is" and the "ought to be." Instead, Bloch argues, drawing on neo-Kantian philosophy, what ought to be is not determined rationally but instead is determined by recourse to a dimension of transcendence that cannot be logically demonstrated and that opens itself onto us in the form of our moral freedom. However, he continues, ensuring the conditions for the moral freedom of the individual, as Kant did, is not enough. Some guarantee is needed that moral actions are correct or that they find their fulfillment through some higher principle. As a result, Bloch argues that the transcendent character of the moral ideas both frees us from the constraints of the Hegelian model of autonomous rationality and, at the same time, puts limits on our freedom. We live, Bloch continues, in the tension created by our freedom to imagine the future as something not yet achieved, as a promise not guaranteed or determined in advance but hoped. This is why for him Utopia is a "supermundane sphere still to be evangelized, still valid over the distance," which stimulates the moral engagement of the individual (179).

Hope, an idea to which he devoted his multivolume magnum opus *The Principle of Hope*, written between 1938 and 1947, allows Bloch to posit the existence of the redemptive moment away from any actuality that might undermine it. If Utopia functions only as a guide to life but is never realizable in actuality, the promise itself loses all meaning, and moral action becomes pointless; if on the other hand Utopia is realized in actuality, freedom itself disappears, Bloch argues. Hence, the messianic moment is bound never to become reality precisely because that would be tantamount to its own extinction. The only situation in which the tension between the transcendent ideal and the immanent real acquires any meaning is that of hoping. Through the category of hope, an idea "illuminated" by "the Jewish eschatological imagination," Bloch opens a third way between the alternatives of freedom and determinism (Mendes-Flohr, *Divided Passions* 105). Hoping for the Messiah's arrival is the typically human response to the paradoxical condition of living in history as free individuals with the anticipation of a final deliverance from the reign of contingency. Similarly, Franz Rosenzweig describes hope as the manifestation of redemption within history: "Hopeful trust is the key word in which the anticipation of the future into the eternity of the moment occurs" (*Star* 252), while Roth defines "home" as the promise of salvation and "hope" as the characteristically Jewish vehicle that points humanity in the right direction. In Judaism, individual moral duty is deeply involved in the divine redemption of the world, as the Talmudic belief that man can redeem God demonstrates (Brod, *Paganism* 32–33), although it alone does not guarantee redemption. The initiative for that rests with God alone, with his mercy, as Brod puts it, which is entreated through prayer, as Rosenzweig argues (*Star* 184) or, in Bloch's secular rendition, through an attitude of hoping.

A more radical moral demand on history is made by Walter Benjamin, whose 1940 "Theses on the Philosophy of History" argues that a strictly rational understanding of history is oblivious to the inherent need for justice that motivates all historical change. In order to evince this dimension of history, Benjamin argues in favor of a messianic interpretation of history that allows the redemptive demand to have final recourse over the outcome of historical events. Just like Bloch, Benjamin promotes the idea of a sovereign will, freed from the empire of rational necessity and legal restraint and capable of making decisions and establishing legal authority through them, something he captures in the concept of "divine violence" that he describes in his earlier 1921 essay "Critique of Violence." Under the influence of Carl Schmitt and Georges Sorel, Benjamin argues that divine violence is the engine of justice, liberating and anti-institutional, while laws and legal violence only establish the power of institutions and mythicize the rational control over the individual (*Reflections* 295). The fact that justice is not a rational or immanent need but instead is a transcendent one, a form of divine mandate to redeem existence, takes precedence in Benjamin's view over our rational projections on history or society. Benjamin uses the "'anarchic breeze' of Jewish messianism" (Rabinbach 63) to reformulate the Marxist philosophy of history and argues as a result that the duty of the proletariat should be to enact its messianic role through "its hatred and its spirit of sacrifice" (*Illuminations* 252) and not wait for its final victory through some kind of teleological rationality of history. The role of the historian is, in this sense, not to establish facts through observation but instead to identify with the transcendent principle of justice in history: "In this structure, he [the historian] recognizes the sign of a Messianic cessation of happening, or put differently, a revolutionary chance in the fight for the oppressed past" (254). Roth too considers the role of the historian in a similar fashion, as he declares it in his 1932 foreword to *The Radetzky March* namely to intervene in the course of history and repair those injustices that were brushed aside by the blind forward march of time. But while Roth's moral restitution does not cancel out history but instead redeems it through the memory act, Benjamin's demand for justice is a "tiger's leap into the past," a literal obliteration of the present through a forceful intervention in the course of history (*Illuminations* 253). For Roth, the moral intervention in history unites the sphere of divine law and the plane of historical existence, whereas in Benjamin's case the demand for justice inaugurates a brand-new era through an apocalyptic and violent event.

The moral responsibility for the work of divine redemption falls upon the individual not only in time, through the obligation to bring justice to historical existence, but also in space. In the 1938 article "Dem Anschein nach" ("Apparently"), Roth writes that "das Leben dieser Erde ist einheitlich, und ein Lebendiges ist, noch über Millionen Kilometer, mit dem anderen Lebendigen verschwistert, und wenn irgendwo das Böse geschieht, ist es überall geschehen. Vielleicht kann es eine wirtschaftliche 'Autarkie' geben; eine sittliche ist unmöglich" 'the life of this earth is unified, and a living being is still kin to another living being even over millions of miles, and when evil happens anywhere, it happens everywhere. Perhaps there may exist an economic "autarky"; a moral one is impossible' (*Werke* 3: 829). The idea that the moral responsibility for all existence is inherent to the relationship between the individual and God is common to other thinkers of the generation as well. Rosenzweig associates moral responsibility with the divine commandment "Love thy neighbor," considering that divine love extends itself toward the human being but that its purpose is to be passed on to the rest of creation. For Rosenzweig, "the neighbor" does not refer strictly to a neighboring person or a specific neighbor. That which is most immediate, humans or things, is what constitutes the neighbor. It can be anyone or anything that steps into the position of neighborliness: "Love goes out to whatever is nighest to it as to a representative, in the fleeting moment of its presentness, and thereby in truth to the all-inclusive concept of all men and all things which could ever assume this place of being its neighest neighbor" (*Star* 218). This versatility of love, its ability to affect any changing context, is what brings it into the living flow of historical change and unending spatial vicinity. Because it is derived from God, from the divine commandment to love, it is eternal, but because it does not fix eternally on the same things or persons, it is universal. As Roth points out in *The Antichrist*, moral responsibility for life on Earth is an obligation that stems from the redemptive promise made by God: "God is our only home. In His sublime presence there can be no evil but only love and justice. Outside of His sublime presence He has given us no home other than paradise and after that the entire earth" (164). This complex narrative of redemption, beginning with the religious transformation of the idea of identity and continuing with its moral manifestations into the realms of history and creation, from the Judaic to the universal, is frequently employed by Roth in his fictional universe.

The Collective-Traditional Dimension of Redemption

As Michael Brenner points out, one of the lessons of World War I was the failure of the old types of community that were built around the nineteenth-century concept of nation-state but also around the idea of a mystical community of blood and soil. The war, carried out in the name of militaristic nation-state interests but also in the name of the supreme idea of nation, was a reminder that the spontaneity of the nation and its spiritual essence should not be hijacked by bureaucratic and hierarchical state institutions, while the freedom of the individual should not be sacrificed to a transhistorical, metaphysical, and eternal concept of nation. The need for a different type of community, one that managed to offer the highest degree of cohesion possible while also maintaining the autonomy of the individual, encouraged the radical reconceptualization of the idea of collective identity among the philosophers and sociologists of the interwar period. For the Central European Jewish intellectuals, this need translated into the search for a community that was traditional and genuine but also open-ended and historically flexible. As Max Brod explains in his 1920 article "Der 'Herderverein'" ("The Herder Society"), the construction of a national Jewish community must be different from the European nations and also be an example of how a community can avoid narrow-minded nationalism (*Im Kampf* 70). Martin Buber too became one the most outspoken advocates of a new type of communitarianism and an ardent opponent of the idea of state (Brenner 36). Joseph Roth also understood the fact that the war resulted from a crisis of collective identity, especially of national identity, and denounced from the very beginning both the bureaucratic mentality of the nation-states and the *völkisch* definition of the nation.

Already in 1919 in the aftermath of the war, Roth condemned the nationalist-bureaucratic mold in which the new Central European states were formed. Facing difficulty in crossing borders that before 1919 did not exist, Roth meditates in the article "Die Kugel am Bein" ("The Ball and Chain") on the nature of the identity conferred by the nation-states: "Er [der Pass] konstatiert nur jene Sorte von Heimat, die durch Polizei, Bezirkshauptmannschaft, Magistrat repräsentiert wird und keine Heimat ist, sondern ein papierener, stempelbesäter Begriff: Staatsbürgerschaft" 'The passport only confirms the kind of residence that is sanctioned through the police, administrative and legal authorities, and that is no true home, but rather a concept expressed through paper and stamps: a state citizenship' (*Werke* 1: 147). The fundamental inability of the nation-state to be a true home results from the mechanistic, empty way in which it treats its citizens, as identical copies of the same abstract national type and without any regard for individual difference or for the spiritual dimension of individual existence. The state exemplifies in Roth's view modernity's basic social contract: one gives up everything in order to enjoy the insider status, some protection, and a sterile identification with a national cultural ideal: "Man muß fühlen, daß man Staatsbürger, Einwohner ist, Registrierter, Katastrierter, unter dem Schutze der Gesetze Stehender, polizeilich Gemeldeter, zehnprozentige Steuer Zahlender, kurz: Kulturmensch mit Niveau und Hemmungen" 'One must feel that one is a citizen, a resident, verified, castrated, a ten-percent taxpayer under the protection of the law, registered with the police, in short: a civilized man with standards and inhibitions,' writes Roth in the 1920 article "Wo ist der Schutzmann?" 'Where Is the Constable?' (*Werke* 1: 364). This diagnostic of the modern state, reminiscent of Freud's *Civilization and Its Discontents*, is common to turn-of-the-twentieth-century political criticism of the state and, according to Werner Sieg, demonstrates an intellectual affinity between Roth and the anarchist ideas of Max Stirner, Sergey Netchayev, and Georges Sorel (94). Analyzing the protagonists of Roth's early novels, all anarchic individuals who reject the state and the compromises one has to strike with modern civilization in order to fit in, Sieg argues that Roth promotes an antibourgeois anarchism with pronounced individualist traits. And yet at the same time, this anarchic individualism did not only reject the state but did express the need for a deeper form of communal solidarity, for a true community.[21]

The anarchist tendencies among Roth's contemporary Jewish intellectuals have also been pointed out by Löwy and Rabinbach. The "religious anarchism" of Buber, Landauer, Rosenzweig, and Scholem translated into a synthesis of religious and political ideas and into the search at the very heart of Jewish spirituality, especially of Chasidism, of a type of community that due to its belief in redemption allowed for a radical combination of individualism and collectivism (Löwy 50). Likewise, Benjamin and Bloch shared, according to Rabinbach, a certain "messianic anarchism," although Bloch later moved away from it toward orthodox Marxist positions (59). Their critique of the rational organization of the state opened up the way for new radical ways of imagining the modern community by using religious and utopian concepts. Using his dialogical-religious model of interpersonal relationships, Buber develops quite early an idea of society in which all the members enter into a meaningful and organic connection with each other, thus ensuring communal peace and harmony. In his 1945 *Paths in Utopia*, Martin Buber returns to his philosophy of society and argues that while societies traditionally relied on their communal spiritual experiences in order to achieve a sense of harmonious belonging, the modern state has confiscated the idea of belonging and subordinated it to its mechanical and rational logic. It was the role of Marxism in its original form, he argues, to liberate society from the state, but instead it replaced the bourgeois state with a new state, run by the revolutionary and party elites. Hence, Buber returns to utopian socialism in order to release that original communitarian potential: "We have seen that it is the goal of Utopian socialism so-called to substitute society for State to the greatest degree possible, moreover a society that is 'genuine' and not a State in disguise" (80). A genuine society that makes the state superfluous is, however, more than just the sum of all individuals or collective values of a national group. For Buber, a society must represent the highest degree of codependency and complementariness of the individual and the group, allowing for both the organic integration of its constituent parts and their individual spontaneity: "a real community is one which in every point of its being possesses, potentially at least, the whole character of community" (*Paths* 145).[22] Buber's utopian community resembles closely Tönnies's notion of organic community (*Gemeinschaft*) and the way in which that is different from contractual society (*Gesellschaft*): "in the *Gemeinschaft*, they [the people] remain essentially united in spite of all separating factors, whereas in the *Gesellschaft*, they are essentially separated in spite of all uniting factors" (Tönnies 65).

Rosenzweig adopts a similar critique of the state and, in *The Star of Redemption*, argues that the modern state is the expression of the desire to find collective redemption in history. He shares Buber's and Bloch's belief that the need for redemption manifests itself naturally within society and is inherent to creation, but, he argues, when peoples believe that they can freeze it into an eternal historical form, they create surrogates of redemption, such as the state. Drawing heavily on the Hegelian notion of state, a notion that in German intellectual history spanned the late nineteenth century and was enthroned as the culmination of civilization by historians such as Leopold von Ranke and philosophers such as Hermann Cohen, Rosenzweig presents the purpose of the state as the collective striving to step outside history, outside itself, and to acquire a meaning that transcends all epochs. But the state is itself historical, he argues. It exists within history but is engaged in a never-ending battle to conquer it: "the state symbolizes the attempt to give nations eternity within the confines of time, an attempt which must of necessity be repeated again and again" (332). Revolutions and epochs succeed each other in an attempt to stop the clock of history, to bring a final resolution to the unending flux of life. "But soon enough boisterous life again overflows the table of hard and fast rules" (333). Hence, Rosenzweig argues, societies need to return to the flux of redemption in history, to the constant dialogue of the historical present and the metaphysical "beyond."

For Rosenzweig as for Brod, Landauer, and Roth, the Jews have the particular mission of restoring society's normal relationship with redemption in history. This mission has naturally alienated them from the workings of the state, which does not acknowledge a higher authority outside itself. Rosenzweig stresses often how divergent the existence of the state and that of the Jewish community are: "the true eternity of the eternal people must always be alien and vexing to the state, and to the history of the world" (334). The state's alien temporality and its fixation on historical forms and desperate attempt to stop the flow of life collide with the existence of a population that is eternal in itself while also being present in history. The Jews do not need the state because they have resolved the problems to which the state attempts to provide the solution. Hence, the state will always persecute them, Rosenzweig continues, will always try to remove any unfamiliar form of historicity or temporality and level all irregularities under its uniform rationality. The problem of the historical persecution of the Jews appears thus to be less determined by anti-Semitism, by prejudice and ethnic hatred, as by the manner in which collectivities decide to resolve the dilemma of their existence in history. The conception of the state as eternity "within the confines of time" discourages individuals from taking moral responsibility for their communal existence, Rosenzweig argues, and thus shuts them off from their redemptive mission (332). Hence, the rejection of the state exemplified by the Jewish communal identity has an anarchic and liberating moral function. For Roth, the fact that many European Jews became stateless in the interwar period is only a confirmation of the same belief that the modern state is incompatible with the idea of home in its moral and spiritual sense. As he puts it in an open letter to Walter Mehring from 1934, "Das Land 'Staatenlos': Dort sind wir zu Hause" 'The country of "Stateless": there we are at home' (*Werke* 3: 517).

A similar critique of the state, whether liberal or Marxist, is waged by Karl Mannheim in his 1929 *Ideology and Utopia*. Mannheim shares Bloch's belief that there exists a seed of utopianism, a "prophetic dream waiting in the head of every thing" (Bloch 203), which explains why societies continuously try to improve themselves, to change their organization. However, Mannheim argues, during the modern period, this utopian seed has been hit by an ideological paralysis, a form of "freezing" of the utopian potential in historical forms that were considered perfect in themselves. For this reason, he argues, the only manner in which change appeared possible was to resort to pure Utopias, to a revolutionary fervor that was, however, divorced from reality and capable only of suspending the continuum of history but never to provide a feasible solution for the future. The modern revolutions are expressions of this repressed utopian consciousness. Mannheim and many other young Jewish intellectuals of his time witnessed the dissolution of the liberal state and the failure of the liberal project to provide a genuine liberation of the Jews. The reason for this was that liberalism was only an empty form, devoid of actual content: "culture in the narrower sense, freedom, personality, are only frames for a content, which, one might say, has been purposely left undetermined" (222). As soon as other political doctrines that were built on a concrete belief (such as nation, working class, and church) challenged its authority, liberalism collapsed. But, Mannheim continues, if the liberal state failed because it froze the promise of salvation into formal principles that lacked substance, the Marxist state failed too because it froze the utopian promise into an oppressive and totalizing ideology. Hence, he concludes, the human need for Utopia, for transcendence, needs to be kept "flowing," alive, and joined with history in a harmonious way that manages to push society forward.

Not just the modern state, in its rational-mechanical form, but also the national idea, in its ethnocentric and racial formulations, annihilates the redemptive, utopian potential intrinsic to human society. During his entire career, Roth never tired of pointing out the logical, historical, and moral fallacies of the ethnic definitions of nationhood or national culture. Whether combating the chauvinism of the early *völkisch* movements in Germany, the Neo-Pagan mystique of the idea of blood community, or the ethnocentrism of Polish, Czech, or Hungarian nationalism, Roth constantly strove to demonstrate the arbitrary nature of nations, the permeability of cultures, and the necessity of building a universal community based on the underlying human need for redemption. It is for this reason that Roth rejected Jewish nationalism and even the Jewish national idea. For him, such a prospect was a compromise of the uncompromisable: the messianic idea. As he argues in the 1937 article "Juden, Judenstaat und die—'Katholiken'" ("Jews, Jewish State, and the 'Catholics'"), the messianic calling of the Jews is to go beyond such definitions and use their privileged position in relation to the other nations in order get to the essence of human existence. In his search for a form of higher spiritual belonging, Roth constantly emphasized the importance of flexible definitions, unpredictable identities, and open-ended cosmopolitan communities that coexisted, however, with strong moral and religious traditions. For Roth too, this conjunction of freedom and necessity was important, as it was for Buber, Bloch, and the others, and was predicated as well on the mutual relationship between history and redemption.

But while criticizing the forms of collective identity that the state or the idea of nation represented did not necessarily require a complex exercise of imagination, offering an alternative, an explicit formulation of an idea of community that met the exigencies of redemption, required time and reflection. If Roth's denunciation of the modern state and nationalism are present from the beginning of his writing career, an expression of the ideal utopian community does not appear until his 1925 visit to southern France. There, "across the fence" of his German culture, he discovers a world in which definitions, principles, and concepts are not as perennial and clear-cut as in Germany but instead are flexible and fluid: "There wasn't the continual endeavor always to have things set in stone. Over there, on the other side, people are continually changing" (Roth, *Report* 72). Roth rediscovers himself in the Provençal world, a world in which all the contradictions that plagued the modernized and industrialized North seemed to be lifted. He is impressed by the cultural diversity of this world, by the coexistence at its very heart of multiple historical narratives of the old and the new, of belonging and estrangement, all living harmoniously together under the inclusive patronage of the Catholic Church and the ancient Mediterranean spirit. Any ideal community, he concludes, must look like that, inclusive and open-ended yet meaningful and authentic: "Each can understand each and their society is open; no one is forced to take up any particular position. This is assimilation at its best: A person may remain as different [*fremd*] as he is and feel at home" (*Report* 109). Roth resorts to the paradoxical formulation of belonging through estrangement in order to paint the portrait of a redeemed form of communal existence.

The reinterpretation of the idea of community as an open-ended, individual-collective construct through the religious notion of redemption is common to other members of Roth's generation. In *Paths in Utopia*, Buber imagines Utopia as a collective aspiration for improvement, an aspiration that is not immanent to society itself although it lives in history and is shaped by it. This aspiration descends upon society from above, so to speak, from a quasi-religious need to redeem the world, but it is given concrete form by the actual historical organization of society. Because it is not rationally produced within society, the aspiration for redemption always displaces society, pushes it forward, beyond itself. Buber sees in this incompleteness of society the sine qua non condition for any utopian form of communal existence. He uses Kropotkin's thesis according to which "we conceive the structure of society to be something that is never finally constituted" as an illustration of this idea of open-ended, changing society (Kropotkin qtd. in Buber, *Paths* 43). But at the same time, just because it is not complete does not mean that society lacks solidarity or a unity of purpose. For Rosenzweig too, the true political constitution of a group has to be simultaneously based on the immanence of historical time and on the transcendence of redemption. As a result, the historical existence of the group is always provisional, never fully finished. Its completion rests on the arrival of the Kingdom. At the same time, the sense of redemption is not strictly individual, although divine revelation is very individualizing in its form of address: "thou." The hope for redemption expresses itself in human action as love for the neighbor, so individual redemption has meaning only within community: "man senses his earthly eternity within the human community . . . and not as individual" (*Star* 291). At the same time, any community is receptive to the promise of redemption only in the neighborliness of the rest of humankind, as a universal community encompassing all of humanity. The "We" of the community seeking redemption, although starting as simply as an "I" and a neighbor, ends up encompassing everyone (325). For Rosenzweig, the principle that unites the individual and the community is the common anticipation of redemption.

This societal openness is not obtained, however, through the denial of tradition but, to the contrary, through the affirmation of an authentic, ancestral, and living tradition that is constantly renovated in the present. For Roth, this interpretation of tradition is the only legitimate way of using tradition: "I have learned here that nothing can continue to exist unless it represents continuity in some way—not necessarily linear or logical, but continuity. . . . In the future is the past" (*Report* 118). The Germanic flaunting of Teutonic traditions is, by contrast, a modern phenomenon, Roth argues, and an example of a false tradition, one that excludes or levels out all differences. As in the case of his dynamic conceptualization of the ideas of individual and collective identity, tradition represents for Roth more than just a ritualistic gesticulation or a freezing into inherited beliefs and principles. It must be open to change, to historical transformation, while at the same time retaining its innermost nature, its spiritual core. In this sense, living within tradition requires constant alertness and moral involvement in reshaping the inherited past. Roth returns to this manner of formulating the ideal utopian community, at the intersection of tradition and historical change, in his reflections on the Jewish community, beginning with the 1927 *The Wandering Jews* and then throughout the 1930s in his ample historical portraiture of the multinational Austrian Empire.

In a similar fashion, for Buber the utopian transformation of society is due to its dual nature, transcendent and immanent to history, both revolutionary and conservative. It creates the new, but the new can only have meaning if it fits into the structure of the old. The brand new, as in Benjamin's philosophy of history, would completely destroy the old, something that Buber wants to avoid because it would also destroy the rational justification of Utopia. This utopian act is therefore a revolutionary conservation of tradition, as Gustav Landauer understood it: "What he [Landauer] has in mind is ultimately a revolutionary conservation: a revolutionary selection of those elements worthy to be conserved . . . for the renovation of the social being" (Buber, *Paths* 59). The conservative aspect of Buber's utopianism is therefore intricately knit into its revolutionary nature in the same way in which for Roth the conservation of tradition is an act of revolutionary change while true rebellion is a reactionary act, as he paradoxically declares in his 1937 portrait of Franz Grillparzer (*Werke* 3: 747). Probably Scholem captures this "Jewish conception" of the idea of tradition in the most edifying manner: "It is the living contact in which man takes hold of ancient truth and is bound to it, across all generations, in the dialogue of giving and taking" (*Messianic Idea* 303). The notion of redemption in the Judaic sense merges the past of the collective tradition with the historical present of individual autonomy, achieving a synthesis between necessity and freedom.

The Historical Dimension of Redemption

The redefinition of identity as a malleable concept rooted in the moral capacity to balance historical contingency and transcendent principles, modernity and tradition, and individualism and communitarianism required a radical reconceptualization of the idea of history, one that was consistent with the restorative potential of the notion of redemption. As Stéphane Mosès demonstrates, the historicist models favored by the nineteenth-century historical sciences, models founded on the assumption that history can be rationally comprehended as a logical process, failed in their predictions about the course of history. World War I, the economic depression, and the crisis of the nation-states were all evidence that history does not follow any preestablished rules and that science alone cannot solve the puzzle of historical change. Many young Jewish intellectuals of the time turned back "to the Jewish experience of history to discover a radically different dimension of historical consciousness and its utopian dimension" (Mosès 13). In Roth's case, the conceptualization of history takes place around the Jewish understanding of time as an intracommunal experience. Precisely because the Jews are rooted in their own inner historical time, a time of messianic expectation, their existence is not dependent on historical forms, such as the modern nation or the state, both modes of existence that, in Roth's opinion, the Jews have already surmounted. For Roth, the internal coherence of the Jewish people is made possible by the use of memory, a memory of the covenant, of the promised redemption, but also of the trials and tribulations of this unfolding promise. Remembering the past unites generations and gives them a common purpose. This unity across time is the unity of redemption living within history. As Rosenzweig observes, "it is a memory which is really not past at all, but eternally present. Every single member of this community is bound to regard the exodus from Egypt as if he himself had been one of those to go" (*Star* 304).

In *The Antichrist*, Roth links the importance of remembering to an idea of redemption that closely resembles the Kabbalistic notion of *tikkun,* or reunification with God: "it is in our innate nature to yearn eternally to become God—because we never forget our origins and are reflections that are always searching for their prototype" (44). If memory is the mechanism through which tradition survives, modernity, on the other hand, thrives on forgetting, Roth argues. Forgetting prompts the individual to cut oneself off from the inherited past and define oneself exclusively in view of the present and of the centrality of the self, in isolation from history and from community. For this reason, "the ability to forget quickly and emphatically" is contrasted by the narrator Roth in the novel *The Radetzky March* with how things were "back then" ("So war es damals!" in the utopian imperial Austria), when "people lived on memories" (*Radetzky March* 112). The logic of modernity, predicated on the autonomy of reason, separates the historical present from the past and conceives of the individual as an insular entity who guides oneself according to abstract rational choices. By contrast, the logic of redemption approaches history as a total phenomenon in which all the moments are still united and in a constant dialogue across time. Everything that happened in the past affects the present in a very immediate and meaningful manner because history is based on the idea of organic growth, just like tradition. As Roth points out in the 1925 series of reports from Provence titled "The White Cities": "Is there not one world again today, welded together by the force of memory? Does the Orient not survive in the Roman arch, in the medieval epic? Are there really distinct worlds? Is there not just one world? What seems to divide, to set apart—does it not in fact unite us?" (*Report* 115).

Because Roth views history as a unitary phenomenon, he rejects the narrative of gradual human development and posits instead the possibility of unforeseen changes, relapses, and even complete reversals in human history. In the 1936 conference "Glauben und Fortschritt," he argues that such unforeseen changes should be interpreted not as derailments from "legitimate history" or as setbacks in the progress of humankind but instead as evidence that history does not follow rational rules, such as progress or evolution: "Man glaubt, die Menschheit wachse wie das Kind mit der Zeit aus den Kinderschuhen" 'It is thought that humankind grows with time out of its infancy, like the child does' (*Werke* 3: 695). Roth argues that the unforeseen nature of historical events is a reminder that humans should not delegate their responsibility for the unfolding of history to rationally produced concepts, such as progress, or institutions, such as the state. They should remember the original, religious purpose of their life in history and use that awareness of their moral responsibility for the promised redemption to navigate the dangerous and unpredictable waters of historical change. In a similar fashion, Benjamin criticizes in his "Theses on the Philosophy of History" the perplexed response of progressive politicians for whom the arrival of fascism in interwar Europe was a historical aberration and not a "logical" historical phase. Benjamin argues that the flow of history is not linear but instead is undercut by messianic currents that can bring in the radically new, whether this is the Messiah or the Antichrist. In using the same imagery of the apocalyptic Antichrist in history as Roth, Benjamin urges the historians to use these messianic undertows to unleash the potential of redemption in history and thus ensure the defeat of evil (*Illuminations* 247–49). Rosenzweig too emphasizes the moral urgency of redemption in history and argues that the idea of progress acts as an obstacle in its way: "Thus the real idea of progress resists nothing so strongly as the possibility that the 'ideal goal' could and should be reached, perhaps in the next moment, or even this very moment" (*Star* 227).

Since the Jewish experience of time is a compressed version of all time into the eternally present expectation of redemption, it results that the past, present, and future are all merged into a moment that is both historical and posthistorical, the time of the Kingdom. It would be hard to rationalize this idea of time using conventional notions. The time of redemption, although eternally present, "a *nunc stans*, not a vanishing moment thus, but a 'stationary' one," is both regressive and prospective, restoring the old and instating the new, as in the case of the unity of tradition and innovation (Rosenzweig, *The Star* 290). Scholem argues that the time of redemption is often rendered in traditional Judaic messianism through the motif of *Moses redivivus*, of the arrival of the Kingdom as a return home and as the end of the *galut* (Scholem, *The Messianic Idea* 53). Hence, in the Judaic tradition, the messianic hope always bears both the mark of the past and that of the brand-new future: "The reason for this is clear: even the restorative force has a utopian factor, and in utopianism restorative factors are at work" (4).

In a similar fashion, Bloch's Utopia restores an old order, no longer valid, in the present through the opening of a glimpse into the millennial future: it explores "*the latency of the primordial secret in itself moving within the Now*, in short the creative unconscious of our spiritual *coronation*" (192). The present contains in essence the very nature of Utopia *in statu nascendi* and represents the simultaneity of the inherited past and the emergent future. The restoration of "no longer" into a time that is "not yet" expresses the idea of expectative hope as a process, always involved in the production of emancipation and yet not an achieved ideal.[23] History is thus permanently displaced, with one foot in the Kingdom and one in the present, an image that evokes the Jewish idea of history: "There's something preliminary, something provisional about Jewish history. . . . Thus in Judaism the Messianic idea has compelled a *life lived in deferment*, in which nothing can be done definitively, nothing can be irrevocably accomplished" (Scholem, *The Messianic Idea* 35). But the fact that history is incomplete should not discourage action and hope, Rosenzweig argues, because finite life is only the "not-yet infinite": "We seek an infinite life, we find a finite one. The finite life that we find is thus simply the not-yet-infinite" (*Star* 223).

Buber's conception of the historical time of Utopia is equally replete with the mystical unity of a now in which past and future coexist. Because Utopia is to be carried out as a rational project, although it is rooted in a transcendent aspiration, its mode of existence is historical. The "here and now" bears for Buber the mark of both continuity and the revolution; it is the space and time in which the action of the individual produces the arrival of Utopia (*Paths* 13). Brod too justifies the redemptive character of human action in the present through recourse to the Talmudic conception of messianic time. Thus, the Talmud asserts the presence of two messianic times: the time of the final redemption of all creation (at the end of times) and the historical time of the redemptive presence of God in the world (*Paganism* 43). The former is more clearly circumscribed to what Brod calls "noble misfortune" and the latter to the "ignoble" one, but not in the sense of two separate forms of redemption: the redemption is one form, and only the times in which it manifests itself are two forms. The presence of God in the world, in creation, produces those everyday acts of redemption that constitute the moments of grace for humankind. Through these moments, humanity's efforts to repair the world are elevated to a redeemed status, confirming the expectative hope of the final redemption of all creation.

A more clearly theological explanation of the redemptive potential of the present moment in history is offered by Franz Rosenzweig in *The Star of Redemption*. In Rosenzweig's view, the triplet world-man-God corresponds theologically to creation-revelation-redemption, which is the mode in which God unveils his actions along a temporal sequence that spans past, present, and future: the world is created in the past, man receives the revelation in the present, and God redeems all creation in a promised future. However, the relationship among these elements is not static: world, man, and God are continuously interacting in the same manner in which creation, revelation, and redemption are constantly reinforcing each other in a construction that unites past, present, and future. Rosenzweig's view of historical existence postulates a unity of the created past and of the promised future of salvation into the time of the present, the "infinite Now" (289). In his view, the time of the now, the time of man, is the moment in which God reveals both his creation and his coming redemption to the individual by addressing him directly through a commandment: "the commandment is purely the present" (177).

This complex configuration of the present moment in the redemptive conception of history raises some questions about the relationship between the experience of life in history and the nature of Utopia. For Roth, the present can stay both under the sign of forgetting, if it is the modern present time, or under the sign of remembering, if it is the present time of the lived tradition, as he encountered it in Provence: "In other cities, living cities, you learn to tell from the present day—which will in time give birth to tomorrow and the day after tomorrow—how much yesterday is different from the day before yesterday. But in Vienne the present was already past" (*Report* 87). The latter manner of experiencing time offers, as he points out, a defense against the sudden, unexpected changes that wreak havoc on the individual who lives the modern idea of present time. It comes as no surprise to him why World War I brought only tears and sadness to Provence and total chaos to Northern Europe (95). The logic of lived tradition overcomes historical traumas through mournful remembering and thus reaffirms the eternity of justice, while the logic of modern historical consciousness collapses in front of historical traumas, leaving the individual devastated and prey to the winds of history. Although Roth acknowledges the final messianic purpose of existence, for him the historical manifestation of the Messiah's final arrival must stay under the sign of continuity, of tradition, but a redeemed continuity in which the individual confronts the challenges of the present with the serenity given by the certitude of the final redemption. The apocalyptic element of the redemptive present is absent from this philosophy of history. For Roth, salvation is best expressed in the Chasidic belief in "the mystical redemption of the individual here and now, i.e., redemption not *from*, but *in* exile" (Scholem, *The Messianic Idea* 195). Critics such as Magris and Steinmann have also emphasized the Chasidic nature of Roth's rejection of revolutionary messianism and his affirmation of the historical present as the medium for the manifestation of redemption (Magris, *Weit von wo* 116; Steinmann, *Von der Würde* 39).

While some representatives of Roth's generation, such as Buber, Rosenzweig, and Brod, shared his belief in the historical nature of redemption, others positioned themselves in a more ambiguous way. Bloch, for example, although a philosopher of hope as the manifestation of the human anticipation of the Messiah's arrival in history, was also interested in the apocalyptic, catastrophic nature of this arrival and in its ability to effect a total and uncompromising renovation of the world and end history. As Boldyrev points out, in Bloch's case "it is not entirely clear how to reconcile the complete and unconditional destruction of the old world with the urge to uncover the mysteries within our soul and to give meaning to the world of everyday life" (99). Landauer too, although fascinated by Chasidism and, like many others, ambiguously intertwining conservative and revolutionary ideas, favored an apocalyptical renovation of history and the rebirth of religion through the chaos of revolution (Löwy 138). This tension between the conservative and the revolutionary elements in the conception of the redemptive "Now time" reflects an older theological debate on the role of messianic thinking within Judaism itself. As Scholem explains in his essay "Toward an Understanding of the Messianic Idea," the Talmudic interpretation of the Messiah's arrival as a time of either complete purity or complete destruction led some to the belief that total renovation is only possible through the total destruction of the world. Hence, the prophecy of the apocalypse became intricately tied into the prophecy of the Kingdom. On the other hand, others resisted this interpretation and insisted on the necessity of refraining from actions intended to hasten the Messiah's arrival (*Messianic Idea* 14–15). The law, they argued, and the tradition are the only guides to the Messiah's arrival, and one should obey them only.

Probably the most representative expression of the apocalyptic nature of the redemptive moment is offered by Benjamin's notion of now (*Jetztzeit*) in his "Theses on the Philosophy of History." While criticizing the "additive" nature of historicism, which collects facts like the "beads of a rosary," Benjamin promotes an understanding of history as a living organism in which the historian can intervene in order to renovate it (*Illuminations* 255). For Benjamin, a Marxist thinker albeit a nonconventional one, the drive for justice and for reparation that characterizes the proletarian view of history executes the exemplary incision into the historical continuum. He mobilizes in his support "the Jewish religious tradition" in order to redefine the role of the historical materialist philosopher as a messianic prophet who can unleash the proletarian Utopia (Niethammer 104).[24] The historian thus has to rely on a messianic idea that prepares history for the sudden intrusion of the Kingdom: "History is the subject of a structure whose site is not homogenous, empty time, but time filled by the presence of the now [*Jetztzeit*]" (*Illuminations* 252). The messianic moment has the power to stop the passage of time and turn back the clocks, to leap backwards into history and start again: "only a redeemed mankind receives the fullness of its past—which is to say, only for a redeemed mankind had its past become citable in all its moments. Each moment it has lived becomes a *citation à l'ordre du jour*—and that day is Judgment Day" (246). For Benjamin, the restorative potential of redemption relies on the denial of the inherited past. Probably influenced by the interest in the history of messianic thinking in Judaism that his friend Scholem was developing at the time, Benjamin explicitly engages in the "Theses" with the apocalyptic interdiction placed by the rabbinic tradition on the interpretation of history.[25] He acknowledges that messianism, although having a long tradition in Judaism, has been regarded with skepticism and even aversion by Jews. However, Benjamin argues that the restorative force of the messianic idea justifies its use in a historical context due to the desperate historical circumstances that required radical, revolutionary solutions. Instead, every moment should be seen as "the strait gate through which the Messiah might enter" (*Illuminations* 255).

Some critics, including Claudio Magris, Markus May, and Bernd Oei, see in Roth's philosophy of history a messianic conception similar to Benjamin's. Particularly the belief that history lies in ruins but can be delivered, that the past can be retroactively repaired through the redemptive unity of time, has constituted one of the main reasons for their joint treatment. Magris points out, however, that while for Benjamin the messianic moment brings an end to history and ushers in a new utopian eon, Roth remains skeptical about the possibility of a new world, limiting himself to the melancholy remembrance of the past (*Weit von wo* 20). Nonetheless, Magris misinterprets Roth's conservative, antiapocalyptical conception of history as proof of his pessimism about history, about the possibility of any real completion of Utopia. In fact, Benjamin's philosophy of history stems from a deeper despair about the future than does Roth's. For Roth, the future can be redeemed regardless of the historical circumstances. What matters above all is the internal reform of the individual, the moral transfiguration of reality into a spiritual truth of a higher kind, one that is not less real but more so than the so-called objective reality: "what we call reality is still an illusion," he argues in *The Antichrist* (37). The type of historical truth that Roth creates diverges from the conventional idea of historical reality. The presence of redemption allows him to reinterpret historical realities not in view of their causes and effects but instead in view of their spiritual meaning. This type of historical consciousness, defined by the reality of redemption, is rendered by Roth in "Glauben und Fortschritt" with a term borrowed from the German idealist philosophy *Geistesgeschichte* (history of the mind), which treats those realities of the higher spiritual order that are not visible to "physical" history (*körperliche Geschichte*) (*Werke* 3: 695). Operating with the historical consciousness of redemption, Roth creates in his work a historical universe that acts as a correction and not an obliteration of the "objective" historical reality.

* * *

This chapter sketched out the general features of the notion of redemption developed by the generation of Central European Jewish intellectuals to whom Joseph Roth also belonged. Understanding this notion's unique character and the historical context of its emergence is crucial for understanding much of Roth's fictional and nonfictional treatment of such key issues as individual and collective identity, modern consciousness, technological civilization, and history. This notion of redemption, one of religious inspiration but "mitigated" through recourse to history, equally emphasizing the importance of divine intervention and the moral responsibility of individuals, paradoxically restorative and prospective, regressive and utopian, individual and collective, is present throughout his work, whether in a nascent form, as in the earlier novels and feuilletons, or in the full-fledged form of the later novels and political articles. Its context of emergence in Roth's work is emblematic for the rise of the idea of redemption within the whole generation and defines the encounter of the young, assimilated Central European German-speaking Jewish intellectual with the world of anti-Semitism, of modern mass politics, technology, secularism, and individual alienation.

The plight of the Central European Jews stemmed in Roth's opinion from the abandonment of the Judaic religious heritage and from the eagerness to conform to the standards of individualism and rationalism that characterize the modern nation-states. The solution he proposed envisions a restoration of these severed bonds with tradition but a restoration that does not isolate the Jews from the actual historical conditions in which they live. The key for Roth, as for the other thinkers analyzed above, is to achieve a fusion of perspectives in which the bond with a redemptive tradition coexists with the given historical conditions, whether favorable or not. For this reason, Roth entertains a view of history that does not explicitly demand the Jews to either assert or deny their historical lot but instead to infuse it with the redemptive expectation of the Messiah's arrival. Similarly, humanity's search for redemption does not rest in the denial of historical reality, in the rejection of the present and the refuge in an idealized past or promising future. History needs to be redeemed in its entirety, neither denied nor uncritically affirmed. It needs to be corrected, remedied, but not necessarily in an ideological or reality-denying manner. Instead, it requires the life-affirming presence of salvation as an everyday act.

Consistent with the idea of redemption as a historical act is Roth's renewed emphasis on the moral responsibility of the individual. Since the universe does not redeem itself by itself but instead requires the active participation of individuals, it follows that people have to break free from both their immediate historical conditioning and any metaphysical fixations and focus instead on the way in which every day can be blessed with the promise of salvation but also filled with the meaningfulness of the moment. This continual search for the redeemed present traverses Roth's work in the form of a persistent aspiration for individual and cosmic deliverance, exemplified sometimes in his fiction and at other times in his journalism. The presence of a constant political dimension in his work should not be seen separately from the wider existential and religious conception of redemption that rests at the heart of his writing. For Roth, the trouble with politics is not a mere result of doctrinaire conflicts but instead is the expression of a full-fledged moral and religious breakdown; hence, any possible political renewal must start from an integral renovation of the individual's relationship with the universe and with God, a renovation that paradoxically binds and liberates.

A consequence of the moral unification of the individual with the universe is the projection of this unity on the political entities that characterize the modern age: the state, the masses, and the citizen. Roth's continuous preoccupation with the rifts between these forms of political aggregation and the ensuing effects, including alienation, authoritarianism, and mob tyranny, points in the direction of a search for reconciliation, for a form of political association that would solve the irreconcilable oppositions ushered in by the modern age. Although his admiration for the premodern political consciousness as a counterforce to the modern one has sometimes been mistaken for political conservatism, it should be noted that Roth does not reject the modern aspiration for self-affirmation and freedom. Instead, he engages the past with the present in order to redeem a historical conception that is predicated on the separation between past and present. He does not challenge the political categories of the modern age per se but rather the way in which they were cut off from any other religious or moral conceptualization of politics. His redeemed political Utopia postulates the ambivalent coexistence of individual and collective aspirations, of personal freedoms and traditional constraints, harmoniously united by the simultaneous moral presence in history and outside of it. Accepting the present in all its immediacy while redeeming it on a religious plane offers the possibility for the resolution of the conflict between self-determination and authority and for the emergence of a space in which the individual and the collectivity, the spiritual life of the community and the political one of the state, coincide with and reinforce each other.

Notes

1. As Hannah Arendt explains, these positions were often associated with the cultural occupations: "An increasing number of sons from well-to-do homes deserted commercial life, since the mere continued collection of wealth was senseless. They

crowded into the cultural occupations; and within a few decades both Germany and Austria saw a great part of their cultural enterprises, such as newspapers, publishing and the theatre, in Jewish hands" (*Jew as Pariah* 115). To George Mosse, the overrepresentation of the Jews in the areas of journalism, the arts, and theater was the result not of an intentional choice but instead of their exclusion from the elite academic "world of mandarins" (24).

2. "It was the secularized version of the ancient Jewish belief that those who 'learn'—the Torah or the Talmud, that is, God's Law—were the true elite of the people and should not be bothered with so vulgar an occupation as making money or working for it" (Arendt, "Introduction" 31). In the same way, Stefan Zweig argues in his autobiography that the real professional motivation behind the second- or third-generation Jewish Austrian bourgeoisie was not the accumulation of fortune but rather the acquisition of status based on cultural achievements: "Subconsciously something in the Jew seeks to escape the morally dubious, the distasteful, the petty, the unspiritual, which is attached to all trade, and all that is purely business, and to lift himself up to the moneyless sphere of the intellectual, as if—in the Wagnerian sense—he wished to redeem himself and his entire race from the curse of money" (13). On the other hand, Volker Henze correctly points out that a career in the humanities was often the only alternative for Central European Jews at the end of the nineteenth century: "Juden waren im Bereich von Kunst und Kultur der ausgehenden k.u.k Monarchie überproportional vertreten—ein Faktum, das vielleicht die Vermutung einer spezifischen jüdischen Prädisposition für alles Geistige und Kulturelle suggerieren könnte, sich zunächst jedoch einfach damit erklären läßt, daß neben dem gewerblich-industriellen allein noch der kulturelle Sektor Juden offenstand, wobei der letztere naturgemäß das weitaus höhere Prestige besaß. . . . [Dies] bedeutete, daß für Juden die höheren Laufbahnen in Armee, Justiz, Verwaltung und akademischer Lehre überhaupt verschlossen blieben" 'Jews were overproportionally represented in the arts and culture of the declining Austro-Hungarian monarchy, a fact that might perhaps suggest the presumption of a specific Jewish predisposition for all things intellectual and cultural, but which can be explained simply by the fact that in addition to the commercial-industrial sector, only the cultural one was still open to the Jews, the latter naturally having the much higher prestige. . . . [This] meant that for Jews, the higher career paths in the army, the judiciary, administration, and academia remained generally closed' (Henze 7).

3. Jürgen Habermas interprets the Jewish "Goethe cult" in the nineteenth century as the expression of a deep belief in the value of education for the purpose of social assimilation as it was represented, among others, by the example of Wilhelm Meister: "It is no accident that the Goethe cult at the start of the nineteenth

century was created in the salon of Rachel Varnhagen, for it is certain that no one else strove with such intensity to live in accord with the model of Wilhelm Meister, who understood the 'cultivation of personality' so peculiarly and so deceptively as an assimilation of the bourgeois to the nobleman, as did those Jews who were also called 'exceptional Jews of culture'" (*Philosophical-Political Profiles* 32).

4. "Der Bruch mit dem von Vater und Großvater eingerichteten bürgerlichen Sein war keineswegs bloß das Aufgeben von etwas, mit dem man wie mit einem natürlichen Besitz frei schalten durfte, nein, es war weit mehr, es war ein Verrat, war Verrat an ihrer Assimilationsleistung" 'The break with the bourgeois existence built by his father and grandfather was by no means merely the abandonment of something with which one could easily dispense as if with a natural possession; no, it was far more, it was a betrayal, a betrayal of their assimilation' (Broch 128). For more, see Hermann Broch, *Hofmannsthal und seine Zeit*.
5. Theodor Lessing demonstrates the arbitrary nature of anti-Semitism in his study *Der jüdische Selbsthaß*: "Und ähnlich ist (je nachdem es gefällt) heute der Sozialismus, der Bolschewismus und morgen der Kapitalismus 'jüdisch.' Oder heute: der Fortschritt, der Radikalismus, die Revolution. Morgen dagegen: der Stillstand, die Stagnation und die Reaktion" 'And likewise (depending on what one likes), today socialism and Bolshevism are "Jewish," and tomorrow capitalism. Or today: progress, radicalism, revolution. Tomorrow, to the contrary: the standstill, the stagnation and the reaction' (112).
6. As Reinhart Koselleck shows, for Schiller the theatrical stage is made into a public moral tribunal that assumes the role of the judge of the corrupt political stage, becoming thus a purer reflection of reality than politics itself (*Kritik und Krise* 82).
7. Arthur Schnitzler voices the disenchantment of the turn-of-the-century generation with the assimilation fantasies of the "liberal generation" of the 1870s and 1880s in his novel *Der Weg ins Freie* (*The Road into the Open*), in which Heinrich Bermann, the son of a liberal Jew, notes about the supporters of assimilation "Heute wäre ja ein solcher Mensch allerdings ausschließlich komisch" 'Today, however, such a person would be purely comical' (273).
8. The Judaic spiritual renaissance of which Rosenzweig was part was concentrated around several centers that gathered some of the most influential figures of the secular Judaic thinking of the early twentieth century. One such center was the city of Frankfurt am Main, where Rabbi Nehemias Anton Nobel mentored a circle of like-minded thinkers. As Leo Löwenthal recounts, "A few names: Martin Buber, Franz Rosenzweig, Siegfried Kracauer, Erich Fromm, Ernst Simon, and several others. The names of the most important members of this circle can be found among the contributors to a festschrift for Rabbi Nobel that appeared in

1921. These names convey a good impression of the sort of Jewish renaissance that developed around Nobel and that later found its institutional continuation in the Jüdische Lehrhaus" (*Unmastered Past* 20–21).

9. Harry Liebersohn has dedicated an entire study to this nexus. See *Fate and Utopia in German Sociology, 1870–1923.*
10. Interestingly enough, the young Jewish generation discovered many of the Kabbalistic sources through German Romantic intermediaries. Because these sources had shaped the Romantic and idealist philosophy of the eighteenth and nineteenth centuries, Habermas considers that not only is the Jewish philosophy of the turn of the twentieth century profoundly impregnated by German Romantic ideas, but these very ideas were also in turn profoundly Jewish in spirit. See "The German Idealism of the Jewish Philosophers" in *Philosophical-Political Profiles* 21–45.
11. A valuable insight into the relationship of Lukács's early work with Dilthey's philosophy and the German neo-Kantians is provided by several representatives of the Budapest School in the collective volume *Die Seele und das Leben: Studien zum frühen Lukács* (*The Soul and the Life: Studies on the Young Lukács*), ed. Ferenc Feher. Arno Münster too explains the influence exerted by Dilthey and Henri Bergson's philosophy of life over the young Bloch but also emphasizes the uneasy relationship he entertained with the neo-Kantian school, whose basic separation between values and facts he tried to bridge through his utopianism. See Arno Münster, *Utopie, Messianismus und Apokalypse im Frühwerk von Ernst Bloch* (*Utopia, Messianism, and Apocalypse in the Early Work of Ernst Bloch*).
12. Volker Henze provides several useful—although sketchy—insights on the complex relationship between Jewish and non-Jewish *Kulturpessimismus*, with particular reference to the works of Oswald Spengler and the early Thomas Mann, suggesting that even if divergent from a sociological point of view, these two directions were related at an intellectual level and had common roots in the German critique of modernity at the beginning of the twentieth century. See Volker Henze, *Jüdischer Kulturpessimismus und das Bild des Alten Österreich im Werk Stefan Zweigs und Joseph Roths* 63–71.
13. The pastorale of the East European shtetl is not a new theme. Much of Yiddish literature is fraught with such oppositions between the corrupt world of the urban ghettos and the pure world of the Jewish shtetl (see Miron). However, Roth's idealization of the shtetl life is not a nostalgic form of literary escapism but rather an allegorical mechanism through which reality itself is called into question and elevated at a moral level.
14. Sebald draws some parallels between Roth's stereotypical portraiture of the Jews and the so-called ethnographical novellas and sketches characteristic of the

nineteenth century. This type of literature—with representatives such as Leopold Kompert and Karl Emil Franzos—bordered ambiguously on sociological study and caricature and often served the mixed purposes of entertainment and satirical commentary but also instruction, especially for a public with little or no exposure to the life of the Jewish shtetl in the first half of the nineteenth century, before the lifting of immigration interdictions and the subsequent massive migration of their population to the West or into the big cities: "Dies sogenannte ethnographische Novelle ist in diesem Zusammenhang hauptsächlich deshalb von Interesse, weil sie, in dem sie geflissentlich das 'Charakteristische' herausarbeitet, zwischen der wissenschaftlichen Studie einerseits und der krassen Karikatur andrerseits ein suspektes Vermittlergeschäft betreibt" 'This so-called ethnographic novella is especially of interest in this context, because, by deliberately bringing out the "typical," it plays a not entirely innocent mediating role between the scientific study on the one hand and the extreme caricature on the other' (Sebald 42).

15. Although Löwy resorts to a similar division in his intellectual history of the generation, his intention is to group the thinkers themselves based on their educational background, intellectual affinities, and political affiliations (26). In the present study, the separation between a secular and religious form applies to the notion of redemption expressed in several concrete cases and not to the thinking of these intellectuals in general. Hence, the way in which the categorizations function in Löwy's study and in this one are different. For example, while this study looks at Buber's theory of Utopia as an expression of a secularized notion of redemption, Löwy includes Buber in the category of religious thinkers.
16. In an interview with Martin Lüdke, Leo Löwenthal reflects on the relationship between Judaism and the messianism of the Jewish theorists of Utopia in Central Europe in the 1920s, including in this nexus also the members of the Frankfurt School, such as Max Horkheimer and Herbert Marcuse. Löwenthal suggests that the framing of Utopia in the realm of the possible, and not the actual, might result from the ancient Judaic interdiction to represent God: "Horkheimer once said—and I believe we were all in complete agreement with him on this—that the Jewish article of faith that one may not pronounce the name of God is very decisive. The unattainable, the unapproachable, the unnamable, which nonetheless contains a sense of longing that one may finally reach the goal, may ultimately speak its name. This conception is certainly very Jewish; it is a motif in our thought even today" (*Unmastered Past* 245).
17. In "Die Juden und die Nibelungen," Roth responds to two of his critics, fellow Jewish émigrés. They reproached him that his attacks on Germany weakened the position of the Jews in the fight against Hitler and alienated the Germans from the

Jewish cause. In response, Roth argued that the Jews had no unconditional allegiance to Germany and that there was nothing that could hurt the Jews more than not admitting that it was not just a handful of extremist Germans who persecuted the Jews; it was an entire nation that voluntarily participated in the anti-Semitic culture of the Third Reich.

18. While acknowledging that Roth felt loyalty for "his 'Eastern Jews'" (*seine 'Ostjuden'*) and had a close connection with Chasidism, David Bronsen argues that the religious dimension of Roth's writings is limited by a fundamental existential vacuum: "Er [Roth] ... bringt sogar einen Überrest von der chassidischen Idee der Allgöttlichkeit der Welt und der Allgegenwart Gottes in sein Schaffen hinein, aber nur um jedesmal diese Tendenzen ad absurdum zu führen" 'He [Roth] ... even brings a remnant of the Chassidic idea of the universal presence of God in the world and of the omnipresence of God into his work, but only to show their absurdity every time' (*Joseph Roth: Eine Biographie* 256).
19. Zionism underwent an existential crisis during and after World War I due to the disrepute in which the idea of nationalism had fallen. Many Jews became suspicious of the prospect of importing the European idea of nation to Palestine, and even Zionists such as Max Brod argued that the new nation had to be in almost every respect different from the "traditional" nations: "Auch als staatsartige Gemeinschaft werden wir anders sein als die andern Völker! ... Man darf vom jüdischen Geist nicht so gering denken, daß man glaubt, er müsse in Palästina gleich ins Philistertum des Nationalismus hinabsinken" 'Even as a national community, we shall be different from the other peoples! ... One may not think so low of the Jewish spirit as to believe that in Palestine it must sink right into the philistinism of nationalism' (*Im Kampf* 70).
20. The relationship between Judaism and Catholicism in Roth's work has been hotly debated by critics. While Steinmann argues that Roth draws inspiration equally from Judaism and Catholicism, Horch rejects the theory of a religious syncretism in Roth's case, arguing that Roth's admiration for Catholicism is circumstantial and superficial in comparison to his authentic anchorage in the Judaic traditions (231). Frey contextualizes Roth's interest in Catholicism and argues that Roth's Judaism is not weakened but instead is strengthened through his adhesion to Catholicism. By using the example of seventeenth-century Kabbalist Sabbatai Zevi, whose apostasy represented the paradoxical triumph of his abjured Judaism, Frey argues that the hostile historical context in which Roth lived made the survival of Judaism possible only through another religion: "um Jude bleiben zu können, mußte man Katholik werden" 'in order to remain Jewish, one had to become Catholic' (172). Carl Steiner too reinforces the idea that Roth's refuge in Catholicism is not motivated by deeply

held religious beliefs but instead results from his increasing political despair and subsequent identity crisis (13). Jacqueline Magnou is even more radical in her opposition to the theory of a "religious" Roth in general. To her, Roth's Judaism represents a marker not of religious identification but instead of ethnic and political identification, hyperbolized by his own identity crisis at a time of great insecurity for the Jews (Magnou 49). For Rosenfeld, Roth's Judaic nostalgia is a melancholy for something that was never there, a fabricated reality that serves to assuage the insecurities of an otherwise assimilated European Jew who cannot harmonize his Jewish and German identities (*Understanding* 96).

21. Jaques Le Rider addresses this paradox of individualism in the Viennese culture of the turn of the twentieth century through a reference to the Nietzschean cult of the individual, who is simultaneously determined by one's own will and by the collective forces that transcend it and make it nonidentical to itself: "It is a strange paradox: the 'cult of the ego' went hand in hand with the discovery of the vacuity and fragility of that very ego. To understand this apparent contradiction we ought probably to return to Schopenhauer and Nietzsche, and distinguish between two meanings of 'ego': ego as individualism and ego as totality. Because the Young Vienna generation was returning, quite deliberately, to the paths first traced by Nietzsche" (*Modernity and Crises of Identity* 44).
22. The nature of the relationship between individual and society in *Paths in Utopia* can more easily be understood in light of Buber's famous earlier work *I and Thou*, first published in 1919. In *I and Thou*, the constitution of society is based on the assumption that any human relationship has to overcome the reification process involved in the subject-object relationship in order to accede to a higher integration and a mutual actualization. This involves the opening of the closed nature of the ego (the "I") and the unhindered connection to the other as an unconquerable entity (the "You"). This form of connectivity allows for a community in which both the I and the You exist as autonomous yet codependent entities in a form of individual-collective continuum. Facing the conundrum of modernity (the lack of a median term between individual alienation and state-run collectivities), Buber turns to connectivity, to the life-generating relation of the I to the You: "True public and true personal life are two forms of association. For them to originate and endure, feelings are required as a changing content, and institutions are required as a constant form; but even the combination of both still does not create human life which is created only by a third element: the central presence of the You, or rather, to speak more truthfully, the central You that is received in the present" (*I and Thou* 95).
23. Although Bloch strove to counter the Marxist objection that Utopias are invariably abstract constructs by sketching a concrete, historical form of Utopia in *The Spirit*

of Utopia, it is the allegorical nature of his messianism, its inability to exist either as an objective reality or as an abstract ideal, that made some doubt its validity. In a letter to Leo Löwenthal from 1921, Siegfried Kracauer writes in connection to *The Spirit of Utopia*: "Meine Kardinalfrage an Bloch wäre . . . : Glauben Sie faktisch an den Untergang, an den Messias, an das tausendjährige Reich? Ist Ihnen das ganz konkret und wirklich? Oder nur so ein Als-ob-Ideal?" 'My cardinal question to Bloch would be . . . : Do you really believe in the doom, in the Messiah, in the millennial kingdom? Is this quite concrete and real to you? Or just such an "as-if" ideal?' (Löwenthal, *In steter Freundschaft* 19).

24. Benjamin's employment of the concept of historical materialism for proving the messianic nature of history is problematic. He adopts historical materialism by counting on its capacity to execute an actual material change through the projection of a moral request over the development of the course of history. This particular understanding of the notion overlooks, however, the determinist character of historical materialism, which postulates not only that history does not evolve according to an idealist speculative model but also that it necessarily follows the objective laws of economic development leading to the final victory of the proletariat and the end of the class-differentiated society. Hence for the historical materialist, any moral claim made in the name of justice must be that of the proletariat, while any other claim is irrational: "If you know in what direction the world process is working, you can either identify yourself with it or not; if you do not, if you fight it, you thereby compass your own certain destruction, being necessarily defeated by the forward advance of history. To choose to do so deliberately is to behave irrationally" (Berlin 66).
25. The correspondence between Benjamin and Scholem indicates that Benjamin manifested an active interest in Scholem's theological research and in his ideas about Jewish mysticism and Chasidism. See Scholem, *Walter Benjamin/Gershom Scholem Briefwechsel 1933–1940.*

Chapter 2

Homelessness, Anarchy, Negative Utopia: The *Via Negativa* of Redemption in Joseph Roth's Early Novels

Joseph Roth's emergence as a journalist and feuilletonist in the Austrian and German literary world of the 1920s is inseparable from the ideology of "cultural despair" popular among many Central European intellectuals of his day.[1] After his relocation to Vienna in 1914, Roth plunged himself into the diverse late imperial cultural and artistic milieu in which forms of experimentalism coexisted with conservative academism and in which the discourse of liberalism and progressivism coexisted with the increasingly more prevalent criticism of rationality and the glorification of nationalism. Somewhat more traditionalist in aesthetical and political convictions, the young Roth was quickly absorbed after World War I into the group of writers associated with *Der Neue Tag*, a periodical dominated by the figure of Alfred Polgar, one of the most important promoters of the late Viennese feuilleton and himself a critic of modern aesthetics and bourgeois values. In Polgar's shadow, Roth became exposed to the writings of other major representatives of the feuilleton and the reportage who investigate in their writings the relationships between bourgeois modernity and the moral crisis of the individual such as Karl Kraus, Hermann Bahr, and Peter Altenberg, luminaries of the Young Vienna circle, and younger writers such as Egon Erwin Kisch and Egon Friedell. Under the influence of his literary and journalistic mentor, Roth developed an early literary style based on belief in the unity of the creative and moral mind, a unity that also confers on the writer the role of social critic and moralist. This early conviction, refined through the next two decades through successive aesthetical and philosophical elaborations, constitutes the foundation on which Roth's future critical investigation of modernity and his philosophy of redemption will be erected.

The popularity of the feuilleton in Viennese literary circles of the time could be seen in a twofold manner: on the one hand, its literary form tallied with an increasing demand for a new form of realism, more condensed and accessible to the readers, a literary counterpart to the growing fascination with the photographic and filmic image that Altenberg exemplified. This development was correlated with a crisis of the classical realist novel, whose overemphasis on characters and psychology was often satirized by Kraus and Polgar. On the other hand, the aesthetical credo of the feuilleton was based on the idea of the necessity of a moral rebirth of the writer, who for far too long had been cut off from the daily concerns of the actual society (Philippoff 11). This new form of realist and morally engaged feuilleton appeared from the very beginning to be motivated by a desire to unify the external world with the moral mind of the individual. Influenced by this aesthetic credo, Roth became interested in identifying and critiquing the social and moral conditions that prevented modernity from achieving this unity. As a result, although some feuilletonists such as Kisch insisted on strictly objective observation and "research," Roth opts for a morally mediated mode of observation: "Roth, einer der einflussreichsten Feuilletonisten deutscher Sprache, sah sich fraglos selbst als Moralist" 'Roth, one of the most influential feuilletonists in the German language, unquestionably saw himself as a moralist' (Frank 477).

Revisiting some of the popular tropes of turn-of-the-century *Kulturpessimismus*, Roth resorts in his early writings to the interpretation of the conflict between tradition and modernity as a conflict between spirit and technology.[2] In "Die Auferstehung des Geistes," an article published in 1920, he makes his convictions clear: the vital search for a spiritual rebirth (a theme common in the years succeeding World War I, partly as a reaction to the sense of social and cultural disintegration caused by the defeat in the war) has been hampered by the materialistic demands made by modern rationality and its attempts to take over the entire spectrum of human experience and subordinate it to the imperatives of social development. Roth's thematization of the conflict between spiritual and materialistic forces takes the form of classical *Kulturpessimismus* (cultural despair) through the opposition he establishes between culture and civilization, which in German intellectual history has a distinct meaning: culture connotes an organic, primal, and direct mode of interaction with the universe, whereas civilization has the subtext of a mechanical, external, and intellectually mediated type of interaction: "Seit Jahrzehnten schon geht die menschliche Entwicklung in dieser Richtung fort, das heißt: rückwärts. Den von den Vätern überlieferten Geist spannte man in das Joch der 'materiellen Kultur' (lies: Zivilisation).

Die Lokomotive des technischen Fortschritts zermalmte das humanistische Ideal von der 'edlen Kraft und Güte'" 'Human development has been going on for decades in this direction, that is, backwards. The spirit handed down by the fathers was forced into the yoke of "material culture" (read: civilization). The locomotive of technical progress crushed the humanistic ideal of the "noble power and kindness"' (*Werke* 1: 277).[3]

The conviction that progress in a material sense is regress in a spiritual sense and the belief that modernity brought above all the loss of a certain humanism and of a sense of nobility and benevolence are motifs that will later develop in Roth's work into a pessimistic philosophy of modernity. As Ward H. Powell points out, Roth's philosophy of culture is marked by "primitivism," or "the tendency of man to think back over the course of his so-called civilized progress and to wonder about the desirability of it all" (4). The civilization-critical tone of Roth's writings represents from the very beginning a pervasive attitude that will affect the formation of the young journalist and novelist and shape his approach and style in a decisive manner. Roth's early emergence as a journalist and feuilletonist is thus characterized by the onset of a series of antimodern and culturally pessimistic themes that set the coordinates along which the later journalistic and essayistic contributions will develop: "Der Ausgangspunkt von Roths Kulturkritik im späten Werk ähnelt durchaus der im Frühwerk formulierten Gesellschaftskritik. Was dominiert, ist ein dezidiert anti-bürgerlicher Grundton, verbunden mit einem vagen Anti-Kapitalismus, der Kritik an Technik und Materialismus mit einschließt" 'The starting-point of Roth's critique of culture in the late work resembles the social critique formulated in the early period. What dominates is a decidedly antibourgeois key tone, combined with a vague anticapitalism, which includes criticism of technology and materialism' (Müller-Funk, "Der Antichrist" 115). Among these themes range the permanent preoccupation with the moral and individual dimension of social and political life; its corruption and transformation in the modern age, especially through the triumph of technology and rationality; the erosion of "culture" through the advance of "civilization"; and equally important, the alienation of individuals through the collapse of the essential relations of belonging and affinity with the surrounding environment.[4]

Roth's early political engagement in the socialist movement has constituted a source of debate among the critics, some supporting the image of the socialist at the expense of the conservative and pessimistic aspects of his work while others considering his socialism a passing episode of no consequence for the conservative ideas that he embraced later in his career.[5] As the present study will demonstrate, the terms "socialism" and "conservatism" are not mutually exclusive in the case of Roth's political convictions, of his values and rhetoric.[6] Their combination can be understood in the context of the emergence at the turn of the twentieth century of a critical discourse within the Jewish intelligentsia that merged the socialist critique of the bourgeois world with the conservative critique of modernity and supported the restoration of the spiritual relationship of the individual with his surrounding world. In this sense, Roth's own early political engagement is inseparable from his critique of modernity and civilization and can only be understood in the context of his anarchic and anti-institutional tendencies, tendencies exemplified by his belief in the moral sovereignty of the individual and his spiritual rebirth. This apparent ambiguity is probably exemplarily conveyed by his own admiration for the representative writer of the Austrian restoration, Franz Grillparzer, whom Roth describes in his 1937 portrait as "a reactionary par excellence, an individual anarchist reactionary" (Roth, *Hotel Years* 246). Because of this ambiguity, Roth's relationship with classical socialism has always been tense and, later in his life, even hostile.

The cultural-pessimistic dimension of Roth's writing is inseparable from a certain redemptive imagination. If the former represents Roth's critique of the phenomenon of modernity in general, the latter expresses his hope in a solution to this crisis. The utopian character of this solution consists in the fact that it tries to overcome the fundamental problems affecting modernity, such as human alienation, excessive rationalization, and moral devastation, in a thorough, decisive, and irreversible manner. The radicalism of this solution resides in the unequivocal rejection of a corrupt reality (in whatever form it might be expressed) and the redemptive expectation of a solution to the misery of history, a misery culminating in modernity itself. Roth's answer to the crisis of modernity postulates the "recovery of lost harmony" (Löwy 2), yet this redemptive philosophy is expressed through three distinct modes that correspond to the three stages of his work and their characteristic response to the crisis of modernity: revolt and retreat, religious experience, and escape from linear history. Chronologically, the early period of Roth's novels (up to *Hiob* and the abandonment of New Objectivity) roughly corresponds to a search for redemption that manifests itself through the revolt of the characters and their retreat from reality.[7] The late period, on the other hand, comprises the novels of both religious and historical expression.[8]

Roth's early novels, often described as *zeitkritisch* (critical of the times), are characterized by the central motif of the homeless, inadaptable, and lonely individual.[9] The motifs of homelessness and isolation also characterize his later novels, but what differentiates them is the nature of the reconciliation of these individuals with their surrounding world. If the later novels provide a *positive* solution to the conflict between the self and the world (materialized in the religious experience or the memory act), then the early ones provide a *negative* solution, which often reiterates the damned condition of the individual beyond any chance of redemption in this world. One of the favorite themes employed in these early novels is that of the returning soldier at the end of World War I. The characters fitting this category exemplify in a more arresting manner the homelessness and inadaptability of the individual. A war veteran himself, Roth was confronted after his return from the Eastern Front with the reality of an altered society, with a collapsed political order and a dire economic situation. As a consequence, his fictional characters express in a more or less direct manner his own reflections on the postwar society. Andreas Pum, the protagonist of *The Rebellion* (1924), as well as Gabriel Dan of *Hotel Savoy* (1924), Arnold Zipper from *Zipper and his Father* (1928), and Franz Tunda of *Flight without End* (1927) have fought in World War I (most of them on the Russian front) and return to Europe at the end of the conflict. Their confrontation with the world they find back home alters them, however, in a decisive manner.

Andreas Pum lost his leg in the war and hopes for compensation from the German state in the form of an easy job in the public sector. However, his expectations are disappointed by a brutal reality that has nothing to offer him except isolation and imprisonment. Franz Tunda and Arnold Zipper represent a different category of veterans: both relatively sophisticated individuals and typical exponents of the young small bourgeoisie, they are faced with their inability to find a place in the new society and to find community and love. While Tunda keeps on drifting from country to country, only to discover the inauthenticity of a world that he nonetheless cannot abandon, Zipper symbolically occupies in his society the role of the kibitzer. The café that he frequents has even assigned a place for him as the spectator par excellence. When he enjoys some attention after his unexpected long absence, it is the attention paid to a spectator, not to an actor: "This welcome delighted Arnold, as did anything which made him aware that someone valued him, even if it were only in his role as spectator. He, who always stood at the fringes, now found himself at the centre for a few minutes" (*Zipper* 184). Zipper has to accept his marginal role because any other is incompatible with either his fundamentally estranged nature or the nature of communally accepted social values.

The contrast between the expectations and the personalities of the characters, witnesses of an unequivocal disaster, the war, and the *Wertvakuum* (value vacuum) of the interwar European societies, ensnarled in petty pursuits and political duplicity, creates a tension that cannot find resolution in either the social field or the emotional field. The characters find themselves ultimately excluded from their societies and family circles because the symbolic hierarchy that they represent (expressed in the traditional and individual order of values and in the emphasis on truthfulness and compassion) is incompatible with the actual hierarchy, in which the laws of survival and gain dominate at the expense of morality.[10] Representing the former, Roth's war veterans cannot reconcile themselves with the moral disarray of the latter. However, the narrator assumes an ironic distance from any kind of rigid moral didacticism. The symbolic hierarchy of the characters is not an idealized moral world, but it is complicated and even distorted by the veterans' personal interpretation of the world. For instance, Pum's own interpretation is ambiguously delusional: "He believed in a just god. One who handed out shrapnel, amputations, and medals to the deserving. Viewed in the correct light, the loss of a leg wasn't so very bad, and the joy of receiving a medal was considerable. An invalid might enjoy the respect of the world. An invalid with a medal could depend on that of the government" (*Rebellion* 2). Tunda's hierarchy is just tentative: "Tunda might be labeled immoral and unprincipled. . . . He did not strive for so-called personal advantage. His ideas were as little egoistic as they were moralistic. If it were absolutely necessary to characterize him by some particular attribute, I would say that his most significant quality was the desire for freedom" (*Flight* 58). And yet in spite of these personal idiosyncrasies, the characters' common denominators are their authenticity and candor, which contrast unambiguously with the value simulacra that characterize the public and socially validated hierarchy.

The characters in Roth's early novels clash with the world to which they return or in which they try to find their place, their inadaptability reflecting Roth's own dissatisfaction with the corruption of the interwar society. As Kesten points out, the focus on the disillusion of the characters in Roth's early novels stems from his unforgiving moral critique of his contemporary society (108).[11] As a moralist and cultural critic, Roth also denounces or satirizes the social state of affairs in his early feuilletons and reports, to which the early novels bear a close stylistic resemblance. His journalistic writings provide him with material—such as episodes, portraits, and situations—for the fictional worlds of the novels. As Klaus-Detlef Müller shows, Roth relied on the examples set before him by Polgar and Kisch, whose feuilletons and commentaries provided, according to Roth, enough material for "twenty-six novels": "Damit ist, pointiert gesagt, der Hiat zwischen Feuilleton- und Romanschriftstellerei geschlossen" 'thus, to put it bluntly, the gap between feuilleton and novel writing disappears' (Müller 209).

The articles dedicated to the nationalist intelligentsia's increasing influence in German society, to the blatant discrepancies between the poverty of the workers and the unemployed on the one hand and the lavishness of the high bourgeoisie on the other, to the isolation and powerlessness of the simple individual in front of a social and political machinery of a colossal and yet irrational power, and to the pervasive hypocrisy of the petit bourgeoisie are just the facets of a generalized critique of modern society that Roth wages under the influence of a culturally pessimistic philosophy of history and a desire for a redemptive transformation of the world. His own feelings of frustration and revulsion in the face of this reality become easily translated into the voice of Benjamin Lenz, the mysterious East European Jew from Roth's first novel, *The Spider's Web* (1923), whose hatred for Europe and everything it stood for is his only motivating force: "He hated Europe, Christianity, Jewry, Monarchy, Republics, Philosophy, Political Parties, Ideas and Nations. He served the Powers only so as to study their weakness, their malice, their cunning and their Achilles heels. He betrayed them more than he exploited them. He hated the stupidity of Europe" (*Spider's Web* 64).

Although undoubtedly one of the most "European" writers of the last century if measured by his extensive knowledge of and professed love for the cosmopolitan spirit of Europe, Roth himself entertained similar feelings toward the Old Continent, often seen as the symbol of a decadence and arrogance that bitterly disappointed the expectations of the young writer. In the 1925 article "Brandes spricht über Europa" ("Brandes talks about Europe"), Roth states that "Europa ist nationalistisch, hochmütig, mittelmäßig" 'Europe is nationalistic, arrogant, mediocre' (*Werke* 2: 375). The fact that Roth the journalist characterizes the spirit of modern European societies in a fashion similar to that of his character Lenz points to the author's own feeling of alienation from this world, a world to which he is attracted as a migrating East European Jew but finds detestable from any point of view, especially from a moral one. In *Flight without End*, Tunda's own words convey the same position of estrangement and maladjustment, which the veteran returning from the Eastern Front experiences in the West: "So this is your world! . . . I feel a stranger in it. . . . I go around with alien eyes, alien ears, an alien attitude to people" (*Flight* 57). Characters such as Lenz and Tunda bear testimony to the extensive continuity between Roth's journalism and his fiction, a continuity that has prompted some critics to consider these characters as a reflection of the author's personal views rather than their fictional transfiguration: "Es hat ganz den Anschein, als ob Roth seine eigenen Sehnsüchte, Ängste, Fremdheitsgefühle und Anpassungsschwierigkeiten an die westliche Welt mittels Figuren wie Benjamin Lenz mehr gestaltet als verarbeitet hat" 'It looks as if Roth uses characters such as Benjamin Lenz to express his own desires, fears, alienation, and adaptation difficulties in the West rather than to fictionalize them' (Müller-Funk, *Joseph Roth* 83).

Active Nihilism and the Negation of Utopia

The debacle of postwar European societies' value hierarchy sets an unsurpassable barrier between these societies and the individuals who believe in the symbolic order. According to Werner Sieg, the conflict between personal assumptions and external reality ("der Widerspruch zwischen persönlichem Anspruch und objektiver Realität") remains a central problem throughout Roth's fictional work (14). When all the possibilities for a compromise between these individuals and the world around them have been exhausted, the only solutions left are either the revolt against the actual order and the sustained effort to undermine it or the passive withdrawal from it. The characters in Roth's early novels choose either one of these options: Lenz and Pum (and to a certain extent Zwonimir Pansin, the rebellious Croatian from *Hotel Savoy*) choose the revolt against the world; Tunda, Dan, Arnold Zipper, Nikolai Brandeis (the Jewish individualist entrepreneur from the 1929 novel *Right and Left*), and Friedrich Kargan (the revolutionary protagonist of the 1929 novel *The Silent Prophet*) choose the abandonment of the world and passive self-effacement. The critical evaluation of modernity and the two attitudes embraced by Roth's characters correspond to the approach to modernity developed by Friedrich Nietzsche. The revolt of the characters reflects Roth's critical view of a world in which not only the traditional hierarchy has been destroyed but also any attempt to assert an alternative value system, to make an unequivocal statement of belief. The modern world is characterized by volatility and triviality, by the simulation of norms and principles, which ultimately leads to the negation of anything permanent and indisputable. This accelerated nihilism, which in Roth's view is specific not only to the social values but also to the entire ethos of modernity, including technical rationality and progress, frames the crisis of modernity in an exemplary manner, as he suggests in his 1936 lecture "Glauben und Fortschritt": "Aber die Zeiten der Hölle erkennt man nicht an der Herrschaft des schlechtweg Bösen, sondern an unserer Ratlosigkeit, zu sehen, was eigentlich Gut und was eigentlich Böse ist. Es ist nicht Nacht, und es ist auch nicht Tag in der Welt. Es ist gleichsam Sonnenfinsternis. Das erzeugt in uns allen das sogenannte 'Weltuntergangsgefühl.'" 'However, it is not in the dominion of the pure evil that one recognizes the infernal times, but in our helplessness to see what is actually good and what is actually evil. It is not night, and it is not day in the world either. It is almost solar eclipse. This creates in us all the so-called "apocalyptic feeling"' (*Werke* 3: 692). This ambiguity, this "eclipse" of the normative criteria of the world, is thus what really characterizes the decay of modern civilization and what finally hinders the representatives of an authentic, clear-cut value system to find their place in the world: "*Mehrwertigkeit* and the uncertainty that it causes cannot be dissociated from each other. When it concerns such questions as purpose and meaning of life, God, religion etc., multivalence leads to agonizing uncertainty" (Mathew 22).

Similarly, in *The Will to Power* Friedrich Nietzsche characterizes modernity not only as the destruction of the traditional value systems, of the metaphysical hierarchy of values, but also as normative ambiguity: "Disintegration characterizes this time, and thus uncertainty: nothing stands firmly on its feet or on a hard faith in itself" (40). Accordingly, Nietzsche distinguishes between an attitude of passive nihilism (specific to those who passively resign themselves to the generalized nihilism of modernity) and active nihilism (specific to those who actively take part in the negation of all values, whether traditional or modern). He further considers that while the former cannot do anything about the inescapable logic of modernity but powerlessly accept it, the latter are actually able to lead to the completion of the task of negation by accelerating it, by pushing it to self-annihilation. This could create the premises for a new beginning and for an assertive attitude toward values, Nietzsche argues. Viewed in this light, Lenz's attitude of active participation in the disaster of the world surrounding him appears as a singular attempt to actually restore the right order to it. He is a nihilist, undoubtedly, but an active one. He acts not out of conviction but instead to study the weakness and malice of his employers so as to better undermine them: "encouraged chaos, incited bloodlust and self-destruction, betrayed one man to another and that other to a third" (*Spider's Web* 64–65). In his contempt and hatred for this world, he decides that the better way to damage it is by serving it, by helping it perform its "values" and attain its self-destructive goals. In a typical Nietzschean fashion, Lenz answers to no one; he is the ultimate individualist who realizes that the only true criterion of value is not to be found in the external world but instead is found in himself: "The name of his god was: Benjamin Lenz" (65). The reconstruction of the moral world starting from the private motivations and values of the individual gives *The Spider's Web* a strong anarchist quality: it is the confirmation of the fact that the nihilism of the outside world can only be countered through an anarchic, individualist attitude that functions as a defense mechanism of the isolated human being in front of a hostile moral world.[12]

Lenz fictionalizes the author's own aversion toward the political environment of the Weimar Republic, an environment described and analyzed in depth by Roth in countless articles and feuilletons published during the early 1920s. Lenz's antagonist, the anti-Semitic cruel, frustrated, and cunning Theodor Lohse, who according to Bernd Oei bears a close resemblance to the instigator of Walther Rathenau's murder, Ernst von Salomon, whom Roth portrays in his series of reports from 1922, embodies the nihilism of the age, which can only be countered by action in kind (Oei 32). If Lohse betrays, murders, and steals, so does Lenz, which explains why Lohse finds in him a kindred spirit. However, what Lohse fails to notice is that his own negation of the world is negated through the surreptitious actions of the individualist Lenz, whose hatred of everything Lohse stands for can only manifest itself in the subversive imitation of his opponent's actions.[13]

However, Lenz's anarchic attitude is not simply the result of an unconquerable hopelessness and disappointment with the world. To the contrary, it is the anticipation of the coming apocalypse and therefore is fraught with redemptive potentiality. In this sense it is reminiscent of the traditional Kabbalistic interpretation of the Torah, which according to Gershom Scholem used the apocalyptical element in order to hurry the Messiah's arrival. The dual nature of the redemptive moment, which was understood in this tradition as both the final destruction of the known universe and the beginning of the everlasting Kingdom of God, created a logical codependency of the two moments. Since the road to deliverance necessarily went through apocalypse, the Talmudic scholars argued that action targeted at speeding up the natural process of the world's decay would actually hasten the arrival of the end times: "the Talmudic teachers were already faced with the question whether one may 'press for the end', that is to say, force its coming by one's own activity" (Scholem, *The Messianic Idea* 14). Viewed in this light, Roth's early anarchism has a religious function, since the apocalypse is not a goal in itself but rather the precondition for the outbreak of the final redemption of a final, uncompromising order of the universe: "Der Anarchismus des jungen Roth, von dem keine soziale, politische und religiöse Hierarchie verschont bleibt, entsteht aus dem Bedürfnis nach einer absoluten Ordnung, die in ihrer Integrität keinerlei Kompromiß, keinerlei Manipulation ihrer Ideale verträgt" 'Young Roth's anarchism, which spares no social, political or religious hierarchy, arises from the need for an absolute order, one that accepts no compromise of its integrity or manipulation of its ideals' (Magris, *Weit von wo* 42).

In a similar fashion, in *The Rebellion* Andreas Pum programmatically becomes a rebel as a reaction against a world that systematically refutes any single illusion about justice and gratitude that he has. Since he conflates the notions of divine and juridical justice—the government from which he expects a recompense for his military deeds is seen as a supernatural force: "something that overlies man like the sky overlies the earth" (*Rebellion* 2)—his rebellion is directed against the state as well as against God. After the quick series of events that leave Pum without shelter or a source of income and with a jail term, he knows that he has nothing left in this world. Not only has he lost his livelihood and freedom, but he has also lost any certainty about the causality of events in the world and any confidence in foundational values or ethical principles: "Im Grunde bestehen keine Zusammenhänge, gibt es nichts zu verstehen" 'Fundamentally, there are no correlations among events, there is nothing to understand' (Düllo 52). Upon seeing his humble hopes broken, this modern-day crippled Job decides to revolt against an absurd and distant order:

> A new hope woke in his soul as he walked out of the station. He saw the joyful bustle of the great metropolis. He saw, over the tangle of carts and horses and people, the new sun of the approaching spring. And even though he was a white-haired cripple, he didn't give up his defiance. Facing death, he clung to life in order to rebel: against the world, against the authorities, against the Government, against God. (*Rebellion* 119)

While Lenz's revolt is meaningful and dangerous (he infiltrates extremist political organizations with the purpose of destroying them and their opponents alike), Pum's rebellion is rather derisory and private: from the window of the public lavatory where he works as a caretaker and toiletry salesman, he imagines himself assisting a fugitive criminal by helping him into the yard through the window.[14] Another time, Pum sees burglars breaking into a store but does not report the event to the police officer standing at the street corner. Pum childishly revels in the destruction of the world around him and unofficially declares himself an ally of all the "heathens," the petty criminals and beggars whom he had initially profoundly despised: "When his newspapers told him about murders and thefts and robberies, he rejoiced. Criminals, the 'heathens', had become his secret allies. They knew nothing of it. But he was their friend, their patron" (134). Readily adopting the label of rebel, Pum is unaware of the tragic-comical effect it triggers when he confesses his condition to his closest ally in the fight against the world order, his trusted parrot Ignatz: "Ah yes, Ignatz, we're rebels, the pair of us" (130).

Much more significant than Pum's revolt against state authority is his rebellion against God, which by contrast emphasizes the tragic condition of the individual who is betrayed even in his hope for religious redemption. Unlike the other homeless "heathens" who suffer social injustices, Pum loses even his belief in transcendent justice and the comfort of divine protection and thus becomes inwardly homeless.[15] It is therefore not surprising that revolt in its pure form becomes the final refuge of a man who lost not only the assurance of external justice but even that of moral or divine salvation. Pum's rebellion symbolically offers a last resort to a man left with none, a paradoxical deliverance from the lack of any possible deliverance. His break with God attains a distorted biblical effect, as the modern Job chooses to berate an absent or indifferent deity: "I have awakened from my servile meekness into red, rebellious obstinacy. I would deny You, God, if I were alive and not standing before You. But seeing You with my own eyes and hearing You with my own ears, I must do worse than deny You: I must revile You!" (141).

The complex significance of this act of apostasy also resounds with Jewish messianic echoes as Andreas Pum takes the act of apocalyptical anticipation to a higher level than Benajmin Lenz. Pum's final gesture recalls the Jewish Sabbatian sect that, in a manner inspired by certain Gnostic beliefs, organized its own logic of redemption around the idea of the apostasy of the Savior, whose gesture signified the mystical triumph over the kingdom of earthly corruption through self-negation. The provoking act of apostasy indicated the redemptive nature of supreme renunciation that, together with that lesser one characterizing the active participation in the disaster of the world, anticipated the messianic promise of salvation: "The catastrophic character of the redemption . . . is pictured . . . in glaring images. It finds manifold expression: in world wars and revolutions, in epidemics, famine, and economic catastrophe; but to an equal degree in apostasy and the desecration of God's name, in forgetting of the Torah and the upsetting of all moral order to the point of dissolving the laws of nature" (Scholem, *The Messianic Idea* 12).[16] Pum's apostasy significantly represents his own voluntary "pressing for the end" and consequent achievement of redemption—even if in a negative way—by annihilating anything that could stand in the way of a total break with the corrupt world, even if this is God. Roth's indirect dialogue with this mystical Jewish tradition will continue in his novels of religious inspiration.

Equally committed to the obliteration of the existing social order is *Hotel Savoy*'s Zwonimir, a good-natured yet slightly naive revolutionary who shares with the main protagonist, Gabriel Dan, a common experience on the Eastern Front during World War I. Even if the spirit of revolt was accentuated in Zwonimir's mind by the revolutionary atmosphere in Russia, it seems that Roth makes from him a rebel without a cause. Zwonimir is a troublemaker who, we learn, always had adjustment issues regardless of environment. As soon as he settles at the hotel, he plans a revolt involving the workers at a local brush factory.[17] Dan, a cynical individualist who does not believe in any form of action against the state, remains nevertheless emotionally attached to Zwonimir, whose courage and honesty he appreciates: "Zwonimir is an agitator, just from a love of trouble. He is a hothead, but honest, and believes in his revolution" (*Hotel Savoy* 65). This attitude reflects the author's sympathy toward the anarchists of the early novels, who embody in their revolt the spirit of uncompromised resistance to the moral disarray of the world. As we shall see, the anarchists of the late novels do not enjoy the same degree of sympathy and are depicted not as antagonists of their world but instead as an organic part of it.

The revolt of Roth's anarchic characters negatively asserts an alternative to the state of generalized corruption characterizing the moral and social world surrounding them.[18] Even though their struggle focused originally on finding a positive solution to the crisis they encounter, all of their efforts are eventually condemned to reasserting their isolation, inadaptability, and hopelessness. Consequently, the negation of everything in this world remains, paradoxically, their last option. Gazing beyond the ruin of history and the corruption of the world, Roth transfigures his pessimism about the world into a hopeful and expectant suggestion of utopian redemption in a manner reminiscent of Jewish apocalyptical thinking: deliverance itself appears only when the actual world has been denied in its entirety. In Gershom Scholem's words, "the apocalyptists have always cherished a pessimistic view of the world. Their optimism, their hope, is not directed to what history will bring forth, but to that which will arise in its ruin, free at last and undisguised" (*Messianic Idea* 10).

Passive Nihilism and the Absence of Utopia

The other category of characters that populate the world of Roth's early novels chooses a different attitude toward the insoluble conflict between individual and society. Although these characters are equally anarchic in their motivations, the nature of their anarchism is different from that of Lenz or Pum. Their response to their conflict with the world, while not positive, is not manifestly negative either: these characters do not choose an active negation of the world, an uncompromised rebellion against everything worldly, but prefer instead to abandon it altogether, to suggest a solution only in the insinuation of a nonworld in which they ultimately disappear. Their solution is not a negation of the world, yet it is negative in that it refuses to provide any explicit course of action, be it rebellious destruction or not. This attitude of passive nihilism is different from that of active nihilism in the sense in which it asserts nothing; it provides no explicit solution and does not advise any form of action. While some critics have seen in it "die melancholische Faszination für die strukturelle Ereignislosigkeit der modernen Welt" 'the melancholy fascination for the structural uneventfulness of the modern world' (Von der Lühe 38), underlining thus the unredeemable nature of the world, Roth is in fact interested in revealing the possibility for redemption negatively—or looking at redemption, so the speak, from the point of view of its absence.

Gabriel Dan, the protagonist of *Hotel Savoy*, embodies the spirit of the returning soldier at the end of World War I. During his return, which is a fragment of a massive westward population movement after the end of the hostilities on the Eastern Front, he is tempted by the comfort of a small-town hotel on the fringes of the world he is returning to.[19] In spite of his desire to continue his travel, he decides to stop at Hotel Savoy for a couple of days in order to rest in a decent setting and maybe replenish his money supply. Nevertheless, the hotel proves to be a trap that is hard to get out of and equally a cause of devastation for anyone staying in it. Allegorically, this hotel represents the temptation of a settled existence for travelers through life—a source of ruin for anyone lingering too long in search for an opportunity. For Jansen the hotel signifies the illusion of stability in life, and he characterizes it as "der vorübergehende unruhevolle Ruheplatz einer Sehnsucht, die sich nie erfüllt" 'the transient restless resting place of a longing which cannot be fulfilled' ("Weltbezug und Erzählhaltung" 77). Dan is an individualist and a man without illusions about the nature of public morality and the duplicity of social life: "I am alone. My heart beats only for myself. The strikers mean nothing to me. I have nothing in common with the mob, nor with individuals. I am a cold person" (*Hotel Savoy* 65). His arrival at the hotel introduces him to its inhabitants, a whole gallery of characters whose generality unambiguously evokes the diversity of human types: some are unscrupulous exploiters, others simply greedy or opportunistic; some are poor and honest, others poor and deceitful; some are intelligent, while others are insane. Dan attempts to weave his way through this web of relations, but he fails; his failure is not the result of a lack of adaptability but instead is a refusal to be part of the squalor of moral corruption and false values. Finally, his confessed individualism proves to be just a mask that hides a warm-hearted individual with a strong sense of values. He socializes with the rich from the lower floors and even obtains a well-paying job, but his heart is still with the wretched inhabitants of the higher floors of the hotel, poor exiles in an ironically inversed world:

> The people from the upper storeys also came to me, and there was no end to this. I saw that none of them lived at the Hotel Savoy of his own free will. Each of them was gripped by some misfortune, and the Hotel Savoy was the misfortune and they were no longer capable of choosing between this and that. Every piece of bad luck came to them through this hotel and they believed that Savoy was the name of their misfortune. (108)

Caught between the misery of the inhabitants of this microworld (the hotel) on the one hand and the superficiality and dishonesty of the rich managers on the other, Dan arrives at a middle position from which he can judge both. However, it is not the suffering itself that most affects him or the opulence of the rich few. The most appalling attribute of this world seems to be the contrast between appearance and essence, between the lack of authenticity of its displayed resplendence (represented mostly by the artificial lifestyle and values of the rich elite and of the duplicitous parvenus) and the unquestionable authenticity of the plain suffering of the many. Dan sees in this an occasion to voice his criticism of the world in general by means of a simile: "This Hotel Savoy was like the world. Brilliant light shone out from it and splendour glittered from its seven storeys, but poverty made its home in its high places" (33). Helped in his always postponed decision to leave by an unforeseen series of events that lead to the burning down of the hotel by the rebellious masses of workers, Dan catches a train out of town to go farther westward, toward an undetermined goal. The final words of the main character—"I think to myself: America; that is what Zwonimir would have said, just America" (123)—should be read allegorically as the promise of a utopian destination toward which the travelers and the homeless will always aspire. Finally, Dan escapes disaster through a miracle but is reminded once again of the treacherous nature of any permanent abode, of the dangers lurking in any form of positive commitment toward this world.[20] His departure from Hotel Savoy signifies the refusal of the world as it is and the option for permanent wandering, which epitomizes Roth's argument for skeptical individualism.

Drawing a parallel between Roth's lonely heroes and the condition of East European Jews in his fictional and essayistic writings, Magris considers the existential solitude of *Hotel Savoy* as being indicative of the uprootedness of Jewish life, incapable of assimilating to modern Western society and, at the same time, unable to preserve its specific identity. This situation, connoted by Dan Miron's metaphorical reinterpretation of the Yiddish term "*luftmenschen*," with which the Viennese Jewish salesmen were often described (24), condemns the individuals to a tragic condition: "So leben sie in einer Art Niemandsland, in einem vorbürgerlichen oder unterbürgerlichen Limbus, in der Agonie einer pikaresken Welt, die schon vom westlichen Räderwerk zermalmt, aber noch nicht verschwunden ist, und das Symbol für dieses Zwischenreich ist wieder das unerschöpfliche Hotel" 'Thus they live in a sort of no-man's-land, in a precivil or subcivil Limbo, in the agony of a picaresque world that, although crushed by the western wheelwork, has not disappeared yet, and the inexhaustible hotel is the symbol of this purgatory' (Magris, *Weit von wo* 51). Other critics, such as Ingeborg Sültemeyer and Thorsten Juergens, have interpreted the novel's ending as an expression of Roth's own skepticism about the possibility of a revolutionary overthrow of the bourgeois order in Central Europe. Zwonimir's failed revolution and the migration of the *Heimkehrers* (returnees) toward the West, possibly toward America, reflect the sobriety brought by the failure of the workers' councils throughout Central Europe at the end of World War I, the stabilization of the currencies and economies of Germany and Austria after 1924, and, equally important, the disappointment with the direction taken by the Soviet experiment in Russia (Juergens 39). Nevertheless, this historicist interpretation fails to take into consideration the existential dimension of *Hotel Savoy*, its examination of the metaphysical sources of human misery. Gabriel Dan's failure is the failure not of a social reformer but rather that of an individual conscience in the modern world; his departure is not an abandonment of the revolutionary promise but instead is the rejection of any positive embodiment of redemption, be it social, moral, or political.

Franz Tunda, the protagonist of *Flight without End*, strives for some kind of existential meaning as well. His life in Austria was interrupted by his participation in the war, and at the end of the conflict he believes that his duty is to try to pick it up from where he left it and take it to its natural completion, in a social but especially emotional sense. His search for love corresponds to the illusory hope for existential meaning that he seeks in various lifestyles and cultures, whose succession only confirms his fundamentally inadaptable nature. In this sense, each woman he encounters represents a type of world in which he futilely seeks happiness.[21] Natasha, his Soviet lover, is depicted by Roth as a simplified and almost caricatured version of the Bolshevik feminist Alexandra Kollontai. Natasha feels contempt for the bourgeois, dismisses the traditional idea of family, is the promoter of a sexuality unburdened by petit bourgeois inhibitions, has revolutionary fervor, and is motivated by a naive desire to enlighten the masses in the spirit of socialism: "Natasha elevated love almost to a revolutionary duty, so giving herself a clear conscience" (*Flight* 20).[22] Tunda's relationship with Natasha corresponds exactly to his relationship with the revolution.

By using the revolution as an ersatz identity, Tunda finds in the Soviet system a good refuge for his own moral ambiguity and lack of resolve. After murdering a priest and six peasants at the behest of the Bolshevik army, he feels no guilt or responsibility, only an unexplained satisfaction enhanced by the fact that the revolution only requires people to execute orders and not concern themselves with their motives.[23] And yet, he feels unhappy both in the position of revolutionary commissar and, later on, in that of bureaucrat in the company of a quiet, simple, and loving Georgian woman, Alja. The limpidity of human relations and the simplemindedness of the ideological mind-set that define his life in the Soviet Union irritate Tunda in a profound fashion. After all, Roth writes, Tunda was "a European, an 'individualist', as educated people say. He required complex situations to enjoy life to the full" (58).

Against this background, Madame G. appears as the promise of a different kind of experience, the Western one. Even if in Baku she seems to embody the charming sophistication of the West European woman, in Paris she is nothing more than the symbol of a world that Tunda ultimately finds snobbish, strange, and cold.[24] Upon meeting her again, he cannot help noticing that "there was no need for any other, any more convincing evidence for the existence of a European culture than this Madame G." (123). By this, Tunda suggests that the European culture is intricately involved with this ideal of inaccessible, cold beauty that cultivates its refinement at the expense of its humanity. In this respect, Madame G. is the opposite image of Alja, the contrast between them recalling the opposition between Western Europe and Eastern Europe that Roth elaborates at the same time in his nonfiction. In *The Wandering Jews*, published in 1927, the same year as *Flight without End*, Roth makes a strong case against the westward migration and assimilation of the East European Jews: "And the name for all this is Western civilization ["westliche Kultur"]. Whoever has it is entitled to despise his cousin who, authentic and uncontaminated, comes from the East. Such an Eastern Jew has within himself more humanity and more divinity than all the preachers can come up with in all the theological colleges of Western Europe" (*Wandering Jews* 22). Tunda's flight and the temptations of his journey therefore could be read as a metaphor for the Jewish migrant experience in interwar Europe, while Roth's treatment of the Jewish migration could in turn be interpreted as a metaphor for humanity as a whole, a humanity in search of simple, clear-cut answers to the complex reality of historical existence.

Irene is more central to the novel because she represents the image that haunts Tunda throughout his restless journey. She is his former fiancée, whom he left in order to go to war and who in the meantime has married another man.

Still, he hopes to find her even though his pursuit is motivated more by a need to justify his constant search and inadaptability than by love. When he eventually sees her she does not recognize him, and he is forced to admit to his unchanging condition of fugitive from life. He never finds his place or his love (which acts as a substitute for belonging in this world) and feels as if his real place is not among the living: "Tunda sometimes felt as if he himself lay there in the ground, as if we all lay there, all those of us who set out from home and were killed and buried, or who came back but never again came home—for it is a matter of indifference whether we are buried or alive and well. We are strangers in this world, we come from the realm of the dead" (*Flight* 130).

Tunda's homelessness is less material than it is emotional: his attempt to find a true belonging in this world fails because his expectations are generated by an ideal order of values that cannot be reconciled with the actual one. According to Heizmann, Tunda's case is exemplary because it epitomizes the inner conflict ("Zerrissenheit") of the modern individual (Heizmann, *Joseph Roth* 94). His place in this world has been erased a long time ago, the author suggests, even though we might never know when that happened. Finally, Tunda realizes that he lives "in a world where he was not at home" (*Flight* 126) but does not undertake anything that might change this situation. Even though he is invited back on an adventurous trip to Siberia by his friend Baranowicz (a lone figure of authenticity in a novel teeming with instances of modern inauthenticity), Tunda declines the invitation and remains instead suspended in the nonworld of his homelessness. Evocatively, the last paragraph of the novel reflects the protagonist's intrinsic incapacity to find a solution to his own estrangement from the world: "He had no occupation, no desire, no hope, no ambition, and not even self-love. No one in the whole world was as superfluous as he" (144). Tunda's search remains trapped in meaninglessness, causing some critics to see in it an anti-Odyssey: "*Die Flucht ohne Ende* ist so auch als Negation, als Widerruf der *Odyssee* mit ihrer glückenden Heimkehr zu lesen" '*Flight without End* should be read as a negation and refutation of the Odyssey with its successful return home' (Wild 44).

Arnold Zipper is another character who passively watches the spectacle of the world and its characteristic negation of everything he was raised to believe in. In *Zipper and His Father*, he is content with the position of marginality that society assigns him and mimics the empty rituals of membership in the social and emotional spheres. Raised in a fairly petit bourgeois and old-fashioned household by a naive but honest father, Arnold joins the war as many other young men did, not out of conviction and patriotism but instead to fulfill the irresponsible fantasies of the older generation, the narrator argues. He is the representative of an entire generation that did not grow to master its own destiny but and had one forced on to it by an obtuse and shortsighted political and social environment. Returning home at the end of the war, the members of this lost generation take the heaviest hit. Defeated on the battlefield, they have to carry the burden of poverty, unemployment, national humiliation, and social alienation: "There is a strong sense . . . in Roth's fiction that a world in which certainty was taken for granted in all things had been irretrievably lost. As in the work of Hemingway and Fitzgerald, theirs is a 'lost generation' for whom the old borders, standards, and measures no longer apply" (Hughes, *Facing Modernity* 54). And yet, their failure is not the failure of their own generation but instead that of their parents' generation, whose obsolete aspirations they embody. If they were prevented from finding their own identity before the war by the paternalistic and bellicose imperial establishment, they are kept away from an identity at the end of war as well, this time by a new generation of postwar profiteers, a generation that functions according to the newly discovered laws of survival, opportunism, and immediate success.[25]

Zipper's feeling of purposelessness in the world he returns to is confirmed by the narrator's concise statement: "I think the war has corrupted us. Let's admit that we were wrong to return. We know as much as the dead, but we have to pretend to be stupid because by chance we stayed alive" (*Zipper* 170). Once again, the characters' homelessness and inadaptability are expressed through the metaphor of a spectral reality to which they might belong and is as different from the world of the living as the symbolic hierarchy they represent is different from the actual one. In front of this blunt realization of alienation from the social world surrounding them, the characters plan to escape to the emotional realm, where hopefully love will provide them with a self-deceiving illusion of belonging. In the dialogue between the narrator and Arnold, the former advises the latter to find a woman:

> "Should I fall in love?"
>
> "Perhaps even that: fall in love. In any case, a woman is a help. She helps you to have the illusion that you still have a goal in this world. She wants dresses and shoes, a home and food and sometimes a child. If you have something to worry about it makes it easier to believe you also have some reason for living." (171)

Zipper follows his friend's advice and pursues Erna Wilder, a shallow and manipulative woman whose only purpose is success and fame as an actress. He voluntarily becomes her servant in the achievement of this goal, even at the price of self-humiliation and unhappiness. His obstinacy in proving himself that he loves this woman equals his desire to find a solution to his estrangement from the world. Fully conscious of the impossibility of this outcome, Zipper does not revolt against his environment, nor does he attempt to manifest his dissatisfaction in a strident way. Instead, he stoically accepts carrying on in the miserable condition of being a stranger in a detestable world. At the end of the novel the narrator gradually loses track of Arnold, whose trips around the world in the service of his ambitious wife make him less and less visible. Arnold's passive disappearance leads Jansen to argue that the main theme of *Zipper and His Father* is the homelessness and uselessness of the individual in real life ("Weltbezug und Erzählhaltung" 110). In a concluding open letter that the narrator addresses to Arnold, we learn that passivity is the natural response of the representatives of this lost generation: "We shall never be able to make ourselves understood. . . . We have been decimated. There are not enough of us. Not enough of us in this world, in which nothing but the sheer physical weight of the masses can make a breakthrough, and not the spiritual energy of an individual person" (245). The narrator decries in this passage the powerlessness of the individual in the era of paradoxical "mass or collective loneliness" of which Buber speaks in *Paths in Utopia* (14).

However, the redemptive significance of the characters' passive attitude becomes visible in the somewhat unexpected turn that Roth gives to the belief that their lives have been "spent in vain": "'In vain,' which means: *apparently* in vain. For, as you know yourself, there does exist somewhere a region in which the traces of our playing are recorded, illegibly, but in some strange way effectively, if not today, then years hence, and if not years hence, then millennia hence" (245). Roth suggests that there is still hope, or maybe even salvation, but not in this world or within ordinary history. The redemption of these miserable destinies can only happen in a deferred, undefined, and vague future. The assertion of this millenarian expectation gives meaning to the passive nihilists' departure from the world. It is not a senseless gesture anymore, motivated by defeatist abandonment and the accepted futility of their life, but instead represents a stage in a teleology of hope whose only positive characteristic is the existence of this hope, the expectation of salvation. Roth's hope for redemption thus echoes Bloch's and Rosenzweig's idea that the present is in essence a "not-yet" Utopia and that even in the midst of despair and purposelessness, our existence beseeches the arrival of a final deliverance.

Right and Left revisits the atmosphere and themes of *The Spider's Web*, with obvious similarities between characters: on the one hand the Bernheim brothers, in their ambition and radicalism, are reminiscent of Theodor Lohse; on the other hand their opposite, Nikolai Brandeis, is similar in his nihilism to Benjamin Lenz. However, while Lohse epitomizes the unscrupulous fanaticism of the nascent fascist movement in Germany, the Bernheims typify the more complex union of interests between the interwar German middle class and the radical nationalist youths. Paul Bernheim is the older brother, interested in success and honorability, the guardian of the bourgeois appearances but ultimately a vain, envious, and hypocritical individual who will compromise any principle in order to achieve his goals. The younger brother, Theodor, is the family renegade: he despises the bourgeoisie and the honorability of the ruling elites and dreams of a violent overthrow of the reviled order. However, just like his brother, Theodor is willing to compromise on issues of principle for the sake of material gains. In spite of family tensions between the brothers, Paul and Theodor represent two sides of the same coin. They personify the apparently opposing social forces characteristic of interwar German society, forces that will collude against the common enemy: the outsider, in this case the Russian Jew Nikolai Brandeis.

Brandeis is also reminiscent of Lenz in that he too is a pragmatic figure who uses his enemies for his own gain but only up to a point. A character introduced later in the novel, Brandeis appears as a counterfigure to the unstable and superficial Paul Bernheim: while the latter is consumed by the selfish and illusory desire to occupy a central place in society, Brandeis is central in society without wanting to be. He consequently tries to abandon this position, always on the run from any form of external conditioning or public expectation. Brandeis's nihilism reflects the option for the anarchic abandonment of prescribed ethical and behavioral models, in favor of a rebirth of the moral person under the sign of one's own freedom and specificity. Through realism and entrepreneurial spirit, this immigrant manages to quickly accumulate a significant fortune and offer a livelihood to large numbers of employees. Additionally, he distinguishes himself through gratuitous gestures of generosity, even toward persons who hate him and would gladly destroy him if the chance arose such as Theodor, Paul's brother.[26]

Brandeis's own early life confirmed to him more than anything else the unstable nature of human beliefs, of social rules and legal regulations. Forced to confront the limit of his own beliefs during the time of the Bolshevik Revolution, he realizes that no one remains unchanged in life regardless of circumstances; instead, there are a multitude of alter egos inhabiting every human being, and accordingly, nothing in this world is changeless: "Ever since that transformation in his life, Brandeis would insist that experience doesn't mature people, it changes their natures. He remembered the lunatic in his village at home, who never tired of asking everyone he met: 'How many are you? Are you *one*?' No, one wasn't just *one*. One was ten people, twenty, a hundred" (*Right* 111). The awareness of the fundamental instability of the world's values alters Brandeis's approach to life: from an idealistic follower of the principle of immutability and conviction, he becomes a nihilist: "Da Ideen so ohne weiteres gewechselt werden können, da man nicht weiß, welche die richtige ist, bleibt nur noch die Feststellung, daß man sich für keine Idee, für keine Ordnung, entscheiden kann. Man muß von Ideen und Idealen frei sein" 'Since ideas can be easily changed, since one does not know which one is the right one, there remains only the conclusion that one cannot opt for any idea, for any order. One must be free from ideas and ideals' (Sieg 84). He leaves Russia and wanders through Eastern Europe for a number of years, assuming different identities and exploiting the volatility of every law and regulation for his own profit. Once in Germany he is again struck by the naïveté of the entrepreneurial and political circles, who seem to act out of ideological and stereotypical beliefs rather than rational and practical spirit. Against this background, he operates with the assurance of the man who knows that self-reliance is the only true value governing the world and that nothing else really matters:

> People strike me as peculiar because in each of them I can find a piece of old, dead Nikolai Brandeis. They still have ideals and principles, schools and houses, identities and passports. They are patriotic and unpatriotic, saber-rattlers and pacifists, nationalists and internationalists. I am none of those things. I had countries, fatherlands in the past, but they went under. I believed in things, they evaporated. (*Right* 115)

And yet, Brandeis temporarily gives in to the fantasy of stability and social happiness: a series of events set into motion by one of his gratuitous acts of generosity brings him in the company of Lydia, a Russian émigré whom he thinks he can love. Once again love acts as the surrogate for identity, as an illusory source of stability in a world without any firmness. Nevertheless, he realizes that the more he builds a life for himself, the more ensnarled he becomes in a morality and a set of rules that are not his but instead are imposed on him by his environment: "Soon the trappings of my power will start to be more impressive than I am. I'll no longer be able to indulge the whims that now are my only pleasure" (194).

These pleasures are the ability to make radical changes in one's life, to deny everything one has built and to start anew, with the singular belief in the power of the individual will.

Once he is reminded of this changeless truth (the only one), Brandeis calmly prepares his exit from this world and his disappearance into a different environment, under a different identity. The force of the demand for change corresponds to the authority of the truth that Brandeis is in possession of: the only authentic drive is back toward the emptiness that actually forms our uniqueness. This moral anarchism is reasserted in the honest words he addresses to his colleague Paul Bernheim: "Everything yields to you, everything's rotten. Leaving it, leaving it is the thing. Even so, I don't have the feeling I'm doing anything extraordinary. Something tells me to move on. Just as something made me come in the first place. It tells me to move on, and I obey" (231). Brandeis leaves the world of the novel and emblematically disappears into a small borderland town, between the East and the West, on a foggy day. The narrator himself leaves the omniscient point of view in order to contemplate this withdrawal in its full dimension: "Brandeis was never seen again. Since that day, there has been no information of his whereabouts" (235). Brandeis's solution to the nihilism of the world is not desperate, nor is it heartbreaking; it is wise and conscious, the result of a long and profound assessment of the meaning of the world. From this skeptical view of the social and moral dimension of modern life emerges the only viable option: taking the volatility of everything human to its natural conclusion by applying it in a conscious manner. In this sense, his gesture of withdrawal from the world could also be interpreted as an active participation in the general normative nihilism.[27]

Some critics have read Brandeis's moral anarchism through the lens of Roth's early feuilletons, as an expression of the author's own political stand on the issue of morality and the bourgeois world. Seen in this light, Roth's belief in the moral sovereignty of the individual relates to Brandeis's own belief in the personal character of all decisions and to his sustained effort to disentangle himself from the web of professional, social, and emotional constraints. For Werner Sieg, such a political attitude is an expression of romantic antibourgeois and anarchic-socialist ideas: "Eine solche politische Haltung ist leicht zu klassifizieren. Sie steht in der Tradition einer bestimmten Spielart des Anarchismus. . . . Es ist der Anarchismus des Anti-Bourgeois, der—frei nach Franz Moor—alles um sich ausrotten will, das ihn einschränkt und hindert, Herr zu sein" 'Such a political attitude is easy to classify. It fits in with the tradition of a certain variety of anarchism. . . . It is the anarchism of the antibourgeois, which, freely adapted from Franz Moor, wants to destroy everything around it that prevents it from being the master of its own fate' (Sieg 94). While this interpretation correctly identifies a continuity in the spirit of the political ideas espoused by Roth, ideas animated equally by an anarchic anti-institutionalism and moral idealism, it leaves unexplained Roth's vacillation between a more politically active attitude, such as that of support for the anarchic socialism of the Munich Soviet Republic, present in such articles as "Schweigen im Dichterwald" ("Silence among the Poets") from 1923 and "Gruß an Ernst Toller" ("A Salute to Ernst Toller") from 1924, and a more passive, contemplative one, already suggested in the novels of the middle period. A possible explanation might be the fact that Roth's anarchism remains largely moral and inner-oriented, even in the case of the more politically engaged writings. As Uwe Schweikert points out, "den Schritt . . . vom aggressiven, das Unrecht aufzeigenden Feuilleton zur offenen Agitation macht Roth nicht" 'Roth does not make the decisive step from the aggressive, moralizing feuilleton to open activism' (44). Roth's engagement with the idea of redemption and Utopia remains attached to a broader religious and existential frame that rejects any ideological, political, or doctrinaire adherence.

Friedrich Kargan, the central character of *The Silent Prophet*, experiences the typical trials and tribulations of the ideologically regimented Marxist revolutionary of the early twentieth century, just to end up realizing the futility of all politics and the changelessness of human nature. Born in Russia but raised in Austria, Kargan possesses that typical Central European versatility that allows him to live between languages and cultures and to better grasp the complexity of human psychology. He is motivated early on in his life by the resentment he feels toward the European bourgeoisie, which he holds responsible for his perceived social and emotional disenfranchisement. Endowed with an adamant perseverance and inborn slyness, Kargan decides to change his destiny by seeking the company of a handful of exiled Russian communist revolutionaries, who initiate him in the practice of ideological self-denial and political cynicism. In the portraits of some of these revolutionaries, one distinguishes similarities with actual historical personages in a sort of roman à clef: the brutal Georgian Savelli recalls Stalin, and the stubborn ideologue L. recalls Lenin.[28]

Kargan is torn between his ideologically colored antipathy for the bourgeoisie and his all too bourgeois infatuation with the typically Viennese Hilde, who displays a mixture of modern feminine emancipation and traditional narcissism. Repulsed by his own lingering bourgeois sentimentalism, Kargan decides to move east to engage in revolutionary action, prompting his proletarian friend Grünhut to remark that there is nothing stupider than to die for a cause: "I intend to suffer for nothing and for nobody. . . . Yes, and to think that there are folk who let their hands be chopped off and their eyes put out for an idea. . . . For Humanity, in the name of Freedom! It's frightful!" (66). Grünhut's words prefigure Kargan's later change of mind and his eventual retreat from world history. On the border between Austria and Russia, Kargan is ambushed by czarist authorities, betrayed most probably out of pure political pragmatism by one of his comrades. Condemned to Siberian exile, Kargan spends one year considering the futility of all ideologies and rediscovering the sense of joy at the simple pleasures of life. At this point, a single plan dominates his actions: "There was at this time only one word that had any meaning: Flight!" (91). He escapes Russia at the outset of World War I and ends up in neutral Switzerland via Austria and Germany. Kargan's flight is similar to Franz Tunda's, as are his psychology and sense of homelessness. There is thus no surprise that Roth makes the narrator of *The Silent Prophet* suggest, in the typically "new objectivist" manner, that he is a friend of both characters and thus most likely also the narrator of *Flight without End*. However, unlike Tunda, whose flight takes him from the East to the West, Kargan ventures into further exploits back and forth before finally settling for the East.

In Switzerland, he reconnects with the communist revolutionaries and follows them in the now-famous secret 1917 train to Petrograd. Back in the newly established Soviet Union, Kargan assumes an ideological role in the Bolshevik army before falling out with his old comrades and choosing once again the individualist solution of flight to the West. This time, Kargan is resolved to rejoin Hilde, whom he meets in Paris. There, the two lovers discover the pleasure of true passion, forbidden until then to both by the vagaries of history, yet soon afterward the relationship runs dry. Hilde is ready to follow him, but he realizes that love is nothing more than a temporary refuge from the inescapable condition of existential restlessness. Like Tunda and Zipper, Kargan meditates upon the untimeliness of his existence, caught between the traditional forms of anchoring to a place or to a social position and a possible future universal homelessness that would be the only authentic type of home for humanity: "I was born too late or too early. I am one of the experiments that Nature makes here and there before she decides to bring forth a new species . . . I shall literally fulfil my fate to be a stranger" (196).

In the end, he acknowledges that his political engagement failed because it was motivated not by true ideological reasons but instead by a purely human pursuit of meaningfulness.[29] Although the narrator admits that all his information about Kargan ends with him rejoining Hilde in Paris, he ventures to speculate upon Kargan's possible final return to the East in the company of his friends Berzeyev and Baranowicz.[30] Unlike Tunda, who declines Baranowicz's invitation in *Flight without End*, Kargan might have accepted it in the form of a politically imposed exile somewhere in Siberia, in the solitude of nature, far from any place where history acts upon human life. If he was exiled against his will and at the hands of the reviled czarist regime the first time, the second time he stoically accepts it, although it is more painful since it is imposed on him by his former communist comrades. His final withdrawal from history is an admission of the pointlessness of any human effort in a world dominated by personal, political, and technological hubris. Kargan, together with the other disillusioned revolutionaries Tunda and Brandeis, brings a confirmation of the fact that, in Roth's view, any reaction against the political world is bound to end in further oppression, as Nadine Gordimer correctly observes (285). The self-obliteration of the ego is the only final gesture of authenticity left to the character and, negatively, is a possible suggestion of another redeemed reality built on rules that cannot be explicitly formulated or that our imagination, so much influenced by the same modern narrative of personal vanity, cannot articulate.

Whether it assumes the generic identity of Europe, of state authority, of legal order and social interaction, or of family or emotional relations, modernity is characterized in Roth's novels through the defining separation between essence and appearance, between the genuine nature of individual emotions and the surrogate values of a world that feeds itself on illusory and selfish pursuits. Left without an authentic connection with the world, the individual loses his sense of belonging and even his certitude of being a complete human being.[31] Roth's novels explore the alternatives left to the isolated individual within this profoundly corrupt universe and single out his desire to bridge the moral chasm between essence and appearance, to restore the lost unity between the private mind and the external world. In this sense, the anarchic attitude of his early characters prefigures a manner in which this redemptive unification could be achieved. However, this redemption remains indefinite because there is no positive resolution of the characters' conflict with the world and no end to their isolation and homelessness. Rebellion constitutes an answer for Pum and Lenz insofar as it manages to negate the world in its social, psychological, and spiritual sense. Their negation starts from the presupposition that everything in this world is the opposite of what it should be, hence a counterideal world, a negative Utopia. By denying the negativity of this type of Utopia, their revolt points in the direction of a double negation, whose final result is the suggestion of the right kind of reality, of a positive Utopia. In the dramatic end of *The Rebellion*, Andreas Pum faces the final judgment in front of the divinity that he reviles. Asked by God where he would like to go next, Pum replies without hesitation "I want to go to Hell!" (*Rebellion* 142). This defiance represents the act of denying an entire world, together with its moral and spiritual values: if indeed divine (and earthly) justice represents only discrimination and mercilessness, then its opposite, hell (and rebellion), must be the real choice for the ideal order of values.

This redemption through negation finds its complement in the redemption through omission that characterizes the passive nihilists Tunda, Dan, Brandeis, and Kargan. This time, the solution to the problem of the world is not its negation but rather its abandonment. These characters do not feel that their symbolic hierarchy is the exact opposite of the actual world and hence do not apply the model of negation without remainder. Their own individualism is not oppositional; it is purposeless. Brandeis's fundamental truth about the volatility of everything, possession or belief, is suggestive of the characters' insurmountable estrangement from this world. Consequently, they cannot negate it or wage a war against it or else they would enter into the same logic of assertion through denial. Their refusal of the world must therefore project itself into an ambiguous promise of a resolution in an undetermined register outside of history and outside of the world, as in Zipper's case. Their sense of untimeliness rests on the belief that they do not belong to this world and time but instead belong to another merely suggested one. If they had chosen active nihilism, as Pum and Lenz had, then they would have indirectly admitted to their belonging to this world, even if simply in order to destroy it. Their disappearance from the narrative and, implicitly, from the world thus represents a negative redemption through omission, a redemption that suggests the promise of something fundamentally different but not opposed.

Out of the Ruins, Redemption

The individual in Roth's novels, even if apparently crushed under the heavy wheels of an absurd social machinery or isolated by a selfish and corrupt world, emerges victorious, at least in a symbolical way. The significance of his final condition points in the direction of a promised redemption, of a utopian reality. In this respect, the messianism of Roth's early novels reminds one of Franz Kafka's messianism. Walter Benjamin and Gershom Scholem spoke of a promise of redemption in Kafka's works, one that manifests itself negatively through the obvious lack of salvation in the narrative world of his fiction.[32] This negativity, Scholem argues, constitutes Kafka's response to classical Judaic messianism and to the postulation of a positive theological order of salvation through the construction of a counterorder, an order of damnation and decay, a *negative theology*: "in Kafka we possess the *theologia negativa* of a Judaism not a whit less intense for having lost the Revelation as a positive message" (Scholem qtd. in Löwy 79). Even if Roth's early work is not as much permeated by religious motifs as Kafka's, an awareness of the corrupt nature of the world is very much present, reaching at times apocalyptic-religious tonalities through its vigor and scope. Additionally, while God is explicitly denied in the early novels, his presence is nevertheless suggested through the negative promise of deliverance.[33] This deliverance bears the undeniable mark of an expectation that exceeds the social and political register in which the plot of the novels unfolds and reaches into the realm of religiosity, a realm more explicitly formulated in Roth's later works. As Leo Löwenthal points out, this negative form of messianism is indeed an expression of Judaic religiosity: "the Jewish article of faith that one may not pronounce the name of God is very decisive. The unattainable, the unapproachable, the unnamable, which nonetheless contains a sense of longing that one may finally reach the goal, may ultimately speak its name. This conception is certainly very Jewish" (*Unmastered Past* 245).

Closely knit into Kafka's negative theology lies a negative utopianism, which answers the political question concerning the role and the mission of the individual in his society: "corresponding politically to the *theologia negativa*, to Kafka's negative Messianism, is a *utopia negativa*, a negative anarchism" (Löwy 81). Kafka's characters almost invariably face a social world governed by self-regulating mechanisms that destroy the individual instead of serving him. This pessimistic allegorical view of reality stems from Kafka's belief that modern rationality has created an insatiable monster, a technological Moloch that acts arbitrarily and destructively while offering the illusion of inevitability and reasonableness. This rationality has its patent expression in the structure of justice, administration, and social organization. The characters fall victim to this awful reality while realizing that the system itself bases its authority in the illusion of authority that the victims themselves bestow upon it. As a result, Kafka's fiction indirectly suggests, only an anarchic revolt of the individual and a reassessment of the pattern of social action starting from a strictly personal and moral view of the world can replace the devastating effects of modernity.[34] If his characters obediently accept the verdict of damnation and annihilation, their conformism acts as a negative indication of what they should ideally do, namely revolt against the external order.

The reality with which Roth's characters are confronted largely exhibits similar characteristics to the one present in Kafka's fiction. First, the logic of the actual world is impenetrable: for Joseph K. of *The Trial*, the legal mechanisms set in motion by the justice system remain unintelligible even though they destroy him. Similarly, Pum is crushed by a legal mechanism that is above the understanding of the average citizen and is absurd and yet unquestionable: "The great grinding wheels of the State were getting to grips with the citizen Andreas Pum, and, before he even realized it, he was being slowly and comprehensively crushed" (*Rebellion* 76). Second, the relationships specific to this world are the opposite of what they should ideally be: the bureaucratic machinery in *The Castle* is not there to make people's lives easier; it is there to make them miserable. As a consequence, objects that are usually the means to the satisfaction of certain ends become ends in themselves like the punishment machine in "In the Penal Colony," which finally reveals itself as the reason for the people's own existence. Similarly, in *Hotel Savoy* the hotel becomes the main source of misfortune for anyone seeking refuge from their own misfortunes: the lives of the people living in the hotel are gradually eroded until they die, impoverished by the merciless manager Kaleguropulos who, in a Kafkaesque twist, turns out to be one and the same person as the liftboy.[35] As an allegory of the world, the hotel's deceiving appearance is another meaningful feature: it seems luxurious on the outside but is the setting of great human suffering on the inside.[36] Ironically, the wretched are also accommodated on the higher floors of the building, emblematically turning the image of an ascent toward heavens into one of a descent into hell:

> Brilliant light shone out from it and splendour glittered from its seven storeys, but poverty made its home in its high places, and those who lived on high were in the depths, buried in airy graves, and the graves were in layers above the comfortable rooms of the well nourished guests sitting down below, untroubled by the flimsy coffins overhead.
>
> I belong to those who are buried on high. Do I not live on the sixth floor and shall I not be driven by Fate onto the seventh? To the eight, the tenth, the twentieth? How high can one fall? Into Heaven and ultimate bliss? (*Hotel Savoy* 33–34)

Third, the world itself is built on illusion, an illusion that nevertheless crumbles at the first sober and independent investigation: Kafka's parable "Before the Law" and his reflection "The Problem of Our Laws" explain that the apparent inevitability and order of the world are actually the result of people treating them as inevitable and orderly. Once one finds the courage to question the justification of inevitability and order, they reveal themselves as simply illusory. Similarly,

Brandeis of *Right and Left* is aware of the fact that nothing in the world is impossible and that much of what actually bears any authority is built on prejudice. One only has to ask, to knock at the door, and the gates of the world will open for him: "Nothing nowadays puts up any resistance. . . . I've realized that it's only the names that frighten people off, with their established and powerful sound" (*Right and Left* 193–94). In *Hotel Savoy*, Gabriel Dan explicitly reflects on the same truth: "They [the people] prepared their own destiny and yet believed that it came from God. They were prisoners of tradition, their hearts hung by a thousand threads and the threads were spun by their own hands" (*Hotel Savoy* 98). Accordingly, all source of authority emerges from the individual, not from the surrounding world. The same anarchic conclusion underlies both Kafka's and Roth's implied political message: "messianic redemption will be the work of human beings themselves, at the moment when, following their own inner law, they bring about the collapse of outside constraints and authorities" (Löwy 77).

Roth's and Kafka's admiration for the Chasidim is well documented, as is their fascination with the world of Chasidic folklore and storytelling. While Roth appreciated the "narrative gift" of the Chasidim in *The Wandering Jews* (47), Kafka even declared to feel "at home" with the Chasidic tales, although he disliked Buber's adaptations (Friedländer 50–51). It does not come as a surprise, then, why the moral anarchism (in the sense of individual redemption of the world through an act of personal moral assertion) present in their work echoes the Chasidic motif of *devekut*, or individual overcoming of the corruption of the world through unification or reunification with the spirit of God. In one of Baal Shem's favorite parables, the illusory aspect of the world's difficulties is revealed only through an act of courage or faith of the individual who dares to push forth and achieve deliverance on his own: once a king built a castle of intricate design, with countless corridors and rooms, and placed the hall of the throne in the middle of it; when the subjects wanted to see him to pay their respects, they were unable to find his room and got desperately lost along the way; when the king's son came to them and showed them that the maze was actually a series of illusions, they were able to find the king very quickly. Baal Shem's allegory gives an active sense to the redemptive force lying dormant inside the individual and expecting to be awoken.[37] At the same time, it confirms a piece of Chasidic wisdom that is captured in Rabbi Nachman's saying "Es gibt kein Hindernis, das man nicht zerbrechen kann, denn das Hindernis ist nur des Willens wegen da, und in Wahrheit sind keine Hindernisse als nur im Geist" 'There is no obstacle which cannot be broken, for the obstacle exists for the sake of the will, and in truth there are no obstacles but in the mind' (Buber, *Die Chassidischen Bücher* 35).

The similar evaluation of the modern world as a corrupt and condemned reality places Kafka and Roth in a position of externality to it, a position in which redemption has already happened, as Theodor Adorno noticed in relation to the Kafkian universe: "Hell seen from the perspective of salvation" (qtd. in Löwy 80–81). This particular vantage point, from which the replacement of the entire world and not just its reformation is formulated, does not, however, bear any positive mark. It is negatively suggested in both authors and conveys their sense of skepticism toward reality and history on the one hand and their messianic expectation and belief in salvation on the other: "Indem Kafka die Welt für absurd erklärt, stellt er zugleich die Frage nach dem Absoluten" 'By declaring the world absurd, Kafka also asks the question about the absolute' (Ausserhofer 38). The belief in the moral power of the individual to transcend the limitations of a corrupt reality and achieve the "restoration, reparation, reformation and the recovery of lost harmony" (Löwy 2) in a personal yet historically meaningful way is pivotal for the interpretation of the works of these two Central European writers, who share a common preoccupation with the question of redemption, a question that as we have seen in Chapter 1 influenced an entire generation of Jewish intellectuals in the first half of the twentieth century.

The presence of the negative redemption in Roth's early novels is a first step in the quest for a positive and far-reaching form of redemption that characterizes the novels of religious and historical inspiration. With the awareness of the failure of the nihilist approach to social, moral, and political questions, Roth's redemptive imagination gradually abandons the individualist and social-critical perspective in order to explore the metaphysical, religious, and historical dimensions of existence in the framework of a collective identity. However, the basic critique of modernity, reality, and human alienation practiced in his early work remains unchanged and provides the background against which the search for a positive variety of redemption takes place in the late novels. This search for redemption defines the fundamental problematics, the characteristic themes, and the general mood of Roth's entire work, regardless of the stylistic changes affecting his writing or the transformation of his political allegiances.

Notes

1. The phrase was coined by Fritz Stern in his famous study *The Politics of Cultural Despair: A Study in the Rise of the Germanic Ideology*. Stern focuses on some lesser-known intellectual figures in turn-of-the-twentieth-century Germany in order to sketch out the birth of a certain type of cultural discourse that grew in influence in

the interwar years and was characterized through a revolt against Western values, modernity, reason, and individualism. The attitude of "cultural despair" resulted from the belief that Germany was sacrificing its most precious possession, its culture, through its democratization and modernization.

2. As Jacques Le Rider points out, "Out of all the artistic and intellectual output of turn-of-the-century Vienna, what appeals to us above all is the evidence of a critical approach to modernity, concentrating on aesthetic, ethical or psychological priorities and questioning certain modernist ideas, such as the idea of progress guided by scientific and technological rationality, or the programme of emancipation envisaged by individuals inspired by Enlightenment optimism" (*Modernity and Crises of Identity* 6). Fritz Harckert too focuses on this Viennese *Kulturpessimismus* and its connection to Roth's critique of culture and civilization.
3. Crucial for the understanding of this distinction in German context remains Norbert Elias's study *The Civilizing Process*: "In German usage, *Zivilisation* means something which is indeed useful, but nevertheless only a value of the second rank, comprising only the outer appearance of human beings, the surface of human existence. The word through which Germans interpret themselves, which more than any other expresses their pride in their own achievement and their own being, is *Kultur*" (4).
4. Jürgen Heizmann considers that the overarching pessimistic themes of Roth's journalistic writings are continued into his early novels: "So ist eines der Hauptmotive in seinen Romanen das *Verschwinden* des Echten und Substantiellen" 'Thus one of the main motifs in his novels is the disappearance of the genuine and substantial' (*Joseph Roth* 7). As early as 1956, Ward Hughes Powell identifies "primitivism" as the core philosophy of Roth's fiction and points out the continuity between the early novels' critical assessment of modernity and the late novels' "primitivist" plunging into a return to tradition and the past (36).
5. For a critic such as Ingeborg Sültemeyer, Roth's early writings demonstrate a clear and even radical leftist affiliation: "Roth's politischer Standpunkt zu dieser Zeit kann in der Nähe des linken Flügels der 'Sozialistischen Partei Österreichs' vermutet werden" 'It can be presumed that Roth's political views at this time were close to the left wing of the "Socialist Party of Austria"' (Sültemeyer 13). Other critics, such as Werner Sieg, reject the "socialist" hypothesis of Roth's early literary career: "mit Sozialismus haben seine Ansichten und diejenigen seiner Hauptgestalten aber nichts zu tun" 'however, his [Roth's] views and those of his characters have nothing to do with socialism' (Sieg 94).
6. For a detailed analysis of Roth's ambiguous relationship to socialism in the context of the social democratic Viennese world of the 1920s, see Rares Piloiu,

"The Paradoxes of Left Socialism in Interwar Austria: Joseph Roth and Austro-Marxism," *Modern Austrian Literature* 40 (2007).

7. The periodization of Roth's novels, based on the author's explicit abandonment of New Objectivity (the article "Schluß mit der 'Neuen Sachlichkeit'!" appeared in 1930), has been correctly challenged by critics who pointed out the continuities between the new objectivist phase and the later more intentionally subjective and allegorical phase. Critics such as Jürgen Heizmann (*Joseph Roth*), Reiner Wild, Andreas Wirthensohn, and Florian Gelzer argue that far from being a pure exponent of New Objectivity during the early phase of his novelistic career, Roth exposes the limits of the aesthetics of New Objectivity and engages the reader with the puzzling complexity of the narrative demarche in general. However, since this work does not emphasize the narratological dimension of Roth's work, we will operate with the traditional separating line between the early and the late novels (favored by Hermann Kesten in the 1956 introduction to the first edition of Roth's collected works), if only because it is the moment when Roth himself officially repudiates the aesthetic precepts of New Objectivity.
8. According to Curt Hohoff, Roth's late period can be further separated into two phases: the first religious one, marked by the novel *Hiob,* and the second conservative and legitimist one beginning with *Radetzkymarsch* (in Magris, *Weit von wo* 15).
9. Rolf Eckart considers loneliness as the core issue of all Roth's novels: "Vor allem die Einsamkeit ist es jedoch, in der Joseph Roth das Ur-Leid des Menschen sieht. . . . Und Joseph Roths Menschen sind einsam, rettungslos einsam" 'However, Joseph Roth sees the primordial suffering of the human being above all in loneliness. . . . And Joseph Roth's people are lonely, hopelessly lonely' (16). Famira-Parcsetich reiterates this idea: "Das grundlegende Problem im Werk Joseph Roths ist folgendes: Der Mensch befindet sich in einem Zustand der Isoliertheit; er ist vom ersten bis zum letzten Tag seines Lebens erbarmungslos allein" 'The fundamental problem in Joseph Roth's work is the following: the human being is in a state of isolation; he is ruthlessly alone from the first to the last day of his life' (125).
10. Sieg talks about a fundamental conflict in Roth's novels between the representatives of different and mutually exclusive value systems. Each character's fixation in one's own system (which Sieg associates with the metaphor of a spider's web) contributes to the basic misunderstanding and clash between worlds: "Die Frage nach der Fixierung ist für Joseph Roth die existentielle Grundfrage seines Daseins" 'The issue of fixation is for Joseph Roth the fundamental existential question of his life' (105).
11. Curt Sanger integrates Roth's criticism of cultural decadence to a wider trend in modern German literature: "Cultural decline or more specifically, the breakdown

of cultural values—'der Zerfall der Werte,' as Hermann Broch calls it—is of paramount concern in modern German literature" (65).

12. Roth's moral and political thinking cannot be dissociated from the general fascination with Nietzsche in the Viennese world at the beginning of the twentieth century. Nietzsche's diagnostic of modernity and ambiguous evaluation of individualism (where the individual is both a result of the crisis of modernity and its lone opponent) generated ardent debates in Vienna in the early decades of the twentieth century. See Le Rider, *Modernity and Crises of Identity* 44.
13. Through this imitation Lenz, the Eastern Jew, enacts the anti-Semitic stereotype of the "dissimulating Jew," whose mimicry of the Gentiles is aimed at undermining and destroying them: "Als ein Jude, der vorgibt, ein anderer zu sein, als er wirklich ist, bestätigt er das Klischée vom Juden als 'Schauspieler'" 'As a Jew who pretends to be another than he really is, he confirms the cliché of the Jew as an "actor"' (Ochse 87). Such intentional employment of anti-Semitic stereotypes against themselves, so to speak, is typical for Roth, who opposes any attempt at exculpatory self-justification as a form of indirect acknowledgment of anti-Semitism. David Horrocks argues that Roth's early journalism contains many instances in which ethnic stereotypes are undermined, most of the time through ironic reductio ad absurdum. As Horrocks points out, Roth is interested in dismantling not only anti-Semitic stereotypes but other racial stereotypes as well ("The Representation" 154). Pamela Saur, on the other hand, acknowledges the presence of ethnic, religious, and gender stereotypes in Roth's work but warns against a "multicultural" reading from the point of view of the present, proposing instead a contextual-historical interpretation through the lens of Roth's "multicultural provincialism" ("Joseph Roth's Multicultural Provincialism").
14. The scenes placing Pum in the public lavatory of a music pub were inspired by a feuilleton written at about the same time (1923) and titled "Der Mann in der Toilette" ("The Man in the Lavatory").
15. Jansen correctly observes that Pum lost the assurance of his spiritual redemption, the "home" of his soul, but through his rebellion he proves that he still has not lost his soul: "Andreas Pum hat zwar die Heimat des Glaubens an Gerechtigkeit und Ordnung verloren. . . . Er hat die *Heimat* der Seele verloren, aber nicht die *Seele*" 'Andreas Pum has indeed lost the basis of the faith in justice and order. . . . He has lost the *abode* of the soul, but not the *soul*' ("Weltbezug und Erzählhaltung" 59).
16. Scholem further explains the role of the apostate Messiah as "dialectical ruin": "His mission takes on a destructive and paradoxical quality which must come into full effect before the positive part of the redemption can become visible" (*Messianic Idea* 62).

17. The motif of the brush factory workers' revolt resurfaces in *The Radetzky March*, even though this time the events are narrated from the other side of the barricade, from the point of view of the authorities.
18. Werner Sieg remarks on the anarchic component of Roth's early novels: "Das Frühwerk, endend mit den Romanen von 1929, ist seiner Intention nach zeitkritisch. Es will politisch aktivieren und vertritt einen radikalen Anarchismus" 'The early work, ending with the novels of 1929, is, according to its intention, critical of the times. It wants to mobilize politically and represents a radical anarchism' (10).
19. Joanna Jabłkowska finds interesting evidence that would confirm Józef Wittlin's statement that the inspiration for the town in *Hotel Savoy* was given by the Polish city of Łódź.
20. Mathew elaborates on the allegorical nature of the novel by stating that "Hotel Savoy is to him [Gabriel Dan] a metaphysical model of the world" (83).
21. Matjaž Birk also remarks on the correspondence between the three phases of Tunda's flight (communist revolutionary, bureaucratic postrevolutionary, and bourgeois) to the three women figures he encounters: "Jede der drei Daseinsmöglichkeiten wird durch eine im Mittelpunkt der Handlung stehende Frauengestalt verkörpert" 'Each of the three possibilities of existence is embodied by a central female character' (116).
22. The writing of *Flight without End* followed Roth's trip to the Soviet Union and was therefore strongly influenced by it. The first part of the novel, narrating Tunda's adventures from Siberia to Moscow and Baku as well as his impressions of the newly installed regime, fictionalizes with a high degree of fidelity Roth's own travel impressions, published serially in 1927. Natasha is endowed with the same characteristics that Roth assigns to the revolutionary-communist women in these travel reports.
23. Jon Hughes makes a somewhat untenable, albeit original, argument that Tunda's murders, together with Brandeis's murder of a priest in *Right and Left*, are similar to protofascist Theodor Lohse's political murders in *The Spider's Web*. Hughes argues, via a whole battery of cultural and gender studies arguments, that the three characters share a "pleasure of heterotopias" due to the fact that their individual responsibility is suspended by the revolutionary fantasies they enact, thus deriving an almost erotic satisfaction from their murders ("Violence, Masculinity and Self" 225). Hughes plays down the moral significance of the murders, a significance that is extremely important in Roth's deployment of the logic of redemption: Tunda and Brandeis were forced into murder by circumstances, while Lohse murdered of his own will. The former, although denied redemption, are still looking for it; the latter is lost forever.

24. Jacqueline Bel focuses on the theme of snobbery in her analysis of *Flight without End*. Drawing on Husserl's *Crisis of the European Sciences and Transcendental Phenomenology*, Bel claims that the spiritual crisis encountered by Tunda in both the East and the West echoes the crisis of the free spirit analyzed by Husserl. A consequence of this crisis, Bel argues, is the rigid and uncritical conformism of the society, expressed in the snobbish adoption of ideas and fashions in vogue at the time (95–108).
25. Jansen suggests that Arnold Zipper is the first truly "Austrian" character in Roth's gallery of Austrian types: his superficiality and inadaptability in the modern world and his old-fashioned and somewhat aristocratic mannerism point in the direction of similar characters in the works of Hugo von Hofmannsthal and Franz Grillparzer ("Weltbezug und Erzählhaltung" 110). However, Franz Tunda was depicted before Zipper more clearly as a distinct Austrian (for instance, during his arrest by the White Guard he is thinking of pastry: "he was an Austrian," Roth clarifies (*Flight* 13). In this sense, Tunda is a precursor of the Austrian characters for whom later the Trottas will provide the archetypal examples in *The Radetzky March* and *The Emperor's Tomb*.
26. Brandeis's story of success fits into a scenario of Jewish life in exile typified by the biblical stories of Joseph, Daniel, and Esther. As Almuth Hammer demonstrates, these scenarios are very important in understanding modern Jewish life in exile and in making sense of successes and failures (41).
27. Mathew compared Brandeis to Lenz in that both have the almost demonic power to stand beyond good and evil and shape a world of their own will: "Modelled on the same lines as Benjamin Lenz in *Das Spinnennetz*, Brandeis stands beyond good and bad, right and left, beyond systems and institutions which he scorns and hates" (120).
28. In his 1966 review of *The Silent Prophet* titled "In die falsche Revolution geraten" ("Getting into the Wrong Revolution"), Jansen suggests that Kargan himself bears clear resemblances to the exiled Trotsky (whose autobiography appeared in 1929, the same year that the novel is dated) and to Roth himself. Another possible source of inspiration, at least for the name, might have been Lazar Moiseyewich Kaganovich, one of Stalin's associates and an early Bolshevik agitator.
29. Sperber analyzes the novel through the lens of the dichotomy revolutionary/rebel. Roth sets out to portray Kargan as a revolutionary but only manages to present a rebel, Sperber argues: "[W]as ist er, wenn nicht ein Revolutionär? Nun, er ist neurotischer Rebell, somit, was auch immer er tun mag, im wesentlichen das Gegenteil eines Revolutionärs" '[W]hat is he, if not a revolutionary? Well, he is a neurotic rebel, and therefore whatever he may be doing is essentially the opposite

of a revolutionary' ("Rebell" 627). Sperber fails to notice Roth's emphasis on the dichotomy ideology/humanity, which is a lot more meaningful in understanding Kargan's fundamental inability to fit in with the other revolutionaries.

30. There are few true friends in Roth's novels, and usually instances of true friendship do not survive because the environment in which they appear is hostile to genuine human attachment. On the other hand, as Rolf Eckart points out, when friendship becomes the focus of a relationship and when it does not disintegrate due to external factors, it collapses from within by proving to be only an empty projection of personal ambitions and therefore false. For Eckart, this is an indication of the endemic lack of human communication and attachment defining Roth's characters: "Joseph Roth verwendet den . . . Begriff Freund immer nur dann, wenn er schildert, daß der und jener keinen Freund habe. Zeigt er aber dann zwei 'Freunde' in seinen Romanen, so sieht man, daß er den Begriff hier im landläufigen Sinn gebraucht. Denn es stellt sich dabei immer heraus, daß jeder dem andern fremd ist und jeder einsam bleibt, daß diese 'Freunde' also meist nur 'Bekannte' oder höchstens 'Kameraden' sind" 'Joseph Roth uses the . . . concept of friend only if he shows that this or that one has no friend. If he then shows two "friends" in his novels, one can see that he uses the term here in an everyday sense. For it always turns out that each one is foreign to the other, and that everyone is lonely, so that these "friends" are usually only "acquaintances" or at most "comrades"' (41).

31. Heizmann associates Roth's critique of modernity with the general antimodern disposition in the beginning of the twentieth century: "Der Verlust von Tradition und Totalität und in deren Folge die Unbehaustheit des Menschen bestimmen das Welt- und Lebensgefühl zu Beginn dieses Jahrhunderts. Auch Roth geht davon aus, daß der Mensch sein Eingebettetsein in eine Überlieferung, in ein geschichtliches Ganzes verloren hat" 'The loss of tradition and totality and, as a result, the individual's homelessness determine the attitude toward the world and life at the beginning of this century. Similarly, Roth assumes that the individual has lost his belonging to a tradition, a historical whole' (*Joseph Roth* 79).

32. Rolf Eckart detects the presence of a certain dialectic between negative and positive judgment in Roth's novels, which explains why misery and decay sometimes unexpectedly turn into their opposites (82). As a consequence, characters sometimes glimpse their salvation, so to speak, from the middle of their damnation. This dialectic relationship confirms the thesis that Roth is interested in finding redemption even when he presents a corrupt reality.

33. Hansotto Ausserhofer argues that in Kafka's and Roth's fiction, God's presence is removed but not entirely denied: "Sowohl bei Kafka wie zeitweise auch bei Roth stehen die Gestalten vor einem Hintergrund, über dem sich 'Gottesfinsternis'

ausbreitet, bei der Gott nicht entschwunden, wohl aber in eine unverbindliche Ferne gerückt scheint" 'Both in Kafka and occasionally in Roth, the figures stand before a background over which "God's eclipse" spreads, in which God does not appear to have vanished, but withdrawn into a distant, passive sphere' (6).

34. Kafka himself had anarchist sympathies, Löwy argues: "Kafka expressed his interest in Ravachol and the works and lives of anarchists such as Godwin, Proudhon, Stirner, Bakunin, Kropotkin, Tolstoy, Erich Mühsam and Rudolf Grossmann" (83).
35. The secret meaning of this inversed world is also absurd and comical, as the identity of the liftboy (a representative of human misery and exploitation) is revealed to be that of the manager. The name Kaleguropulos was most likely suggested by that of Nikolaus Kalogeropoulos, the Greek prime minister whom Roth ridicules in a text from 1921 ("Hellas"). Roth ironically claims in this article that his high school Greek teacher would have made him decline the name Kalogeropoulos had this teacher still been alive (*Werke* 1: 505). In *Hotel Savoy*, Roth actually declines it: "Kaleguropulos, Kaleguropulu, Kaleguropulo—a vague recollection of boring school periods; of a Greek master resurrected from forgotten years in a bottle-green jacket" (12).
36. Magris talks about a closer resemblance between Hotel Savoy and Hotel Occidental from Kafka's *America*: the huge number of rooms, the unknown number of floors (Roth mentions, however, that the hotel has seven floors), and the mixture of existential mystery and administrative organization (*Weit von wo* 52).
37. Baal Shem's parable and its relationship to *devekut* is discussed more comprehensively by Scholem in *The Messianic Idea in Judaism and Other Essays on Jewish Spirituality*.

Chapter 3

Transgression, Confession, Atonement: The Search for Redemption in Joseph Roth's Fiction of Religious Inspiration

Joseph Roth's 1925 trip to southern France, with a climactic end in Provence, represents a significant moment for the evolution of the young novelist and journalist. In its wake, a series of articles about France appeared in the *Frankfurter Zeitung* (*Frankfurt Gazette*), the newspaper that sponsored Roth's trip, as did a set of travel essays grouped under the title "Die weißen Städte" ("The White Cities"), which would remain unpublished until 1956.[1] These essays testify to the revelation that Roth has upon his encounter with the ancient Mediterranean and Catholic culture of the French South. If until 1925 his travel essays as well as the political articles and feuilletons are mostly focused on the critical evaluation of the postwar European world, on the moral discrepancies of a world torn apart simultaneously by a frantic desire to modernize and by a reactionary and nationalist culture, then the essays dedicated to the white cities of the Provence reveal, maybe for the first time, a profound satisfaction with a cultural climate that seemed to be the exact opposite of everything Roth had written about until then. A man of the North and the East, as he identified himself until that point, Roth discovers in the southern lifestyle and ancient traditions the solution to many of the problems that plagued the industrialized and fast-changing societies of Central Europe. This first encounter with the world "across the fence" (*Report* 72) would constitute the turning point for the articulation of his mature philosophy of history and culture, a philosophy that informs a considerable part of his later work.

Witness to a devastating world war and to accelerated social and political transformations, such as the disintegration of the major Central and East European empires, the emergence of new nation-states, the subsequent ideological transformation of their cultural milieus and the industrialization and "massification" of their societies, Roth encounters in Provence a world that apparently suffered very little or not at all from these transformations, a world still deeply entrenched in a culture and mentality that seemed millennia old: "How little the world knows of the avalanches that are in store. Will they not come this far? Will their force be already broken? Will the new culture, prefaced by waves of destruction, stop in front of the living monuments of the old, as once before, and strike a compromise?" (*Report* 75). A certain mixture of nostalgia and hope encases Roth's rhetorical questions. Nostalgia results from the awareness of having found in the culture of the French South a living relic of his own childhood, of a world that he considered long disappeared under the destructive impetus of modernity and history: "When I reached the age of thirty, I was finally allowed to see the white cities I had dreamed of when I was a boy" (70). Hope, on the other hand, is expressed in the burgeoning desire to extrapolate the specific formula that Provence used in its defense against the dehumanizing forces affecting the northern part of Europe and develop it into a redemptive principle for humankind as a whole.

Insulated from the specialization and formalization of interhuman relations affecting Roth's rapidly modernizing world, the Provençal culture functions according to temporal cycles that stretch across centuries and bear witness to the succeeding waves of social transformation, from the ancient Roman fascination with the spectacle and the grandiose to the medieval piety of the Catholic spirit, from the exuberance and vitality of the popular peasant temperament to the traditional tolerance and multiculturalism of the Mediterranean spirit. The world that Roth discovers with fascination is able to turn even morally questionable aspects into centuries-old virtues: prostitution becomes an extroverted manifestation of love, and commerce becomes a community-building trade: "traders at a time when trade was heroic, and every transaction served not just a material purpose but also a historical one, broadening the horizon, establishing communications among people!" (100). In Roth's idealized Provençal world, even poverty loses its grimness. Far from dehumanizing, poverty gives people a certain dignity, a certain humanity and permanence, attributes with which he would later build some of his fictional figures, among whom beggars play a central role. In a letter from Avignon to Benno Reifenberg, Roth writes that "I am at home in the Palace of the Popes, all the beggars live in the most wonderful castles, I should like to be a beggar and sleep in its doorways" (*Joseph Roth: A Life* 45).

The feeling of permanence that the South inspires and the inflexibility of ancient traditions seem to transcend the fleeting preoccupations of the industrializing world with oneself, with questions of national specificity, and with the desire to dominate and usher in a totalizing, ideological, and technological culture on the ruins of the old ones. The ancestral Mediterranean world has seen the desire for total domination at different moments in history, Roth argues; it has seen its rise and demise and wisely filtered all these experiences into the few values with general-human validity, such as tolerance, godliness, love of life, stoicism, and tradition. This coexistence of various traditions is harmoniously tied together by the cosmopolitan spirit of Catholicism, to which Roth begins to draw closer on this occasion: "It [Avignon] is a Catholic city. And just as Catholicism is a cosmopolitan religion that embraces all peoples, so Avignon is the fortress of the Catholic Church, a cosmopolitan, organic fusion of all sorts of traditions and styles. It is Jerusalem and Rome, it is classical and medieval" (*Report* 99).[2]

The Provençal world managed, in Roth's view, to achieve a synthesis of the divergent human needs for belonging and diversity, something that modernity failed to accomplish. The drama of his early novels centers around this impossible synthesis and showcases either isolated individuals to whom a sense of belonging in the modern society is denied (Tunda, Zipper, and Brandeis offer the best examples of estrangement) or "mass" individuals who fit in, are part of a group, but at the cost of the exclusion of all the other different individuals (Lohse and Bernheim are the insiders in a society that rejects any form of deviation from its norms). The reason for this incapacity of reconciliation of the one with the multiple lies, as we have seen, in what Roth considers to be the moral breakup of the individual's relationship with society and in the larger more comprehensive social atomization and separation of rationality from the sphere of traditional life. To the modern world, devoured by problems of domination, stratification, and profit, the Provence offers the alternative of a simple, commonsensical, and traditional life, inclusive and diverse, ancient and yet lively: "I would take pleasure in seeing what European Catholicism had brought about, the wonderful mixing of races. . . . Each can understand each, and their society is open; no one is forced to take up any particular position. This is assimilation at its best: A person may remain as different as he is and feel at home" (108–9). This double condition of identity, which requires both distance and belonging, specificity and commonality, constitutes the recipe of moral restoration of the individual's relationship with the surrounding world that Roth will apply in the novels of religious and historical inspiration. In Provence, being "rooted," Roth argues, is the same as being a stranger. This paradoxical matrix of individuality is also highly significant because it constitutes an alternative to the assimilation crisis that the Jewish author experienced personally.[3]

Roth's idea of diversity is nevertheless not synonymous with that of open-ended experimentation, of personal originality or social transformation, as some critics have correctly observed: "Die oft beschriebene Idealisierung der Multikulturalität bei Roth meint vor allem ein klares Nebeneinander im Vielvölkerstaat mit klaren Autoritäten und kein echtes Durcheinander und Dazwischen" 'The often-described idealization of multiculturalism in Roth's work means, above all, a clear side-by-side existence in the multiethnic state with clear authorities, and no genuine intermixing and between-ness' (Lughofer 86). Roth considers the tolerant culture of the French South to be the result of a strict submission to an ancient tradition and not of a contradiction of its inherited values: "Everything is passed on from generation to generation—the house, the silver, the morals" (*Report* 139). For this reason, diversity concerns strictly the ethnic and social divisions and does not extend to personal preference, lifestyle, or even gender relations. After all, it is the patriarchal nature of this world, with its millennia-old customs, clearly defined gender roles, and widespread devoutness, that ensured the survival of its truly general-human values. A thoroughgoing revision of this tradition would represent nothing else but a sliding into the lawlessness and instability of the modernizing world ("the relative nature of . . . things themselves"), with its irrepressible pursuit of self-assertion and domination (*Report* 74). In Provence, the lively and assertive existence within an inherited tradition, optimistically affirming the eternal truths of humankind, such as the permanence of love, suffering, and desire, finds its metaphysical counterpart in a pious and stoical Catholicism that establishes a harmonious relationship between the individual, the community, and God. For this reason, the arrival of the socially estranged and civilization-skeptical Roth in southern France functions as a return home, to a feeling of belonging and familiarity that his previous experiences in an individualist, mercantile, and brutal modern European world denied him. Above all, however, this experience exposes Roth to the essence of a redeemed utopian humanity he had been seeking from the beginning of his writing career: "That for me is the highest stage of human evolution [*Humanität*]. And human evolution [*Humanität*] is what Provençal culture is all about" (109).[4]

Roth's travels to southern France open new vistas for the literary development of the Austrian author, especially by confirming to him that far from representing a hindrance in the liberation of the individual from the authoritarian social and moral impositions of the modern world, tradition and religion may constitute the only escape routes into a harmonious relationship with the universe. They appear capable of taking the focus off the individual and the immediate world and opening up a space of coexistence at a communitarian level, where the permanence of collective memory and the transcendent horizon of the sacred are still possible. The solution to the private individual's conflict with the modern world could acquire thus a positive, substantial character, beyond the nihilism of self-destruction or self-effacement that framed much of Roth's early fictional universe. These travel essays can therefore be read as "the documentation of the narrator's attempt to cast off this debilitating skepticism, to re-engage with the world as a historical continuum, an ideal 'Gemeinschaft' in which, as Benjamin would have it, the present may be 'read' in the past: 'eine mit Jetztzeit geladene Vergangenheit'" (Hughes, *Facing Modernity* 44). By taking a leap into the redeemed horizon of tradition and religion, by extricating the fictional world from the entrapments of the present, Roth envisages the possibility of a positive solution to the conflicts besieging modern consciousness.

By 1926, Roth had established a logical connection between the paradoxical spirit of the Provençal world, predicated equally on identity and difference, and the search for a spiritual home for his typical fictional stranger, with whom he identifies as an East European Jew faced with a deceiving promise of assimilation in an increasingly exclusionary and racist Europe. Instead of opposing the unruly specificity of the individual moral conscience to the sense of collective identity and tradition, the Provençal spirit united them, providing a restored identity of the individual and the world. This redeemed form of identity, however ambivalent, represents for Roth the only possibility of solving both the problem of individual estrangement and that of collective conformism. The spirit of the Provence provides a unified, redeemed view of the world and overcomes the aporias of modern rationality by joining novelty and convention, freedom and tradition, the present and the past. This redemptive horizon, described only "in the negative" in the early novels through the characters' impossibility of achieving it, acquires for the first time a clear, positive formulation in the cultural template of Provençal France, the world of harmoniously coexistent contrasts.

As a consequence, Roth promotes a new model of identity, one shaped in the image of his philosophy of redemption. By defining himself through a series of paradoxical terms, he hints at a symbolic overcoming of the formal distinctions characterizing traditional identity (insider/outsider) and through this at a larger obliteration of the oppositions characteristic of the rational, actual world (reason/religion, revolution/reaction, nationality/cosmopolitanism): "I am a Frenchman from the East, a Humanist, a rationalist with religion, a Catholic with a Jewish intelligence, an actual revolutionary," writes Roth in a letter written only one year later, in 1926, to Benno Reifenberg (*Joseph Roth: A Life* 88). Through this self-identification Roth creates an artificial identity for himself, an identity that does not correspond to an actual (geographical, rational, national) identification but instead to an ideal one, based on a set of elective affinities that transcend the limitations of conventional understanding. To him, this type of spiritual, redeemed identity is more authentic and accurate than a formal one, imposed by objective classification. After all, how would one characterize the Provençal identity, an identity resulting too from an overlay of diverse, even divergent, ethnic and cultural traditions? This predilection for viewing the world from the perspective of redemption rather than observation is relevant in explaining Roth's preference for counterfactual histories or transfigured, allegorical realities.

Belonging does not just "happen" to the individual, Roth suggests, but instead results from an act of coparticipation in a common set of values, including in his case religion, tradition, freedom, rationality, and humanism. In the spirit of his interpretation of Provençal culture, Roth sees a codependency among these values, which are contradictory only on the surface: true revolutionary freedom is the one obtained in a community of faith, rationality is the wisdom bequeathed through tradition, and Judaism can only authentically exist within the frame of a general humanism. The key for this *coincidentia oppositorum* lies in the evolution of Roth's early anarchic beliefs. His early moral anarchism, which advocated a breakdown of the external moral scaffold of society and its reconstitution on individualist moral foundations, finds its completion in the conservatism of his late conception of redemption. In Roth's view, no beginning is possible in a moral void, and no moral law is valid as long as it does not approximate the individual's inborn anarchic desire for freedom. In this sense, tradition is the most radical challenge to moral convention insofar as it is critically assumed and used for the purpose of liberating the individual from external social conditioning. For this reason, in his 1937 portrait of Franz Grillparzer, Roth considers that true rebellion is that which is led in the name of the genuine traditional values and their rightful hierarchy: "He [Grillparzer] never revolted, because he was in permanent rebellion. He rebelled out of conservatism, as a supporter of hierarchical order and a defender of traditional values" (*Hotel Years* 240). In Roth's conception of the self and the world, identity requires diversity, and this diversity merges into a whole of organically connected elements. Thus, by placing himself beyond the historical and logical discontinuities of modern rationality, Roth generates the model for a redeemed identity of the individual. Only here, in the implicit space of redemptive imagination, do all contradictions disappear, and the private condition of the human being unites with the general-human, collective dimension of social existence.

Roth endows the Provençal world with all the attributes of redemption that other Jewish thinkers of the time articulated in their philosophy. The ability of the community to be simultaneously collective and individual, the same and different, satisfying both the need for organic belonging and for private freedom, is similar to Buber's notion of utopian community, which is a "living togetherness, constantly renewing itself," where "the unity that was felt in public permeated all personal contacts" (*Paths in Utopia* 135). Similarly, Provence's distinctive mixture of conservatism and novelty recalls very closely Buber's idea that Utopia relies on "revolutionary conservation: a revolutionary selection of those elements worthy to be conserved and fit for the renovation of the social being" (*Paths in Utopia* 59) or of Mannheim's notion of "relative utopia," a reality capable of harmonizing the inheritance of the past with the revolutionary vision of the future. This intertwining of the old and the new bears also upon the notion of time, which is simultaneously present and past. Roth observes that in Provence "the present was already past," in contrast to the linear and irreversible conception of time characterizing modern societies (*Report* 87). This time is the time of redemption, similar to Rosenzweig's "infinite Now" (*Star* 289) and Benjamin's "*Jetztzeit*" (*Illuminations* 252). Through it, the Messiah arrives every day but not in an apocalyptical manner. Instead, this arrival is "*the primordial secret in itself moving within the Now*," as Bloch argues (192). It happens all the time through the eternal convergence between the created world and the promised world, or as Rosenzweig put it, its coming is "always" (224). Roth confesses that the Provence has revealed to him the truth of this essential unity of the world: "I have learned here that nothing can continue to exist unless it represents continuity in some way. . . . In the future is the past" (*Report* 118). The reality of redemption as an everyday moment that is simultaneously past and future, eternal and changing, brings to mind the Chasidic notion of salvation, as a "neutralized" form of messianism, as Scholem observed (*Messianic Idea* 176). Therefore, it is not surprising why, next to Provence, Roth would find similar expressions of redemption during his trips to Galicia. He even indirectly hints at this symbolic Provençal-Galician synthesis when he declares himself "a Frenchman from the East, . . . a Catholic with a Jewish intelligence" (*Joseph Roth: A Life* 88).

The same redemptive imagination that begins to alter Roth's approach to his existential themes after his visit to southern France is also responsible for the gradual transformation of his literary style. Roth begins to question some of the aesthetical precepts of New Objectivity as early as 1927, such as the claim that literature should be able to reflect external events in a report-like style without involvement and with no moralizing intentions. In "Nur echte Erlebnisse" ("Only Real Experiences"), an article from 1927, Roth argues that the writer has an obligation to turn to experience in order to give it a universal, representative meaning through literary work and stop seeing empirical events as belonging to an order different from that of the "poetical," abstract creation (*Werke* 2). He contends not only that the goal of pure documentary writing is unrealistic but also that it impoverishes the existential function of storytelling, which is to re-create reality and impart a sense of human authenticity to the reader, an effect that can only be realized through a recourse to value judgments and moral processes. Roth therefore begins to argue that the writer has an almost moral responsibility for both the narrated story and the reader, that he has a role and a goal, that offering access to his judgment and moral discernment is the destination and the truth of any auctorial enterprise. The writer creates a world through his novels and is responsible for it not only as an observer but also as an "understander," as the magician who not only reflects a world but also transfigures it and gives it moral meaning. The moral reality of the fictional world is for Roth—as he writes in the 1930 article "Schluß mit der 'Neuen Sachlichkeit'!"—the necessary complement of the "reflected" reality: "Der Erzähler ist ein Beobachter und ein Sachverständiger. Sein Werk ist niemals von der Realität gelöst, sondern in Wahrheit (durch das Mittel der Sprache) umgewandelte Realität. ('Real' ist unter gewissen Bedingungen . . . auch die sogenannte 'phantastische' Welt)" 'The narrator is an observer and an expert. His work is never detached from reality, but in truth, transformed reality through the medium of language. ("Real" is under certain conditions . . . also the so-called "fantastic" world)' (*Werke* 3: 157). This new literary awareness is inseparable in Roth's case from his growing interest in transferring the weight of his philosophy of history and culture into the realm of redemption by looking at the world more and more through the eyes of salvation itself, thus transcending the endless entrapments in the ill-fated world of actual history and modern existence.[5] Because of this transformation, the themes and atmosphere of Roth's novels undergo a significant change, while the search for redemption, a search that traverses his entire work, abandons the themes of revolt and retreat in favor of the religious and existential themes of sin, expiation, and absolution.

The present chapter will investigate the role of religious experience in mediating between a corrupt phenomenal reality and the promise of redemption from it. The nature of Roth's theodicy, his relation to Chasidism, and the role of the Christian idea of salvation will be analyzed in several of his later novels and short stories. The thematics favored in these works, including religious stoicism and pious existence as well as transgression and atonement, postulates the existence of a positive notion of salvation in contrast to Roth's early work, where salvation is formulated apophatically. The characters of his later work are offered an actual solution to the moral, social, and personal ruin of the world they inhabit through a tangible liberation from suffering.[6] Unlike the early characters, whose destinies are determined by blind, mechanical social and political forces and whose only escape is either anarchic revolt or the ambiguous disappearance, these later characters are morally free individuals whose possibility for redemption rests on the fact that they live "mit einem eignen, der Transzendenz verbundenen Schicksal" 'with their own, transcendentally conjoined destiny' (Trommler 295). Writing from the perspective of a clear, positive notion of deliverance, Roth no longer needs the societal and psychological scaffolding of the early novels in order to establish the authenticity of his stories. Instead, he constructs his stories in a symbolic way, according to an implacable teleology of redemption, in which the characters stage exemplary, quasi-mythical situations. For this reason, the passage from the early forms of realism (such as New Objectivity) to the fabulous realism of the late period describes the transition from the earthly perspective of unachievable salvation to the mythical perspective of acquired salvation.

An important motif in the novels of religious inspiration is represented by the reality of suffering and its theological justification. In novels such as *Job: The Story of a Simple Man* (1930) and *Weights and Measures* (1937) suffering occupies a central role, as it does in the early novels, but unlike them it is not treated as the result of external factors, such as social decay, the lack of human communication, or the purposelessness of history. Suffering is presented in these late novels as the ontological condition of the individual, as the identity-giving horizon of human existence (Blanke 59). By stoically accepting this condition, suffering itself is paradoxically transfigured into its opposite, redemption. Mendel Singer and Anselm Eibenschütz, the protagonists of the two novels, inquire into the metaphysical rationale of their suffering and, in spite of their private speculations and interpretations, cannot harmonize the divine notion of justice with the actuality of the pain they experience. The same inability to articulate a reasonable theodicy affected Andreas Pum (of *The Rebellion*), but in his case the result is an inverted salvation (salvation qua damnation), whereas Singer and Eibenschütz receive in the end a positive measure of divine comprehension and resolution, however symbolical this might be.

Job and the Road to Earthly Saintliness

Job, the first novel written after Roth's break with New Objectivity, abandons the social-political thematic of the early novels and revisits the biblical motif of Job in the context of the mass migration of East European Jews to America.[7]

Mendel Singer, a pious Jewish Torah teacher, lives a simple life in a small Russian shtetl, Zuchnow, together with his wife and four children. The daily existence of the Singer family runs according to an undisturbed routine involving eating, praying, and fasting, a routine that displaces the time of the novel into an almost mythical and eternal present. The remoteness of their location, the poverty of their household, and the equanimity of their spiritual life appear in the beginning of the novel as a testimony to the resilient nature of a community with a strong sense of belonging, rooted in an archaic tradition and in a lifestyle that does not seem to be affected by the major social and moral turmoil sweeping the urban life of modern Europe: "At the end of each week the Sabbath dawned thus, with silence, candles, and song. Twenty-four hours later the Sabbath sank into night; the grey procession of weekdays began, a weary circle" (*Job* 7).

Mendel Singer's religiosity confirms his harmonious relationship not only with an unquestionable divine force ("Every morning Mendel thanked God for his sleeping, for his awakening, and for the dawning day") but also with a simple and poor world: "He had nothing to regret, and he coveted nothing" (*Job* 4). Singer is content in his poverty and, living in the refuge of the ancestral traditions of the shtetl and the metaphysical and moral assuredness of the Torah, feels in complete agreement with the social, personal, and religious facets of his life. His stoicism, consolidated by an Oriental Judaism that in Roth's view is more than a religion, namely a modus vivendi,[8] instructs him to faithfully accept his fate and unswervingly refrain from serving the earthly powers committed to changing it while at the same time maintaining an unwavering hope in the reality of divine redemption. Unavoidably mixed with superstition and obscurantism, Singer's religious stoicism prevents his newborn child, the epileptic Menuchim, from receiving the necessary treatment: "No doctor can cure him, if God does not will it. Should he grow up among Russian children? Never hear a holy word? Eat milk with meat and chickens roasted in butter, the way people get them in the hospital?" (10). The conflict between tradition and modernity exemplified by this moment in Singer's life will develop, however, into the theological conundrums that *Job* poses: how can God's plan of salvation be respected if one undertakes actions directed against it? Additionally, how can one obey the divinely sanctioned paternal obligation toward the well-being of one's children if the actions resulting from it contradict God's will?

Deborah, Mendel Singer's wife, shows flexibility on these questions and sees no irresolvable conflict between divine salvation and the human plans to act on it or even influence it: "in ihrer Glaubenshaltung entspricht sie dem Chassidismus" 'in her belief system, she comes close to Chasidism' (Schmidjell 18). Consequently, she takes responsibility in her own hands and resorts to the means available to a simple Jewish woman from a Russian shtetl: prayers to the dead and securing the blessing of a rabbi who works miracles. The figure of the miracle-working rabbi (*der Wunderrabbi*), already developed by Roth in the 1927 collection of essays *The Wandering Jews*, is representative for a Chasidic culture that represents, in the author's view, the Eastern Jews' response to the problem of salvation in Judaism. Overwhelmed by the burden of their miserable lives and not entirely detached from a mystical, supernatural interpretation of nature, the explanation of signs and the summoning of wonders become a practical way of entreating a permanently postponed promise of deliverance: "For the hasids, however, the wonder-rabbi is the intercessor between man and God," writes Roth in *The Wandering Jews* (28). A messenger of God's divine plan, the voice of the rabbi must therefore carry an almost oracular weight: Deborah learns that Menuchim will be saved and will grow to be the pride of Israel; "his eyes will see far and deep," and his mouth "will announce good tidings" (*Job* 16).

Consistent in his stoicism, Mendel Singer remains nevertheless skeptical about the rabbi's prophecy. Singer's skepticism about the prospects of any earthly solution to life's problems has been interpreted by some critics as evidence of a kind of ancient wisdom that is responsible for his "stoische Ataraxie" 'stoic *ataraxia*' (Hüppauf 40). In his orthodox relationship to God and to the Judaic law (the Torah), Singer refuses to accept that a human mind could penetrate the secret of the divine plan: "His modest piety required no mediator between God and men" (*Job* 18). As Hansotto Ausserhofer points out, Roth subtly introduces here one of the most problematic aspects of Eastern Judaism, namely the conflict between the orthodox interpretation of the laws, represented by Singer, and the more popular-pietistic one supported by Chasidism, represented by Deborah (262).[9] Although in *The Wandering Jews* Roth describes this conflict with sociological and even psychological means, he is in fact more interested in stressing the cultural unity of Jewish religious life in the East. United by a rich tradition of piety and by religious humanism, the East European Jews rise above the theological differences among them through the fervor with which they expect the final redemption of phenomenal existence. Even though Roth, following a trend of the times, often expresses admiration for Chasidism for its spirituality and existential intensity (as certain essays from *The Wandering Jews* or later stories such as "The Legend of the Holy Drinker" demonstrate), in *Job* as in *The Wandering Jews*, he does not elevate Chasidism above Jewish orthodoxy, showing more interest in the religious phenomenon in general. The conflict between Singer's orthodoxy and the Chasidic interpretation of the law will prove, in the end of the novel, to be irrelevant in comparison to the real conflict that defines our age: that between innovation and custom, or between modernity and tradition.[10]

However, Singer's confrontation with the modern world and its characteristic problems does not limit itself to the dilemma of Menuchim's medical treatment. Singer's adamant persistence in the Judaic tradition and the otherworldly order of salvation is further challenged by his other three children's response to the pressures and temptations of the world outside the shtetl: while the daughter Miriam cannot resist her erotic curiosity about the young Cossacks from a nearby barrack, the son Jonas expresses his desire to assimilate into Russian society by willfully signing up for military service. The compulsory draft in the czarist empire represented, for a variety of reasons, one of the most terrible impositions on the Jewish population, more oppressive than the taxes, the bureaucracy, or the discriminatory and restrictive legislation. On the one hand, it deprived poor families who relied on their older sons for financial support of their basic livelihood, and on the other hand, it violated the traditional Jewish interdictions concerning military participation in the service of an earthly power. Roth already emphasizes this issue in *The Wandering Jews*: "Not only was it stupid to die on behalf of some kaiser or czar or other, it was also a sin to live far from the Torah and in opposition to its teachings. It was a sin to eat pig meat. To bear arms on the Sabbath. To drill. To raise a hand, never mind a sword, against a stranger who has done them no harm" (*Wandering Jews* 94).

By unreservedly joining the czarist army, Jonas rejects and offends the Jewish tradition as well as his own family. Singer's third son, Shemariah, resolves, however, to escape the draft by illegally leaving the country and immigrating to America, an alternative that in many cases constituted the initial cause of the subsequent mass migration of Jewish families to the new world.[11] Shemariah's choice exemplifies the other side of the assimilation process into which Mendel Singer's family is gradually drawn, namely the Western style of assimilation, which offers access to a contractual, prosperous, and sophisticated society that represents the counterpart to the arbitrary and brute force of a discriminatory and harsh society such as the Russian one. Hansotto Ausserhofer sees in the assimilation of Singer's children three ideal types (developed in a separate sociological study by Artur Ruppin): liberal, represented by Miriam, who willfully adopts the influence of modern civilization; freethinking, represented by Jonas, who rejects the religious tradition of his community; and agnostic, represented by Shemariah, who assimilates into the modern society as an "enlightened" Jew (285).

Aware of the hopeless destitution and sorrow of her family's life in Russia and encouraged by the children's desire to leave the closed world of the shtetl and experience emancipation in the secular world, Deborah seizes the opportunity created by Shemariah's escape and pushes for the migration of the entire family to America. Once again, Mendel resists her suggestion by holding on tight to his stoic belief in divine purpose. He feels that amid a changing world, a secret bond of permanence is tying him to his little son, Menuchim, who had been so ruthlessly punished by a crippling disease: they are the only ones who do not want more, who do not expect a positive change of their ordinary existence and are satisfied with the dictates of a fate that remains, in spite of all the prayers and fasting, impenetrable: "The sons disappeared. Jonas served the Tsar in Pskov, and was no longer Jonas. Shemariah bathed on an ocean strand and no longer was called Shemariah. Miriam gazed after the American, and wanted to go to America, too. Only Menuchim remained what he had always been since the day of his birth—a cripple. And Mendel Singer remained what he had always been—a teacher" (*Job* 74). And yet in spite of his hesitations, Singer gives in to his wife's pressures and to her hope of improvement and salvation in a different world.[12] From the moment of their decision to emigrate up to the actual departure, the Singers have to go through the bureaucratic nightmare of obtaining the necessary papers from the Russian officials and almost fall through the cracks of an incompetent, arbitrary, and corrupt administration. Finally they manage to bribe their way out of the country, a procedure described with an exactness and humor rivaling some of the finest pages of Anton Chekhov's satires. Roth's portrayal of the Singers' departure from the shtetl represents, next to Sholem Aleichem's similar story of the cantor's son, Mottel, one of the most touching and amusing stories about the Russian Jews' migration to America.

The emigration of Mendel Singer's family happens, however, at a price: little Menuchim, physically retarded and incapable of speaking, must be left behind, as he might not be able to withstand the challenges of a hazardous trip. Firm in his belief that only God can help his youngest son, Singer decides to leave Menuchim in the care of another family in spite of the feelings of compassion and remorse that are tearing him up on the inside. Through his decision Singer disavows the rabbi's prophecy, which foresaw a miracle and encouraged the parents to watch closely over their child. Instead, Singer takes refuge in the mystery of God's purpose and delegates the misfortune of the child to an impenetrable logic of divine chastisement, which precludes any secondary doubts about parental responsibility and love: "When we sin, though, He can punish us" (*Job* 104). As Deborah attempts to inquire into the rationale of this punishment, Singer rejects her question and desperately tries to find solace in his orthodox faith, even though his conscience does not allow him any tranquility: "'Why does He punish us now? Have we sinned? Why is He so cruel?' 'You blaspheme Him, Deborah. Leave me in peace—I cannot talk with you any longer.' And Mendel Singer buried himself in a pious book" (104). Mendel Singer's new life in America starts under the sign of the betrayal of his son and of a destiny over which he has no control. The fact that the divine Beyond remains incomprehensible to him makes it practically impossible for him to make a rational decision when he is confronted with a dramatic choice, such as that between his obligation toward his family's happiness and his paternal obligation toward every one of his children, especially the helpless ones. The drama of modern Job starts to unfold under this condition of incomprehensibility of divine judgment and with the unavoidable transgression of God's law.

The narrative of decline begins at the onset of Mendel Singer's settlement in New York City. Living in the middle of a strange world, urban and cold, a veritable technological Moloch, Singer feels insignificant and isolated, a simple Jew trying to recompose his traditional lifestyle and the imperturbable cycles of prayer and fasting. The values of the new world, which place success, money, and progress at the top of the social hierarchy, cannot affect him, a man formed in the spirit of the simple virtues of the shtetl, such as piety, compassion, and respect: "mixed with his admiration for the future was a nostalgia for Russia. . . . He did not know why he felt so. But it eased him. He was already too old for these new things, and too weak for triumph" (151). While Miriam and Shemariah (assimilated as "Sam" in the United States) enjoy the pleasures of the secular world at their fullest, completely forgetting the world from where they came, Deborah and Mendel start to gradually suffer from the absence of little Menuchim, whose trail they slowly lose.[13]

Against this background of private discontent with the lifestyle and the values of the new world on the one hand and the relative material success and social improvement on the other, fate follows its cruel course and strikes the Singer family. Shemariah is drafted into the army and shortly thereafter falls fighting for the American side in World War I; Deborah suffers a stroke and dies after hearing the news about her son's demise. A few days later, Miriam loses her sanity and has to be confined to a mental asylum. Left all alone, Mendel contemplates his situation and fatalistically concludes that he lost everyone, including Jonas and little Menuchim, abandoned to their fate in a hostile Russian world. Beginning to understand the source of his tribulations, Mendel remorsefully looks back at his decision to immigrate to America, at the offense he brought to the laws of divine design and omnipotence: "If only we had stayed there—thought Mendel—nothing would have happened. . . . Mendel had never wanted to go. Deborah, Miriam, Shemariah—they had wanted to go, to travel about in the world" (174).

However, Singer cannot find his refuge in the Torah anymore. He knows that he has committed a sin, and yet he cannot quite understand the nature of his sin; God's law remains impenetrable and distant, offering him no sign of intelligibility. Singer's judgment, however flawed and partial, cannot reconcile the piety and misery of his entire life with a cruel punishment that refutes any norm of justice or conception of divine love: "God said: I have punished Mendel Singer! For what has He punished him? Why has He not punished Lemmel, the butcher? Why not Skovronnek? Why not Menkes? He punishes only Mendel" (179). The persistent question that he refused Deborah, namely the question of the rationale of divine punishment, returns to Singer, confirming the inescapable conflict between Judaism's religious hermeneutic compulsion and the impenetrability of its divinity's mind. That the book of Job is the ultimate expression of this contradiction (May 253) is made clear through the parallel between Singer's fate and Job's. When his other Jewish friends try to console him by suggesting a comparison to the biblical Job, whose faith was tried by God through the most terrible misfortunes, Singer virulently rejects the analogy. Unlike the other Jews, who believe in a God whose judgments are simultaneously punitive and gratifying due to the unity and mystery of divine mind, Mendel Singer sees God as an arbitrary force, brutal and merciless, temperamental and capricious, a veritable Russian official whose benevolence can never be ensured:[14]

> Only the weak He gladly destroys. The weakness of a man tempts His strength, and obedience awakens His scorn. He is a great, brutal *ispravnik*, a real Russian official. Follow the laws, and He says you have but done it for your own advantage. Break but one of His commandments, and He persecutes you with a hundred chastisements. Seek to bribe Him, and He brings a judgment against you. Deal uprightly with Him, and He is impatient for bribes. (*Job* 181)

Singer's desperate words evoke Andreas Pum's own quarrel with an absent God, and as in the case of the protagonist of *The Rebellion*, Singer's actions try to provoke or retaliate against divine authority: "I want to burn God" (*Job* 180). He stops praying and even violates his dietary prohibitions by eating pork, all in an attempt to "irritate God" (187). He even goes as far as attempting to burn his inherited old praying kit consisting of the phylacteries, the prayer shawl, and the prayer books but stops short of doing so; his final hesitation, together with the remorse he feels for his transgressions, emphasizes the tragic condition of the individual who can only find justice in hurting himself and the things he loves and lives for: "Yet he suffered because he did not pray. His rage hurt him, and the impotence of his rage" (189). After all, God could not be touched by either faith or by anger. His remoteness remains absolute, and the individual is condemned to isolation from divine grace on his side of the world, at least until the arrival of the Messiah: "Hate could move Him no more than piety" (189).

Nevertheless, Singer's fate takes another unexpected turn: in the middle of his remorseful resignation to a cruel fortune, salvation appears unexpectedly as his long-lost son Menuchim emerges under the identity of the Russian composer Alexis Kossak. Menuchim unveils to his father the secret of his auspicious fate after the departure of the rest of the family to America, tells him about his miraculous healing and professional success, and instills hope in him about the chance of reunification with the other two children, Miriam and Jonas. Menuchim also reveals his intention of gathering the family and returning to their old house in the now-Polish Zuchnow, thus restoring the equilibrium to the Singer family: "Die Sphäre der Lebenskraft ist die des Familienkreises, durch den sie genährt, gesteigert und gleichzeitig auch begrenzt wird" 'The sphere of vitality is that of the family circle, through which it is nourished, increased and, at the same time, also limited' (Magris, *Weit von wo* 130–31). Elated, Mendel Singer follows his son with a rediscovered equanimity that would comfort his last years of life, metaphorically transcribed by Roth into the peace he feels before falling asleep in the last lines of the novel.

Menuchim's return bears all the signs of redemption, and the portrait of the character approximates that of a Messiah. His eyes were "old, and at the same time young"; a "few thousand years" shone in them. "[T]hey knew everything; the whole world reflected itself in them"; they "were full of light," and "God Himself had spoken" to them (*Job* 212). The revelation of Kossak's real identity is accompanied by the imagery of an unfolding miracle: the children start to cry, the candles begin to flicker, and people are left breathless. "A miracle has happened!" cries a witness, and as if beholding the resurrection of a Christ, Singer rushes to touch his son in order to make sure it's not just an illusion: "Mendel sinks down before Menuchim; he searches with impatient mouth and waving beard for the hands of the son; his lips kiss whatever they touch, the knees, the legs, the waistcoat of Menuchim" (227). Charged with Judeo-Christian significance is the fact that the son appears during the Passover celebration, as a promise of redemption from the anguish of both life in a distant land and this-worldly suffering.[15] The return of the lost son bears further religious echoes to the story of Joseph in the book of Genesis, as Menuchim returns to the ones who have abandoned him and showed no mercy for him, only to save them from their wretched lot. In a telling image, he bathes his father and dresses him, thus humbly showing him a profound filial love and respect.

Facing the materiality of redemption, Singer admits to the error of mistrusting the Chasidic rabbi's prophecy and also to that of revolting against God: "I have committed grave sins; God has closed His eyes. I called Him an *ispravnik*. He held His ears. He is so great that our badnesses seem to him very small" (229). Not only does Singer admit to his religious offenses, but he also admits to his broader violation of the law of stoicism, in which the traditional notion of love and affirmation of life is contained: he confesses that he was wrong to oppose his children's desire to assimilate outside the shtetl—"Jonas was right! . . . You were right to become a Cossack!" (174)—and that he had mistakenly looked at the world outside his narrow faith and household as inimical and dangerous: "he would no longer be afraid of dogs. . . . Careless of beetles and snakes, of toads and grasshoppers, he would be prepared to lie upon the naked earth" (206).[16] He acknowledges that the desire to escape the universe of the shtetl and look for rescue in the promise of prosperity and well-being equally represented a sin: "Peace had been at home there, youth had been at home there, and familiar poverty" (174). Singer's realization of what salvation means does not limit itself to a reassertion of his faith in God or to a return to the strict observance of the Torah; his conception of redemption is tantamount to a life-affirming attitude, stoical and tolerant, which encourages the individual to use the present as a vehicle to the permanence of salvation instead of searching for a solution outside of what life offers.[17] Only this new synthesis between the immanent and the transcendent is capable of offering Singer a reconciliation with the world. It spans the divide between his expectation of deliverance from suffering and the actual fulfillment of this expectation ("*Erwartung und Erfüllung*"), a divide within which the whole story unfolds (Vom Hofe 80).

Singer's redemption is not otherworldly; it does not require the abandonment of this world. To the contrary, it is acquired through an instance of what Max Brod, in his analysis of the nature of miracles in Judaism, calls "this-worldly miracle" (*Diesseitswunder*): the miracle reaffirms the world but in a redeemed manner (*Paganism* 100–101). Following the Talmudic legend of Simeon bar Yochai, Brod concludes that the act of redemption achieves its full meaning only when the world of creation is reaffirmed, not denied, through the reality of the revealed divine mercy. Menuchim's arrival has the role of redeeming this world, not of destroying it. He causes his father to rethink his attitude toward everything that caused him so much anguish in the past. Singer returns to his old world and to his old religious practices but not in the same way. He returns as a redeemed individual who will no longer use the Torah as a barrier between himself and the world around him but instead will use it as a window opened by God to the world. Singer will now be open to tradition and to change as well, in a union of a higher spiritual order. As Ludger Schwienhorst-Schönberger points out, the new world to which Mendel Singer returns is the redeemed world of creation that God also shows the biblical Job at the end of his trials (233). It is the world of reconciliation in which the miracle of creation is present once again. In this new world the old contradictions are lifted, including that between the strict rabbinic law and the reformed Chasidic interpretation or that between the necessity of maintaining a traditional Jewish identity and stoically facing the challenge of history.[18]

Roth's idea of redemption appears thus to be inseparable from that of tradition, albeit in a manner that opens up tradition to change, "in einer Struktur, die gleichwohl Veränderungen und Anpassungen zulässt" 'in a structure that nevertheless allows for changes and adjustments' (Hartmann 122). For him, religiosity materializes in the practice of virtue and not so much in the belief structure, because ultimately Roth is interested not in any theological construct but instead in the active affirmation of holiness through life. This explains why the formal conflict between a more orthodox interpretation of Judaism and a marginal one, such as Chasidism, is not directly relevant to him, but the conflict between traditional Judaism and assimilated Judaism is: tradition represents a modality of actively living the communal values, whereas assimilation feeds on the fundamental separation between modern, secular individuals and their inherited faith.[19] In this sense, Mendel Singer's sins are objective, not theologically dogmatic; they represent the breakdown of tradition, of the routine, of the cosmic cycles. For him, the daily affirmation of life and piety is alone the place where God is present: "One ought to stay at home, be fond of horses, drink spirits, sleep in the fields, let Miriam run with the Cossacks, and love Menuchim" (*Job* 174). In Singer's revelation, the dilemmas posed by the contradictions between God's will and the legal religious interdictions or between the need to make actual life-changing decisions and the commandment to give priority to spiritual salvation are solved at a different level, allowing him to reach the "Humanismus eines praktizierbaren Glaubens" 'humanism of a practicable faith' (Oei 98).

Although some critics have suggested a theological interpretation of the novel, arguing that the much-expected miracle of redemption eventually happens as if to confirm the triumph of the Chasidic worldview over the "Othodoxie des Gerechten" 'orthodoxy of the righteous' (Hartung 429), Roth actually seems less interested in doctrinal questions than in spiritual ones in general. In the end, the protagonist of the novel is not offered an indication of which attitude is the right one in addressing God's will—listening to the letter of the scriptural law or listening to the advice of a *Wunderrabbi*, stoically accepting his earthly suffering or actively trying to remove it—but is illuminated in regard to his moral responsibility toward these fundamental dilemmas from which he tried to escape. In his attempt to divine and judge God's purpose, Singer committed the same mistake that biblical Job committed in believing "that His knowledge is like our knowledge or that His purpose is like our purpose," as Maimonides argues (qtd. in Glatzer 21). Singer's sin results not from his mistaken interpretation of the divine will but instead from his refusal to accept the incomprehensibility of this will and the existential implications of this incomprehensibility. His final revelation allows him to see that his religious responsibility toward God starts with and cannot be distinguished from his moral responsibility for the basic aspects of life and that sin is not a violation of some abstract theological laws but instead is a violation of the accountability for the problems of real, simple existence. As Claudio Magris points out, "Religion als fideistische Instanz interessiert Roth kaum . . . sie gilt ihm als Lebenssitte, als Kraft des Menschen" 'Roth is not interested in religion in a fideistic sense . . . but as a way of life, as individual fortitude' (*Weit von wo* 127). Religion is affirmed in a moral and existential, not theological, manner. This moral foundation of religion contradicts Alexander Stillmark's belief that Roth's notions of good and evil are derived directly from religious tradition: "Roth hält, ähnlich wie Dostojewskij, an den durch die Religion überlieferten Vorstellungen von Gut und Böse fest" 'Roth, like Dostoevsky, adheres to the religiously inherited ideas of good and evil' ("Die Literarische Beichte" 75). For Roth, the concepts of good and evil take on a religious function but only insofar as religion is to be understood as moral practice, an objective exercise, and not as revelation, a theological construct.

Other critics see in Roth's antitheological approach to the Job metaphor a specifically neo-Chasidic attitude (which Claudio Magris insightfully associates with Martin Buber's original synthesis between Chasidism and existentialism) that aims at the liberation from ethical conflict through the fusion of the mundane and divine spheres of existence.[20] Roth's approach to the problem of suffering and its theological justification is indeed influenced by popular Jewish pietism such as Chasidism, but his theological stance cannot be stamped as Chasidic per se. Instead it is mixed, as in Buber's case, with a variety of secular philosophies, among which existentialism and Romanticism are primary, as well as with elements of Christian pietism, such as self-sacrifice and healing love. The fact that tradition plays such a central role for Roth stems from a philosophy of history and culture that asserts the primacy of the spiritual unity of the moral and phenomenal world rather than from a theological conviction. Singer's Judaism, as in the case of Provençal Catholicism, plays an important role not as a body of theological laws but instead as an expression and guarantee of tradition, as a vehicle for the redemptive conciliation of the individual with his world.[21] The significance of suffering appears thus in the light of Roth's philosophy not as a purely theological problem, as it did for the biblical Job, but instead as a moral one: the pain resulting from the simple existence of the individual in this world is not true suffering but rather the fear of suffering, the desire to finish it and escape from it.[22] Singer's story suggests that the individual cannot really escape his moral condition, which is the horizon of his simple existence, with everything that belongs there: virtue, error, grief, and even sin. True redemption results from the stoical assumption of this condition, a condition of fallible humanity, that makes suffering unavoidable: "Hiob ist das Epos dieses Stoizismus" 'Job is the epopee of this stoicism' (Magris, *Weit von wo* 159).

In his study of Jewish *Kulturpessimismus* in Roth's works, Volker Henze compares Ernst Bloch's reflections on the story of Job (from *Atheismus im Christentum* [*Atheism in Christianity*]) with Roth's *Hiob* to conclude that while for Bloch Job is the herald of a new time to come, a revolutionary time of redemption as opposed to the eternal time of the inaccessible Yahweh, for Roth Job is a reaffirmation of eternal principles in opposition to any future prospect of redemption in history (181). According to Henze, Bloch's Job is forward-looking and messianic, while Roth's is backward-looking and orthodox-conservative. However, Henze fails to understand that Singer's redemption is not only a simple return to old convictions but is also a different return, a return with the present and the future in mind. Singer discovers the time of redemption by participating in the "this-worldly miracle," as Brod calls it, a miracle that has meaning in this world, in the present. As a result, Singer's very attitude toward history is altered in the sense in which nothing can now upset his harmony with the world because it is filtered through the life-changing experience of redemption. Singer looks forward to his old life but in a different light. For Singer, contrary to what Henze argues, redemption is not a way out of this world but instead is a way of living in the "here and the now."

This neo-Chasidic attitude brings Roth in closer vicinity to philosophers such as Bloch and Buber, who emphasize in their work the fact that redemption is ingrained in the simple condition of individual existence. Instead of withdrawing from this condition into either secular rationality or contemplative Salvationism, they argue, the individual should welcome the moral unity with the world and take charge of history because, as Rabbi Nachman teaches, God manifests himself in multiple ways, and one encounters him everywhere (Buber, *Die Chassidischen Bücher* 17). Roth's traditionalism proves once again to be only apparently backward-looking. His conception of tradition is that of lived morality, of active participation in the continuum of past, present, and future, in which continuity and change are not mutually exclusive. That Roth stands here in Chasidism's religious proximity is evidenced by Gershom Scholem's description of the Chasidic conception of redemption, which sees daily life as the threshold through which messianic salvation takes place (*Messianic Idea* 240). For this reason, Singer's return home is simultaneously a restoration of the past and a leap into the future, an affirmation of life. As Ronsenzwieg argues, existence is linked with the past through tradition and with the future through redemption; we bear responsibility for linking these two segments in the present by making it our own time, the time of our own moral decisions:

> Every day stands between a yesterday and a tomorrow, and all that lives proves it is alive by not standing still one certain day but making of that day a yesterday, and setting in its place a tomorrow. Peoples, too, stay alive by constantly transforming their today into new customs, into new eternal yesterdays, while at the same time they lay down new laws structured out of their today, for the service of their tomorrow. . . . In addition to their own soil and their own language, the increase in custom and the renewal of law give them the final and strongest guarantee of their own life: a time of their own. So long as a people computes a time of its own—and it computes this time according to its still living store of customs and memories, and the continuous renewal of its lawgiving powers, its leaders and kings—just so long has it power over time, just so long is it not dead" (Rosenzweig, *Star* 303).

Roth's emphasis on the present moment should not be seen as a glorification of the actual present, of the historical succession of mundane events. As Ilse J. Lazaroms argues, "Roth did not envision the solution to the European crisis to lie in the present, but in a reinsertion of the values of the past into an as yet unrealized future. Yet, at the same time, he advocated a full immersion into the present as means to reach this goal" ("The Double Bind" 703). This present represents the time of a redemptive synthesis of a vivid tradition and moral law with a historical world that always configures new situations. The resulting synthesis, at the same time historical and modern, appears to constitute the only possible source for the emergence of both a creative relation to the past and an auspicious emergence of the future. This manner of conceptualizing time is simultaneously monistic and pluralistic in that it lessens the indeterminacy of the future while opening up the past to new possibilities. The present carries in it the seed of the coming redemption, an idea that closely resembles Rosenzweig's "synchronic time": "only an absolutely synchronic time can allow the actualization of the most distant future in the flash of the present instant, in other words, anticipating Redemption" (Mosès 58).

Roth redefines the notions of sin, suffering, and expiation and originally reinterprets the traditional theodicy by shifting the emphasis from the divine justification of suffering to the human reaction to it. The moral responsibility for dealing with the misery of the phenomenal world is what may ultimately constitute the real source of suffering for the individual: trying to evade this responsibility by denying the encompassing reality of existential torment leads to the actual cause of suffering. Only through full consent to the inescapable horizon of human misery, to the traditional confrontation with this reality, can a life-affirming, positive redemption from suffering be realized. In the same way, the violation of the ingrained moral responsibility for human existence represents a sin, because divine law is not separated from the individual and instead is part of the daily act of life. In Chasidism, the idea of incarnate law contrasts with the more traditional theological conception of the law as an external imposition from an eternally impenetrable Beyond. In his 1927 collection *Die Chassidischen Bücher*, Buber writes that "Alles äußere Gesetz ist nur ein Aufstieg zum inneren; der letzte Zweck des Einzelnen ist, selbst ein Gesetz zu werden. In Wahrheit ist die obere Welt kein Außen, sondern ein Innen" 'All external law is but a rise to the inner law; the ultimate purpose of the individual is to become a law himself. In truth, the upper world is not an exterior, but an interior' (*Die Chassidischen Bücher* 16). Therefore, refusing the inescapable unity of the moral mind and the physical world represents for Roth an act of violation of divine law and a deadly sin. Running away from their historical lot, from the misery of daily existence, the Jews who seek deliverance in the West are pushed into a metaphysical transgression: "Why do you people always go wandering around in the world! The Devil drives you from one place to another" (*Job* 99), the Cossack Sameshkin points out to Mendel Singer. Expiation appears thus to be possible only through an act that restitutes the unity of the traditional world and reaffirms the identity between the law and life. Sin, suffering, and atonement do not strictly concern the individual's relationship with divinity but are concerned with the moral horizon in which any redemption and expiation in general is possible.

Job's treatment of an important moment in Jewish history, the dissolution of the shtetl and the mass migration to the West, has prompted some critics to analyze the novel in the wider context of the Yiddish literature devoted to the same problem (e.g., Magris, *Weit von wo* 19). The gradual erosion of shtetl life under the influence of modernization and immigration is perceived in this literary tradition, as in Roth's case, as a catastrophe of cosmic proportions, an element in the millenarian chain of suffering and *galut*, comparable to the destruction of the Jerusalem Temple:

> Just as the Spanish Expulsion has been regarded by contemporary Jewish historians and theologians as a catastrophe similar in magnitude to the destruction of the Temple and the fall of the Jewish Commonwealth, so too the destruction of the shtetl was now to be interpreted as a link in a chain of major national disasters, a chapter in the continuous story of woe and bereavement, of life in the vale of tears. (Miron 22)

However, unlike the Yiddish authors who integrated the destruction of the shtetl into a narrative of decline of Jewish existence, Roth uses the crisis of the shtetl as an existential metaphor with general-human validity, as the illustration *in nuce* of the wider crisis of modernity.[23] The life of Jews in the East represents for Roth the living expression of a traditional humanism that, like that of Provence, managed to withstand the onslaught of nationalist modernity and should be preserved even beyond the East European shtetl. Roth rejects the idolatrous attachment to places or abstract ideas and welcomes instead a transformative view of history in which inherited traditions change the future and open up new possibilities. This is evidenced by the fact that Roth rejects the unproblematic idealizations of the East and even admits the possibility of assimilation as legitimate in some of his articles. In his 1934 article "Der Segen des ewigen Juden," he argues that the East European Jews were right to migrate when their suffering became unbearable (*Werke* 3: 531). Similarly, the protagonist of *Job*, Mendel Singer, reaches at the end of the novel the conclusion that his opposition to his children's assimilation into Russian society was mistaken, although he experienced himself the failure of assimilation in America. Roth's nostalgic, antiassimilationist views cannot be interpreted in a conventional ideological or even political fashion without soon running into internal contradictions or irresolvable ambiguities. They express a conviction of moral-religious nature that transcends the immediate historical and social context and at the same time eludes ossification into static or didactic forms.

Redemption as the Quest for Moral Adequacy

The novel *Weights and Measures* also deals with the thematic of human suffering yet in addition develops the problem of justice, human and divine, and its relation to the justification of suffering. Anselm Eibenschütz, the protagonist of the novel, is a state employee recently relocated from the western provinces of the Austro-Hungarian Empire to the small eastern district of Zlotogrod, on the Russian border. An orderly man with a military education and a rigid sense of justice and discipline, Eibenschütz inspects the weights and measures of the local merchants. On the remote fringes of the empire, where imperial authority gradually fades away and where the local unwritten laws of illegal trade and fraud dominate ("the people of this district regarded all those who made inflexible references to law, statute, justice and the State as born enemies," *Weights* 12), the inspector Eibenschütz honestly attempts to apply the law of the state, which harshly punishes any forgery: "Thus the State made manifest its intention to use arms, if necessary, to punish cheats, in accordance with the commandment proclaimed in the Holy Scriptures, which considers a cheat to be the same as a thief" (7). Through this clarification Roth suggests that secular law claims the same authority as divine law, and Eibenschütz is intent on guarding and employing it without derogation.

The inspector lives a petit bourgeois life, together with a wife he does not love and who does not love him back, conscientiously fulfilling only his official obligations. Although he realizes that his life is not satisfying, he does not undertake any action to change it. Eibenschütz is a man who lives according to the laws of the institutions he is part of and refuses to see that beyond the formal obligations lie human passions and unwritten rules of overwhelming force. When his wife cheats on him with his own clerk Eibenschütz does not forgive her, nor does he leave her; he does not want to break the law of the marital institution. Instead, he forces her to live in a separate room and shuts himself off from her completely. As she delivers the baby conceived in the act of adultery, Eibenschütz does not relent—even though he once thought about having a child himself—and remains indifferent, feeling at most a mixture of pity and contempt.

The public service does not offer Eibenschütz much professional satisfaction either. Confronted with a hostile community of small cheats, corrupt officials, and concealed criminals, he attracts their collective enmity. He indiscriminately penalizes poor merchants who counterfeit their weights and measures in order to survive (such as the Jewish Frau Czaczkes and Mendel Singer, a character patterned in the image of *Job*'s Singer) and well-off ones who steal out of habit, pleasure, or greed (such as the murderer Leibusch Jadlowker): "Like the cholera he raged in the land, did Inspector Eibenschütz" (125). The scrupulous inspector does not apply the law of the state moderately, even though deep inside pity and compassion stir his repressed emotions: "the law's the law," observes gendarme Piotrak, his deputy (132). Eibenschütz's incapacity to temper the arrogance of a rational law that considers itself unassailable in the face of human needs, suffering, and passion metaphorically represents the source of ruin for any individual who rejects reality and gives priority to regulations over emotions.

Incapable of offering or receiving compassion or affection from the world in which he lives, Eibenschütz desperately plunges himself into a deceptive love for a duplicitous woman, Euphemia, who does not love him and cannot escape her own petty motivations and conformist habits. After an outbreak of cholera his wife and her illegitimate son die, leaving him all alone in a hostile world without love, friends, or any professional gratification: "Inspector Eibenschütz felt as if he had been abandoned by God and the world" (117). Gradually any motivation for living disappears inside of him, and the inspector engages into self-destructive drinking and disregard for the decorum required by his office. He does not cease, however, to be a representative of the central government. To the contrary, he continues to exert his authority indiscriminately and with even more alacrity, like an automaton guided simply by the law of the state: to proof the weights and measures and to punish the offenders.[24] Already dead on the inside, Eibenschütz finds his physical death at the hands of the unscrupulous Jadlowker, who takes revenge in the end of the novel for the inspector's penalization of his violation of the commercial laws. In the agony of dying, the inspector has a final revelation in which God appears to him in the disguise of a Great Inspector of weights and measures (significantly bearing a physical resemblance to Singer, the symbol of honesty—however that is possible—in the novel), who mysteriously declares Eibenschütz's own measures at the same time false and correct, as a confirmation of the incomprehensibility and incongruence of the notions of personal, earthly, and divine law.

Weights and Measures further develops Roth's stoic philosophical attitude and philosophy of redemption. The novel presents a parable of the elusiveness of justice and the relativity of moral norms, with the purpose of revealing, at least symbolically, a higher standard of virtue through the assertion of this very relativity as the only moral ground on which the individual can exist in harmony with the surrounding world: "Da vor dem Absoluten nichts Bestand hat, können göttliche und menschliche Gerechtigkeit nicht zusammenkommen, sich wechselseitig gar nicht erfassen" 'Since nothing endures in front of the absolute, divine and human justice cannot agree, remaining mutually incommensurable' (Blanke 80). The main character of the novel represents the paradoxical fusion between the evasion of moral judgment, expressed in the passive nostalgia for the military career ("In the army, everything was prescribed," *Weights* 20), with the self-righteousness of the worldly judge, who does not doubt the validity of the prescribed institutional laws ("The law is the law," 125). Instead of demonstrating moral assertiveness and earthly stoicism, he displays exactly the opposite, namely moral powerlessness and official hubris, which leads to his eventual downfall. Eibenschütz's unhappiness and suffering result from this incapacity to challenge the law through personal moral judgment and to stoically accept the reality of the world without the conceit, vanity, or confidence of the absolute judge: "He was very unhappy, was Inspector Eibenschütz" (102).

The inspector's confrontation with the mentality and customs of the new district is emblematic of the conflict between modernity and tradition, or between order and contingency (Chertenko 58), a central theme in Roth's fiction. While modernity holds its own standards to be absolute, a fact demonstrated by Roth's ironic conflation of state law with biblical law, tradition purports no absolute benchmark of virtue: honesty and corruption are ambiguously tied together. If Eibenschütz holds himself to be thoroughly honest ("Anselm Eibenschütz did not cheat," 18), Singer represents a combination of fraudulence and kindness: while he counterfeits his measures and sells blemished merchandise he is also pious, and even the inspector admits that "in spite of it all he's an honest man!" (132). Even the murderous Jadlowker is capable of showing tolerance and understanding for Sameschkin, the poor Bessarabian chestnut salesman who is formally married to Euphemia but spends most of his time peddling his merchandise from village to village, content with a meal and a shelter. In these characters' world, the official legal standards apply only partially or even not at all, hence the notions of peace and justice held by the state authority and by the locals are mutually exclusive: the inspector arrests Jadlowker because he was a disturbance to state authority, while Jadlowker considers that "if Eibenschütz did not exist, one could live in peace" (139). Confronted with his feeling of inadequacy in this world, Eibenschütz feels deserted by God and admits to his incapacity of understanding the normative intelligibility of the world. In one of the rare moments of introspection, he asks himself "Who really reigns over the world?" (95).

The confrontation between tradition and modernity is further illustrated by the relationship between the inspector and the Jewish world of the shtetl. Eibenschütz is an assimilated Jew who represents a secular and modern power and has only distant yet familiar memories of the traditional life of his family:

"He himself was of Jewish stock. He still remembered his grandfather, who had worn a big beard and had died when he, Anselm, had been eight years old" (59). In his capacity as a state employee Eibenschütz nevertheless applies the abstract and unfamiliar official law to a community that only tries to make its poverty slightly more tolerable, as it has done for centuries, through small tricks and evasions of the law. On the other hand, the figure of Mendel Singer is revelatory for the traditional Eastern Jewish world and its values: a simple Torah teacher plagued by abject poverty, he is a pious and humble man, entirely dedicated to divine matters and to helping people with advice. His simple life and good heart are for Roth the symbols of a superior and traditional morality and an ancient lifestyle. By contrast, Eibenschütz's institutional laws seem superficial and insignificant. For this reason, the inspector feels as if he has somehow committed a sin by fining him: "'We shouldn't have done that!' said Eibenschütz to Piotrak" (132). Eibenschütz feels that although irreproachable at a formal level, modern law is tantamount to a sin if applied against traditional law, which supports a different hierarchy of virtue, one based on the truly significant aspects of human existence. This is why Dorothee Gelhard considers that Eibenschütz's sin is to no longer recognize the commandment of tradition, which is a violation of religious proportions in Judaism: "Eibenschütz' Sündenfall ist, die 'Sprüche der Väter' פרקי אבות (Pirke Avot) nicht mehr zu kennen" "Eibenschütz's original sin is to no longer know the Ethics of the Fathers, פרקי אבות (Pirke Avot)" (98). Eibenschütz's dilemma is exemplary for a phenomenon that occupies a central role for Roth, namely the impact that modernization has on the individual. Caught between traditional forms of religious and moral judgment on the one hand and the "zunehmende Standardisierung gesellschaftlich-wirtschaftlicher Abläufe durch wissenschaftliche Verfahren und Messprinzipien" 'increasing standardization of socioeconomic processes through scientific methods and measuring principles' on the other, Eibenschütz feels unsettled and alienated (Winiwarter and Haberl 396).

Nevertheless, the closing scenes of the novel are evocative of the moral convictions of the author, who constructs a setting reminiscent of Pum's final judgment in front of an enigmatic deity. In his final moments of life, Eibenschütz receives the epiphany of God; however, God appears to him as the Great Inspector of weights and measures, and Eibenschütz himself appears as the merchant whose weights are being proofed. God looks a little bit like Singer and exclaims mockingly "Duty is duty! Now we shall test your weights!" (148). The mysterious verdict of the divine inspector synthesizes the moral ambiguity of actual existence, or "die Verrätselung der Welt" 'the mysteriousness of the world'

(Maier 41): "All your weights are false, and yet they are all correct. So we shall not report you!" (149). In these final lines rests the key to Roth's novel. They suggest that the attempt of the earthly powers to assume absolute divine authority in the application of the standards of justice is absurd and abusive.[25] The ambiguity of divine justice proves that no standard is absolute, thus justifying the ambiguous traditional standards of conduct of the Zlotogrod district, a typical Galician place where, as Roth noted in his 1924 travels to Polish Galicia, "die strenge Form lockert sich volkstümlich" 'the strict procedure loosens according to local customs' (*Werke* 2: 288). Roth deliberately conflates the traditional conception of morality with the divine one, suggesting thus that the only way to access the perfection of divine judgment is through the imperfection of traditional moral thought.[26] The transition from imperfection to perfection is realized by Roth through the means of his redemptive conception of the present as the moral coming together of earthly life and divine law. The imperfection of tradition appears as such only when judged against a rigid standard, such as the one imposed by conventional jurisprudence. However, seen from the perspective of redemption, in which the formal antagonisms between prescriptive norm and contravention to norm have been surmounted, this imperfection functions as the standard of perfection. Perfection is not a prearranged concept for Roth; it is challenged and continually reinvented in the simultaneity of moral law and actual existence. Bernd Oei captures this idea in his belief that "Das rechte Maß zu halten lässt sich auch auf die Ethik beziehen" 'Keeping the right measure is also a matter of ethics' (159).

The motif of the measurement unit, popular in the Chasidic imagination, is used by Roth in order to offer a response to the traditional religious interpretation of the significance of the law. The Chasidic tale of Rabbi Menachem Mendel from Rymanov offers an example of the established conception of the law, according to which the authority of the law is not subject to interpretation or derogation, being eternally and transcendentally established (Buber, *Die Chassidischen Bücher* 495). Once, a rabbi envoy went out to proof all the weights and measures at the last day of the month. He found them all in order except for those belonging to one rich man, who had a false volume measure. The man defended himself, saying that he used it no more; yet the rabbi's man argued that even if that were the case, it should not be tolerated in the store. The rabbi punishes the rich man by refusing to invite him to prayer. Understanding his violation, the man begs for forgiveness. The moral of this tale confirms the notion that in the evaluation and application of the law, the principle matters, not the fact. The authority of the rabbi, both earthly and divine, is a metaphor of the categorical nature of the law, whether secular or religious. Roth's *Weights and Measures* represents a parody of this traditional conception due to the inversion of the standard hierarchies of authority and justice. This confirms that beyond the actual Chasidic influences, Roth infuses his later novels with an original philosophy of redemption that surmounts the typical polarities between preestablished moral authority and submission to it. Roth's transfiguration of reality rescinds the absolute religious separation between the transcendent authority of the law and its immanent application, suggesting that true redemption is possible only in the union between the realm "beyond" and the one down here: "Die Frage nach dem rechten Gewicht ist metaphysisch betrachtet zwischen Immanenz und Transzendenz anzusiedeln" 'Considered metaphysically, the issue of the right weight is to be placed between immanence and transcendence' (Oei 166).

The religious significance of *Weights and Measures* touches, as in the case of *Hiob*, on the problems of human suffering and sin understood not in a strict theological sense but instead as objective occurrences in a world of lived spirituality. It is not the understanding of the divine motivation of human suffering that interests Roth—or, put differently, a theodicy that justifies the coexistence of absolute divine goodness and human suffering—but rather the human incapacity to grasp the inscrutability of this problem. Roth does not pose the question of human suffering and sin as violations of divine law but instead as the failure to engage with the ambiguity of lived morality and with the everyday nature of divine redemption. As Albrecht Weber points out, Eibenschütz's Last Judgment is a revelation of human proportions, not one of transcendent awe and glory. God appears to him as an inspector of weights and measures who resembles the humble Jew Mendel Singer, an indication of the fact that the religious law is measured in its earthly application, as "transcendent immanence": "[eine] Immanenz, die transzendiert, aber hierorts, an den Grenzen und in den Vorstellungen des Irdischen, ohne Jenseits" '[an] immanence that transcends, but here, within the limits and representations of this world, without "beyond"' (82). Since humans partake in the act of suffering, the rationale for suffering does not lie outside of the human world but instead is organically linked to human practice, to the way divine law is actualized and reinvented in the moral practice of everyday life, as a living testimony to how inseparable our religious and moral existence is from the existence of the external world. According to this neo-Chasidic religious conception, any departure from the present moment, from the continuity of tradition understood as living redemption, is a violation not only of moral laws but also of religious laws. Stoicism, understood as the assertion and full embrace of the present, proves itself to be the only acceptable attitude leading to an objective redemption in the "here and now." For this reason, *Job* and *Weights and Measures* are seen by some critics as the Jewish response to the problem of salvation.[27]

Job's Mendel Singer and Anselm Eibenschütz commit a sin by opposing the order of redemption represented by the world of tradition. However, they commit this infraction due to a fundamental lack of insight brought about by self-righteousness, which causes them to live the drama of the incongruity between their private interpretation of the law and the reality of this law. Acknowledging the existence of this normative fracture constitutes the condition for the salvation of the characters, whether in life or in death. The two protagonists do not, however, restore the state of redemptive unity with the world through an act of personal sacrifice, through expiation, but instead restore it through revelation, through an unexpected enlightenment. If Singer is enlightened about his transgressions by the revelation of his son's return, Eibenschütz learns about his hubris from the final revelation coming out of God's own mouth. There is nevertheless an alternative form of religious redemption present in Roth's fiction, one obtainable through reparation and repentance. This approach is emblematically emphasized in three other novels and a short story: *Tarabas: A Guest on the Earth* (1934), *The Hundred Days* (1936), *Confession of a Murderer: Told in One Night* (1936), and "The Leviathan" (1940).

Tarabas explores the problem of religious redemption against the background of conventional East European small-town life and singles out the tension between the autonomous modern self and that of the traditional community. Nicholas Tarabas is a Russian émigré who lives in New York City after his personal and professional life failed deplorably in his homeland, due mostly to his impulsive and adventurous personality: "He was jealous, wild, and tender, as ready with kisses as with blows" (*Tarabas* 5). Incapable of assimilating to the new world, he prefers the company of fellow nationals such as the young Katharina, whom he believes he loves and for whom he commits a violent crime: feeling prevented from pursuing his emotional relationship by her rigid employer, who despises him, Tarabas beats him up in a fit of rage and leaves him unconscious, hovering between life and death. As Tarabas mistakenly believes that he murdered the man, he uses the outbreak of World War I as an opportunity to escape from the United States and return to Russia, where he joins the army.

Rejected by his strict father, who does not approve of his son's reckless temperament, Tarabas goes onto the front with nothing to return to at the end of hostilities and no expectation for the future: "the war had become his vast and bloody home" (41). In spite of his lack of concern for his own life, Tarabas manages to come out of the conflict alive, as if "a higher power kept watch over him and preserved him to live his strange life out" (42). However, his fierce personality finds in the war the ideal outlet, so even if the war ends, Tarabas does not disband his company and leads his own personal campaign of plundering in a chaotic Russian hinterland caught in the grips of the civil war. The protagonist embodies the typical attributes of the anarchist hero of Roth's early novels; he does not believe in any order, enjoys the confusion that political turmoil brings about, and above all he is the master of his own will: "In his troop he was the Tsar" (43). Returning to his unnamed home province, which after the war became one of the newly created Central European states, Tarabas is hired as a colonel in charge of the garrison of the small town of Koropta, a position through which the authorities hope to temper the danger that he and his company pose to the security of the new country.

Things take a turn for the worse as Tarabas proves to be incapable and unwilling to keep his men in line. While some desert the army, others launch individual raids into the town and plunder the local peasants. Even Tarabas enjoys the feeling of absolute authority that he has over the town—"the terrible king of Koropta" (84)—a position from which he abuses the services of the local innkeeper, Nathan Kristianpoller. The latter, an industrious and simple Jewish entrepreneur, represents the spirit of stoicism of the traditional Jewish community faced with the ever-changing earthly authority; he does not question Tarabas's illegitimate power and takes it as a fact of life, a passing misfortune that should be avoided as much as possible: "as time went on he very soon grew accustomed to the altered aspect of the world, and, like many of his brethren, he contrived to avert all danger from himself and his" (68). During one of the rebellious outbreaks of his company a group of soldiers, manipulated by the devious and murderous renegade Ramzin, abusively occupies the inn and, after getting drunk, starts target-shooting at one of the walls, accidentally uncovering a painted image of the Virgin Mary that lay hidden behind the wall lime. Ramzin, whose power over the mind of the crowd has a devilish quality—"The devil was in it" (125)—incites the soldiers and Christian peasants to a pogrom against Kristianpoller and the Jews of Koropta, whom he accuses of desecrating the image of the holy Virgin. Tarabas, incapacitated by his drunken stupor, cannot stop the mob that plunges into an orgy of destruction and lynching on a Friday night while the Jews are preparing for the Sabbath. The scene of the pogrom is described with an insightful yet generalizing eye that reveals the psychological and sociological mechanisms of the pogrom practice in Eastern Europe in general: "A wild fury, scarcely known even to themselves, implanted in their hearts from earliest childhood, caught in the blood and driven into every vein, awoke now and grew strong within them, fed by the alcohol they had consumed that day, increased by the excitement of the miracle they had experienced" (130).

The reaction of the mob, instinctually stimulated by the "sight of the red blood" (138), constitutes a moment of collective psychosis, while the destruction of the Jewish houses is a response emerging from a deeply entrenched collective fear. The image of the flames engulfing the Jewish shtetl on the eve of the Sabbath is reminiscent of the pogrom images in the Yiddish literature, which all refresh the original trauma of the burning of the Jerusalem Temple.[28] By the break of dawn, when Tarabas's belated intervention occurs, the destruction of the Jewish homes is almost complete, and the "evil spell" (145) of mass fury has dissipated. Tarabas's failed responsibility awakens in him the feeling of remorse and the realization that he was, at least morally, accountable for the destruction visited upon the innocent Jews. After an enlightening conversation with Kristianpoller, who plainly confesses that being a Jew is not a matter of choice but instead is a matter of chance, Tarabas regains his sense of reality but at the same time the certitude that until that point his life has been wasted in a vain effort to assert oneself in the world, to selfishly give priority to his will before that of any other person. For the first time in his life he experiences the suffering of other people and another man's view on life, which explains why, by comparison, everything he ever undertook appears now irrelevant and immoral: "For a moment his loud, heroic life showed itself to him in all its worthlessness, stupidity, and emptiness; he wondered if he ought not rather envy the despised Kristianpoller his unfailing reason and the well-ordered existence that he doubtless led" (162). Once again Roth stresses through this revelation a conviction that he already made clear in some earlier novels such as *Job*, namely that the pursuit of personal or social ambitions corrupts the soul and confuses the mind of the individual. According to John Heath, this worldview, common to many Roth novels, is a legacy of the European Baroque tradition. It condemns personal ambitions as the cause of life as an "errant way" (*Irrgang*) and relies on the motifs of memento mori and *vanitas* in order to promote an attitude of stoicism and skepticism.

Intent on ensuring the order in Koropta, Tarabas declares a curfew for the Jews, whose lives could be endangered by the masses of Christian peasants who start to pour into town in a pilgrimage to the miraculous icon of the Virgin Mary. The sexton of the synagogue, Shemariah, "of all unhappy Jews the most unhappy" (171), does not, however, respect the interdiction. A pious old man "full of zeal and diligence" (172), he worries above all about the fate of the Torah scrolls in the burned-down synagogue and decides to save them from defilement.

On the way back from the synagogue Shemariah, who is carrying two scrolls in his arms "like two dead children" (184), runs into Colonel Tarabas, who wants to take the scrolls away from him and send him back home. Humiliated and powerless, Shemariah desperately attacks Tarabas in an "absurd and heartbreaking" (187) scene that makes him look like a helpless clown. Infuriated, the colonel feels possessed by a vicious desire to debase the man and "in a scene redolent of Dostoyevsky" (Rosenfeld, *Understanding* 60) mercilessly pulls off clumps of red hair from his beard, a sacrilege against everything it stood for: Jewish faith, old age, and dignity.

Filled with a devastating regret for his transgression, Tarabas tries to find a way to atone. In his opinion, tarnishing the poor old man's honor is worse than murdering him: "I am worse than a murderer. . . . And have been for years and years, but I only see it clearly now. I'll atone for everything" (199). Tarabas decides to leave everything that his life represented until then, authority and ambition, egotism and reckless passion, and start a new life dedicated to the single and humble goal of finding Shemariah and apologizing to him for his offense. In pursuing this difficult objective, Tarabas has to go through a gradual process of detachment from the demons that have dominated his entire life, expiating not only for the crimes committed against the Jews of Koropta but also for the arrogance and contempt with which he treated friends and family. He becomes a beggar, the lowest form of social existence that, precisely because it is opposed to everything that modern hubris represents, bestows on the individual a stature of dignity and holiness. Roth uses this occasion to express his moral judgment of modern society, a society caught in the blind pursuit of progress and in the hope of happiness through social advancement, both illusions of a fundamentally unstable human fate. The condition of homelessness is exemplarily expressed by the beggar and the tramp, who represent through their marginal, wandering lives a metaphor of existential dimensions.[29] In their stoical march through life, they represent the true moral law that governs mankind's relationship with the metaphysical Beyond, with the notion of redemption as moral participation in the simplicity of existence: "the unrest of the factories and machines, the windiness of dwellers on the sixth floor, the deceptively settled ones in their here-today and gone-tomorrow instability, can no longer bear the thought of the honest, calm, unceasing movement of the good and aimless wanderers" (202). In typical Roth fashion, the ideas of fixity and migration are transformed into their opposite: stability is deceitful, changeable, whereas migration and movement are permanent, like the moral law with which they identify. For Roth, the condition of migration is tantamount to that of holiness, as "The Legend of the Holy Drinker" explicitly demonstrates.

Tarabas expiates for his transgressions through humility and pain, deprivation and introspection, the latter a quality that he now discovers for the first time and that brings him close to the moral insightfulness that, in the case of many beggars, is taken for insanity: "he enjoyed his torments, and wished to prolong them if he could" (206). At the end of the novel after a brief encounter with the pious and charitable Shemariah, Tarabas obtains closure when the old Jew confesses that he has forgiven him. Released from the burden of his unbearable sin, Tarabas dies in a monastery with the satisfaction of having reestablished order in the symbolical world of moral values that he had previously desecrated.

The religious significance of the novel rests, as in the case of *Job* and *Weights and Measures*, in the positive resolution of the conflict between two different worldviews: on the one hand, the moral debacle of the historical and social world, with its displaced values and arrogant self-centeredness, represented by the selfishness and moral blindness of the hero; on the other, the order of tradition, the stoicism of a moral life regulated by the measure of redemption as an everyday event. In *Tarabas*, Roth allows the character an actual salvation from the condition of moral decay in which he was brought by a tumultuous history and an impetuous life. His salvation rests equally on the recognition of the order of tradition as the only authentic alternative to individualism and modern historical change and on the act of expiation for the denegation and offense brought against this order. As a transgressor, Tarabas can only enjoy the condition of final reconciliation in death by abandoning historical life itself. As Frank Joachim Eggers observes, "die Stationen Schuld, . . . Erkenntnis und Umkehr, Reue und Buße kulminieren schließlich im märtyrerhaften Tod des Protagonisten. Sie bilden die theologischen Fixpunkte der Handlung" 'The stations of guilt, . . . insight and contrition, remorse and expiation finally culminate in the martyrdom of the protagonist. They form the theological reference points of the action' (127). His death represents a paradoxical return to the real life, a symbolic transmutation into the order of redemption in which characters such as Kristianpoller, Shemariah, and the other Jews in the novel already live. In death, the "guest on Earth" symbolically returns home, to "eine andere Heimat . . . in die der Gast . . . zurückkehren kann" 'a different home . . . in which the guest . . . can return' (Heimerl 282).

The order of redemption that Roth offers as an alternative to the tragedy of the modern ego is the world of life within tradition, which is represented not only by the Jewish world but also by the entire horizon of traditional experience. This type of life, exemplified by Kristianpoller's stoicism and joyful *amor fati*, enforces Roth's neo-Chasidic philosophy of moral redemption in the simplicity of everyday life: "He knew, the Jew, that the sun went down in the west, and that on every cloudless day it shone upon that rack, yet in that moment he drew solace from the most everyday, the most familiar things" (*Tarabas* 81). Equally part of this horizon of redeemed tradition are the Christian perpetrators of the pogrom, whom Roth does not oppose to the order of authentic morality; they act as simple pawns in the game of fate, under the "spell" of evil tidings, yet they are not intrinsically anti-Semitic. Roth's idea of tolerance, which he extolled in the case of southern France, is a concept derived from his typical philosophy of culture, which does not oppose murder to virtue, or violence to harmony and humanness, but instead opposes the cultural order of tradition to that of modernity. The pogroms are preferable to the false promise of assimilation because they are traditional and more honest; they express the rawness of humankind's relationship to nature and to one another, which in Roth's moral order is preferable to the hypocrisy of equality contained in the modern idea of nationality. In *The Wandering Jews*, Roth observes that "wherever there are devout Christians is a place where Jews can live as well. Because the fear of God is still more dependable than so-called modern humanism" (91).[30] The act of violent repression of the Jews by the Christians from Koropta does not represent for Roth a calculated act but instead represents simply an unexpected stir of passion, which he stereotypically associates with the ardent Slavic soul: "the pious peasants cherished no thoughts of vengeance and violence today" (*Tarabas* 176).

Roth inserts a religious interpretation through the very distinction he draws between a Christian traditionalism, complexly tied into structures of segregation or sacred purification that often allowed for crimes but represented nonetheless a general human metaphysical effort to establish harmony between the individual and the universe on the one hand and heathen modern rationalism on the other. In his opinion, this modern rationalism, although formally claiming to have overcome the exclusion of the individuals through its concepts of citizenship, equality among nation-states, and universal humanity, produces de facto discriminations and rigid restrictions that are irremovably rooted in the hubris of control and instrumental reason. In the 1937 article "Emigration," Roth contends that the difference between traditional and modern anti-Semitism reflects the difference between the redeemed world of traditional rituals and the corrupt one of modern rational actions: "der Antisemitismus der Inquisition war ein religiöses, ein metaphysisches Mißverständnis; der Antisemitismus aber des heutigen deutschen Barbarismus ist kein metaphysisches Mißverständnis, sondern die logische Folge eines heidnischen Rationalismus" 'the anti-Semitism of the Inquisition was a religious, a metaphysical misunderstanding; however, the anti-Semitism of today's German barbarity is not a metaphysical misunderstanding, but the logical consequence of a pagan rationalism' (*Werke* 3: 759).

Religious anti-Semitism is, in Roth's view, an element within the horizon of tradition that people have lived by for centuries and have almost gotten used to. The mention of the pogroms in most of his novels conveys a sense of apocalyptic destruction but is always accompanied by a careful delineation between the order of traditional life, in which suffering as well as enjoyment are seen as inescapable dimensions, and the order of modernity, which deepens the sense of suffering precisely by trying to circumvent it. In the posthumously published novel fragment "Strawberries" dating from 1929, Roth describes the pogroms as passing events in the life of the shtetl: "There were occasional little pogroms. In the general hurly-burly, they were soon forgotten" (*Collected Shorter Fiction* 136). Even for the Jews of Koropta, the pogrom was a "trivial" fact of life that they were used to and that only represented a direct consequence of the inescapable fate that had also caused the Jerusalem Temple to burn: "Whatever else of shame and ridicule and suffering may come their way is but the consequence of that bitter fact" (*Tarabas* 170). The rooting in an ancient tradition makes the resilience of the Jews into an element of existential proportions, expressed in the wise stoicism with which circumstantial misfortunes are judged in the great plan of religious salvation: "Die Widerstandsfähigkeit des Brauchtums wird zum Symbol des Überlebens der jüdischen Welt" 'The resilience of tradition becomes the symbol of the survival of the Jewish world' (Magris, *Weit von wo* 140).[31]

Religion has a soothing power in the traditional community, but it is not itself the key to the redemption that Roth is looking for. Rather, the stoical life of the traditional community acquires a religious, redemptive function in the theological economy of the novel. Christianity is relevant to the author not because of its teachings but because of its power to offer a living relationship between individual and God, exemplified in the paradoxical capacity of the image of the Holy Virgin to both incite to ethnic murder and to atone for this transgression: "The memory of all those things vanished before the picture's holiness" (149). Judaism is, similarly, relevant not as a religious dogma—after all, God's design remains impenetrable to Kristianpoller: "He guides us as He wishes us to go, and we know nothing. We do not understand His cruelty, nor His goodness either" (163)—but as the commandment to abide by the law of the Torah regardless of circumstance, to resist by the power of the messianic expectation the temptation to change one's destiny by means of earthly ambition. As in the case of *Job*,

Roth does not try to undo the mystery of the divine mind, nor does he try to answer the crucial question of the mystic ("can we ever understand the divine mind?") but instead uses it as such, as a social and moral guide for the individual's everyday existence. This stoicism, which Kristianpoller expresses in his resigned submission to Tarabas's abusive will, represents the true moral alternative through which the individual's relationship with the world can assume an eternal, redeemed status: "The Jew Kristianpoller gave praise to God for His miracles. Great He was, though His ways defeated comprehension, very great His inexplicable lovingkindness" (116). As Katharina Ochse points out, rather than stressing the differences between Christianity and Judaism, in *Tarabas* Roth is interested in demonstrating their similarities and in arriving at a new kind of universal religious syncretism: "Die Unterschiede zwischen den beiden Religionen treten zurück gegenüber ihren Gemeinsamkeiten zugunsten eines universalen Menschheitsgedankens" 'The differences between the two religions become secondary in comparison to their similarities, which favors a universal idea of mankind' (197).

Tarabas's life in Koropta escalates to a confrontation between his stormy personality and the conservative lifestyle of the traditional world, not necessarily due to hostile circumstances, as he claims, but instead to the divergence between the selfish world of personal purpose and the communal world of inherited values. His violation of the order of tradition is not only a social offense; it is also a religious sin. By debasing the symbolic order in the act of humiliating Shemariah, Tarabas commits an act of sacrilege against all humanity, whose hope of salvation is reflected in the piety of a simple Jew. Only an act of expiation can ease Tarabas's guilty conscience and bring harmony to his relationship with the world. The fact that he becomes a beggar is an indication that atonement can only be realized through the abandonment of the private will: by becoming inexistent for the social world, Tarabas reasserts the principle of stoical suffering and humility, the joy of the simple things and of every day lived on Earth. Only when, after his encounter with Shemariah, his mighty will is reduced to a humble wish for a piece of bread is his mission accomplished and the old Jew can forgive him. Through this element of positive salvation, Roth offers in *Tarabas* an actual model of redemption. Individual consciousness and the world become reconciled through the restorative act of expiation: "Es ist das typische Thema von Joseph Roths Spätwerks: der Autor erzählt die Humanisierung eines Menschen als 'Heimkehr' in den christlichen Glauben, die Wandlung eines Ethos des Krieges und der Wehrhaftigkeit in das der Humanität, Schwäche und Wehrlosigkeit" 'It is the typical theme of Joseph Roth's late works: the author tells the story of the humanization of an individual as a "return" to the Christian faith, the transformation of an ethos of war and fierceness into that of humanity, frailty and vulnerability' (Eggers 114).

Tarabas's story of "return" reiterates the idea of the search for the restoration of a lost harmony, of *tikkun*. However, this restoration can only happen through moral metanoia, through a return to oneself as the person in charge of one's conscience, through what Brod, in *Paganism, Christianity, Judaism*, calls lifting the "ignoble misfortune" (77). Consistent with Brod's interpretation of what moral obligation represents in Judaism, Tarabas assumes responsibility for his own actions and tries to lift his burden with humility and with the awareness that his action in itself is not a guarantee of his final absolution. He becomes morally active but also beseeches divine mercy, which will come in the form of Schemariah's forgiveness. Tarabas's attitude of hopeful expectation epitomizes the right approach to the promise of salvation and recalls Bloch's and Rosenzweig's idea of hope as a mixture of action and expectation. Tarabas's final conversion, from a lover of the self to a lover of the other, also reiterates Rosenzweig's idea of neighborly love, which is understood as an extension of God's love onto the immediacy of creation. In the sense favored by Rosenzweig, the love of one's neighbor, a love disbursed indiscriminately on anyone close, regardless of ethnicity or religious belief, is a form of coparticipation in the redemption of the world (*Star* 218). Seen in this light, Tarabas's amends redeem the world as a whole, not only himself.

The thorny issue of the conflict between individual will and the external world preoccupies Roth due to its moral significance. In a modern era that breaks away from the authority of the divine will and its earthly correspondent, the will of the monarch, the individual becomes more and more important as a source of decision making and authority. The resulting drama of moral responsibility is what interests Roth in the first place, particularly the individual answer to this responsibility. Singer and Eibenschütz avoided their moral responsibility and deferred all questions of judgment and decision to external sources of authority, whether religious or secular. As a consequence, they became alienated from their world and were finally crushed by it, their deliverance being possible only through the recognition of their failed accountability for those around them. On the other hand, Tarabas embraces his power to make decisions and succumbs to the belief that his will is more important than any other external authority. In the end he is also crushed by the weight of his decisions, by his fiery resolve, and seeks redemption in renunciation. In both cases, the search for salvation is possible only through a process of awakening, remorse, and atonement and through the affirmation of the necessity of conciliation between self and world, or between individual will and external conditionality, whether this conditionality takes the form of tradition, nature, or divine will. Roth's conception of redemption is reflected in the characters' ability to repair the broken unity of existence: they correct the abuses of history through recourse to higher eternal principles but also mitigate the chiliastic temptation of absolute, ahistorical truths through a constant return to "here and now." This ability to balance the historical and metaphysical planes of existence is reminiscent of Karl Mannheim's preference for a "relative" conception of Utopia in which "the relationship between Utopia and the existing order turns out to be a 'dialectical' one" (199).

The same redemptive scenario is vividly played out in the novel *The Hundred Days*, a novel staged against the background of Napoleon Bonaparte's famous Hundred Days between his return from exile in Elba and his final abdication after the defeat at Waterloo. The novel stands out from the rest of Roth's novels in that is it not set against a Central and East European backdrop. Conceptually it is a "transitional" novel, bridging the religious and historical thematics of his later work. Considering the attention to detail in the historical reconstruction of the scenery and atmosphere as well as the preoccupation with history as a source of moral questions, one might even consider the novel historical in the same way in which *The Radetzky March* and *The Emperor's Tomb* are. However, given the fact that the reconstructive impulse behind the story is not corrective, in the sense that it does not try to deliver the past itself from the injustice of history, and considering the emphasis on the ideas of sin, renunciation, and atonement, *The Hundred Days* appears to resemble more closely the other novels of religious inspiration.

The novel is structured into four parts, symmetrically reflecting the destinies of its two main protagonists: the first and the third parts are dedicated to Napoleon himself, and the second and fourth parts are dedicated to a humble laundress in the service of the emperor, Angelina Pietri. Although the two characters lead parallel lives, occupying opposite positions in the social hierarchy and having only chance encounters with each other, their destinies are mysteriously united. The novel opens with Napoleon's return from exile and the flight of Louis XVIII. The people of Paris adapt themselves quite easily to the change of rulers, as they did when the king returned and the emperor left for Elba less than one year before. They change their loyalties in the same way that they change the colors and the symbols adorning buildings and uniforms. Their volatility is Roth's constant reminder that people do not believe in ideas, in principles, and are easily swayed by pragmatic considerations and by concerns for their own safety and fortune. They typify the irresolvable tension between the whims of history and the permanence of human nature, a tension present in Roth's other novels. The departing king is aware of the volatile nature of public opinion, which is why he leaves without much hesitation or regret over people's shifting loyalties: "Do not make my heart heavy, my children!" he says to servants kneeling before him (*Hundred Days* 6).

But the returning emperor is not the same person as before. He is aged, hesitant, mistrustful, and lonely. He is pressed by time and by the gathering armies of his enemies and is devoured by his desire to avenge himself on them. Feelings of injured vanity gather inside him, both as an emperor and as a father and husband who has been forced by his enemies to never see his exiled family again. The implacable passage of time is the constant reminder of the urgency of his actions: "Time was flying, time was running out" (16). He knows that he has to skillfully navigate among court intrigues, people's expectations, the unpredictability of the enemy, and the vulnerabilities of his army. He knows what people want, and he is ready to deliver: food, drink, and patriotic euphoria. He stages himself again as a common soldier, as one of the people, but also as the exceptional leader called to rule the French in the name of the enlightened principles of the French Revolution. And yet at the very moment when he does all this, he feels that the old connection with his people and his trust in his leading role are dead: "But he, the Emperor, was alone. With increasing solitude he sat before his maps" (43). He knows that during his entire life he relied only on his sovereign will, but this self-reliance is now crumbling, and the emperor finds himself alone, without support from anyone around him or even from God. However, the emperor is bound to a duty, the duty to carry out his destiny, to heed the call of his own will to power.

Angelina Pietri, on the other hand, is a small satellite revolving around the overwhelming personality of the emperor. A simple girl from Corsica, she is employed at the imperial court as a laundress and secretly harbors a devouring love for her fellow Corsican master, Napoleon. In her desire to be closer to him, she even steals the emperor's military handkerchief from the pile of clothes that she is supposed to iron. The handkerchief is a common item, identical to those used by the soldiers, and alongside millions of other objects manufactured by imperial decree, it carries a symbolic meaning: it depicts the map of Napoleon's battles. She will keep and cherish this item for a long time. As was the case for many girls of humble condition in Paris at that time, she begins a relationship with a soldier who begets her a son but refuses to marry the child's father. Her heart is set on Napoleon alone, and her own son becomes an army drummer boy in the service of the emperor. However, in spite of her proximity to and affection for Napoleon, their paths meet only several times and even then accidentally. The most meaningful of these encounters happens when, according to a common practice at the court, she is invited into Napoleon's bedroom to satisfy the emperor's sexual needs but, to her humiliation, is rejected by him. Although angry, she still retains her fondness for him. After Napoleon's exile to the island of Elba, she leaves the imperial palace and finds refuge in the home of a veteran of Napoleon's mercenary army, the amputee Wokurka, who falls in love with her and wants her to move with him back to his native Poland. Although she initially accepts, once Napoleon returns she changes her mind and returns to her old job at the court.

However, Napoleon's return ends in defeat. The Battle of Waterloo puts an end to his quest for domination and to his reign. Roth does not deal with the battle itself but instead with its aftermath and with Napoleon's state of mind in the hours following the defeat. The narrator focuses on how difficult the process of finding closure is for someone whose only manner of dealing with difficulty has been confrontation and self-assertion. Left with nothing in the end, Napoleon loses all his greatness, his arrogance, and his pose. The old warrior in him would like to find a glorious end in death on the battlefield, as a final testimony of his sovereign will, but even his own death eludes him. The peasants who see him on his way back to Paris do not believe it is him: "That's not the Emperor Napoleon! He's Job" (147). The Job motif returns as a reminder of the inscrutability of the divine plan and of the frailty of the human will. Gradually Napoleon realizes that he is no longer interested in holding on to anything, to power, to ambition, and he welcomes his own fate: "For the first time in his life since he had become powerful, he felt the bliss that renunciation brings. In the midst of his speech he was overcome by the grace of humility" (157). He humbles himself and recognizes that all he ever wanted was wrong because it was the result of an infatuation with his own will. Before turning himself over to the English and serenely accepting his final exile to the island of St. Helena, Napoleon has the religious revelation of a dream in which the old pope and his own mother reveal to him his hubris, his inebriation with his own ambition, but forgive him in the end all his trespasses.

Napoleon's downfall is also Angelina's downfall: she loses her son in the Battle of Waterloo and has to leave the palace together with the fugitive emperor's suite. The faithful Wokurka returns to her, trying to convince her one more time to leave with him, but she knows that without Napoleon there is no life for her either. Wokurka explains to her that she is wrong to tie her life to the caprices of big history, that it is the small histories that are the most relevant for people. His insight reflects Roth's conviction that history is a deceitful force and that its power relies on violence and lies. Instead, the only truth is the reality of redemption in the here and now, the humble acknowledgment of one's own insignificance, the joy of the small things in life, and the love for the people around us. But Angelina is set on a course opposite to that of Napoleon, "moving from belief in God to offer herself as a meaningless sacrifice to the Napoleonic myth" (Broerman 41). While Napoleon finds redemption in his atonement, Angelina dies unredeemed. As if possessed by a superhuman will, she runs onto the streets of Paris, already teeming with crowds celebrating the flight of the emperor and the return of the king, shouting "Long live the Emperor!" She is quickly lynched, and the novel ends with Wokurka crying over the broken body of "little Angelina Pietri."

In Roth's demonology of modernity, Napoleon Bonaparte plays an important role alongside other historical figures, such as Martin Luther, Friedrich the Great, and Otto von Bismarck. In his 1937 portrait of Franz Grillparzer, published one year after the novel *The Hundred Days*, Roth bitterly reflects on the dissolution of the medieval world order, on the disappearance of the universalist, inclusive, and Catholic Europe and the rise of Protestantism and nation-states, "the Europe of the Reformation and the French Revolution, the Europe of Napoleon and Bismarck" (*Hotel Years* 244). For Roth, the narrative of historical decay is typified in the ambition of raising the particular above the general to single out the individual mind and the individual will. The Reformation, with its emphasis on the individual connection with God, on linguistic and national particularism, and the French Revolution, with its antiabsolutist and antimonarchic ideology, its faith in reason, secularism, and popular will, embody these basic features of modernity. Napoleon, the inheritor of the ideas of Enlightenment and the French Revolution, the anticlerical warrior whose goal was to rid Europe of its medieval monarchies of divine right, is therefore a promoter of ruin and damnation, fundamentally opposed to the order of redemption that the world of Roth's novels aspires to. What makes Roth, then, attempt to redeem Napoleon, to extricate him from this genealogy of infernal destruction?

In a way, Roth suggests that there is a possibility for salvation even for individuals such as Napoleon, that they too are subject to the same temptations but carry in them the same individual potential for deliverance as anyone else. In Napoleon's case, the source of perdition and also of his own misery is his will. The novel is focused more on depicting the torments brought about by this passionate will than on narrating a particular course of events. Although static in this way, *The Hundred Days* stands out through its consummate technique of external and internal portraiture and through the intense internal dialogue. Particularly meaningful is the internal dialogue between Napoleon and God, emphasized during the key moments of the novel. Earlier in the story, we witness a weak and insecure emperor fighting his aging and his own doubts. Back in the palace, he stops in front of the altar where the fugitive old king used to pray every morning, an altar that the servants have not yet had time to remove. He gazes at the crucifix for a moment while pondering the futility of any reliance on divine intervention and then exclaims "Away with it!" and knocks it down on the floor, breaking it into pieces (*Hundred Days* 17). But the very next moment he feels regret, and when his minister of police, the treacherous Fouché, enters the room, Napoleon ineffectively tries to hide the broken crucifix behind his boot. Roth contrasts the fragility of the small figure of Christ on the cross with the toughness of the larger-than-life figure of the emperor, a figure augmented by the propaganda paintings adorning the palace. However, as is often the case in Roth's novels, the contrast is real only if seen in reverse: the crucifix is small but resilient and glorious in its message, while the emperor's colossal stature is only hiding his weakness.

Napoleon's very claim to power is flawed by the illegitimate nature of his resolve. Unlike the French king, who inherited his title by divine right, the emperor is a usurper, a soldier who gained his imperial title by the force of his weapons. In his vanity, he forgot his humble origins and his reliance on luck, believing that everything was possible to an exceptional individual such as himself. He showed no regard for tradition, for the natural course of the world, instead pushing everything in the direction he wanted. His own mother reproaches him for his impatience, his consuming desire. In the vision he has at the end of the novel, Napoleon converses with the pope (a possible reference to Pope Pius VII), who reveals to him that Napoleon's weakness has consisted in his strength, in his use of force. God, who represents the power of the meek, of the humble, is stronger than any emperor: "The weak defeat the mighty!" (188). Napoleon is his own biggest enemy, the pope continues, because he showed no self-restraint, no wisdom: "You shine too brilliantly! Your light consumes itself as it shines!" (188). In his absorbing preoccupation with his own military and political goals, he also neglected people, especially those around him who loved him and whom he used as a means to fulfill his desires. The love of "little Angelina" for him is hinted at here indirectly, thus casting a new light on her own destiny. In the end, Napoleon admits to his sins and yearns for powerlessness, for submission: "It is impotence that I love." In a return to the motif of the crucifix, he admits his defeat and his desire for humility, a reason why God forgives him: "I hold a scepter but I wish for a cross" (158). His religious transfiguration points in the direction of another redeemed kingdom: "Sein 'neues Reich' liegt aber nicht mehr im Diesseitig-Realen, sondern im Jenseitig-Verklärten. Der Welt- und Machtmensch ist zu einer religiösen Figur geworden, dem die höchste Gnade der göttlichen Erkenntnis zuteil wird" 'However, his "new kingdom" is no longer in this earthly reality, but in a transfigured otherworldly reality. The power-hungry man of the world has become a religious figure to whom is bestowed the highest grace of divine insight' (Steiner 98).

The idea that the inadequacy between individual will and external conditionality is a source of sin is emphasized in *The Hundred Days* in many instances. Napoleon's manner of relating to the universe is telling of his hubris: for him there are no countries, only maps. The mountains and plains and the hills and rivers play for him the role of tools in the logic of military action—they exist to be used to one's own advantage. The elements—the sun, the rain, and the snow—are for him just conditions that can prove advantageous or disadvantageous in battle. Instead of admiring the miracle of divine creation and accepting it as an entity valuable in itself and worthy of reverence, he debases it by putting himself above it. The manner in which Napoleon relates to the passage of time itself is another instance of this inadequacy. Time for Roth is a central concern, which explains why his novels abound with individuals dealing with the puzzle of the passage of time. His historical novels in particular deal in depth with the question of temporality, historical change, and aging. Roth creates in his novels two kinds of temporality that reflect on his larger separation between the order of damnation and that of redemption. On the one hand there is the linear historical time, the time that flows incessantly and that constantly separates ages and stages, "die *fugacitas* der Geschichte" 'history's *fugacitas*' (Magris, *Weit von wo* 278); on the other hand there is another time, a time of simultaneous presence of all moments and ages. The first kind of time is the time of the rational conception of the self, of the individual who takes over the universe in order to master it and assert oneself. For Roth, this kind of temporality leads to alienation and misery, to a constant need for time in order to achieve one's goals. Although the individual is at the center of the universe in this conception of time, no moral responsibility is demanded from him. Instead, the logic of historical change itself provides a substitute for moral decision making: history decides what is right and what is wrong. The second kind of time leads to the stoic renunciation of the self and the embrace of the moment as a source of fulfillment. Although it is predicated on the idea of abandonment, this type of temporality demands the moral participation of the individual in history precisely because this abandonment is assumed by the morally free individual through an act of sovereign decision making. This is the temporality of redemption.

Napoleon stays under the sign of the first kind of temporality. For him, time moves in one direction alone, faster and faster. The hourglass is the recurring motif of the little time left to him to build his empire and defeat his enemies: "On the table was an hourglass of polished beryl.... Thus the emperor had his enemy, Time, constantly before his eyes" (*Hundred Days* 24). Napoleon sees time like a modern individual, as something outside of himself and as the only measure of success or failure. He never has time to enjoy the things and people around him. In the end, he cannot endure the tormenting pressure of time and yearns for a standstill. The carriage transporting him back after the defeat at Waterloo symbolically represents the ineluctable passage of the time that traps the emperor. He wishes that the wheels turned more slowly: "He needed a little more time to think things over but the city was nearing rapidly, increasingly fast as though it were approaching him so as to meet him halfway, with its teary face and its spectral throne. He wanted to shout 'Slow down! Go slowly!'" (150). Once he accepts his fate, Napoleon transitions to the time of redemption, a long continuous time of contemplation of past, present, and future in a single moment. On deck of the English ship that takes him on his final exile, he takes the time to consider all the death and destruction he has caused and to watch the remote shores of his beloved homeland. He orders the clocks stopped in an emblematic gesture against the modern, sinful temporality of history and opens the window to let a seagull stand on his windowsill: "Damit ist die Herrschaft des Kaisers, eine moderne, charismatische, machtvolle, gebrochen, sie wird geradezu überwölbt von einem vormodernen Zeitmaß" 'Thus, the Emperor's modern, charismatic, powerful rule, is broken; it is basically overtaken by a premodern tempo' (Schlüter 52).

The other characters in the novel place themselves differently in relation to the binomial redemption/perdition. Angelina, the other main protagonist, falls prey to her own passion for Napoleon. In the beginning of the novel, she appears as the embodiment of the simple virtues of tradition: she prays to the crucifix hanging over her bed, has no ambitions beyond her condition, and is truthful and loyal. She is, however, dominated by love for the emperor, a love that changes her life. She gradually stops praying; becomes indifferent to the love and kindness of those around her, such as the Pole Wokurka; and even sacrifices her only son to the emperor's military ambitions. In the end, she dies at the hands of a mob of monarchic supporters. Her fate is tragic and indicates that misplaced love can be destructive, that the dream of greatness is elusive and condemns the individual to self-annihilation. Her love for Napoleon is a love for the person but also for his political persona, a love for the hubris of history and, as Wokurka explains to her, a sin.[32] Her inability to hold on to her true self, to the reality of redemption, seals her fate in a disastrous way.

Other characters, such as the veteran Wokurka, the emperor's mother, and King Louis XVIII, distinguish themselves from Napoleon and Angelina through their acquired redemption. They possess the wisdom characteristic of the position of moral intelligibility brought by redemption and see clearly, without confusion, through the deceptive veil of history. Wokurka has known the war and has suffered the loss of a limb; he has seen his hopes crushed and has come to the realization that history is not worth living for. Instead, he only desires a quiet life back in his homeland next to a person he loves. Napoleon's mother appears at key moments in order to help him regain the sobriety of his true self, to remind him that he is a man of humble origins and the son of a common woman, not a God. The king too is portrayed by Roth with open sympathy: "He was a good king. Few loved him, but many in the country liked him" (*Hundred Days* 6). He epitomizes the idea of virtuous albeit lackluster living. He has known the whims of history and the misfortune of exile too well to have any ambitions for himself or for the world around him. Instead, he displays the virtues of religiosity such as humility and forgiveness, both marks of a true redeemed existence. In more than one way, the king is reminiscent of Emperor Franz Joseph of *The Radetzky March*: he is old and wise but also dull and uninterested in military action. He does not need to conquer the world in order to rule over it. His own divine mandate, handed over to him by illustrious ancestors, gives him this distinction. He is thus different from the modern men of ambition, from the usurpers of Napoleon's kind. What sets all these characters apart is their harmonious coexistence with forces they cannot control, such as history or God, and their moral abandonment of ruinous ambition. This redeemed existence is also possible for Napoleon but only through a work of atonement and self-humility, through the abandonment of the irresponsible logic of history and the embrace of moral responsibility for the world.

Another novel that exploits the theme of redemption through reparation is *Confession of a Murderer: Told in One Night*. This novel is, however, the story of failed moral reparation and of the repentance and subsequent ethical insight resulting from this failure. In a manner similar to *Tarabas*, *Confession* focuses on a Cossack's transgressions against the order of redemption, transgressions that lead to his spiritual and objective damnation and finally to the desperate search for salvation through expiation. Also analogous to *Tarabas* is the identification of the Jewish world and of a pious and virtuous Jew with the universal order of deliverance, an allegorical figure with a powerful impact on the symbolism of the novel.

Semjon Semjonovitch Golubchik (whom the narrator lends the narrating voice under the pretext of reproducing someone else's story, a device through which Roth returns to a technique reminiscent of New Objectivity), the illegitimate son of the Russian prince Krapotkin, unsuccessfully tries to acquire recognition of his noble ancestry and remains bound to his identity as the successor of the Cossack forester Golubchik. Unhappy with his modest and, in his opinion, unjust condition, the hero resolves to employ all possible means in order to gain the honor and status he deserved by birth: "I was a Krapotkin, and, by God, I had the right to call myself Krapotkin" (*Confession* 29). In pursuit of his vain goal, Golubchik leaves his native Volhynia and heads for Odessa, where the prince keeps his permanent residence. The clash between the expectations of a simple Russian peasant and the sophisticated and perverted urban world reveals a familiar conflict in Roth's writing, namely that between tradition and modernity. Golubchik learns on this occasion the bitter lessons of duplicity, indifference, and vicious manipulation, which constitute the modern world's basic principles. In his innocence and eventual failure, he brings to mind the similar misadventures of Menahem-Mendl in Odessa, Sholem Aleichem's paradigmatic simple Jew who tries to find his luck outside of his shtetl.

Exhausting all the legal channels, being rejected by the prince himself, and being mistreated by an abusive police force, Golubchik decides to embrace the principles of the corrupt modern world in order to take revenge on everyone responsible for his misery: "for the first time the desire for vengeance, that twin-sister of hate, awoke within me" (75). His cynical attitude recalls that of Benjamin Lenz, the protagonist of *The Spider's Web* who rejects everything in the corrupt interwar German society yet decides to participate in its destruction by adopting its very values. Golubchik becomes a member of the Ochrana, the infamous czarist secret police, which bestows on him the authority to arbitrarily decide over other people's destinies. This job brings him a particular satisfaction, as he becomes involved in all sorts of conspiracies and diversions that he uses in his own interest or for the simple amusement that he derives from causing others anguish and misfortune. Golubchik's moral transformation is characteristic of Roth's late Christian conception of the pleasing, tempting nature of evil. As a result, Steinmann correctly points out that *Confession* is a novel strongly impregnated by the spirit of the discussion about the nature of evil: "Die Vorstellung vom Machtcharakter des Bösen prägt die Erzählhaltung . . . dieses Romans" 'The idea about the powerful nature of evil characterizes the narrative mind-set . . . of this novel' (*Von der Würde* 95).

Falling in love with a pretty but superficial French mannequin, Lutetia, who seems unable to harbor any real emotions, Golubchik uses his influence to weave a web of deception around her in order to ensure if not her love then at least her dependence on him. Under the false identity of Krapotkin he moves his center of operations to Paris, where he indefatigably pursues his impossible love and the objective of avenging himself on Prince Krapotkin. Golubchik fails, however, in both pursuits, as Lutetia proves to be more receptive to money and glamour, while the attempt to frame the prince's actual successor as an enemy of the state remains unsuccessful. Although his profession turns him into a man with no scruples, Golubchik discovers during one of his missions a long-lost sense of humaneness, of compassion and purity. He has to entice a young Jewish woman, Channa Lea Rifkin, who lives in exile in Paris, to return to Russia under the pretext that this return would condition the release of her brother, unjustly accused of sedition. Golubchik's encounter with Rifkin awakens, however, an unexpected feeling of empathy for the woman, who represents the icon of innocence and suffering in a world of petty vanities and treachery: she had a "pale, broad, innocent face, in which the sufferings of all our Russian Jews lay plain to read" (169). Bewildered by her integrity, love of family, and spirit of sacrifice, Golubchik decides not to betray her.

In spite of his decision, the machinery of deception of which he was part manages to trick the woman, and before he can do anything to stop her, Lea Rifkin returns to a gruesome fate in Russia.[33] Disappointed by his own irresponsible behavior and lack of firmness in helping her as well as by the realization that his criminal connivance has only managed to hurt the innocent instead of affecting the scoundrels, who proved to be too powerful and cunning to be touched, Golubchik gives up on everything he fought for, including Lutetia and his desire for revenge, and leaves for Russia. His moral self-deception, the arrogance of his purported anarchism, and the vanity of his passions disintegrate in front of the image of innocence and faithfulness that Rifkin represents. The incapacity to help her and his indirect betrayal awaken feelings of remorse that cannot be extinguished: "Death despised me. . . . I had murdered, and I could not die. . . . At that time I longed for it. For I believed then that death was an agony by which one could atone. Only later did I begin to realize that it was a deliverance. I had not earned it; and therefore it had not come to deliver me" (213). Incapable of obtaining closure, Golubchik returns at the end of World War I to Paris, where he resumes his life next to a resentful Lutetia in a gesture that represents the penitence that he imposes on himself.

The novel's thematic structure continues and develops the philosophy of moral redemption that Roth had already outlined in earlier works, such as *Job*. The stoical acquiescence to human suffering, the humility of judgment, and the appreciation of tradition are contrasted to a world engulfed by the self-deception of grandeur and the viciousness of overconfidence. Golubchik's desire to become more than he was meant to be, his social and ethical hubris, constitutes his source of despair: "der Sündenfall heißt vor allem Bruch und Nichtbeachtung des Maßes, das dem Individuum gesetzt ist; wer es überschreitet, verliert sich selbst" 'The capital sin is above all the breaking of and disregard for the limits placed upon the individual; whoever oversteps them loses oneself' (Magris, *Weit von wo* 189). In Roth's view, even the desire to obtain justice from a dishonest social world amounts to an act of aggressive self-assertion, which constitutes a vice and not a virtue: "I thirsted after justice. And whoever desires absolute justice, has already fallen a victim to the lust for revenge" (*Confession* 78). Golubchik becomes aware of his moral blindness in the moment when he realizes that even without his intention, Lea Rifkin fell victim to the machine of repression of which he is an integral part. This insight overturns his moral assuredness, and from perceiving himself as a victim who justifiably pursues his revenge, he starts to see himself as the perpetrator of an atrocious crime, a villain who is in no way better than those he despised and hated.

The association of Golubchik's newly discovered identity with that of Judas Iscariot is evident in the protagonist's own words, and through it the biblical motif of the sacrificing of the innocent is further reiterated (Steinmann, *Von der Würde* 105): "One who has never taken a reward for a betrayal may perhaps think of 'blood money' as an empty phrase. I not. I not" (*Confession* 202). Roth develops his story of transgression and expiation around the theme of the Cossack's murder of the innocent Jew, a central image in both Yiddish literature and Chasidic storytelling that symbolically inverts the founding myth of traditional anti-Semitism (the murder of Christ by the Jews) in order to evince the changeless nature of mankind's victimization of the blameless.[34] In one of Buber's Chasidic tales, a limping Cossack returning from the front shoots without reason through the window at a praying rabbi, who dies shortly thereafter. The name of the Cossack, Armilus, or the Jewish Antichrist, brings true the prophecy about the killing of the Messiah's son, Joseph (which was the actual name of the murdered rabbi), thus delaying the moment of salvation. This traditional Chasidic rendition of an old Judaic eschatological motif gives a historically contextual explanation to the postponement of final redemption and offers the Cossacks a role in the narrative of the Messiah's arrival (Buber, *Die Chassidischen Bücher* 646).

The end of the novel, in which Golubchik tries to restore harmony to the order that he breached through his actions, bears testimony to Roth's conviction that salvation from the disaster of the world, even if not certain, can only be found through an act of humble, everyday entreating of the Kingdom of

God. Golubchik reasserts the order of tradition in his decision to abandon his narrow ambitions, a fact symbolized by his eventual acceptance of the name Golubchik—"'Ah, Golubchik,' he called when he saw me. . . . 'Yes, it is I,' I said" (*Confession* 215)—yet he knows that the crime against Lea Rifkin cannot be expiated by any gesture. Instead, the only substitute left for the hero is to live with the trauma of his violation as a constant reminder of the impossibility of reaching atonement. In this act of repentance, the sense of redemption is figuratively asserted as the understanding of what sin is, regret for committing it, and recognition of the victim. Even though Golubchik cannot find actual closure, the state of permanent mourning in which he lives demonstrates that he has restored the moral unity with the world and assumed his responsibility for his actions. This form of existence in the present with the past in mind, "citable in all its moments," represents a manner of living every day as a "Judgment Day" (Benjamin, *Illuminations* 246). Through his contrition Golubchik entreats the arrival of the Kingdom, which can happen any time and may lift his burden in eternity. Although Rifkin is Jewish and Golubchik is Christian (a scenario repeated in *Tarabas*), Roth suggests that the search for redemption through repentance is universal and includes the entirety of humanity: "'We' in whose community the individual recognizes his sin, can be nothing less than the congregation of mankind itself" (Rosenzweig, *Star* 325).

The paradigmatic example of Roth's conception of religious redemption is probably the allegorical short story "The Leviathan," published in its entirety posthumously in 1940. Its simple, almost didactic structure and archetypical characters are an indication of the author's intention to provide a straightforward illustration of his philosophy of redemption. The thematic of the story is similar to that of his religious novels and deals with the problem of temptation by evil, transgression of the moral order of redemption, and expiation for this sin. Nissen Piczenik is a modest Jewish coral merchant from a small Russian shtetl, Progrody. He is renowned in the whole region for the good quality of his merchandise, with which he has a special relationship: "Yes, for Nissen Piczenik corals remained alive, even when they had been cut, polished, sorted and threaded" (*Collected Shorter Fiction* 262). A secret bond ties him to the corals that he polishes and sells in which not only his honest effort is contained but also the history of the trade itself, that of the people wearing the corals, and the mystery of the undersea world from whence the corals came. Cossacks from far and wide come to see him in a pilgrimage-like procession; in purchasing their corals, they look not only for aesthetic quality but also for good omens for the future, for a consolidation of their relationship with divinity.

In this traditional, almost magical world, the life of the coral merchant unfolds at equal pace, yet a deep longing to understand the secret of the corals' existence lives inside him, a secret buried deep down in the undersea world. Piczenik imagines the corals as a living treasure guarded by the mythical marine giant, the Leviathan, who embodies the supreme principle in his imaginary pantheon: "until the coming of Messiah—he [Jehovah] had left the supervision of all the animals and plants of the sea, and in particular of corals, to the care of the Leviathan" (262). As Almuth Hammer points out, the Leviathan's significance is closely connected in the Talmud with the messianic expectation for the redemption of the world: "die Figur des Leviathan [ist] mit der 'Utopie' des jüdischen Glaubens schlechthin, dem Eschaton konnotiert" 'The figure of the Leviathan connotes the "Utopia" of the Jewish faith par excellence, the eschaton' (144). This suggests that the attraction exerted by this mysterious world over Piczenik has a higher redemptive meaning, manifested in the ending of the story. This deep-seated desire is also reinforced by Piczenik's curiosity to know what else lies outside of the narrow confines of his world and by the lack of emotional commitment to his childless family life. Longing and alienation, both central feelings for Roth, typify the yearning of the individual living in a closed tradition to experience the novelty of the world, its diversity and sense of history. That this yearning also points the way out of the shtetl for many Jews (including Piczenik) and is, according to Roth, a source of great misery to them becomes apparent already in his 1927 study *The Wandering Jews*: "They follow a vague call from elsewhere . . . , the desire to see something of the world and escape the supposed constraints of home" (10–11). The ambivalence of Roth's redemptive imagination manifests itself here through the tension between the prospective messianic promise (the Leviathan) and the retrospective persistence of tradition (the shtetl), a tension affirmed also in Buber's notion of Utopia.

However, Piczenik's business is endangered by the competition with the store of Jenö Lakatos, a Hungarian dealer who owns a chain of stores in which he sells corals at very enticing prices. Piczenik soon learns that the secret of Lakatos's business is celluloid (the corals that he sells are artificial) and lets himself be tempted by the Hungarian merchant into mixing celluloid corals among his natural ones. Soon after this dishonest deal, the granddaughter of a peasant who commissioned a chain of corals in order to avert evil spirits and to whom Piczenik offers artificial corals dies. He realizes then the sin he has committed, burns the celluloid corals, packs the real ones, and decides to immigrate to the new world. The ship that he boards sinks, however, and Piczenik drowns. His end is rendered by Roth in a mythical key as a return of the old merchant to the world he loved so much: "But as far as Nissen Piczenik was concerned, who went down at the same time, one cannot simply say that he was drowned along with the others. It is truer to say that he went home to the corals, to the bottom of the ocean where the huge Leviathan lies coiled" (*Collected Shorter Fiction* 290).

Piczenik's story epitomizes, on the one hand, the individual's struggle with the temptation of success and false virtue that modernity and society offer (a temptation of the incarnate forces of corruption) and, on the other hand, the desire to participate in the multiplicity of the world and in actual history. While the former lure represents the act of sinful gratification of the wrong passions—the problem of the evil is evinced in Lakatos's satanic offer: "And that was how the Devil first came to tempt the choral merchant Nissen Piczenik. The devil was Jenö Lakatos from Budapest" (284)[35]—the latter provides an indication of the inescapable horizon of man's desire to expand his experience, to escape the narrow conditioning of tradition and conventional laws. Piczenik's desire to leave his shtetl poses an existential dilemma because it represents a force that bears an ambiguous status, representing both the inauthentic drive to escape from ritualized life (as in Golubchik's case) and the mark of the authentic confrontation of the inherited moral law with the challenges of history (as in Mendel Singer's case). However, this desire alone does not constitute the source of Piczenik's ruin but instead offers the dimension of the character's humanity, of his paradoxical longings and existential inconsistencies.[36]

The choral merchant's transgression, which represents a betrayal of his own credo and trade, is unambiguously the expression of a moral weakness. Although an infraction of actual small proportions in the secular reality, his decision to sell artificial corals is tantamount to a catastrophe of cosmic proportions in the complex network of magical forces acting in the traditional world. Piczenik's betrayal is a breach not only of vendor-customer trust but also of an ancient tradition of the spiritual laws of his community, a betrayal of the corals themselves, which represent the symbol of an ineffable purity of the redeemed universe: the peasants stop visiting him, the real corals lose their charm, and even his relationship with God becomes insignificant: "He recited his prayers mechanically every morning and evening" (289). Remorseful for his offense, which brought with it a gradual erosion of all aspects of his life, Piczenik must reestablish order by an act of sacrifice: he renounces his earthly possessions and dies a symbolical death through a reunification with the world of pure metaphysical principles, the world of the corals and of the Leviathan.[37] Only in death can Piczenik find closure for his sins, and hence death carries a redemptive sense: he does not soar to the skies but instead, in an inverted image of salvation, sinks to the actual undersea world, where he would "join his corals, the real corals" (291).[38] The significance of the end of the story rests in the constant preoccupation of Roth's late work with providing a sense of conciliation of the individual with the world, a sense of positive redemption. This solves the apparently irresolvable conflicts that tore Piczenik's life apart and constituted the source of his tribulations:

> Dort, im Reich des Leviathan, werden sämtliche Spannungen aufgehoben sein: die zwischen wahrer, natürlicher Kultur und künstlicher Zivilisation; zwischen einer Welt von fruchtbaren und animierenden Frauen und der Welt des in Grund und Wesen unfruchtbaren Ehelebens; zwischen dem jüdischen Außenseiter und der slawischen Gesellschaft; zwischen dem Künstler und Händler und der Welt seiner Kunden, denen nicht so sehr an der Schönheit des Produkts gelegen ist, sondern an dessen Nützlichkeit. (Shaked, "Kulturangst" 295)

> There, in the Kingdom of the Leviathan, all tensions will be abolished: those between true, natural culture and artificial civilization; between a world where women are fecund and rousing and the world of an essentially infertile marriage life; between the Jewish outsider and the Slavic society; between the artist and dealer and the world of his customers, who care not so much about the beauty of the product, but about its usefulness.

For Roth, true redemption is possible only when the dissonance of modern existence is lifted and the contradictions brought about by secularization, individualism, and rationality are definitively surmounted. By finding his redemption in death, Piczenik joins the same gallery as Tarabas, *Job*'s Mendel Singer, and Eibenschütz, who all experience deliverance in or shortly before death in a gesture of expiation or reconciliation with a world in which they have rediscovered their sense of salvation. According to Hans-Jürgen Blanke, "nur im Tod, scheint Roth ausdrücken zu wollen, ist jene letzte Erlösung und Befreiung von allen irdischen Ketten möglich; dem Lebenden bleibt sie versagt bis er seinen Leidensweg durchmessen hat" 'Roth appears to say that only in death is that last redemption and liberation from all earthly chains possible; the living person is denied it until he has gone through all his pains and sorrows' (65). And yet for Roth death is seldom a defeat, a conclusion of the individual's futile search for redemption or for meaning. It is more often a successful completion of this search and the anticipation of a deferred yet certain promise of a final renewal. What is exhausted in the end is not the life of the individual but rather the meaninglessness of mundane historical existence. Life ceases to exist as it was before, but a new redeemed life appears on the horizon. This is why the order affirmed through Roth's characters' final expiation or revelation is the order of redemption in this life, the restoration of the possibility for a hopeful existence in the here and now. In this sense, Hansotto Ausserhofer considers Mendel Singer of *Hiob* and Nissen Piczenik "Propheten des messianischen Reiches" 'prophets of the messianic kingdom' (329).

"He Has Borne Our Griefs and Carried Our Sorrows": *The Beggar Messiah*

"The Legend of the Holy Drinker" (1939), a short story written just a couple of weeks before Roth's death, expounds a slightly different approach to the notion of religious redemption without, however, altering the substance of its understanding. The structure of the narrative, like that of "The Leviathan," is schematic, and the author tries to build a simple yet exemplary story, a legend. Andreas Kartak, a Polish migrant worker who has gradually slipped into alcoholism and lost his employment, lives under a Seine bridge in Paris and acquires his livelihood from begging. One day his path crosses that of a stranger who offers him two hundred francs, which Kartak, a man of honor, offers to repay at a later time when his budget will allow. The man directs him, however, to donate the money to a Paris church in the name of a saint, the little Thérèse de Lisieux. A series of unexpected events makes Kartak successively waste and regain his two hundred francs, but the hero seems to never be able to repay the stranger in spite of his determination to do so. Anytime Kartak finds himself in the possession of the sum various events intervene that make him spend it, yet every time he miraculously manages to recover the money. In the end of the story Kartak, half drunk, has a vision of Saint Thérèse de Lisieux, whom he erroneously identifies in the person of a simple girl who displays a striking physical resemblance to his own mental image of the saint. Insisting on repaying her the money, he collapses unconscious and is dragged into the nearest place that could offer minimal help to a dying beggar. By astonishing coincidence, this place happens to be exactly the church where he has been trying to go for days. Kartak dies in the church while trying to reach for his money and repay his debt.

Andreas Kartak's story represents, according to Esther Steinmann, the author's own religious testament (". . . ein Mann von Ehre" 59). Just like the protagonist of the story, Roth spent the last years of his life in a state of acute material need in small and cheap Paris hotel rooms, hardly affording any self-care and in an almost permanent state of inebriation. As Hermann Kesten recollects, "leidenschaftlich war auch sein Hang zur Selbstzerstörung. Er war einer der gewaltigsten Trinker seiner Zeit" 'His propensity toward self-destruction was also passionate. He was one of the most tremendous drinkers of his time' (105). Kartak's irreparable condition of exile and his stoical reception of the misery of existence represent Roth's transfiguration of his own suffering and moral condition. According to any traditional concept of morality and propriety, he is a sinner, an irresponsible drunk, but in the hierarchy of Roth's conception of virtue, Kartak is a holy man because he treats life with the honesty of one who has nothing to lose or gain. In Steinmann's opinion, Kartak's virtue is ontic and not moral: he displays "eine ontische Integrität, die ihn gegenüber moralistischen Anwürfen unverletzlich macht" 'an ontic integrity that makes him immune to moralistic accusations' (*Von der Würde* 114). For this reason Kartak always ends up even, neither losing nor gaining. An invisible divine will arranges that anytime profit might swerve him out of his stoical poverty and awaken in him the love of money, he loses his money in the same way as he gains it anytime he is about to drift into the melancholy of the loss. He cannot fail the moral test of his existence because Roth made him into an already redeemed human being, a living saint.[39] This condition affords him a radical form of freedom in which he reevaluates the notions of sin and virtue and reinvents them away from social and conventional codes. While his behavior cannot be considered virtuous in the traditional sense, it cannot be said to be immoral either (Steinmann, ". . . ein Mann von Ehre" 61).

The Christian motif of the simplicity of holiness, *sancta simplicitas*, acquired through poverty and integrity is united in "The Legend" with the Chasidic notion of saintliness as joyous affirmation of the plenitude of life, beyond discriminatory or expedient moral judgments about the nature of the world. The story of Rabbi Jaakob Jizchak from Lublin illustrates this notion. One day while walking in the street with his pious apprentices, he meets a man known for his unreserved sinful behavior. To the astonishment of his disciples, the rabbi chats friendly with the man and then continues his walk. Asked by the disciples why he showed such affability instead of harsh judgment, the rabbi replies that sinners who repent and return to their wicked ways are worse than those who at least indulge in their sin; the latter's unreserved actions create a certain joy about them that encourages everyone and uplifts their spirit: "der Glanz seiner Freude überwältigt mein Herz" 'the radiance of his joy overwhelms my heart' (Buber, *Die Chassidischen Bücher* 482). Chasidism's practical notion of salvation, a salvation immanent to everyday life, is exemplified through Kartak's morality, a morality produced in the immanence of participative, joyful existence. That Kartak is holy and redeems the world in his own humble way illustrates the conviction that the Messiah arrives even in misery and desolation, which is another expression of the Chasidic belief in the Messiah's "destruction of exile by its spiritualization" (Scholem, *Messianic Idea* 195). W. G. Sebald argues that the motif of the beggar-Messiah, common in the Chasidic literature but also in that of Kafka and Döblin, finds in Roth its patent expression: "In ihm hat sich ein Archetyp des Exilierten gebildet, . . . eines Gottes im Elend" 'An archetype of the exile formed in him, . . . of a god in misery' (92). Through the combination of Christian and Chasidic motifs, Roth confirms Eggers's conclusion that the "Legend" is religious but not in a confessional sense: "Deutlich wird bei allem die Distanz des Autors zu dogmatischen Positionen. Ein Bruch gegenüber dem katholischen Gattungsverständnis ist darin zu sehen, daß Roth seine Legende nicht nach konfessionellen Rezeptionsbedingungen ausrichtet, sondern gewissermaßen religiöse Literatur mit 'offenen Gemeindegrenzen' produziert" 'In the first place, Roth's distance from dogmatism becomes evident. A break away from the Catholic understanding of the genre can be seen in the fact that Roth does not construct his legend according to the expectations of a confessional readership, but produces, in a way, religious literature with "open congregational borders"' (129).

The death of the character, premonitory of the death of the author himself, is unexpected and light, almost as a confirmation of the redeemed nature of his life, of the intrinsic holiness of his existence. Kartak does not suffer, nor does he realize that he is dying; he seems to simply alter his state while his substance remains unchanged and holy because holiness represents everything that he undertakes. In the final line of the story, Roth symbolically ties himself into this wondrous narrative of salvation by entreating God's mercy for his own deliverance: "May God grant us all, all of us drinkers, such a good and easy death!" (*Three Novellas* 109).[40] Indeed, Roth died a fast death shortly after finishing the legend of Andreas Kartak and, not unlike his hero, tried in the last part of his life to live with the conviction that redemption is a daily condition that compels the individual to participate in the disaster of history with the hopeful expectation of its final deliverance and to entreat this deliverance by morally engaging with the world.

Forced into Parisian exile by the Nazi occupation of Austria, Roth lived the last years of his life in a state of profound anguish and disenchantment with the course of European history, which seemed to confirm his worst apprehensions about the dangers of modern industrial and mass societies. Even if some critics argue that Roth sought to escape the disaster around him by finding refuge in the reality of his fictional work, in reality he never saw the fictional world as a separate entity from the real one. To the contrary, he conceived of them as two sides of the same coin and consistently carried the reality of his fictional world over into the empirical world and the other way around, his political concerns into his fiction. Roth never lost the sense of hope that his fiction captures beyond the appearance of ontological destitution and despondence that it communicates. Active in a variety of Austrian exile and antifascist organizations, he put his philosophy of redemption in the service of democratic resistance through an optimism that stemmed from his firm belief that redemption is more real than reality, that salvation, albeit fictional, has the power to influence lives in a more decisive manner than pragmatic skepticism or realism. A letter dated October 10, 1938, seven months before his death, and addressed to his friend Stefan Zweig gives expression to his optimism, to his active commitment in the reality of salvation in spite of the unfolding disaster around him: "I don't see, dear friend, why you describe our situation as 'hopeless.' If it is, then only because you make it so: we have the duty, the absolute duty, to show *not the least* pessimism" (*Joseph Roth: A Life* 527).

By advocating a redemptive unification between the individual mind and the phenomenal world, Roth's moral philosophy bears significant similarities to that of other Jewish intellectuals of the time, such as Buber, Bloch, Rosenzweig, and Scholem. Influenced at the same time by Chasidism and Romanticism, existentialism and Christian mysticism, Roth tries to find a larger, more inclusive synthesis between the religious dimension of humankind's basic hope for salvation and the ethical questions concerning the individual's existence within society and history. As Moshe Idel points out, the redemptive reunification of the holy sparks that form the unity of God and man, an idea central to the Kabbalistic motif of *tikkun*, is a question of convergence between divine law and individual morality. If "our forefathers would not have understood the separation of human morality from God's truth," then the modern individual has lost this bond (Idel, "Rosenzweig" 164). Hence, its renovation constitutes the most urgent undertaking for all the mentioned thinkers, including Roth himself. The issue of modern selfhood, detached from the constraints of tradition but also unable to find a satisfactory, substantial moral engagement with his world, troubles Roth from the very beginning of his writing career. The crisis of modernity appears to him right from the start as a moral crisis that affects more than just questions of normative validity or adequacy of virtue; it also destroys the individual's metaphysical assuredness and hopefulness, which constitute the spine of humankind's essential relationship with the sphere of religious redemption. His early novels testify to this profoundly felt crisis of the individual who loses all hope of salvation in this world or in the hereafter. The characters' revolt and flight from the world represent, through negation, the only redemption possible.

While the concern for the complex crisis that affects the modern individual remains unchanged in Roth's late career, he envisages a different positive solution in his late novels. He concludes that raw revolt against a corrupt order cannot affect the inner mechanisms characterizing this order and can only further the fracturing of the connection between the individual and world, the isolation from community, and the egotism of self-righteousness. Instead, a restoration of this broken state, a restitution of the moral harmony between individual and the world, is the only manner in which not only the question of moral adequacy could be answered but also that concerning the general-human horizon of religious hope for final deliverance. In his 1937 article "Grillparzer," Roth writes that

> The unreliability of the world is a consequence of its inadequacy. You don't oppose its pressure, its mood, its despotism, by open revolt, which can have no other outcome than catastrophic inadequacy, in other words: disorder, the greatest of all dangers to a human, but by a retreat into the depth, into the cave of the self. . . . He [the human being] doesn't live off to the side, but in the depths. From below he sees more accurately, with a juster bitterness and a moral bitterness, the facility, the poverty of the high-ups, and more clearly the summit of heaven. (*Hotel Years* 247–48)

In Roth's late novels, the most common experiences that his characters undergo in order to achieve salvation center on the restoration of a broken bond with tradition, with inherited values, with the most simple, almost primary experiences that tie humanity together and prepare it for the confrontation with the unpredictable.

Roth's late work also marks a shift in perspective, from the existential anguish of the failed search for redemption encountered in his early novels to the equanimity of the certitude of redemption of the late ones. The turbulent, tormenting nature of the world seen from the perspective of the characters' own futile struggles gives way to a calmer exemplary and almost mythical world in which the individual struggles are seen from the point of view of their denouement. In his late novels, Roth no longer poses the problem of the crisis of modern consciousness from the perspective of the individual caught in it but instead poses it from that of redemption as a de facto experience. The characters' search for reconciliation with their own universe becomes thus a teleological story—a story seen from the perspective of its own end—and the experience of redemption is no longer posited virtually or through negation but actually and as a positive solution.

Notes

1. The 1989 edition of Roth's collected works published the newspaper articles under the original series' title "Im mittäglichen Frankreich" and the essays under the title "Die weissen Städte." See Roth, *Werke*, ed. Klaus Westermann, Vol. 2, 1989. The 2004 English translation reproduces the article series under the title "In the French Midi" and the essays as "The White Cities." For more, see *Report from a Parisian Paradise.*
2. The Jewish fascination with the Mediterranean world is, according to Asher Biemann, a cultural trope distinct from the German fascination with the French South: "Jewish Italophilia, in this respect, was more than a *fatigue du nord* and more than a search for personal rebirth. It was more than travel and more than refuge. It was, rather, nothing less than the affirmation of a new identity, a plurality of identities, as only the sites of the Mediterranean could offer: A new, de-intellectualized cosmopolitanism rooted in the land itself and emerging from the cultural connectivity of the Mediterranean, from its archeological simultaneity and historical mobility, from its capriciousness, allegro, and mutability" (256). This characterization applies fully to Joseph Roth's view of the Mediterranean world.
3. It is therefore not surprising why some critics see in the social estrangement of Roth's early fictional characters the drama of a failed Jewish assimilation. See Magris, *Weit von wo* 51.
4. According to Bernd Hüppauf, Roth's travels to France were responsible for the author's turn toward an attitude of skepticism that would be influential in his late work. This skepticism, which Hüppauf defines in relation to the philosophical skepticism of Michel de Montaigne and Pierre Charron, is characterized by realism, individualism, and hostility toward ideology: "Seit etwa 1926 entdeckt Roth auf unsystematische und intuitive Weise für sich, was in der philosophischen Tradition des Westens seit Montaigne und Charron als *Skeptizismus* bezeichnet wird. Den ersten und auf Roth befreiend wirkenden Anstoß dazu lieferte bereits seine Reise nach Frankreich" 'Since about 1926 Roth has discovered in an unsystematic and intuitive way what is termed "skepticism" in the philosophical tradition of the West since Montaigne and Charron. The first impulse in this direction was already provided by Roth's trip to France and it had a liberating effect on him' (30–31).

5. Alfred Pfabigan proposes a highly original interpretation of Roth's initial adoption and later abandonment of New Objectivity. Pfabigan argues that the aesthetics of New Objectivity, through its alleged "technical" literary method, allowed a decoupling of the individual from the work. This was particularly important for Jewish authors whose works were frequently dismissed in the German-speaking world as "Jewish" due to the popularity of the traditional Romantic view of literature as being the product of a national or ethnic spirit. New Objectivity had the potential of offering something close to a "democratic" aesthetic form, similar to jazz (105). However, as Roth began to associate modern aesthetics and democracy more and more with Germany and with the pathology of modernity (or with the Antichrist), he sought out more and more a conscious and intentional identification with the Jewish auctorial identity. In this sense, his abandonment of New Objectivity is consistent with his more general turn toward the ideas of religious salvation and moral autonomy.
6. Hermann Kesten insists that in spite of Roth's shift from the novels of social orientation to those of religious inspiration, the fundamental issues remain unchanged: "Der zornige Pessimismus, die heitere Erbitterung, die revolutionäre Ironie gegen ein Schicksal, das hier Gesellschaft, da Gott hieß und die beide vielleicht stärker als das Individuum sind, die es zerbrechen, aber nicht ändern können, diese ganz wunderbare Klarheit eines Mannes, der alles gesehen, alles geprüft, alles in seiner Welt verworfen hat, und nicht gesonnen ist, mit dieser Welt zu paktieren, dieselbe tapfere Verzweiflung und derselbe vernünftige Mut, in einer unvernünftigen Welt vernünftig bleiben zu wollen, prägen die Art aller Romane Roths" 'The angry pessimism, the cheerful exasperation, the revolutionary irony against a destiny called society here and God there (both being perhaps stronger than the individual, able to break, but not change him), this quite marvelous clarity of a man who has seen and inspected everything, who has rejected all things in his world, and is not disposed to pact with it, the same brave despair and the same rational courage to want to remain rational in an irrational world, all of these characterize the style of all Roth's novels' (109). Kesten focuses exclusively on the existentialist significance of the conflict between individual moral mind and the external world, a problem present throughout Roth's entire fictional work. However, Roth envisions different solutions to this conflict in the early and late novels, moving from the narrow perspective of the individual to the sphere of metaphysical questions, aspects that Kesten does not address.
7. Due to the centrality of the themes of uprootedness, disintegration of the shtetl, and conflict between tradition and modernity, *Job* has been relegated by some critics to the "shtetl literature" category alongside works by classic Yiddish and

German-language authors such as Sholem Aleichem, Isaac Leib Peretz, Mokher Sforim, and Karl Emil Franzos (Rosenfeld, *Understanding* 44).

8. In an article titled "Wailing Wall" published in 1929, one year before *Hiob*, Roth writes that "Religiosity becomes an organic function of the individual Jew. A Jew fulfills his 'religious duties,' even if he doesn't fulfill them. Merely by being, he is religious. He *is* a Jew" (*What I Saw* 48).
9. Eva Raffel objects to the common identification of Deborah's religious practices with Chasidism. In Raffel's view, Deborah is intentionally depicted as a proponent of assimilation, and only in this sense is she an opponent of Mendel's orthodoxy. Rather than a religious figure, Deborah "verkörpert die typische jüdische 'Mamme,' die sich um alles Irdische kümmern mußte" 'embodies the typical Jewish "Mamme," who had to look after all the mundane things' (209).
10. Certain interpreters, such as Esther Steinmann and Hans-Jürgen Blanke, focus primarily on Roth's Chasidism and Catholicism. However, they fail to emphasize that for Roth, the religious phenomenon in general is more important than particular religious doctrines, which are subsumed by him under the umbrella of tradition. See Steinmann, *Von der Würde des Unscheinbaren;* Blanke, *Joseph Roth: Hiob; Interpretation von Hans-Jürgen Blanke.*
11. "It is rare to find a Jewish family in the East that doesn't have an uncle or cousin in America. Somebody emigrated, twenty years ago, say. He fled the draft. Or he received his call-up papers and deserted," writes Roth in *The Wandering Jews* (*Werke* 2: 879). It is significant that in Sholem Aleichem's *Adventures of Mottel, the Cantor's Son*, the same fear of military service determines the immigration of Mottel's family to America.
12. Using Deborah Singer's case, Katja Garloff contends that the temptation of assimilation is a typically feminine attribute in Roth's work. Garloff makes a case for a psychoanalytical reading of the anti-Semitic stereotypes about Jewish assimilation as a form of feminization and hence interprets Roth's antiassimilationist rethoric as a fear of emasculation. However, her interpretation ultimately falls short of explaining Roth's complex civilization critique, of which the critique of assimilation is only one subcategory.
13. Magris correctly contends that Roth does not try to present America in a sociological or even historical manner but instead, as in the case of the other historical-political entities of his work such as Austria, France, and Germany, presents it symbolically: "Seiner höchst europäischen Perspektive bleibt Amerika eine fremde Welt, wirkungsvoll in ihren charakteristischen Zügen gezeichnet, aber als absolute Alterität aufgefaßt" 'From his very European perspective, America remains a foreign world, effectively portrayed in its characteristic features, but perceived as absolute alterity' (*Weit von wo* 153).

14. "Das Hiob-Wort ['Der Herr hat's gegeben, der Herr hat's genommen; der Name des Herrn sei gelobt!'] wird in Mendels Mund dahingehend verfremdet, daß der göttliche Wille, den der biblische Hiob als Einheit von geben und nehmen verstanden und dergestalt ungeteilt auf sich bezogen hatte, dichotomisch aufgespalten wird: geben und nehmen verteilen sich auf verschiedene Personen als das ungleiche Maß der unberechenbaren Unbegreiflichkeit Gottes" 'Job's saying ["The Lord hath given, the Lord hath taken away; blessed be the name of the Lord!"] is in fact alienated in Mendel's mouth by the fact that the divine will, which the biblical Job had understood as a unity of giving and taking, and applied it thusly, undivided, upon himself, is divided in two: to give and to take are distributed to different persons as the unequal measure of the unpredictable incomprehensibility of God' (Steinmann, *Von der Würde* 40).
15. According to Hans-Jürgen Blanke, even the name Menuchim is derived from the Hebrew "m'náchejm," which means "the soother" (54). For a full interpretation of the novel's Jewish "*Soziosemiotik*," including the more or less overt biblical references, see Shaked, "Wie jüdisch ist ein jüdisch-deutscher Roman?" ("How Jewish Is a Jewish-German Novel?").
16. According to Magris, a characteristic of Yiddish literature, also present in much of Roth's fiction, is to depict nature as fundamentally opposed to the Jewish search for meaningfulness and salvation; its chaotic, dangerous character is a metaphor for the very condition of *galut*: "Die Natur ist also eine große Metapher für das Exil" 'Nature is thus a great metaphor for the exile' (*Weit von wo* 194). Similarly, Andrei Oişteanu shows in his study *Imaginea evreului in cultura romana* (in translation, *Inventing the Jew: Antisemitic Stereotypes in Romanian and Other Central-East European Cultures*, U of Nebraska P, 2009) that the Jew's fear of dogs is a recurring motif in the representations of the Jew in Central and East European cultures such as the Romanian one (238). Sidney Rosenfeld argues that the image of nature in *Hiob* reflects the mental and spiritual situation of the characters: "der russische Wald ist 'ewig in seinem verwurzelten Bestand'; die Juden dagegen sind entwurzelt, sie sind auf dieser fremden Erde nicht 'daheim'" 'the Russian forest is "eternal in its rooted constancy"; the Jews are, to the contrary, uprooted; they are not "at home" on this strange earth' ("Joseph Roths *Hiob*" 492). Singer's yearning for nature is a yearning for a return to a form of belonging that was always there but that he mistakenly ignored.
17. The motif of the stoic renunciation of the worldly ambition and return to the pacified harmony with one's fate is common to East European Jewish literature of the turn of the twentieth century. In spite of the difficulties that forced the East European Jews into exile in the West, the nostalgia for the native places remains,

often transfigured into a return to the home village, a return that carries a moral meaning. In Karl Emil Franzos's short story "The Picture of Christ," Bocher David, the young Jew who traveled the world in search of an identity, returns to his home shtetl, Barnow: "In the old days I had worked for name and fame . . . but my own sorrow taught me to feel for others. . . . So I came back to Barnow, to the people who had been so kind to me in my childhood, and to the graves of my parents. . . . It was an unspeakably deep, an unspeakably anxious, longing for a firm support to which I could cling in the darkness, sorrow, and confusion in which I was plunged. . . . I have not made a name for myself, as was once my ambition, but have become a poor and simple tender of the sick. . . . I am now at peace, and am therefore happy: I have learnt renunciation!" (291–93).

18. Singer's final revelation bears the power of example for European Jews at the turn of the twentieth century who, torn between the desire to assimilate and that of asserting their specificity, forgot about their moral obligation for individual historical existence. Heinrich Bermann, one of the characters from Arthur Schnitzler's *Der Weg ins Freie,* expresses a similar view: it is not the assimilation to the norms imposed from the outside nor the self-centered assertion of a distinct ethnic specificity that the Jews should search for; instead, they should turn toward themselves and assume their individual, concrete historical condition. Doubting the legitimacy of the Zionist solution, Heinrich argues that "Ich glaube überhaupt nicht, daß solche Wanderungen ins Freie sich gemeinsam unternehmen lassen . . . denn die Straßen dorthin laufen ja nicht im Lande draußen, sondern in uns selbst. . . . Dazu ist es natürlich notwendig, möglichst klar in sich zu sehen, in seine verborgensten Winkel hineinzuleuchten!" 'I do not believe at all that such peregrinations into the open can be undertaken together . . . for the roads there do not run in the country outside, but in ourselves. . . . For this, it is, of course, necessary to see as clearly as possible within oneself, to illuminate one's most hidden corners' (276).

19. It is relevant to emphasize Roth's contempt for Zionism, which although aimed at the emancipation and defense of the Jews from the discrimination and segregation they faced, especially in Central and Eastern Europe, was still a secular national doctrine. As he writes in *The Wandering Jews,* life next to Christians, however difficult, was preferable to this modern illusion of redemption: "An Orthodox Hasid from the East will prefer a Christian to a Zionist" (31).

20. Magris sees the same tendency in other Jewish writers, such as Isaac Leib Peretz: "So erarbeitet also die literarische ostjüdische Kultur eine Art Synthese zwischen Nietzscheanismus und Historizismus unter dem Zeichen einer ruhigen—nicht trunkenen oder exaltierten—Bejahung der effektiven Realität der Dinge, wie sie sind" 'The literary East European Jewish culture develops thus a kind of synthesis

between Nietzsche and historicism under the sign of a calm—not inebriated or exalted—affirmation of the actual reality of things as they are' (*Weit von wo* 170).

21. Kesten even argues that fundamentally Roth was an atheist, and his inclination toward religion corresponded to his philosophical revolutionary conservatism, which simultaneously emphasized redemption and tradition, freedom and order (113–14). However, Roth's relationship with religion, even if unconventional, could hardly be characterized as "atheistic": he attempted to reinvent the religious question as a moral question.
22. Roth's conception of suffering borders on the Chasidic one, which assigns it a positive role in the great narrative of redemption. However, while human suffering is important in Chasidism as a harbinger of the redemption that will end it (a typical Kabbalistic interpretation), for Roth it is relevant in itself, a position that brings him closer to the Catholic doctrine of suffering as the promise of salvation. In Chasidism, final salvation occurs only when all the possibilities for a redress here on Earth have been exhausted, which explains why God intervenes to alleviate pain: his unexpected gestures of benevolence actually postpone the final arrival of the Messiah (Buber, *Die Chassidischen Bücher* 653). For Roth, on the other hand, suffering carries with it already a sense of salvation, reminiscent of the Pauline transformation of weakness into strength. In this regard, G. P. Butler's conclusion that Mendel Singer's suffering is pointless and that his salvation has only a mocking effect is erroneous: "Nothing really comes or came about to save him, his kind, the simple man at the end of his tether" (232).
23. Marcel Reich-Ranicki correctly points out that Roth's depiction of the life of the Galician Jew does not have much to do with actual reality, representing more of a transfiguration of his own literary imagination: "Das von Roth entworfene, reizvoll-dekorative Bild Ostgaliziens hat mit der Wirklichkeit soviel und sowenig gemein wie Chagalls berühmte Visionen mit der realen Stadt Witebsk" 'The charmingly decorative image of East Galicia that Roth sketched has as much and as little in common with reality as Chagall's famous visions with the real city of Vitebsk' (*Nachprüfung* 225). Ritchie Robertson compares Roth's depiction of several representative figures of the Galician shtetl, such as the *Fehlmacher*, the *melamed*, and the *tsaddik*, to their depiction in the traditional ghetto fiction and concludes that Roth intentionally adopted formulaic presentations that distorted reality in order to obtain a theatrical atmospheric effect (199). This, he argues, is the result of a modernist, almost expressionist response to ghetto fiction.
24. Telse Hartmann, who analyzes the novel through a postcolonial lens, draws a comparison between Eibenschütz and Kurtz of Joseph Conrad's *Heart of Darkness*. Analyzing Eibenschütz's fascination with the "native" Euphemia, his

self-destructive drinking, and the influence of an exotic landscape and a hostile climate over his psyche, Hartmann speaks even of a case of "going native" (57).

25. Blanke considers that the reluctance of the religious Jews to accept the law of the state as a legitimate one has to do with a general mistrust toward earthly authority: "Der Staat, der nicht die *civitas dei* repräsentiert und sich nicht auf göttliche Legitimation berufen kann, wird vom orthodoxen Juden mit Skepsis und Befremdung betrachtet" 'The state, which does not represent the *civitas dei* and cannot invoke divine legitimacy, is viewed by the orthodox Jew with skepticism and alienation' (41). Roth starts from this assumption in order to sharpen the contrast between modern rational law and traditional law.
26. W. G. Sebald argues that *Weights and Measures* provides an indication that order and right cannot be equated with the sense of justice, which is of an ineffable, almost divine nature. The relativity of the measures and the generosity of the masters are proof that the organization of traditional societies is more just and authentic than any imposed law: "[Die Parabel] will sagen, daß durch den sogenannten Fortschritt der Zivilisation und die Zunahme von Recht und Ordnung weit größeres Unrecht und Unglück über uns kommt als das natürliche, an dem wir ohnehin leiden" '[The parable] wishes to say that the injustice and misfortune brought upon us by the so-called progress of civilization and the increase of law and order are far greater than the natural ones, from which we suffer anyway' (63).
27. Helmut Famira-Parcsetich identifies two types of solutions to the religious problems that Roth's novels portray: Jewish, marked by the promise of redemption either in this world (*Job*) or in the next (*The Rebellion*, *Weights and Measures*), and Christian, where this-worldly ambitions must be abandoned in order to obtain redemption in the hereafter (*Tarabas*, *The Hundred Days*) or the man must expiate for his sins (*Confession of a Murderer*) (126).
28. "Characteristically, in the 1880s and later the literary reaction to pogroms would almost inevitably involve the employment of the fire metaphor" (Miron 18). Miron argues that in all of these images, the archetype of destruction is that of the burning down of the Jerusalem Temple and the beginning of the exile.
29. Roth's 1929 article "Für die Staatenlosen" ("For the Stateless") describes in polemical terms his preference for the stateless, refugees, and people without national or institutional identity. He sees in their fate the expression of a moral resistance of the uncompromising traditional spirit in front of the corruption that modernity brought with it, a modernity represented by national states and by racial and ethnic exclusions. Consistent in his theory of national alienation, Roth writes in the 1937 fragment "Emigration" that "Ich, der ich noch eine politische Heimat habe, bin stolz darauf, unter den Heimatlosen sprechen zu dürfen" 'I, who still

have a political homeland, am proud to be able to speak among those who have no homeland at all' (*Werke* 3: 754).

30. Manes Sperber also emphasizes the fact that piety and poverty often bridged the gap that mutual suspicion and cultural difference created between the Jews and Ruthenians of Galicia: "Dissimilar as they were, they shared poverty, their common technological backwardness, and finally the very different yet equally profound all-permeating faith in God brought them closer than any outsider could have guessed" (*God's Water Carriers* 38).
31. Kati Tonkin considers *Tarabas* a story of hope but also, at the same time, a cautionary tale about the dangers of anti-Semitism ("A Parable of Germany" 162). She interprets the novel, written shortly after the Nazi takeover of power in Germany in 1933, as a parable of Germany's ability to overcome anti-Semitism but also as a warning about the dangers awaiting it if Germany would not do so. Tonkin's analysis does not, however, take into consideration Roth's wider moral philosophy of history, in which the search for redemption is more important than the sin itself and in which the general-human interpretation takes precedence over any historical or contextual interpretation.
32. Bastian Schlüter considers the scene of Angelina's death in the context of Roth's critical view of historical transience and progress. Schlüter therefore draws a comparison between her death by the Seine River and the image of ruin left in the wake of the flow of history that pushes Walter Benjamin's angel of history onward (53). He is right to compare Benjamin's view of history to Roth's due to their common skeptical evaluation of what linear time and additive progress mean for humanity.
33. Dieter Kliche argues that Roth's Jewish characters are animated simultaneously by noble feelings and by defenselessness in front of a hostile world: "Seine jüdischen Romanfiguren sind von besonderer Reinheit, Güte, moralischer Kraft und Überlebensfähigkeit, aber auch Schutzlosigkeit, Verletzbarkeit und fataler Eignung zum Opfer" 'The Jewish characters in his novels are especially pure, good, morally strong and fit for survival, but also defenseless, vulnerable and fatally susceptible to become victims' (792).
34. Some of the most gruesome pogroms and bloody repressions against the Russian Jews were perpetrated by the Cossacks since the seventeenth century. *Ritualmord in Ungarn*, Arnold Zweig's 1915 expressionist tragedy, employs the motif of the sacrifice of the innocent Jew by the anti-Semitic masses and by the political villains who manipulate them. Zweig emphasizes the tragic condition of the Jews who cannot be accepted as Jews or achieve assimilation in Central and Eastern Europe, being thus forced into a renewed affirmation of their unique destiny as eternally persecuted and eternally "chosen." This paradoxical condition of being both pariah and

"chosen" is famously analyzed by Max Weber, who sees in it the secret of Jewish resilience: "The Jews' theodicy of disprivilege was greeted by the pitiless mockery of the godless heathen, but for the Jews the theodicy had the consequence of transforming religious criticism of the godless heathen into ever-watchful concern over their own fidelity to the law. . . . The Jew was naturally prone, as a result of his lifelong schooling, to casuistical meditation upon the religious obligations of his fellow Jews, on whose punctilious observance of the religious law the whole people ultimately depended for Yahweh's favor" (497).

35. A character with the same name tempts Golubchik in *Confession of a Murderer* to sign some documents that, unbeknown to him, would lead to Lea Rifkin's death. In this novel, Lakatos is also described as the devil: "I feared Lakatos as the actual emissary of Satan who had thought out for me, for me especially, a little private devil" (193). In the 1935 novella "Triumph der Schönheit," another character named Jenö Lakatos is presented as a superficial gigolo, a home wrecker, a "human type, not a personality" ("ein Typus, keine Persönlichkeit") (*Werke* 5: 653).

36. Ausserhofer considers Piczenik's secret longing for the undersea world as the aspiration for redemption, the final goal of his existence, from whose achievement he is temporarily obstructed by Lakatos's temptation: Piczenik betrays himself "weil er die Erfüllung seines Sendungsauftrags infrage stellt" 'because he calls into question the fulfillment of his mission' (305). This interpretation emphasizes the significance of the coral merchant's search for religious self-fulfillment and not that of his search for expiation for his violation of the order of redemption.

37. Heizmann analyzes Piczenik's fascination with the sea and the Leviathan as an indication of the need to restore a mythical time that has been disturbed through history's intrusion ("Mythen und Masken" 203). The conflict between different conceptions of time is once again present here. However, the time that is restored through the final return to the world of the Leviathan should not necessarily be understood as a return to a static or cyclical time outside of history. According to Tamás Lichtmann, the Leviathan, as a messianic symbol, announces a future Utopia and therefore conveys the hope of a final redemption of history itself: "Die Heimat der Juden ist in die messianische Zukunft (Utopie) verlegt, die einzige Heimat des Korallenhändlers ist der Grund des Ozeans, er gehört zu den Korallen" 'The homeland of the Jews is displaced into the messianic future (Utopia); the only home of the coral merchant is the ocean's bottom, he belongs to the corals' (51).

38. Roth's religious conception of sin and redemption is different from the theological-Christian emphasis on subjective, intentional processes. For him, as for the Judaic tradition from which he draws inspiration, sin and redemption are objective occurrences in which the individual participates almost without volition, guided

by a divine plan that exceeds the capacity of human understanding or subjective perception. In a 1937 article titled "Emigration," Roth voices this conviction by using the case of the Jewish refugees: "ein vertriebener Jude—selbst, wenn er ohne Rassengesetze in seiner Heimat ein SA-Mörder geworden wäre, bleibt doch ein Vertriebener, und wir, die wir an Gott glauben, müssen an diesen Vertriebenen die göttliche Gnade erkennen, die ihn verhindert hat, ein Mörder zu werden—und wir haben nicht nach seinen verhinderten Intentionen zu urteilen, sondern nach seinem Schicksal. Arm ist er, elend ist er, er verdient nicht nur Hilfe, er fordert sie mit Recht" 'an expelled Jew, even if he had become an SA [short for *Sturmabteilung*, or Storm Detachment] murderer were there no racial laws in his homeland, remains yet an expellee, and we, who believe in God, must recognize in him the divine grace that has prevented him to become a murderer. We should not judge him by his foiled intentions, but by his fate. Poor is he, miserable he is, he does not only deserve help, he rightly demands it' (*Werke* 3: 756). Destiny has the power to bring about transgressions but also redemption through divine intervention and often in spite of the individual efforts. Kartak is a compelling example of this type of redemption through the power of destiny.

39. Kesten sees in "The Legend of the Holy Drinker" a confirmation of Roth's pessimistic philosophy of eternal damnation: "er beweist, daß dem Verlorenen durch nichts zu helfen ist, nicht einmal durch eine wunderbare Kette von Wundern" 'he proves that nothing can be done to help the lost, not even through a wonderful chain of miracles' (113). Similarly, Düllo argues that the apparently redemptive ending of the story should not deceive the reader into believing in the possibility of a real transfiguration. Roth is far more interested in demonstrating the circularity and hopelessness of history: "Denkt man an Roths ausdauernden und so vielfachen literarischen wie journalistischen Diskurs über das Thema 'alt/neu' . . . dann sind wir an einem ernüchternden, alles anders als versöhnlichen Schluß angelangt, darüber sollte auch die tröstend-melancholische Kehre am Ende der Novelle nicht hinwegtäuschen" 'If one thinks about Roth's persistent and diverse literary and journalistic discourse on the subject of "old/new" . . . , we arrive at a sobering, and in no way conciliatory, conclusion; the soothing and melancholy twist at the end of the novella should not deceive us' (308). What the two critics fail to observe, however, is the transfiguration of the earthly notion of damnation into salvation—from the perspective of achieved redemption, everything that in reality is condemned appears as saved and vice versa. Steinmann correctly reminds us of the Christian significance of this inversion as it appears in the Epistle to the Corinthians (3:19): "the wisdom of this world is foolishness with God" (*Von der Würde* 118).

40. The same Chasidic fascination with the holiness of the simple life of the beggar and drunkard is also illustrated in Manès Sperber's memoir *God's Water Carriers*. Urtschy, the old village beggar and drunk who lives on people's almsgiving, pays an unexpected visit to the author's father one night to ask him for help with a night prayer whose lines he could not remember. The piety of the drunk leaves an indelible mark on the young author's memory: "He was not acting from fear of angering God through an omission; rather, he was driven by that peculiar Hasidic love for God, who is the worshipper's giving, serving older brother and comforter" (*God's Water Carriers* 66). From this perspective, Kartak's sense of duty for the mission he needs to carry out appears not as an external necessity but instead as an internal necessity, related to the holy unity between the character and God.

Chapter 4

Memory, Restitution, Justice: The Search for Redemption in Joseph Roth's Historical Fiction

At the end of the novel *Zipper and His Father*, Roth expresses, through the voice of the narrator, his resignation about the incapacity of the modern world to understand and accommodate the unfortunate Central European "lost generation," a generation educated in the spirit of the imperial values and confronted at the end of World War I with a totally changed reality. The meaninglessness of the life of this generation appears to him as a metaphor for the alienation of the individual in the modern society, alienation that could find a solution only in the hope of a redemption beyond the limits of chronological time, in a utopian future: "there does exist somewhere a region in which the traces of our playing are recorded, illegibly, but in some strange way effectively, if not today, then years hence, and if not years hence, then millennia hence" (*Zipper* 245). The tragic condition of the lonely individual is not visible to the other members of society, who are blinded by their own historical hubris and pay no attention to the existential and moral corruption of the world around them. For this reason, the present, understood as the uncritical investment in the immediacy of the empirical, cannot offer any hope for redemption to the individual. If on the other hand this individual condition may "leave traces" that will become visible only in a distant, uncertain future, it results that any possibility for reparation resides in the future's ability to observe the past and do justice to it. As Roth declares in a 1928 letter to Stefan Zweig, modernity strips the individual even of the ability to experience his own tragic condition in an authentic way, for which reason this condition becomes visible only from the point of view of the historical process itself: "I had qualms, I have qualms about that 'tragic' component, I think our postwar man no longer has that 'classical' capacity for tragedy, which is no longer a component of character but is still present in the 'historical view'" (*Joseph Roth: A Life* 116). As a consequence, the "historical view" ("historische Betrachtung") and reconstruction of the past is the only means through which justice can be imparted to the victim. This act of recognition through historical reconstruction manages to conjure up the trauma of the past and heal it through a gesture of identification and ethical comprehension.

This convergence between the ethical intelligibility of the world and its historical reconstruction constitutes a dominant concern in Roth's late novels and is highlighted particularly in the novels of historical inspiration. Some of Roth's late novels, particularly those of religious nature, already touch on the problem of time in relation to humans' redemptive potential. By developing an understanding of tradition that goes beyond the conventional confinement to the heritage of a given past and to its resistance to change, these novels emphasize a form of active stoicism in which the individual does not seek refuge from the challenges of history through restorative or escapist fantasies but instead engages with them in a morally responsible manner, rooted in the awareness of the challenges of the present. This unconventional idea of stoicism stems from a Judaic conception of individual moral responsibility, a conception that attempts to reconcile the inscrutability of divine will and the purposefulness of human action. In this sense it is reminiscent of Franz Rosenzweig's notion of active expectation, Bloch's hopeful expectation, or Max Brod's fusion of "activity" and "waiting in humility" (*Paganism* 78). Roth's conception of tradition as "living" tradition, bequeathed from the past yet continually reactualized in the present in the form of moral responsibility, allows him to bridge the gap between past and present in what some critics saw as a neo-Chasidic moral contemporaneity of all times, of which Scholem also spoke: "Mit dem anamnestischen Bewußtsein universaler geschichtlicher Solidarität ist Roth der jüdischen Tradition verpflichtet" '[In his use of] the anamnestic consciousness of universal historical solidarity, Roth is beholden to the Jewish tradition' (Steinmann, *Von der Würde* 15). The moral unity of the world functions for Roth in the "here and now" of every new event that connects humanity across time and space. As he points out in the 1938 article "Dem Anschein nach," "Vielleicht kann es eine wirtschaftliche 'Autarkie' geben; eine sittliche ist unmöglich" 'Perhaps there may exist an economic "autarky"; a moral one is impossible' (*Werke* 3: 829).

The fact that for Roth the autarky of the moral mind is not possible has definite implications for his conception of history. Insofar as the course of modern history is based on the notion of linear progress and on emancipation from the past through the dissolution of the ties between individual and community, between the explicit laws of reason and the unwritten laws of tradition, and between private freedom and ethical norms, moral judgment becomes necessarily confined to a particular viewpoint that is absolute in itself but totally relative in relation to other viewpoints. This factionalism of values appears for Roth as a source of moral incapacitation and the ideal ground for the emergence of those cataclysmic disasters that shook the foundations of modernity. This state of affairs is described in his nonfictional novel *The Antichrist* through the metaphor of the inverted Babel tower: if in Genesis the tower failed because people's languages and, as a consequence, views on reality were confused, now even the awareness of this basic incommunicability no longer exists. Instead, everyone shares the illusion of a shared goal that is in reality a complete illusion. The metaphorical tower of modernity stands because it is rooted in its own self-delusion, in its complete separation from the past and from the others. It suggests a unity of purpose and a clarity of mind but hides the moral confusion on which it is built. It represents, in brief, not just confusion but instead confusion with the aspect of clarity ("confusion *within* the clarity itself," *Antichrist* 36). Against this fragmentation of the moral mind, fragmentation rooted in incommunicability, hubris, and forgetfulness, Roth raises the spectrum of memory and revision as a means to achieve a reunification of the moral consciousness of humanity. Memory and historical revision act as a defense against the ethical neutrality of instrumental rationality, a rationality that proceeds blindly ahead, in oblivion of the injustice it commits on those who are leveled under its march.

Roth's religious novels demonstrate that the deliverance of the individual from the disaster of history, a disaster in which he unintentionally participates, is possible only through the acquisition of moral clarity in relation to the world. His redemption, which is the deepest metaphysical longing of the human being, is dependent on the moral clarity that brings together the far and the near (Rosenzweig would say God and the Neighbor) and thus joins the religious and mundane dimensions of existence. The fact that for Roth salvation is simultaneously this worldly and otherworldly is an illustration of his belief in the necessity of reunifying the rational and theological dichotomies between self and world and between earthly existence and spiritual salvation. In this sense, the historical dimension of Roth's late novels is inseparable from the religious one: the meaning of historical reconstruction is tightly knit into the demand for moral clarity, for justice, and thus for redemption. This unification of the historical and the metaphysical is profoundly indebted to the Chasidic belief in the dialectical unity of the "*hitlahavut* (ecstasy) and *'avodah* (divine service)" where, in Martin Buber's words, "*hitlahavut* embraces God beyond time and space, [whereas] *'avodah* is the service of God in time and space" (qtd. in Mendes-Flohr, *Divided Passions* 86). The Jewish effort to unite these two twin aspects of existence provides Roth, as in Buber's case, with a model for humanity as a whole: the "most fundamental experience of the Jew [is the] 'striving for unity.' It was this striving for unity—within the personal, the political, and ontological spheres—[Buber argues], 'that makes Judaism a phenomenon of mankind, that transforms the Jewish question into a human question'" (Mendes-Flohr, *Divided Passions* 86).

Even though Roth's philosophy of history is not cohesively united into a solid theoretical text, it can be reconstructed from the smaller essays, articles, and epistles that deal with the problem of history. A brief sketch of Roth's philosophy of history will facilitate a clearer understanding of the redemptive nature of his historical novels, the role he assigns to memory, nostalgia, and mourning but most of all to moral clarity and the demand for justice. Because of Roth's emphasis on moral processes, the question of scientific accuracy that some critics raised in relation to his fictional reconstructions of past social, cultural, and individual phenomena appears to be *une question mal posée*.[1] By understanding the real objective of Roth's historical writings, which is to infuse history with a moral dimension that goes beyond mere empirical observation and objective historiography, one can interpret the liberties that the author takes in shaping his version of historical truth as a logical consequence of his philosophy of redemption.

Within the framework of Roth's pervasive critique of modernity, a special place is occupied by the logic of progress. Skeptical about the discourse of human progress in history from the very beginning of his writing career, Roth associates the optimistic logic of modern social and technological advancement with the hubris of a simplified conception of life. As early as 1920 he considered progress a blind, exclusionary force that eliminates any alternative modes of thinking or feeling. In "Die Auferstehung des Geistes," he decries the leveling work done by "die Lokomotive des technischen Fortschritts" 'the locomotive of technical progress,' which eliminated the traditional worldviews and values (*Werke* 1: 277). This logic, for which he finds the patent expression in American popular pragmatism, a logic "des grobkarierten Fortschritts, der Grammophonkultur und des Wolkenkratzers" 'of the uniform progress, the gramophone culture and the skyscraper,' as he writes in his 1921 article "Humanität" ("Humanity"), annihilates anything spiritual, especially the moral intelligibility of the world, and provides instead an ersatz ideology of reason that is supposed to offer the individual a simple, immediate answer to the most complex existential questions (*Werke* 1: 631). At the same time, the Soviet Union and its Bolshevik ideology represent the Eastern counterpart to the American ideology of progress. In 1926 Roth undertook a trip into the heart of the Soviet Union and concluded that "die frische, ahnungslose, gymnastische-hygienische rationale Geistigkeit Amerikas"

'America's fresh, unsuspecting, gymnastic-hygienic rational spirituality' characterizes the land of the revolution and its people who, instead of being liberated, were chained by the more severe mental chains of a philosophy of unswerving progress and material development that repressed humanity's deep longing for moral meaningfulness and the hope of redemption (Roth, *Der Neue Tag* 223).

The arrogance of autonomous rationality, its impetuous break with anything traditional and overconfidence in the laws governing a totally new age of humanity, led, in Roth's opinion, to a catastrophic evolution that is equally responsible for the rise of nationalism, world wars, economic depression, and social alienation. This modernity is "the Antichrist," as Roth explains in his apocalyptical nonfictional novel that shares the same name. The hubris of self-affirmation, which in the religious novels constitutes a source of decay and damnation for the individual, becomes in the historical novels a destructive force that devastates collectivities and entire civilizations. The restorative political fantasies that affected the European interwar period and that appeared as a reaction against social fragmentation and democratic alienation, such as fascism, are not, in Roth's opinion, the result of a desire to return to a premodern cultural and political matrix but instead are the extreme result of modernization and the culmination of its process of self-destruction.[2] The glorification of the mystical forces of the nation, the exclusionary logic of racism, and the hysteria of personal political ambition characterize the age of modernity, Roth argues in the 1936 lecture "Glauben und Fortschritt," an age that has severed all the bridges linking it to the traditional world:

> Nein, meine Damen und Herren, die Schrecken unserer Tage sind nicht etwa 'ein Rückfall'—sondern viel eher authentische blutige Zeugnisse gegen unsere Neuzeit; vielleicht sogar ein *Probe-Ausfall* in die Zeiten, die noch kommen werden. Sie vermitteln uns, diese neuzeitlichen Schrecken, keineswegs etwa einen *Nach*geschmack des Vergangenen, sondern, so fürchte ich, einen entsetzlichen Vorgeschmack des Kommenden. (*Werke* 3: 694)

> No, ladies and gentlemen, today's horrors are not "a relapse," but rather authentic bloody evidence against our modern times; perhaps even an inroad into the times that are yet to come. They convey to us, these modern horrors, by no means an aftertaste of the past, but I fear, a dreadful foretaste of what is coming.

The cause of this degeneration rests with the very principle of progress, which excludes alternative developments, including the possibility of historical relapse, and suppresses marginal and traditional modes of understanding the world:

"[die geschichtliche] Dynamik, die beiseite drängt, was dem schnurgeraden Positivismus eines undialektischen Fortschrittdenkens nicht in den Weg passt" '[the historical] dynamics that pushes aside what does not fit into the dead straight positivism of a nondialectical philosophy of progress' (Pauli 37). This conception of progress, Roth argues, fails to understand that humanity does not grow uniformly and that history does not unfold linearly; instead, each follows a logic of its own. The ideology of progress is not interested in the moral development of the individual; it follows the logic of material growth and mistakes technological progress for actual human advancement: "Man glaubt, die Menschheit wachse wie das Kind mit der Zeit aus den Kinderschuhen" 'It is thought that mankind grows with time out of its infancy, like the child does' (*Werke* 3: 695).[3] Progress without moral development—that is to say, change produced outside of the spiritual tradition bequeathed by the past generations and without the aspiration for redemption—is an act of sinful conceit motivated by the desire to escape the moral responsibility with which we come into the world: "Ich bedauere es . . . einfach deshalb, weil alle Erfindungen . . . uns nicht einen Schritt höherbringen werden; im besten Fall zehntausend Schritte weiter" 'I regret it . . . simply because all inventions . . . will not take us a step higher; in the best case ten thousand steps further' (699). This view of progress leads Magris to the conclusion that "Roth sieht den Verlauf der Geschichte als einen Triumphzug des *esprit bourgeois* in den verschiedensten politischen Formen; der *esprit bourgeois* und sein unaufhaltsamer Sieg sind in seinen Augen Beweis und gleichzeitig Metapher für die Geschichte als Involution und Rückshritt, für die Natur als Stand der Sünde und der Verderbnis" 'Roth sees the course of history as a triumphal procession of the *esprit bourgeois* in the most varied political forms; the *esprit bourgeois* and its unstoppable victory are, in his view, proof of and at the same time metaphor for history as involution and regress, for nature as a state of sin and corruption' (Magris, *Weit von wo* 187).

While Roth declares himself not to be the adversary of reason and progress per se, he claims that they should assume the role that God intended for them, namely that of providing humanity with a tool for improvement in view of the redemptive hope that awaits at the end of history. He thus strips the concepts of reason and progress of their secular meaning and characteristic autonomous function and fuses them into the redemptive logic of history, in a manner reminiscent of Bloch's unification of rationality and Utopia. In a 1934 article titled "Eine Gewalt hat sich zwischen uns und die Gnade der Vernunft gestellt" ("A Force Came between Us and the Grace of Reason") Roth writes that "Der Verstand ward uns gegeben, damit wir mit seiner Hilfe die schwere

Not unserer Hände entlasten und damit wir allmählich lernen, unsern Kopf, der nach dem Ebenbilde Gottes geschaffen ist, aufrecht zu tragen, immer aufrechter, damit er dem Himmel entgegenrage, wo er gleichsam sein erhabenes und ewiges Spiegelbild findet" 'The intellect was given to us so that we remove the heavy burden of our hands with its help, and thus we gradually learn to hold our head, which was created in the image of God, upright, and still more so, so that it approaches heaven, where it finds, as it were, its sublime and eternal reflection' (*Werke* 3: 567).

Historical change becomes meaningful only when it serves the moral comprehension of the universe, and this moral comprehension rests, unlike the rational comprehension of the universe, on unification and not on separation, whether it is the unification of the present and the past or that between the distant and the near. Roth's 1925 travels to southern France bear testimony to the crystallization of these ideas of redemptive unity of all space and time into a continuum that makes the individual part of the whole world and of the entire history. The segregation of nations and countries that forms the core of the modern states is transgressed in Provence by traditional forms of human solidarity and communal life that go unchanged for millennia. Roth discovers here a form of belonging that reaches deeper than any other form of identity, precisely because it is rooted in humanity itself. Everyone is at home in southern France; countries and nations, the faraway and the near, dissolve into a single entity: "That's how small the world is. And if you think some of it is foreign, you're mistaken. Everywhere is home" (*Report* 40).

Tightly knit into the spatial unity of the world is its temporal unity. In southern France history lives in the present; it is not a reality encountered in museums or history textbooks. Unlike Northern Europe, where yesterday is separated from today and today from tomorrow in an unsurpassable logic of temporal irreversibility, time appears here to be the same, almost static. Instead of a succession of separate moments, the temporality of this world is distinguished through its metaphysical unity. The connection with the redemptive Beyond, with God, is what unites all the moments of this world, from Roman antiquity to the present and to the future: "In essence all these constructions were the same: in their pure lack of aim, which is at the same time the highest aim of all: to reach God" (*Report* 87). This "contemporaneity for all tradition," as Scholem put it, has the ability to protect the individual from the vagaries of history, from the "avalanches that are in store," by offering not an escape from time but rather a connection with time, one that was severed by modern rationality and linear history: "Happy land in which one can dream again, and learn to trust the energies of the past, which we thought—like so much else—a mistake and a lie in our schoolbooks!" (75). This notion of time reenthrones the individual moral conscience in history, makes it take responsibility for the past, present, and future. Hence, the purpose of history is to prevent injustices from remaining without repair and our advance into the future from being a blind march forward that leaves a pile of disasters in its wake. As in Benjamin's philosophy of history, for Roth, as he puts it in "Glauben und Fortschritt," history can emerge in its true dimension only when this injunction of messianic redemption takes place inside the historical continuum and when humanity gives itself its true value, that of the way that goes "nach der Tiefe und nach der Höhe: dem Glauben also; *dem Vertikalen und nicht dem Horizontalen*" 'to the depth and to the height: to the faith, thus; to the vertical and not to the horizontal' (*Werke* 3: 700).

The regressive longing therefore corresponds to a redemptive desire, which Roth contrasts with the progressive ideology of modernity. This is the manner in which the past can be brought back to life and understood, recognized, in order for the present to absolve itself from the burden of its own sinful forgetfulness of those past lives that were annihilated in the course of linear history. Magris draws a valid parallel between Roth's view of history and that embraced by Walter Benjamin: "Ohne auch nur von weitem an die Tiefe Benjamins heranzukommen, . . . versteht auch Roth tatsächlich die Geschichte als Geschichte der Besiegten" 'Without even remotely approaching Benjamin's profoundness, . . . in fact Roth also understands history as the history of the vanquished' (*Weit von wo* 45). Reconstructing a painful past can open the way for a moral restoration of history to its normal course. In a review of Hans Tietze's book *Wien* (*Vienna*) of 1932, Roth uses his regressive historical conception to show that history has committed a gross injustice against the Habsburg monarchy and against the emblem of Austrian culture, Vienna. The role of fiction or memoir, Roth argues, is to "show" history the disaster for which it is responsible, to moralize it in view of a possible reparation and conciliation with its own past: "Wenn es möglich wäre, der Geschichte die Sinnlosigkeit vorzuwerfen, mit der sie die österreichische Monarchie im Jahre 1918 behandelt hat, so würde es genügen, ihr die Stadt Wien zu zeigen" 'If it were possible to reproach history the senselessness with which it dealt with the Austrian monarchy in 1918, it would be enough to show it the city of Vienna' (*Werke* 3: 444). This act of rehashing the past, of "taking history for a walk" through the old times that are no more, as Roth himself put it, has a regenerative function. The sense of historical reconstruction acquires thus a religious significance for the Austrian writer, being intimately connected with the demand for justice and deliverance: "Als religiös qualifiziert erweist sich die Literatur Roths nicht nur in ihrem schöpferischen Sprachverständnis, sondern auch in einer chronikalischen Erzählung, die um die Erlösende Kraft der Erinnerung weiß und sie in den Dienst derer stellt, die in den Annalen der Weltgeschichte gerade nicht verewigt sind" 'Roth's literature proves itself to be religiously qualified not only through its creative understanding of language, but also through a chronicle-like account that knows the redemptive power of memory and puts it in the service of those who are not immortalized in the annals of world history' (Steinmann, *Von der Würde* 14). It is the responsibility of the historian, as Benjamin and Bloch understood this profession, to show that "there are . . . clearly 'negative aspects' to empirical reality which the historian must not only acknowledge but negate through pointing to the possibility of an alternative, 'transcendent' reality" (Mendes-Flohr, *Divided Passions* 375).

Past, Present, and Future: The Eternal Time of Redemption

Roth's 1932 novel *The Radetzky March*, considered a masterpiece of interwar Austrian literature and by many the author's most important work, reiterates the same problem of moral reparation for a historical past that disappeared much too quickly and unjustly under the flattening force of modern history. The novel feeds on the assumption that the passage from the imperial world of prewar Austria to the republican interwar period inaugurated a paradigmatic shift not only in the political, social, and cultural practices of all of Central Europe but also in the existential rapport between the individual and his surrounding world and equally in the type of historical time to which the individual is subjected. While the early novels focus on the alienation and moral breakdown of interhuman relations, they also emphasize the schizophrenia of the modern mind, torn between the longing for communitarian identification and the drive toward individualist self-affirmation. This constant dehumanizing impulse is caused in these novels by an underlying logic of progress and competition that parts history into victors and losers, butchers and victims, and pushes characters such as Tunda, Zipper, Brandeis, and Kargan through an unknown, meaningless life. *The Radetzky March* offers, by contrast, an alternative both to the social and moral relations framing the individual and to the type of historical time that conditions these relations. This alternative expresses the possibility for a conciliation between the individual and the universe, at social and moral levels, and offers, in a similar manner to the novels of religious inspiration, a positive solution to the crisis of modernity through the redemption of life in history.

The contrast between the passage of time in the old premodern world and in the new modern one often touched on in the novel is rendered by Roth in moral terms: the old world was based on remembrance and on the moral agreement with traditional values, while the new world is based on forgetfulness and rapid change. In the new world the individual is urged to pursue his ambitions alone, while society is regulated by mechanical and rational laws that have no support in tradition. The discrepancy between a "communitarian" premodern world and a "social" modern one (to borrow a Tönniesean distinction) acquires for Roth a moral significance: the imperial world is the world of the redemptive unity of the individual and the world, whereas the modern republican world represents the failure of this unity. Like Buber, who strives for a "real community" (*Paths in Utopia* 145), Roth yearns for an ideal community in which the contradictions of modern society are being lifted while simultaneously the harmony of the past is being restored, ushering in a new redeemed present. Naturally, his depiction of the imperial world is not the same as the "objective" political or social reality of the Dual Monarchy: "Nicht als eine politische Realität begriff er also die Donaumonarchie, sondern als Idee und Vision, als Chiffre und als eine rückwärts gewandte Utopie: Kakanien als Wille und Vorstellung" '[Roth] does not understand the Dual Monarchy as a political reality, but as an idea and vision, as a cipher, and as a backward-looking Utopia: Kakania as will and representation' (Reich-Ranicki, *Nachprüfung* 224).

The intentions of the author, expounded in the introduction to *The Radetzky March*, are explicitly moral: by resurrecting a deceased world, Roth taps into the historicity of the old redeemed world in an attempt to break the course of linear history that generates modern oblivion and indifference. The act of memory is not simply a nostalgic recollection of the imperial Austrian world, in the manner in which Stefan Zweig practices it in his memoir *The World of Yesterday*, but instead is a trial against history itself, whose insensible progress annihilated anything that stood in its way: "Ein grausamer Wille der Geschichte hat mein altes Vaterland, die österreichisch-ungarische Monarchie, zertrümmert" 'A cruel will of history has shattered my old fatherland, the Austro-Hungarian monarchy' (*Werke* 5: 874). In the same introduction, Roth ironically uses Schiller's notion of history as a "world tribunal" (later made famous by Hegel) with the intention of demonstrating, against the poet's belief that the course of history is an unfailing test of the logic of the world itself, that history can make judgment errors, as can any other earthly instance, and that an appeal is necessary in Austria's case: "Den Willen der Weltgeschichte erkannte ich wohl, ihren Sinn verstehe ich nicht immer. Wenn sie wirklich das Weltgericht ist, so erscheint sie mir zuweilen nicht weniger frei von Rechtsirrtümern und -fehlern als ein gewöhnliches Bezirks- oder Landesgericht" 'To be sure, I recognized the will of world history, but I do not always understand its meaning. If indeed it [history] is the tribunal of the world, it appears to me that sometimes it is no less free from legal errors and mistakes than an ordinary district or regional court' (874). The historicity of modern times is characterized by a blind onward progression, a progression that leaves behind a trail of ruin, Roth argues, in a manner reminiscent of Benjamin's metaphor of the angel of history: "Die Völker vergehn, die Reiche verwehn. (Aus den vergehenden besteht die Geschichte)" 'The peoples pass, the kingdoms scatter. (Of those that pass does history consist)' (875). It is therefore the author's responsibility to suspend the time of conventional history and redeem those destinies cut short by its oblivious march through reminiscence: "Er [der Roman] hat die erhabene und bescheidene Aufgabe, die privaten Schicksale aufzuklauben, welche die Geschichte fallen läßt, blind und leichtfertig, wie es scheint" 'It [the novel] has the august and modest task to scoop up the private destinies that history dropped, blindly and frivolously, as it seems' (875).[4] The author bears a moral responsibility to remind the readers of a prematurely obliterated reality, achieving thus the utopian emancipation of history by uniting the present moment of readership to the past in a simultaneously regressive and redemptive gesture: "[Die Erinnerung] darf nicht bloß Bild des Gewesenen sein, sondern soll Hoffnung des Kommenden sein, so wie auch der Mensch durch die Zeit nach vorn treibt, ins Kommende" '[Memory] must not be merely a picture of what has been, but should be the hope of what is coming, just as the human being is pushing forward through time' (Treitler 211).[5]

The obligation to remember the past takes on a particularly Jewish significance, as the act of remembrance is not a mere act of memory; it is imbued with the presence of redemption and with the imperative of justice and moral judgment. Historian Yosef Hayim Yerushalmi makes this clear when he asserts that Israel's past cannot be simply left to the whims of an imperfect memory. The act of remembering is a collective obligation: "Memory is, by its nature, selective, and the demand that Israel remember is no exception" (10). What history leaves in its path is not simply dead but rather the living trace that links the present with the past, which is why the modern individual has the obligation to face the historical past in moral terms. As the Hungarian Jewish philosopher Agnes Heller argues, the difference between mere memorialist archaeology and the act of remembrance consists in the fact that the former does not connect the present with the past, while the latter does. The act of nostalgia best represents this attitude: "It is nostalgia that resurrects the dead past. It cannot resurrect the dead . . . but it makes the dead speak and act as if they were alive" (40). Nostalgia is the act of remembrance that brings back to memory the injustices of the past that were inflicted on the forerunners in the form of their historical finitude, of their failed projects or unachieved goals. It continually feeds on the feeling of distress that accompanied the original acts of injury and allows the present individuals to still relate to their past in a direct, almost organic manner. The same sense of moral responsibility informs the fellow Galician Jewish author Manes Sperber's memorialist impulse, which stays under the sign of the advice his family gave him as a child: "Gedenk! Erinnere dich! Tizkor! Since earliest childhood, I had been cautioned to 'remember' in three languages [Yiddish, German, Hebrew]: . . . Whenever you set foot in the place where you did an injustice to someone else, you shall feel the woe that you were, are, shall be guilty of'" (*God's Water Carriers* 36). The contemporary Hungarian Jewish author György Konrád also derives his own nostalgia for Central Europe from the moral obligation to relive the past, an obligation inscribed in the Jewish theme of remembering the past, of repentance and redemption: "accepting also means wanting to remember, and suffering. We get the entire past of our chosen community, a past that includes all its monstrous figures" (80). In the same manner, *The Radetzky March* shapes the reconstruction of imperial Austria on a memorialist urge that has its roots in the Jewish philosophy of memory or, as Almuth Hammer put it, in the Judaic connection between divine election and remembering ("Verknüpfung von Erwählung und Erinnern," 69).[6]

The Radetzky March is, however, not a novel of glorification of the historical Habsburg past or of the utopian harmony between the individual and his contemporary world. It is a novel of decay, in the same manner in which many of Roth's earlier novels were. It is a metaphorical testament for a world in decomposition whose main protagonists, the three generations of the Trotta family, illustrate the gradual collapse of their world.[7] Aside from the three Trottas, the novel hosts a wider gallery of characters, including Emperor Franz Joseph I, with the intention of focusing on larger social and cultural phenomena that exceed the confines of private psychology or individual destiny. The multiperspectivism of the novel successively shifts the focus from the personal experience of history to the collective one, successfully managing to combine the view from "above" with that from "below" (to employ Georg Lukács's typology of the historical novel).[8] Along with its sequel, the 1938 *The Emperor's Tomb*, but also a few other novels and short stories staged against the background of the Austro-Hungarian dualist society, such as *The Tale of the 1002nd Night* (1939), *Weights and Measures*, "Stationmaster Fallmereyer" (1933), and "The Bust of the Emperor" (1935), *The*

Radetzky March builds a comprehensive gallery of typically Austrian characters, a veritable "*comédie autrichienne*" in which some saw a proof of continuity with the classical Austrian literature of Franz Grillparzer and Johann Nestroy (Kesten 101).

The novel opens with the mythical inception of the Trotta house in the fictional act of heroism of the infantry lieutenant Joseph Trotta during the Battle of Solferino. There on the battlefield, he single-handedly saves the life of the then young Emperor Franz Joseph, who had been recklessly exposed to enemy artillery fire by his staff officers. Due to his heroic act, the simple Slovenian peasant from Sipolje is raised in rank, knighted by the emperor, and quickly assimilated into the ranks of the Bohemian petty nobility: "Captain Trotta was severed from the long procession of his Slavic peasant forebears. A new dynasty began with him" (*Radetzky March* 6). The old peasant inside Trotta proves, however, to be too inflexible to let himself become entirely absorbed into a world characterized by the unwritten laws of monarchic governance, by the sophistication and grace of an office that bears no actual function, only symbolic function. When the second generation of Trottas comes into the world, he learns that the story of his simple act of heroism is used for propagandistic purposes by being turned into a tale of legendary proportions that children had to learn in school. Outraged by this falsification, he petitions the authorities, including the emperor himself, in order to restore the accurate truth to the actual story, yet he invariably receives the same answer: a story is never bound to a factual truth but instead is bound to the context in which it serves, to the moral that can be derived from it. In an official response from the ministry of education, it is stated that while the truth of the story must be retained in general lines, its didactic rendition should not be "dry" or "devoid of any spur to the imagination and any patriotic sentiments" (10). The emperor himself suggests that "people tell a lot of lies," and if one can learn something useful from a lie, why not accept it? (10). The image of the empire as an imaginary construction, propped up by a general moral attitude rather than by reality, thus confirms Hermann Broch's belief that imperial Austria "sich auf den Traum stützen musste, um real sein zu können" 'had to rely on the dream to be able to be real' (133). Jacques Le Rider draws on this paradoxical aspect of *The Radetzky March* when he analyzes the process of a "deconstructive construction" ("*dekonstruktiven Konstruction*") at work within the novel: "Indem Joseph Roth den Habsburgischen Mythos im *Radetzkymarsch* auf- und ausbaut, entmystifiziert er ihn zugleich durch den Hinweis auf die Lüge, die die Legende vom Helden von Solferino von der historischen Wahrheit entfernt hat" 'As he constructs and expands the Habsburg myth in *The Radetzky March*, Joseph Roth also demystifies it by referring to the lie that has detached the legend of the hero of Solferino from the historical truth' ("Arbeit" 26).

Incapable of grasping the symbolic nature of the establishment he represents, the now Baron Trotta withdraws to the isolation of his estate and leaves the scene open for his son, Baron Franz von Trotta und Sipolje, who represents the middle, golden age of the Trotta dynasty and around whom most of the novel revolves. Unlike his father, Franz Trotta follows an administrative career, becoming a district commissioner in a small Moravian town. In his provincial location, Baron von Trotta conscientiously acquits himself of the official and aristocratic responsibilities incumbent to his office, demonstrating in a manner different from that of his father his ability to represent the symbolical nature of imperial authority, an authority based on the preservation of the social and political status quo through a paternalistic yet tolerant supervision. The fine balance between the administrative and symbolic type of authority that he represents reflects the situation of the emperor, his hierarchical superior, who represented in the empire both the political authority of the state (although only nominally) and the religious one, as a successor of the lineage of Holy Roman emperors going back to Charles the Great. As a representative of imperial authority, Baron Franz von Trotta emulates the character and role of the emperor in the smallest details, with Roth intending to create in his person a mirror image of the emperor himself: his German was nasal, like that of Austrian "higher officials and lesser nobles" (26); his "elastic step" was similar to that of the kaiser (154), and even his whiskers were cut like those of Franz Joseph (26).[9] Through the person of the baron, the second-generation Slovenian peasant assimilates completely and freely assumes the solemnity and decorum characteristic of his social position.

Baron Franz von Trotta represents, however, a sad, almost quixotic figure. Although he embodies the symbolical principles of the imperial world, such as moderation, grace, loyalty, and traditionalism, he is confronted with the gradual corrosion of these values in late Austro-Hungarian society. He slowly and painfully realizes the anachronistic character of the type of authority that he represents and the unavoidable extinction to which his world is subjected in order to allow for a new ethos, characterized by the nationalism of the various ethnic groups within the empire, to take its place. In spite of his stern opposition, the baron, an exponent of an aristocracy of spirit more than of blood, acknowledges his defeat and realizes that the world he represents is destined to disappear in the darkness of historical forgetfulness, a realization accentuated by the failure of his son, Carl Joseph, to continue his role. Baron von Trotta's final death, simultaneous with that of Emperor Franz Joseph, unequivocally expresses the end of the Trotta dynasty and of the world that it stood for: "'I would like to have added,' said the mayor, 'that Herr von Trotta could not outlive the Kaiser. Don't you agree, Herr Doctor?' 'I don't know,' Dr. Skowronnek replied. 'I don't think either of them could have outlived Austria'" (331).

The third generation of Trottas, represented by the young Lieutenant Carl Joseph Trotta, the other central character of the novel, represents the decline of the Slovene dynasty against the background of normative confusion generated by the social, political, and above all moral transformation of the Austrian world. Raised by his father in the spirit of a strict discipline and respect for the values of the Habsburg hierarchy, Carl Joseph receives a military education in an attempt to reconnect the Trotta family with the military caste from which it derived its honor and standing. Carl Joseph is nevertheless a victim of this education, as his lack of parental affection alienates him from an emotional point of view and turns him into a melancholy figure incapable of coming to terms with his own identity and social role. In the figure of the young lieutenant, Roth expresses the personal side of the confrontation between the individual and society, demonstrating that the values that his father considered immutable and binding cannot, in themselves, guarantee individual happiness and meaningfulness.

Unlike Baron von Trotta, Carl Joseph is the free individual par excellence. He is not destined to become anything, to fill any predetermined office or to assume the fate of his surrounding world. As a result, he is the subject of unpredictable changes of fortune and is unlucky in almost everything that he undertakes: "Ahead of him lay a life of grief. He braced himself to endure it, pale and resolute, as befits a man" (38). His first adversity is caused by the death of Frau Slama, the wife of a local constable with whom Carl Joseph had his first love affair. The fate of the woman, who died trying to give birth to Trotta's progeny, places the young lieutenant before the experience of death, which is going to stay with him until the end of the novel. Incapable of experiencing any authentic emotion due to the conservative nature of his family and work environment, he measures the meaning of life in relation to the overriding presence of death, which offers a fitting outlet to his melancholy personality. Detached to a Moravian regiment after graduating from the cavalry military school, Carl Joseph is exposed to the rough life of the lower military echelons, where alcoholism, promiscuity, and decadence in general are rampant. This sharpens his sense of existential despondence, and only his friend, the Jewish doctor Max Demant, manages to temper it through his warmth and wisdom.

The relationship with Max Demant is short-lived, however, as the doctor dies in a duel over the honor of his wife, a duel for which Carl Joseph is indirectly responsible. Seeing himself once again responsible for the death of another close person, Lieutenant Trotta feels an overwhelming guilt: "He could never have put it into words, but we may say that he was unspeakably afflicted by the thought of having been a tool in the hands of misfortune" (114). Confused and disheartened, he abandons himself to the caprices of life, a young man who "lost his youth" in the stream of an incomprehensible destiny that promised him meaningfulness in the service of an abstract and distant power but actually offered him only the grief of death (39). The imagistic presence of death is emphasized by Roth in many instances that involve the young Trotta, such as that of his arrival at a remote Galician garrison, where he is transferred after the incident leading to Demant's death. There in the seclusion of the borderland where the Austrian world gradually melts into the Russian czarist one, the officers of both the Austrian and Russian armies occasionally celebrate together, unaware of the cruel fate awaiting them in only a few years' time. Carl Joseph's arrival seems, however, to bring the certitude of death a little bit closer: "not one of the czar's officers and one of His Apostolic Majesty's officers knew that Death was already crossing his haggard, invisible hands over the glass beakers from which the men drank" (132).

Lieutenant Trotta's life in the small borderland garrison proves to be a continuation of his earlier misfortune. The Galician district in which Roth places his hero is populated by characters who recall other novels, such as *Hotel Savoy*, *Weights and Measures*, and *The Silent Prophet*, while the description of the region bears remarkable resemblances to those in *Job*, *Tarabas*, and "Strawberries." Carl Joseph is confronted in the borderlands with a confusing world, split between the tumult of modernization and the peaceful atemporality of traditional lifestyle. The same ambiguity characterizes the moral sense of the people inhabiting this area, suggestively called by Wiebke Amthor *Grenzgänger* due to their ability to live between worlds and to challenge any conventional idea about the rule of law, the permanence of the nation-states, or the separation between right and wrong ("An den Toren Europas" 120). While some are honest and generous, such as the soldier Onufrij, others are unscrupulous, such as the usurer and smuggler Kapturak, a character present also in other Roth novels, including *The Silent Prophet* and *Weights and Measures*. The proletariat of the area, impoverished and exploited, is at the same time mutinous and violent. During a revolt at the local bristle brush factory, the ill-fated Carl Joseph is put in charge of the squadron that is supposed to disperse the demonstration. When without his intention the situation runs out of control, the soldiers shoot at the workers. The order to fire into the crowd came from Lieutenant Trotta yet without his will, as if a higher authority exerted command over him: "Someone, he believed, raised his hand, someone else's voice coming out of him repeated the order—'Fire!'" (210). Pardoned by the emperor in grateful recollection of Carl Joseph's grandfather's act of heroism, Trotta muses over the meaning of the events that destiny prepared for him: "Fate had prepared this political demonstration for him. That was why he had wound up at the border. He was certain now that a scheming, treacherous fate had granted him his furloughs in order to destroy him upon his return" (204).

In his remote area of the empire, Lieutenant Trotta's life degenerates gradually. The noble progeny of two generations of Austrian barons loses any sense of decorum and moderation, drifting into alcoholism. Pushed into further difficulties by a reckless commitment to take over a considerable financial debt that a friend incurred over a game of cards, Carl Joseph extricates himself from this dirty business only when the emperor himself, at Baron Franz von Trotta's petition, agrees to cover for the son's debt. Profoundly disillusioned by his own life, Carl Joseph eventually comes to the realization that leaving the army would be his best option. A sense of general meaninglessness and decline characterizes his bitter recognition that military life cannot offer him a direction or a concretion of any of the virtues that it was supposed to instruct, such as loyalty and honor. Baron von Trotta experiences his son's resolution as a catastrophe of existential proportions: "Everything, everything in the world seemed meaningless. The end of the world was nigh!" (235). Carl Joseph's decision is reinforced by the reaction of imperial Hungarian officers at the news about the assassination of Archduke Franz Ferdinand in Sarajevo: instead of mourning the news they celebrate it, giving vent to their nationalist and separatist ambitions and provoking Lieutenant Trotta's unexpected furious reaction. Significantly enough, it is in this moment that the young Trotta feels his military and aristocratic vocation awoken for the first time; in his reaction against the detractors of the throne, he feels a genuine expression of the spirit of his ancestors, defenders of the monarchy and of the emperor: "He felt as one with his grandfather. He himself was the Hero of Solferino" (299).

Carl Joseph's reaction has a cathartic function for him, and he turns suddenly from a pawn in the hands of destiny into an independent individual with his own will. This revelation, presented by Roth in the style of the other epiphanies that make characters such as Piczenik of "The Leviathan" and Golubtschik of *Confession of a Murderer* reach a religious insight into the source of their own misery, contributes to Lieutenant Trotta's sober awareness of the necessity of leaving the army and starting a simple life in a Galician village. By beginning a new life in the posture of a simple peasant, Carl Joseph brings evidence of his moral transformation, which reassigns him the role of moral judge of his own life. His quasi-religious metamorphosis, indicative of the desire to give up ambition and empty formalism, brings him back into the fold of a tradition that is meaningful for him, that of his Slovenian peasant ancestors: "Each morning he strolled through the adjacent villages. 'Praised be Jesus Christ!' said the peasants. 'Forever. Amen!' Trotta replied. Like them he walked with slightly bent knees. That was how the peasants of Sipolje had walked" (308).

Redeemed from his moral decay on a spiritual level, Carl Joseph finds his death shortly thereafter during the hostilities of World War I, in which he fights as a drafted civilian. His death, which occurs during an unsuccessful attempt to bring water to his ambushed platoon, does not result from a heroic deed that would place him in his grandfather's illustrious lineage. Instead of being glorious, it is humble: Carl Joseph dies for the simple soldiers while trying to quench their thirst, not save their lives. The trivial death of the character is reminiscent of that of Tarabas and Eibenschütz and expresses Roth's conviction that the redemption that the individual experiences in the world can take final form only in death, in the eventual abandonment of every earthly ambition. Unlike his progenitor, Carl Joseph must find his own sense of deliverance by atoning for the moral debacle of an entire world of which he represents an integral part. In this sense, he embodies the condition of the characters from the religious novels: "The end of the grandson of the Hero of Solferino was a commonplace end, not suitable for textbooks in the elementary schools and high schools of Imperial and Royal Austria. Lieutenant Trotta died holding not a weapon but two pails" (320).

The tripartite structure of the historical narrative of *The Radetzky March*, divided among the first, second, and third generations of the Trotta family, corresponds to a sequence of rise, zenith, and decline of Austria's late imperial stage, which Roth analyzes from a moral-sociological perspective, using the actual historical development of the Austrian Empire in a selective and figurative manner. The author adopts this method with the purpose of re-creating a type of historical intelligibility that corresponds to his own moral projections. A proof of this "distorted" historical effect is the countertempo of the development of the Trotta dynasty and that of the Austrian Empire: the accession of the Slovenian Joseph Trotta to the ranks of the nobility is evocatively rooted in the 1859 Battle of Solferino, which marked the beginning of the end for the multinational Austrian Empire. In the aftermath of the defeat Austria lost Lombardy and in the following decades started to lose other provinces as a result of the pressure from other empires and of the rise of national consciousness throughout Central Europe. Roth exposes the factors leading to the gradual erosion of the empire through his openly hostile remarks about the growing influence of Prussia and the rise of nationalism (especially Hungarian nationalism, which led to the dualist compromise of 1867), yet he creates a sense of majestic permanence through the immobility of the Trottas' attachment to the monarchic contract, which made some critics consider *The Radetzky March* an anti-*Bildungsroman*.[10]

The making of the Trotta dynasty, with its rise in the age of actual imperial decline, offers a moral counternarrative to the social dynamics of the late Austrian Empire. The ascent of the newly ennobled Slovenian family to a position of authority in the second half of the nineteenth century corresponds, on the one hand, to a decrease in the influence of the aristocracy and, on the other, to the actual historical rise of the Austrian liberal bourgeoisie (Schorske 5). The political growth of a culture of enlightened capitalism created many frictions between the old nobility and the urban high and petit bourgeoisie (dramatically pitched against each other during the Revolution of 1848), concluding with the limitation of aristocratic authority and the gradual transformation of Austria from a feudal society to a relatively modern one in only several decades. And although historically antagonistic, in *The Radetzky March* the bourgeoisie and the nobility do not clash with each other. The friendship between Dr. Skowronnek and Baron Franz von Trotta bears testimony to the "harmonious accord" between two distinct social strata (233). Although belonging to different social categories, they form a small community based on an "aristocracy of the spirit" ("die Aristokratie des Geistes") (Wörschnig 94) that unites them in their moral relationship with the world:

> That was a stern time, as we know. But it recognized exceptions and even liked them. It was one of the rare aristocratic principles, such as that mere commoners were second-class human beings yet certain middle-class officers became personal adjutants to the Kaiser; that Jews could claim no higher distinctions yet certain Jews were knighted and became friends with archdukes. (*Radetzky March* 187)

Roth's novels do not reject social mobility and the bourgeoisie a priori, although in many cases the secular tendencies associated with the bourgeois world constitute a source of social criticism. He is actually more interested in the moral content of the actions undertaken by the various social actors and not in their social position. Roth's nuanced employment of the term "bourgeois" brings evidence to this, as Magris shows, being pejoratively connoted in reference to Germany but positively connoted in Jewish and Austrian context (Magris, *Weit von wo* 124). The Trottas' assimilation into the noble class offers proof of the acceptability of social mobility, which constitutes one of the virtues of the permissive imperial world, yet Carl Joseph's own return to the peasant roots of the family demonstrates that assimilation is not a virtue in itself. For Roth, any social position has to be in a moral balance with the individual's personality in order to avoid becoming a source of corruption and suffering.

By associating the imperial authority with the liberal bourgeoisie in the name of higher moral principles, Roth also touches on a social reality of the late imperial world, namely the political dependence of the bourgeois strata on the person of the monarch, whose authority they acknowledged, although they felt at odds with the royal petty nobility that always claimed actual political power: "because of its weakness, it [the Austrian bourgeoisie] remained both dependent upon and deeply loyal to the emperor as a remote but necessary father-protector" (Schorske 7). However, Roth glosses over the political causes and implications of this dependency that he celebrates as a source of moral convergence between two worlds that, in spite of their differences, retained a common attachment to the simple morality of life, the dignified asceticism of authority, and traditional humanism. The true usurpers of the aristocratic world are, in Roth's opinion, the representatives of the mass ideologies of the late nineteenth and early twentieth centuries who pursue the replacement of the transcendent authority of the monarch with the secular one of the class or the nation: "Vom Kaiser aus führt ein näherer Weg zum bosnischen Maronibrater und zum galizischen Talmudjuden als zum sudetendeutschen Historiker der Wiener Universität" 'A closer route leads from the Emperor to the Bosnian chestnut roaster and the Galician Talmud Jew than to the Sudeten German historian from the University of Vienna' writes Roth in his 1939 "Rede über den alten Kaiser" ("Speech about the Old Emperor") (*Werke* 3: 940).[11]

Roth further distorts the social reality of Austria at the end of the nineteenth century through his moral polarization between aristocracy and bourgeoisie on the one hand and the mass ideologies of socialism and nationalism on the other. Although Baron von Trotta grows suspicious of the nationalist and socialist agitation—"Long ago, in the quiet years . . . there had been no autonomists, no Socialists, and relatively few 'suspicious individuals'. And as the years wore by . . . those groups were growing, spreading, and becoming dangerous" (*Radetzky March* 142) just like another character, Count Morstin of "The Bust of the

Emperor," who has as "only evident passion . . . his opposition to the 'nationality question'" (*Collected Shorter Fiction* 241)—in fact the expansion of the nationalist ideology was directed first and foremost against the democratic and capitalist bourgeoisie and not against the aristocracy. In his rallying cry under the banner of German nationalism, Georg von Schönerer, a second-generation aristocrat, appealed to the metaphors of feudal Austria: "He rejoiced in epithets redolent of chivalry: 'Knight George' or—after his estate in Lower Austria—'the Knight of Rosenau.' The official song of his party, *Ritter Georg hoch*!, was sung to the tune with which the Austrians traditionally honored their military hero, Prince Eugene of Savoy" (Schorske 120).[12] Similarly, the political strategy of Karl Lueger, the anti-Semitic mayor of Vienna at the turn of the twentieth century, was to create "a coalition of the aristocracy and masses against the liberal middle class" (136). When Roth fails to acknowledge the ideological and reactionary character of the alliance between the interests of a gradually weakening nobility and those of the populist and nationalist movements of Austria at the end of the nineteenth century, he intentionally creates a distorted social reality that corresponds to his own concepts of tradition and aristocracy, which are to be understood in a moral, not actual historical, sense: "Klassizismus und Adel sind darüber hinaus Metaphern einer metahistorischen Haltung und stehen in diesem Sinn bei Roth eng mit der leidenschaftlichen jüdischen Ablehnung der Geschichte, die ja Exilgeschichte ist, in Beziehung" 'Moreover, classicism and nobility are metaphors of a metahistorical attitude, and in this sense, in Roth's work they are closely related to the passionate Jewish rejection of history, which is a history of exile' (Magris, *Weit von wo* 121).

Even the emperor's general connection to the interests of a conservative clerical political structure, which was not especially welcoming toward the petit bourgeoisie and toward the Jews, does not sway Roth from his idealized attachment to Emperor Franz Joseph. Although Roth admits, in the same "Rede über den alten Kaiser," that the old emperor rejected the Jewish bourgeoisie, he considers his open contempt for the vulgar anti-Semites to be more revealing of his actual character: "Nun, wenn man auch nicht sagen kann, Kaiser Franz Joseph hätte die Juden geradezu geliebt, ganz gewiß ist es, daß er die Antisemiten verachtete" 'Well, if one cannot say that Emperor Franz Joseph really loved the Jews either, it is quite certain that he despised the anti-Semites' (*Werke* 3: 944). The emperor's invalidation of Karl Lueger's election as mayor of Vienna, motivated by political reasons, and his eventual recognition, motivated by equally political reasons, represent for Roth proof of Franz Joseph's moral stance. Roth is interested not in explaining the political mechanisms that facilitated the racist mayor's victory or the creation of a coalition of feudal and nationalist interests that threatened the liberal and Jewish bourgeoisie but instead in emphasizing the moral superiority of the old emperor who allegedly did not offer Lueger the courtesy due an elected mayor: "er empfing den Bürgermeister nur zweimal in Audienz. Und Kenner versichern, daß er ihn zweimal mit den Worten empfing: 'Sein S'stad!'" 'he received the mayor only twice in audience. And connoisseurs swear that twice he received him with the words: "be quiet!"' (944). Roth's disregard for Lueger's eventual victory, which represented undeniable evidence of the pervasiveness of anti-Semitism in late imperial Austrian politics, an anti-Semitism that had its roots in both the modern nationalist ideologies of the nineteenth century and the Catholic clericalism of the feudal nobility, is reminiscent of Stefan Zweig's denial of the anti-Semitic significance of the mayoral triumph of 1897: "Even when Lueger, the leader of the anti-Semitic party, became burgomaster of the city, no change occurred in private affairs, and I personally must confess that neither in school nor in the world of literature, have I ever experienced the slightest suppression or indignity as a Jew" (25).

For a reader familiar with Roth's late rhapsodizing of the imperial Austrian world and its characteristic representatives, the nobility, the military, and the emperor, his early articles criticizing the very same ruling hierarchy would appear as a surprising expression of an early socialist mind-set. However, these articles express not the viewpoint of an ideological socialist but instead that of a moralist, a perspective common not only to his late work but also his early work. In pages reminiscent of the tone of his later writings, Roth criticizes in these articles the immorality, incompetence, and absurdity of the Austrian imperial establishment.[13] In "Teisinger" (1920) and in "40 Mann = 6 Pferde" ("40 Man = 6 Horses") (1923), Roth denounces the madness and indifference that have pushed the masses of young men into the trenches of World War I as well as the irresponsible behavior of the Austrian officer body, who treated the mass of mobilized soldiers as nothing more than abstract figures in an odious war game. "Der Prinz" ("The Prince") (1922), on the other hand, mocks the indolent lifestyle and affected superiority of the aristocracy and gleefully hints at its anachronism and unavoidable disappearance, a situation that is mournfully presented in the late works. In "Kaisers Geburtstag" ("Emperor's Birthday"), an article from 1925, Roth reminds the reader that although the postwar republic did not turn out as revolutionary as they might have wanted, at least they should take solace in the fact that they witnessed the fall of the monarchy and in the realization that "was wir für Marmor hielten, Gips war" 'what we believed to be marble, was in fact plaster' (*Werke* 2: 336). If indeed, as Leopold Decloedt argues, in the young Roth "wird das Monarchische als Verkörperung des Überkommenen, des Bösen und Schlechten gesehen" 'the monarchy is seen as the incarnation of the conventional, of the evil and the bad' (272), how can the later change of heart be justified? Although Decloedt points to Roth's "zwiespältige Trauer" 'ambivalent grief' as a contiguous form of nostalgia that the aging Roth feels for his youth and, by implication, for the monarch but also to financial motivations, he fails to notice the consistencies behind the inconsistencies. They point to the fact that for Roth, it is not the actual historical or social identifications that bear significance but rather the moral constitution of reality, which often tolerates noticeable contradictions in the name of an allegorical view of the world.[14] The aristocracy that he criticizes in his early works becomes an object of veneration in his late works, because what Roth means by "aristocracy" in the late works is primarily the "aristocracy of spirit," an allegorical version of aristocracy that incorporates equally the emperor and the Galician Jewish peasants.

The moral tone of Roth's early articles is retained in the late work, yet the object of criticism shifts from the inherently corrupt nature of the imperial system to its external corrupting causes.[15] Thus, the spirit of the feudal world is no longer responsible for the ills that led to national oppression and eventually to war. Instead, the spirit of modernity, a spirit that corrupted the old world and led it almost unwillingly to immoral acts of a nearly religious significance, is responsible. In *The Radetzky March*, the intrusion of the demonic into the redeemed order of moral harmony is represented by the unstoppable advance of modern history into the historical tempo of the ancien régime: "The whole world had changed. . . . Yes, the whole world!" concludes Baron Franz von Trotta (*Radetzky March* 174), while Count Chojnicki decides in one of his melodramatic moments that "this is the age of electricity, not alchemy" (163), declaiming "How much longer, how much longer? This era no longer wants us!" (161). The new era, in which nations and classes take the place of simple humanity and universal moral standards, is ushered in by individuals acting as instruments of a higher impersonal power in which Roth sees the Antichrist as the will of history, as an inauspicious destiny in which humans are paradoxically involved: "It is a hellish blindness, for although we were blinded we think we can see," writes Roth in *The Antichrist* (29).

Carl Joseph's incapacity to master his own destiny and his subjection to an incomprehensible and illicit will epitomize the characteristically modern disconnection between moral understanding and human action, a motif that Roth places at the center of his critique of history and civilization. Carl Joseph's ill-fated role as a herald of death and disaster for those around him transforms his actions into objective sins, for which the character tries to find a "self-imposed penance" (*Radetzky March* 114). The emperor himself is a passive spectator of the collapse of the world around him. The principle of responsibility that he represents cannot find its meaning anymore, so the emperor becomes a tragic pawn in the hands of a destiny that points unavoidably toward annihilation: "Now not even the Kaiser bears responsibility for his monarchy. Why, it even looks as if God Himself no longer wishes to bear responsibility for the world," Dr. Skowronnek concludes in an apocalyptical tone (243). Alienation, intolerance, and above all war, realities that formed the early Roth's basis for criticism of the Austrian imperial establishment, are now delegated to a different spiritual authority, which bears responsibility for the downfall of the whole world. This authority, demonic in its religious character and modern in its historical appearance, forces the representatives of the utopian, redeemed order to commit transgressions against their will. In his "Rede über den alten Kaiser," Roth argues that the Austrian emperor accepted World War I against his will: "'Ich habe es nicht gewollt!' sagte Franz Joseph, als der Krieg ausbrach" '"I did not want it," said Franz Joseph when the war broke out' (*Werke* 3: 940). In his *Twilight of a World*, Franz Werfel gives a similar account of the kaiser's signing of the 1914 declaration of war against Serbia, which is forced upon him by a zealous and nationalist officer body. Consistent with Roth's own idealization of the old emperor's moral rejection of violence, Werfel argues that the kaiser's wisdom made him hesitate before such an act—"None of them know what war is like . . . I know . . . at Solferino" (Werfel 28)—yet his isolation and advanced age prevented him from resisting it. In *The Radetzky March* Roth presents the act of war as a sin that the emperor consciously takes upon himself, fulfilling thus a tragic destiny of self-obliteration: "'War is also a sin!' he said aloud. But the priest didn't hear him. . . . 'Let it end!' said Franz Joseph. No one heard him. 'If only I'd been killed at Solferino!' he said. No one heard him" (*Radetzky March* 329).

Roth does not highlight in his depiction of the Austro-Hungarian Empire the historical factors leading to its decline but does highlight the moral and religious significance of this decline, which is presented as an apocalyptical event. According to Frank Joachim Eggers, Roth is more interested in presenting the "civilizational decline" of the world, which is only exemplified through the case of Austria-Hungary: "Der *Radetzkymarsch* handelt vom 'Kulturverfall', der am fiktiven 'Untergang' Österreich-Ungarns exemplifiziert wird" '*The Radetzky March* is about the "cultural decline," which is exemplified by the fictitious "downfall" of Austria-Hungary' (146). The insidious forces of moral corruption that modernity ushers in lead to a fall from the historicity of redemption into secular history. Count Chojnicki underscores the religious significance of the social and national revolutions taking place inside the empire, revolutions that are responsible for the subversion of the old regime: "This era wants to create independent nation-states! People no longer believe in God. The new religion is nationalism. Nations no longer go to church. They go to national associations. Monarchy, our monarchy, is founded on piety, on the faith that God chose the Hapsburgs to rule over so and so many Christian nations" (161–62).Chojnicki's remark that monarchy is religious should not be understood as a reference to a particular religion or to the relations between state and church; it should be understood as a reiteration of the actual lived spirituality that characterizes the experience of redemption. Chojnicki is interested not in questions of theological or sociological significance but instead in the foundational, moral questions that also fascinate Roth the author. In a 1935 open letter sent to and published in the periodical *Der Christliche Ständestaat* (*The Christian Corporate State*), Roth reiterates the opposition between the order of redemption, represented by Austria, and the modern logic of nations and patriotism: "Der 'Österreichische Gedanke' ist kein 'patriotischer', sondern beinahe ein religiöser" 'The "Austrian idea" is not a "patriotic," but almost a religious one' (*Werke* 3: 674).[16]

Understanding the deep moral significance of the transgressions produced by the modern age constitutes the purpose of the historical reconstructions in Roth's fiction. Going beyond the "contextual" causes that led to the downfall of Austria, he tries to focus on the structural causes of the demise of the traditional world. Even though Roth's investigation of imperial Austria's demise goes beyond the surface causes, it does not focus on depth phenomena in the manner suggested by social historians but instead focuses on moral and civilizational experiences, on the philosophical and redemptive intelligibility of history. For this reason, triggering moral reactions in the reader is by far more important for Roth than providing a historical intelligibility of the narrated events. Understanding the blame for Austria's historical trauma, not simply its social and political causes, constitutes such a moral reaction to the past. For this reason, Roth often refers in his articles to the "historical" and "moral" blame for the "execution" and "rape" of Austria, as he does in the 1939 article "The Execution of Austria:" "Historical liability [*Schuld*] is old. . . . This should not be overlooked when you want to understand how Austria could be so violated. All iniquities are too profound and deeply rooted in the past for our 'sense of the present' to perceive them" (*On the End* 76–77). The ethical transparency of history, which allows the interpreter to understand and judge the practical offenses committed in the past, can provide a regenerative experience by redeeming history from its past injustices.

Roth's alternative moral history of Austria offers a selective re-creation based on the author's own philosophy of history and moral convictions. The question about the novel's claim to historical authenticity is therefore irrelevant. Hartmut Scheible argues that in *The Radetzky March*, Roth intentionally created an ambiguous temporality ("verwischte Konturen der Zeit"), a temporality that does not match any actual historical chronology of the late Austrian Empire (*Joseph Roth: Mit einem Essay* 148). In this way, the narrative does not lay claim to any external criterion of veracity but instead owns its own "innere Wahrheit" 'inner truth' (Scheible, *Joseph Roth: Mit einem Essay* 152). Jon Hughes's emphasis on the diegetic character of Roth's narration reinforces this idea: "The bridges to the 'real' world, to the past as it 'actually' happened, are burnt at the outset, leaving the text to function solely according to its own internal dynamics, not 'Geschichte' but 'eine Geschichte'" (*Facing Modernity* 171). By contrasting the world of the "aristocracy of the spirit," of which nobility, the middle class, and even peasantry constitute an integral part (in *The Emperor's Tomb,* connected in their loyalty to the imperial world are a high bourgeois, Franz Ferdinand Trotta; a proletarian Jew, Manes Reisiger; and a Slovenian peasant, Joseph Branco),[17] with a society of mass mobilization, which includes elements of the nationalist bourgeoisie and the proletariat, represented in the notions of "rights," "elections," "the people," "resolution," or "revolution," all words that awake Baron Franz von Trotta's scorn (*Radetzky March* 141), Roth transgresses any ideological, political, or historical polarization. The political and historical elements of his narrative are transfigured into the moral allegory of a clash between a world of harmonious tradition and honorable conservatism and a world of frenzied self-affirmation, vain ambition, and intolerance. For Roth, this allegorical transfiguration is more real than observed reality because it stems from a deeper insight into the moral structure of the world. Realpolitik, on the other hand—that is, pragmatic and rational explanations—is mere blindness, he argues (*Werke* 3: 951).

The attempts by various critics to interpret Roth's attachment to the imperial world as an expression of political conservatism and reaction are as mistaken as those coming from interpreters who see in his early work the presence of a socialist outlook.[18] In fact, Roth places himself beyond any clear-cut ideology or doctrine, adopting instead political self-characterizations that defy conventional understanding and demonstrate the limited validity of the established political labels. Even if he defines himself as reactionary, he does so in a highly idiosyncratic manner. Thus, when Roth declares in 1930 "I am a skeptic. . . . I am a reactionary" (*Joseph Roth: A Life* 153), he does not see himself as a defender of the political order of the ancien régime, as a defender of the feudal social system or glorifier of monarchic absolutism in a conventional sense. His conservatism is targeted at the preservation of a moral relationship with the universe, which in itself defies any confinement to actual historical or political categorizations. This redemptive unification of the individual mind and the external world surpasses any theoretical and ideological opposition and appears simultaneously as conservative and revolutionary: "I am . . . a Catholic with a Jewish intelligence, an actual revolutionary," writes Roth in a 1926 letter to Benno Reifenberg (*Joseph Roth: A Life* 88). At its core, the responsibility for this unification is personal and rests, as Kliche argues, on Roth's appeal to individual morality and on his contempt for mass politics and collective ideologies (Kliche 787–88).

Roth's notion of conservatism is indissolubly tied into the idea of revolt insofar as any moral restoration is a revolutionary act, which simultaneously breaks down the order of decay and reestablishes the order of redemption. For him, this typically Austrian quality of political conservatism is exemplified in the person of "revolutionary" Franz Grillparzer: "He was the classic instance of a rebel who is at the same time a true reactionary: a phenomenon which the recent fashion of labelling everything rebellious and indignant, everything consciously eccentric and apart, as 'revolutionary' is incapable of understanding" (*Hotel Years* 246). Roth's original manner of conceptualizing politics allows him to reverse the classical political terminology: conservatism can be truly revolutionary, while classical revolutions can be reactionary. Such a clearly anti-ideological interpretation of politics has prompted some critics to consider Roth's writing as a fitting illustration of Kurt Bartsch's thesis that Habsburg literature is marked by *Ideologieskepsis* (Tonkin, *Joseph Roth's March* 65). This skepticism toward political ideologies, Helmuth Nürnberger argues, sets Roth and his Austrian literary precursors apart from the enthusiastic nationalism of the German literary tradition (91).

Roth represents through the vanished "world of yesterday" and through the portrayal of imperial Austria his own conception of redemption in the form of a no longer existing Utopia, which explains why some critics, in failing to notice its transhistoric function, characterized it simply as a "backward-looking Utopia" (*rückwärts gewandte Utopie*) (Wörschnig 90). "Things were different back then," remembers Skowronnek in *The Radetzky March*. "It was easier in those days! Everything was so secure" (*Radetzky March* 243). The permanence of that world, which Stefan Zweig refers to as "the Golden Age of Security," results from the experience of time as a slow, pervasive phenomenon, which offers all participants a mutual intelligibility of personal history (Zweig 1). The utopian quality of that time consisted in its capacity to be both changing and stagnant and to achieve a moral simultaneity of all past moments in the present. Unlike those days, the modern times are based on forgetfulness and isolation, on looking forward but never around or backward, as the narrator points out in *The Radetzky March*: "That was how things were back then. Anything that grew took its time growing, and anything that perished took a long time to be forgotten. But everything that had once existed left its traces, and people lived on memories just as they now live on the ability to forget quickly and emphatically" (*Radetzky March* 112).[19]

However, Roth's melancholy evocation of the utopian *illo tempore* is not simply regressive or "backward-looking," as Wörschnig argues. The time of the empire is not only evoked but also *invoked*, or summoned into the present through a séance-like process of reawakening the ghosts of a lost world. The Utopia of the past is brought into the present and is activated through a contemporary audience who remembers that world and thus restores justice to it. Hence, if the utopian time of the empire fused the past and the present, so does the restoration of that time into the present of the narrative. Its function is identical then and now, and the very act of remembrance in which the narrator involves the reader restores that Utopia. Roth charges the reader with the active role of redeeming, not restoring, the historical past: "der Leser des *Radetzkymarsch* findet und bekennt den ihm gültig scheinenden Textsinn im Ereignis seiner Verarbeitung der ihm zur Verfügung gestellten historischen und narrativen Informationen" 'The reader of the *The Radetzky March* finds and affirms the meaning of the text that seems valid to him in the act of processing the historical and narrative information made available to him' (Spieth 284). In this sense, Roth's evocation has a redemptive function that affects the present but also the future, since any future recollection will be an activation of that time. This simultaneity of times in the present moment is an illustration of the redemptive time envisioned by Benjamin, Buber, Bloch, and Rosenzweig and a reaffirmation of the Judaic belief that remembering the past is not a passive act but rather one of active participation into it, an act of appropriation of the past, of actualization for moral and religious purposes. As Yoseph Hayim Yerushalmi asks, somewhat rhetorically, about the act of remembrance in Judaism, "Is it possible that the antonym of 'forgetting' is not 'remembering,' but *justice*?" (117).

Equally important for the feeling of security that the imperial world offered was its strict sense of hierarchy, which encompassed everything from the official structuring of social relations to private moral values: "There existed in my vanished world of the old Monarchy those precious and priceless, unwritten, unrecognized and impenetrable rules . . . which were cast in a bronze more enduring than written rules themselves," confesses the first-person narrator-character Franz Ferdinand Trotta of *The Emperor's Tomb* (64).[20] This hierarchy, rooted in a utopian conception of tradition, did not, however, limit the individuals in their aspirations but instead provided them with a sense of measure that, in Roth's view, constituted the true condition for the exertion of freedom. The fact that the social hierarchy, in spite of its apparent strictness, could be broken through social assimilation into a higher class is an indication of the fact that the true hierarchy that matters to the author is a "hierarchy of the spirit," one that goes beyond mere social customs and characterizes the truer moral constitution of the world. The sense of integrity and honor and, more important, the wise exercise of virtue constitute the moral insights that define a balanced world, a world that knows how to guard its traditional values and how to respond to the challenges raised by historical change.

Emperor Franz Joseph is the guardian of this order and the embodiment of the idea of service code, or *Dienstpragmatik*, as Roth writes in his 1939 "Rede über den alten Kaiser": "Er verliert sich in Formalismen, der alte Kaiser" 'He gets lost in formalisms, does the old emperor' (*Werke* 3: 941). In *The Radetzky March*, the emperor knows his role and plays it in all occasions, to the point where the official persona takes over the private person: "The Kaiser disguised his wisdom as simplicity: for it does not behoove an emperor to be as smart as his advisers" (*Radetzky March* 215). His relationship with his subordinates reflects the moderation that suits the respectability of the office he represents, so he never punishes anyone too strictly, nor does he express his enthusiasm too unreservedly, although human emotions often overwhelm him. Ernst Kantorowicz analyzed this position of the monarch through the concept of *persona publica*: "He is, and acts as, a *persona publica*. And in that capacity he is expected to consider all issues with regard to the well-being of the *res publica*, and not with regard to his *privata voluntas*" (Kantorowicz 95). During a military pass in review, the emperor realizes that time passes too fast for him to keep pace with it and is short not only for himself but also for the world around him. Silently and with a heroic sense of duty for his position, Franz Joseph acquits himself of the proper duties and carries on with the fulfillment of a destiny written in advance:

> He no longer felt like striding along the lines, but he had to go on lest people realized he was frightened by his own age. His eyes, as usual, peered into the distance, where the edges of eternity were already surfacing. But he failed to notice that a glassy drop appeared on his nose, and that everyone was staring, spellbound, at that drop, which finally fell into his thick, silvery moustache, invisibly embedding itself—And everyone felt relived. And the march-past could begin. (*Radetzky March* 226)

The image of the kaiser in *The Radetzky March* is centered on the idea of permanence, order, and decorum on the one hand and on the relationship between the private individual and his social role on the other. The external image of the monarch, visible to the public and standardized into the icon of the empire, is represented in the picture of Franz Joseph, which Carl Joseph encounters everywhere in the country in honorable and less honorable places, a paternal figure that guards over the destiny of its children from the remoteness of its ahistorical location. Together with the ubiquitous march of Radetzky, that veritable "*Marseillaise des Konservatismus*" 'Marseillaise of conservatism,' as Roth calls it in the 1928 article "Konzert im Volksgarten" ("Concert in the Public Garden"), the emperor's portrait constitutes one of the most powerful symbols of the Austrian world (*Werke* 2: 923). For the young lieutenant, the picture inspires contradictory feelings of distance and yet empathy with the one who decided the lot of the entire Trotta family through an accident of destiny: "the Kaiser seemed to have aged suddenly, within a single day, within a very specific hour, and since that hour he had remained locked in his eternal, silvery, and dreadful senility as in an armor of awe-inspiring crystal" (*Radetzky March* 70). The *persona publica* of the monarch, carefully guarded by the imperial establishment and by tradition, represents what Kantorowicz, drawing on medieval law, calls the "Body politic" of the king (Kantorowicz 7). The "Body politic" of the monarch pertains to the religious sphere through its nonhistorical, immortal, and invincible quality. Roth confirms this idea in his "Rede über den alten Kaiser": "Kaiser Franz Joseph der Erste gehörte zu jenen österreichischen Gestalten, denen die Legende schneller entgegenkommt als die Geschichte" 'Emperor Franz Joseph the First belonged to those Austrian figures who find their place faster in legend than in history' (*Werke* 3: 938). The "Body politic" represents the divine authority on Earth and therefore transcends all earthly institutions and laws. Its purely symbolical, formal function inspires lifelessness, so the person of the emperor appears to Carl Joseph as nothing more than an effigy on official documents or on coins, a veritable *deus otiosus* who inspires the novel's general feeling of abandonment: "gradually the Supreme Commander in Chief developed the indifferent, habitual, and unheeded countenance shown on his stamps and coins" (*Radetzky March* 69). Similarly, Bruno Schulz describes the countenance of Emperor Franz Joseph as the "symbol of ordinariness" but also "the ultimate within the bounds of possibility, the guarantee of unpassable frontiers within which the world is enclosed once and for all" (Schulz 33).[21]

Fused into the "Body politic" of the emperor lies also his "Body natural" (Kantorowicz 7). This complementary notion refers to the earthly, human character of the monarch, which is subject to injury and death. The human side of

Franz Joseph is stressed in close connection to his official side. As the public is focused exclusively on his public persona, Roth provides an insight into the moral life and psychology of the emperor: "Once he had read a book about his life, which said, 'Franz Joseph I is no romantic.' . . . But I love campfires. He would have liked to be an ordinary lieutenant, to be young" (*Radetzky March* 218). A generous figure and a genuine bon vivant, the emperor (whom Werfel also describes as an ill-fated romantic) enjoys the simple pleasures of life—a good meal and "ein frisches Krügl Bier" 'a fresh mug of beer'—which explains why Roth presents him in his 1939 "Rede" as a typical exponent of Austrian "*Gemütlichkeit*" (*Werke* 3: 944). Throughout *The Radetzky March*, the feeling of powerlessness that the aging emperor experiences and that constituted a major source of public ridicule from writers who described him as senile (such as Karl Kraus in *The Last Days of Mankind*) is never externalized but instead is closed inside as a sad reminder of the fragile and mortal nature of the monarch's other body, the "Body natural." The progress of the Trotta dynasty appears from the emperor's perspective as a constant memento of time's irreversible passage, and his difficulty in identifying each generation of the Slovenian family in relation to the Hero of Solferino is an indication of his decaying abilities. Even his legendary blue eyes, immortalized in the standard portrait displayed on coins and stamps, hide in actuality a warm paternal love, which Carl Joseph discovers almost unexpectedly during the Corpus Christi parade in Vienna: "The porcelain-blue eyes of the Supreme Commander in Chief—eyes grown cold in so many portraits on so many walls in the empire and now filled with a new fatherly solicitude and benevolence—gazed like a whole blue sky at the grandson of the Hero of Solferino" (*Radetzky March* 192).

The particular conjunction of the "king's two bodies" takes in Franz Joseph's case the form of a paradoxical identity between the lord and the vassal, a position that makes the emperor simultaneously sovereign and subject: "as a public person he, the Prince, is at once *legibus solutus* and *legibus alligatus*, is at once *imago aequitatis* and *servus aequitatis*, at once lord and serf of the Law" (Kantorowicz 96). For this reason, Roth presents the person of the monarch as a prisoner of his own royal body, himself the most humble subject of the law he embodies. Werfel characterizes the monarch in a similar fashion: "Even at a time when personality was the object of snobbish reverence, when the irregular and the arbitrary were the rage, Franz Joseph triumphed over his own originally impatient and capricious temper; he reduced it to the impersonal, to order and rule" (Werfel 19). His behavior must always reinforce the idea of military discipline, his lifestyle the austerity of a civil servant: his living quarters are "dürftig" 'meagre' (Roth, *Werke*

5: 341), and he prefers the routine of military life to the comfort that his entourage provides for him. In his "Rede über den alten Kaiser," Roth stresses the same idea: "'Spartanisch' nannten die Historiker sein Leben . . . weil er um vier Uhr morgens aufstand, weil er auf einem kurzen, einfachen, harten Eisenbett schlief, in seinem Arbeitszimmer" 'The historians called his life "Spartan" . . . because he got up at four in the morning and slept on a short, simple, hard iron bed, in his study' (*Werke* 3: 944).[22] The emperor does not overstep his role, nor can he intervene in matters of social and political relevance in order to preserve his position. His role is to guard the monarchic law, the feudal-vassal contract, and not to oppose the will of the majority or the course of history; when the pressure of modernity on his empire increases to the point where a fundamental change becomes inevitable, his responsibility is to stoically take his duty to the end: "He saw the sun going down on his empire, but he said nothing," remarks the narrator in *The Radetzky March* (213). Although he understands the catastrophic nature of the changes engulfing his world, the emperor must represent the monarchic principle of neutrality and remain distant from the petty pursuits of a morally decaying political class. His wise aloofness confers on him a patrician air, which connects him with the "aristocracy of the spirit" represented by his lower-rank subjects: "They just don't want to be ruled by me anymore! thought the old man. What can you do? he added to himself. For he was an Austrian" (225).[23]

Roth recasts the monarchic principle of neutrality in moral terms, transforming thus the person of the emperor into the symbol of a moral law that presupposes both a stoical attitude in relation to the course of mundane history and a direct participation in the preservation of the order of tradition that the throne represents. This "indifference" in matters of social or historical importance, combined with the involvement in the symbolical order of the world, constitutes for Roth the mark of an aristocracy of the spirit that always resides in the realm of redemption, in which the contradictory notions of stoicism and participation are reconciled and unity is restored to the spiritual relation with the world. For this reason, Emperor Franz Joseph can engage in apparently contradictory actions that in reality are united in the realm of redemption. For instance, he is interested in the imperial routine, in the ceremonial functions and figurative expressions of authority, rather than in authority itself: "He didn't like wars (for he knew that one loses them), but he loved the military, the war games, the uniforms, the rifle drills, the parades, the reviews, and the company drills" (216). Reaching the unity of redemption also presupposes an unambiguous withdrawal from the course of actual, profane history: "he [the emperor] allowed people their errors, and he believed less in the permanence of the world than did the wags who told jokes about him in his vast empire" (216). The same aristocratic and moral detachment characterizes Franz Joseph's loyal subjects, in which Roth sees the exponents of the same type of ethical patriciate. The East European Jews, together with the Trottas, the Slavic peasants, and the humanist bourgeoisie, partake in the emperor's moral authority: "In their own way they are aristocrats, because the mark of an aristocrat is, above all, his indifference; and nowhere have I seen more indifference than among my Polish Jews!" exclaims Count Chojnicki's brother (*Emperor's Tomb* 29). Roth fuses thus both the monarch and the subjects into his concept of aristocracy that unites them in the redemptive realm of spiritual accomplishment and moral lucidity.

Most of the characters in *The Radetzky March* fall within the same template as the emperor: they represent lower echelons in a hierarchy ending in the person of the monarch, yet all are caught in the same feudal-vassal relation, and they all pertain in the dual condition that their social role and unique individuality purport. According to David Bronsen, subordination relationships are crucial to the structuring of the novel: "im Radetzkymarsch ist 'herrschen und beherrscht werden' von kritischer Bedeutsamkeit" 'In *The Radetzky March* "to rule and be rule" is of critical importance' ("Das literarische Bild" 135). In an emblematic manner, the annihilation of the private individual for the benefit of the social persona ties together the baron and the emperor and is reflected in almost every one of their actions. The baron's ceremonial interactions with his own son, Carl Joseph von Trotta, expressed in their brief and almost official dialogue about the military rules of subordination and in their repetitive and empty epistolary exchanges, further highlight the ethics of decorum and tradition that Roth affectionately assigns to his characters.[24] In their inflexible sense of official duty, the emperor and the baron recall Roth's other characters, such as Count Morstin in "The Bust of the Emperor," the Postmaster in "April" (1925), and Jacques, the baron's butler.[25]

The virtue of conservatism thus brings together representatives of the aristocracy and of the petit bourgeoisie, of the peasantry and the proletariat, under the common denominator of noblesse, sense of responsibility, and wisdom.[26] Like his emperor, Baron Franz von Trotta is a "Spartan" but also an "Austrian," a paradoxical combination of asceticism and refinement (*Radetzky March* 25). Unlike the emperor, however, the baron does not have the encompassing view that reaches beyond time, at the "frontier between life and death" (213). For this reason, his historical presence is more accentuated; he is an active defender of the monarchy from the onslaught of modernity, and only the gradual exposure to the inevitability of disaster and to the insurmountable antagonism between the two clashing worlds bestows upon him the same aristocratic stoicism. When Count Chojnicki mysteriously declares to the baron that "the Fatherland no longer exists," he is bewildered and asks for an explanation. "'I assumed you wouldn't understand,' said Chojnicki. 'We are all no longer alive!'" (161).[27] The death to which the count refers is the anachronism of the aristocratic world ("aristocratic" in moral sense) in modern times and its inability to make a meaningful gesture, dramatic or heroic, that would affect the course of history. The very transformation of the times crushes the protagonists and renders them invisible, ghostlike creatures in a world that is unavoidably heading to its demise: "Indeed this occasion seemed utterly familiar, the realization of something he had often dreamed of. The Fatherland of the Trottas was splintering and crumbling" (298).

The symptom of the meaninglessness of the times manifests itself most clearly in the person of Carl Joseph von Trotta, who cannot harmonize his public persona with his private existence.[28] Incessantly failing in all attempts to live up to the moral responsibility of his position, he experiences the drama of alienation at its most devastating intensity. Ultimately he has to break through the barriers imposed by both tradition and modern history to reinvent himself as a man of his times, a moral conscience who single-handedly breaks with the world and withdraws in the nonhistoricity of his private self, a tragic figure reminiscent of Roth's early characters, whose only possibility of finding redemption was to completely desert their world. By renouncing the "Body politic," which a now meaningless tradition imposes on him, Carl Joseph von Trotta does not remain, however, a purely "natural body," as other characters before him did such as Franz Tunda, an unredeemed entity vacillating endlessly into the continuum of history. Carl Joseph finds redemption only through his newly discovered social identity, the peasant one, which constitutes the young lieutenant's true aristocratic individuality. In this capacity history regains meaning for Carl Joseph, whom Roth condemns to a prosaic death at the end of the novel. His death is, however, only a confirmation of his accomplished redemption.

In a certain sense it might even be argued that Carl Joseph, although the exponent of the decadent and final phase of the Trotta dynasty, is the only member of his family who succeeds to find closure and a sense of redemption. His return to the true origin of his family, the peasant one, brings him a sense of composure that allows him to confront history in any form it might come, be it favorable or calamitous. Not the same can be said about his grandfather and father, who are not able to arrive at this state of redemption within history, which explains why the actual unfolding of historical events affects them negatively and leads to their ultimate and painful downfall. Lieutenant Joseph

Trotta dies unappeased, estranged from the social position into which he was forced by historical circumstances, lonely, and disillusioned. Baron Franz von Trotta dies with the monarchy, alienated from and defeated by the rise of a new and unfathomable modern world. Their inability to live within history, regardless of history's turns and whims, points to the persistence, even in the heart of an apparently redeemed world, of an element of corruption. For Roth, this corruption might paradoxically be represented by the very historical stagnation and sense of personal self-sufficiency that are otherwise highly praised throughout the novel as guarantors of continuity and ancestral virtue. Roth suggests that therefore redemption is not a static concept and that any idea of perfection, however justified, will eventually degenerate and lead to pain and corruption. One has to own redemption, to fight for it, to involve oneself morally in its shaping and give it meaning in history regardless of circumstances. In this sense, only few characters manage to achieve a state of salvation in historical exile, one that recalls the Chasidic notion of redemption in the *galut*. Carl Joseph Trotta, the butler Jacques, and Emperor Franz Joseph seem to be the only characters capable of accepting their fate with equanimity, to face death under hostile historical circumstances with the certainty of a higher moral intelligibility of the world.

The Demant family represents a third layer of subjects in the symbolical hierarchy of the novel, after the emperor and the Trottas. A purely bourgeois Jewish family, the Demants also rose to a position of social prominence through three generations, spanning a period similar to that of the Trottas and also in the protective shadow of the same old Emperor Franz Joseph. The oldest of them, a tavern keeper, was an Orthodox Jew whose presence is still felt throughout the novel, an almost formulaic character built in the same template as other small-town Jewish entrepreneurs, such as Nathan Kristianpoller of *Tarabas* and Manes Reisiger of *The Emperor's Tomb*. A strong and pious man, the tavern keeper represents in the novel the heritage of an ancient Jewish tradition, paralleling Joseph Trotta's peasant tradition. The nobility of the Demant family, consisting in its moral integrity and loyalty for the monarchy, was continued by a second generation represented by the postal employee Demant, whose simple life and death as well as patriotism place him in the same category with other small imperial clerks, such as the postmaster in "April" and the lawyer Lakubeit of *Tarabas*. The third generation, represented by the regiment Dr. Demant, a mirror image of Carl Joseph, is confronted with the same problem of inadaptability that Lieutenant Trotta faces: miserable in his career, surrounded by a hostile and decadent world, he is unhappily married and has been "tired for years" (102).[29]

Demant's friendship with Carl Joseph is a friendship of despair, and bad luck unites Demant with Trotta through a community of destiny. Dutiful guardian of his social role and honor, the doctor finds his death through a duel that he stoically accepts with the conviction that he does not belong to the actual world any longer: "This death is senseless. . . . As senseless as my life was," he concludes briefly before his death (102).

The intergenerational function of tradition is emphasized in the dynastic fate of the Trotta and Demant families, whose heritage bestows a heavy burden on the young offspring. Carl Joseph's tribulations are constantly analyzed by Roth in relation to the moral legacy of the old Baron Joseph von Trotta, whose portrait hangs in the district commissioner Trotta's study. A mysterious presence for the young lieutenant, the portrait of the old baron seems to bear testimony to a deeper truth about the destiny of the family and the world, like a voice stretching from the past to the present, "familiar but unfathomable" (33). The schematic portrait of Dr. Demant's grandfather, reminiscent of the fascinating portrait of Kristianpoller's grandfather in *Tarabas*, suggests a similar ambivalent feeling of belonging to and estrangement from a distant tradition that reaches down to the regiment doctor. Likewise, the ubiquitous presence of the emperor's portrait, remote yet familiar, induces in the minds of the two grandsons ambiguous feelings of incertitude with regard to their own existential meaningfulness. The call of the past and the duty to keep it alive in the present are metaphorically expressed by Roth through the motif of the portrait, of the ancestor's face, which he developed in a 1929 review of the book *Das Menschengesicht* (*The Human Face*) by Max Picard. In this article, Roth claims that the revelation of truth is a rediscovery, an eerie experience that somehow points to the concentricity of the experiential world. In the family portraits, Roth discovers an intimation of the repetition of the truth of a face but always displaced, like a rediscovery:

> ich, eingeladen in einem beliebigen Haus eines Zeitgenossen und das zufällige Bild seines Großvaters an der Wand oder auf dem Tisch betrachtend, von einer unbekannten Gewalt gezwungen war, es mit dem lebendigen Antlitz des Enkels zu vergleichen. Erschüttert stellte ich fest, daß dieser nicht die Züge von jenem trug, sondern die Schatten der Züge, als wäre der Enkel nicht der Nachfahr, sondern der Schatten seines Ahnen. (*Werke* 3: 147)

> When invited into his house by one of my contemporaries, and looking at the random picture of his grandfather on the wall or on the table, I felt compelled by an unknown force to compare it with the living countenance of

> the grandson. Shaken, I realized that the latter did not bear the features of the former, but the shadows of the features, as if the grandson were not the descendant, but the shadow of his ancestor.

This "shadowy" quality of the offspring is what determines Roth to place Carl Joseph and Dr. Demant in the shadow of their grandfathers, as if the destiny that the latter represent can only find its fruition through the life of the successors. This approach is consistent with Roth's notion of tradition as "lived" tradition, as reactualized experience, and with the idea that the past truth is present in the "here and now" of history: "nach der Wahrheit zu suchen—nicht um sie als etwas Neues zu finden, sondern als etwas Altes, Ewiges wiederzuentdecken" 'to search for the truth—not to find it as something new, but to rediscover it as something old, eternal' (147).

In *The Radetzky March*, Roth transfigures the feudal society into a utopian community that redeems history from its wretched course. The imperial Austrian world, with its "aristocracy of the spirit," its strict unwritten laws and yet permissive, generous, and humanist political practices, preoccupied by a symbolic representation at a religious rather than historical level, a nation of none and a country of all, reconstitutes, as if in an immense kaleidoscope, the redemptive imagination of an author disenchanted with the course of actual history and firmly anchored in a moral judgment of the modern world. Roth's attempt to turn the Austrian "unity in diversity" into an ideal, redeemed national identity (in his 1938 article "Requiem Mass," Roth defines Austria as "uniquely [catering] for a maximum of differences and a minimum of antagonisms," *On the End* 34) reiterates an idea formulated already in the mid-1920s, during his trip to southern France: any true, harmonious, and unitary identity is possible only under a paradoxical circumstance of uprootedness and belonging, of historical mobility and moral inflexibility. The Austro-Hungarian multiethnic state, a state determined, on the one hand, by the historical spontaneity of various nations of equal standing and, on the other, by the submission to the authority of the same monarch, represents for Roth a perfect social counterpart to individual identity, which is determined by private freedom and, at the same time, by collective tradition. For this reason, the Jewish identity appears to Roth as quintessentially "Austrian" because just like the emperor, it is rooted not in a particular arbitrary territory but instead in the idea of a country united by the monarchic principle: "So erweist sich das Jüdische als Essenz der mitteleuropäischen . . . Kultur" 'thus, the Jewish culture proves to be the essence of the Central European . . . culture' (Magris, *Weit von wo* 161).

In *The Radetzky March*, the imperial Austrian world is opposed to social revolutionary unrest, to the agitators who, louder than "frogs" and "larks," "in all languages . . . exhorted the bristle workers to stop working" (174), but also to the rise of Pan-Germanic or Pan-Slavic nationalism: "The district captain felt as if the whole world were suddenly made up of Czechs—a people he viewed as unruly, hardheaded and stupid and as the inventors of the very concept of 'nation'. A lot of peoples might exist, but no nations" (228).[30] The stoicism of morality and the strength of tradition are opposed to the sinful ambition to change the world, to pursue goals that defy the moral unity between the individual and the world, to push forward with the blind march of historical change and progress. At the same time, this moral stoicism is also opposed to decadent self-sufficiency, spiritual immobility, and indifference. The flimsy and carefree Austrian aristocracy, which Roth often describes with irony but also sympathy, as in the novel *The Tale of the 1002nd Night*, is engaged in equally immoral behavior because of its hedonistic pursuit of individual gratification. Through their "skeptical frivolity" and "wicked insouciance," which constitute the "pride of the doomed," and the symptom of "the disintegration which at that time we still did not see coming," as Franz Ferdinand Trotta puts it in *The Emperor's Tomb*, the exponents of this decadent world violate the principle of ethical participation in the world, a principle upon which rests the possibility of redemption (14).

The absolutist monarchic world is, on the other hand, an alternative to both types of moral transgression, through hubris and through passivity. Its defining characteristic is the ability to combine stoicism with moral participation in a manner that recalls Rosenzweig's notion of "active expectation." This attitude also accounts for the way in which historical change takes place in the world of redemption that Austria represents. If the ideologies that modernity ushers in, such as nationalism, socialism, and liberal individualism, fail to meet the criteria of redemption due to their emphasis on private will and disregard for the inherited world of tradition, a stubborn freezing in tradition, as Baron Franz von Trotta occasionally displays in relation to his son, may lead, on the other hand, to an a priori rejection of private moral freedom and end up in a powerless and melancholy relationship with the world. Roth proposes the middle way—Siegfried Wlasaty spoke of a narrative "Zwischenstadium," a position between yesterday and today (qtd. in Juergens 135)—consisting in the capacity of the individual to produce change through recourse to tradition, in the redemptive simultaneity of the past, present, and future.[31] In *The Radetzky March*, the pace at which the emperor accepts change is the pace of wisdom, of a moral reconciliation between the individual and the world, which is alone capable of redeeming the eternal present of historical reality: "Our Kaiser, God bless him and keep him, is not so old-fashioned as some people think. Of course, the so-called conservative forces aren't all that wrong either. You have to proceed slowly, take your time, think it through. Just don't rush things!" (*Radetzky March* 122). This conception of change within tradition recalls Mannheim's support for a mitigated form of revolutionary utopianism that does not deny but instead affirms the immanent reality.

The monarchy provides for Roth the symbol of a paradoxical moral conservatism that represents, through its radical and uncompromising emphasis on the harmony between traditional values and the historical world, a genuine revolutionary force targeted at the reformation of the most profound rapports between the individual and the universe. This paradoxical blend of conservatism and radical renewal represents for some critics one of the most problematic aspects of Roth's political ideas, due to its conceptual closeness to the "conservative revolution" favored by many interwar fascist movements throughout Europe.[32] However, unlike the proponents of ideological reactionary-revolutionary movements of the time, Roth's concepts retain a basic symbolical function, targeting above all a moral renewal and only secondarily a political one. The monarch's moral radicalism consists precisely in his opposition to any radical change, which places him, Roth argues, in opposition to the modern idea of change. Roth's concepts of reaction and revolution are exactly the opposite of those customarily used for political purposes, representing instead his protest against a world of inverted value hierarchies. The technique of pacification, of postponement, the slow pace of change, what Werfel plastically termed the policy of "*Fortwursteln*," constitutes—in an ironical way—the late imperial Austrian conservative revolution, a utopian revolution that constantly reaches toward the moral settlement of the conflict between tradition and the historical world.[33]

Roth's particular reconstruction of the Austrian world is a projection of his own moral philosophy, and in this sense its claim to truth should be sought in his particular conception of truth, which is indissociable from redemption, and not in a conventional historiographic tradition.[34] In *The Radetzky March*, the emperor's attitude toward the notion of historical truth best captures Roth's own attitude. His relativization of what historical truth is, which Baron Joseph von Trotta refused to accept, represents not an endeavor to control or falsify history but instead a moral answer to the strict delimitation between truth and falsehood that our commonsensical or societal norms dictate: "He had lived long enough to know that it is foolish to tell the truth" (*Radetzky March* 216). A representative of a redeemed conscience, the emperor does not operate with ready-made moral notions and instead inscribes his own meaning of morality into the world according to the exigencies of a utopian, integral spiritual harmony between the individual and society. The emperor is not interested in the historical truth, that is, in what counts as historical truth from a purely rational point of view; he is interested only in the higher truth of the moral relationship of the human being with the world.[35] As a consequence, the social and historical reality of the late Austrian Empire should not be equated with the literary topos developed by authors such as Roth, Werfel, and Zweig. Their metaphorical renditions and idealized memoirs would easily be contradicted by historical testimonies of politicians and intellectuals of the time such as Thomas Masaryk, who decried the rampant discriminations to which national minorities other than German or Hungarian were subjected, or the author Karl Emil Franzos, who was barred from pursuing an academic career due to his Jewish ethnicity. Where some critics saw enlightened tolerance and a conservative politics of "*Fortwursteln*," the social democrat Viktor Adler saw "Absolutismus, gemildert durch Schlamperei" 'absolutism tempered by negligence.'[36]

In *The Radetzky March*, Roth does not reconstruct a lost world and instead reconstructs the significance of this loss from the point of view of his own time. Sigmund Freud described this psychological mechanism as melancholia in that the individual is attached not to the lost object but rather to the significance of the loss: "He had suffered a loss in regard to an object; what he tells us points to a loss in regard to his ego" (Freud 585). As a result, the very construction of the novel bears the mark of Roth's emotional involvement. Instead of building from the outside in, from evidence collected over time and subjected to the test of verity, as a historian does, Roth builds from the inside out, from the perspective of redemption, and only retrospectively rearranges the puzzle of evidence in order to find its confirmation in reality. However, this does not pose a problem of validity for Roth, since the reality of redemption, albeit allegorical, is more real to him than the observed, historical reality. Walter Benjamin does not explain what the research of what he calls a "materialist historian" in the "Theses on the Philosophy of History" might actually look like, yet his reliance on the messianic experience of justice will always favor, as it does for Roth, a "redeemed" perspective upon history, one that makes any resort to historical evidence and refutation irrelevant.[37] For this reason, *The Radetzky March* can be seen as a "historical" novel only to the extent to which all history is seen through the lens of redemption, as *Heilsgeschichte*: "So stellt sich zum Schluß des Romans ein archaisch-episches Weltverständnis ein, das einen Ausblick auf die Totalität des Universums und den vom religiösen Standpunkt her bestimmten 'Sinn' von Geschichte bieten möchte. Der Roman kann unter diesem Aspekt nur bedingt als 'historischer' behandelt werden, da er Geschichte letztlich als 'Mysterium' begreift" 'Thus, an archaic-epic understanding of the world appears at the end of the novel, which wants to provide an outlook on the totality of the universe and on the religiously determined "sense" of history. From this point of view, the novel can be treated as "historical" only conditionally, since ultimately it conceives of history as "sacred mystery"' (Eggers 161).

The sequel to *The Radetzky March*, *The Emperor's Tomb* (1938), one of Roth's last novels, is a continuation of some of the main motifs that the author already developed in the first part, complemented by a critique of modern history and culture from the point of view of the events that took place in Austria between 1932 and 1938. During this period Roth spent most of his time in exile, especially in France, and witnessed with despair the rise to power of the national socialists in Germany, the increase of fascist sympathies in Austria, and the eventual Anschluss of Austria to Germany in March 1938. *The Emperor's Tomb* revisits the theme of Austrian agony, or *finis Austriae*, of an Austria that falls once again victim to a merciless fate. The protagonist of the novel, Franz Ferdinand Trotta, is Baron Franz von Trotta's nephew and an exponent of the Viennese high bourgeoisie. Franz Ferdinand's family connections with native Slovenia are kept alive through his cousin Joseph Branco, a simple farmer with whom the assimilated progatonist has nothing in common except for an imaginary national identity and the loyalty to the same Austrian monarch. The first part of the novel focuses on Franz Ferdinand Trotta's discovery of the imperial provincial world, represented by Joseph Branco and by Manes Reisiger, a Galician Jew and friend of Branco. Trotta, the young socialite and insider of the aristocratic circles of late imperial Vienna, leads a lighthearted, "carefree" lifestyle, marked by "skeptical frivolity" and "melancholy curiosity" (*Emperor's Tomb* 14). This fashionable melancholy for the "authentic" and "archaic" makes him and his friends invest Branco and Reisiger, two pragmatic peasants without urban longings, with the pure attributes of "imperial Austrianness," in which the company of patrician friends sees the much-needed counterbalance to the newly emerging demotic nationalism. Loyal to the belief that "Austria's essence is not to be central, but peripheral," Trotta embarks on a trip to the eastern parts of the empire at the invitation of the Galician Manes Reisiger, where the outbreak of World War I finds Trotta (17). Fascinated by his spiritual kinship with the simple provincial world, he decides to fight in the same battalion as his Slovenian cousin and Jewish friend.

After falling prisoners of war and escaping Siberian captivity, the three friends return to a changed world in which new nation-states appeared from the ruin of the old empire. As each one returns to his province (now belonging to a different country), Trotta has no choice but to go back to his native Vienna and to his wife, Elizabeth, whom he had married shortly before going to the front. His marriage, however, falls apart, as his love remains fundamentally unreciprocated. Elizabeth proves to be a shallow and selfish woman, like most women with whom Roth's war veterans fall in love, and Trotta sees himself a stranger in a new world in which he is incapable of finding any meaning.[38] His old company of friends suffers from the same existential meaninglessness, resulting from the conviction that "we were dedicated to death" (15). As the group of friends disintegrates and the hostile destiny brings about the final demise of the world, the protagonist has lost every possession or connection with the old society and is "no longer bothered with the world" (150). The German Anschluss finds Franz Ferdinand destitute and homeless, spiritually adrift and hopeless. This state contrasts with his symbolic return to the tomb of the Austrian emperors in the last pages of the novel in an emblematic yet melancholy reclaiming of a lost utopian identity.[39] Trotta's final line—"So where could I go now, I, a Trotta?"—restages the existential futility of Roth's early characters such as Franz Tunda, whose lack of conciliation with the world excludes the possibility for actual redemption (346). Given the circumstances of the Nazi takeover of Austria in 1938 and the prelude to the upcoming war and the Holocaust, Trotta's existential despair takes on, however, a different and more dramatic and ominous meaning: it is not only the rhetorical questioning of an absent redemption but also the questioning of the very possibility of survival.

The Emperor's Tomb follows the structure of Roth's early novels, although in this case that nebulous feeling of belonging and existential meaningfulness that the early characters desperately seek takes on a concrete shape: imperial Austria, a concept that has already been articulated in all its complexity in *The Radetzky March*. Similar to novels such as *Flight without End*, *Zipper and His Father*, and *Right and Left*, the hero is incapable of finding his place within the new postwar society and wanders aimlessly inside a ruined reality.[40] However, unlike the characters in the early novels, Franz Ferdinand Trotta, Roth's fictional alter ego, nostalgically projects his yearning into the past of the Dual Monarchy, a past that cannot be resurrected anymore yet offers him the certitude of a symbolic redemption. Even if he constructs his "*civitas imaginalis*" during the time of the old monarchy, he does so with the certitude of the historical inevitability of its final collapse: "Perhaps in the hidden depths of our souls there slumbered that awareness which is called foreboding, the awareness above all that the old Emperor was dying, day by day with every day that he lived, and with him the monarchy—not so much our Fatherland as our Empire; something greater, broader, more all-embracing than a Fatherland" (15). Thus, in *The Emperor's Tomb* the motifs of *felix Austria* and *finis Austriae* overlap, as in *The Radetzky March*.

The utopian Austrian world depicted in *The Emperor's Tomb* values the same aristocratic self-sacrifice to the sense of duty that *The Radetzky March* emphasizes: Count Chojnicki observes religious holidays not out of piety but "because he felt that his noble estate in duty bound him to follow the established pattern of religion" (32).[41] Furthermore, the imperial world, hierarchical and repetitive, is a reiteration of the same Viennese imperial standards, from the train stations to the small clerks and pubs, just as in *The Radetzky March* the sound of "Radetzky March" and the emperor's portrait summoned the presence of the same imperial authority in all the towns and villages of the empire.[42] Franz Ferdinand's visit to the eastern parts of the empire occasions his remark that he "was just as much at home in Zlotogrod as [he] was in Sipolje or Vienna" (38–39). The purely "imaginary" nature of this community (in the sense of Benedict Anderson's "imagined community") is intentionally rendered as imaginary by Roth: "A whole land, a Fatherland, is something abstract" (27). In opposition to the generally accepted view that national identities are rooted in an objective unity of blood and soil, Roth argues that all collective identities are imaginary, the only difference being the moral effect that each of these imaginary communities has on the individuals. The national one, "daemonic," as Werfel characterizes it (Werfel 7), is a destructive fantasy: "Austria will perish at the hands of the Nibelungen fantasy," concludes Count Chojnicki, the brother of the homonymous count from *The Radetzky March* (*Emperor's Tomb* 17). The imperial identity, however, is a moral community, structured around the concept of tradition, continuity, and normative stability.

The imaginary character of the national community is illustrated by Count Chojnicki's belief that one "cannot love every single field of wheat and rye, or every Polish lady or gentlemen," but "there are people who may have been born in China, Persia or Africa whom [he] would call fellow-countrymen. . . . A true fellow-countryman is sent to one as a sign of grace from heaven," the count concludes (27–28). The idea of belonging as an expression of a deeper elective affinity, of a spiritual community, reiterates the concept of identity that Roth first formulated during his trip to southern France, a concept that encapsulates his philosophy of redemption. The same type of community characterizes the "aristocracy of the spirit" that, in *The Radetzky March*, brings together the political aristocracy, the bourgeoisie, and the peasantry. In *The Emperor's Tomb*, Roth's belief that the emperor is closer to the Bosnian chestnut roaster or Galician Jew than to the German nationalist professor from Vienna, a belief expressed in the 1939 "Rede über den alten Kaiser" (*Werke* 3: 940), is concretized in the characters Joseph Branco and Manes Reisiger, the former a seasonal chestnut roaster and the latter a Galician Jew, who together with the aristocrat Chojnicki and the bourgeois Trotta form a microimage of the Austrian Empire.[43] Franz Ferdinand decides to give up on the privileges he would have enjoyed during the war due to his social position just to be with Branco and Reisiger precisely because he feels that only together with them is the ideal, utopian community that the empire represented realized: "I wanted to die with Joseph Branco, my cousin Joseph Branco the chestnut roaster, and with Manes Reisiger the *fiaker* from Zlotogrod, not with a lot of waltzers in uniform" (*Emperor's Tomb* 62). Count Chojnicki explains the symbolic value that the chestnut roasting profession represents, in spite of its humble and prosaic nature: "This gentleman has sold his chestnuts everywhere, in half the European world, one might say. And wherever people ate his roasted chestnuts, it was Austria, and Franz Joseph was on the throne" (140).[44]

When the idealized Austrian world disappears entirely and Franz Ferdinand is left without any actual support, he cannot reconcile with the new society. He feels that he "is not a man of [his] time," and he cannot find a replacement for his lost world (7). The woman he loves is just a temporary and deceitful shelter from existential homelessness (in the same way that Arnold Zipper's love is), while his social and personal relationships crumble due to general moral and emotional fatigue. The agonizing memory of the historical trauma becomes the only certainty that can offer him a sense of identity. He knows what he is not and what he cannot be any longer, for which reason the last part of the novel is pervaded by a feeling of melancholy. His disengagement with the world and his incapacity of assuming a meaningful identity make him an extraterritorial, ghostlike creature who disappears into the night that history brings over his beloved Austria: "I was obsolete; obsolete indeed. To be obsolete among the living means something like being extra-territorial. I was extra-territorial among the living" (152).

The historical perspective developed in *The Emperor's Tomb* reflects the unredeemed relationship between the modern individual and his historical consciousness. Franz Ferdinand Trotta illustrates this dramatic condition of broken unity resulting from the temporal displacement of the moral and societal dimensions of existence. Forced to live in a detestable historical reality by an impersonal force of change that operates on the principle of exclusion, struggle, and empty volition, Trotta remains firmly anchored in a vanished world that survives only through the painful memory of its own disappearance. Werfel characterizes this condition as the schizophrenic situation of the entire postwar Austrian generation: "They belong to two worlds: to that dead one which, living in them, is not quite dead; and to the world of its heirs, who took over the property like goods after a sale" (Werfel 4). The protagonist's incapacity to break through the barrier separating his social life from his moral convictions results in his feeling of damnation and in his exposure to the most agonizing aspects of historical change. Franz Ferdinand Trotta therefore partakes in the same unhappy consciousness that characterizes the early characters or even Carl Joseph Trotta (before his revelation and moral conversion). As in Carl Joseph's case, the decline of the world is seen from the midst of chaos itself. Even if Franz Ferdinand projects his deliverance into a historical Beyond, he cannot actualize the redemptive function of this Beyond in a messianic act similar to those present in Roth's later novels. In this sense, even if the perspective of redemption is positively described in the novel through the reality of the Austrian Empire, the hero cannot find access to its regenerative potential, while the historical perspective remains caught in the unending gesture of melancholy.[45]

Redemption as the Quest for Historical Adequacy

In contrast to the historical perspective of *The Emperor's Tomb*, that of "The Bust of the Emperor" offers a wider outlook on history, similar to that of *The Radetzky March*. The trials of the quixotic Count Franz Xaver Morstin, feudal lord in a remote Galician village, illustrate a different manner of relating to historical consciousness and even offer the perspective of redemption within history. Count Morstin's story begins in the time before World War I, when his moral authority among both the local peasants and officials allowed him to intervene in juridical matters that officially concerned only the representatives of the imperial power. His interference with the course of standard legal procedures is motivated, however, by the genuine desire to help and to offer gratuitous services to the neediest members of his community. Simple peasants and clerks benefit from his generosity, a generosity that, the narrator argues, stemmed not from any personal form of compassion but instead from the "hardening" of arbitrary charity "over the generations" into an aristocratic "form of duty and tradition" (*Collected Shorter Fiction* 239). Bound to his own duty toward the helpless members of his community, the count spends his time involved in purely symbolic activities meant to enforce the emperor's authority in the province: he inspects the police, meets with the religious representatives of various communities, and organizes the imperial military maneuvers that take place in his district. During one of these maneuvers in which Emperor Franz Joseph himself visits Count Morstin's village, a local young peasant sculpts a bust of the emperor, which the count praises as evidence of the loyalty of the masses for their ruler by divine right.

However, with the outbreak of the war, Count Morstin goes to the front and stores the bust of the emperor in his mansion's cellar. At the end of the military hostilities he returns to his village, which has in the meantime become a part of the newly established Polish Republic. Back home, the count loses his aristocratic privileges, and his authority becomes a mere shadow of what it used to be, hardly kept alive by the people's goodwill and appreciative recollection of the count's generosity. Although surrounded by the same environment as before the war, the count does not feel at home anymore in his village: "What is home, anyway?" the count often asks himself: "Was I not . . . so much at home in this place because it belonged to a master who owned just as many different places that I loved as well? No doubt about it!" (244). From his reflections about the nature of national identity, the count concludes that his old country provided him with a sense of belonging precisely because it used to be a country of no specific ethnic group, a country of "orphaned nationals." This paradoxical formulation, in which the idea of belonging ambiguously coexists with that of homelessness, constitutes one of Roth's favorite literary topoi precisely because it stems from a view of redemption as the utopian reconciliation of the irreconcilable. By contrast, the corrupted modern world operates with ethnic exclusions and builds its idea of the state on the premise of one nation's preeminence. Hence, after the war the count is confronted with the impossibility of being at home while having no roots anywhere. Eternal wandering (another expression of redemption for Roth) tragically turns into mere homelessness: "Now everywhere around me they speak of their new fatherland. And they think of me as *déraciné*. I always have been. Oh, there once was a fatherland, a real one, the only possible fatherland for orphaned nationals. And that was the old Monarchy. Now I am a homeless man who has lost the true home of the eternal wanderer" (244).

Nostalgic and sorrowful about his lost spiritual home, Count Morstin decides to travel abroad, where he accidentally witnesses an event that will produce a major change in his attitude about the vanished Austrian world. While having a drink in a fashionable Zurich bar, he observes a group of drunken people who were entertaining themselves by passing a crown from one to another and mockingly dancing with it on the top of their heads. When he hears that the crown in question was the crown of Saint Stephen, the Habsburg symbol of authority, the count is overcome by anger and attacks the frivolous and decadent party. Roth compares the group to a pack of scavengers living off the historical ruin brought about by modernity: "a selection of the type of persons who were temporarily put in charge of administering the inheritance of the lost world, only to deliver it a few years later—at profit to themselves—to the still more progressive and murderous inheritors" (246).

Profoundly appalled by the corruption of the modern world, Count Morstin returns to his village, determined to don the official imperial uniform and post the bust of the emperor in front of his house. This gesture of defiance of history itself, interpreted by the simple people as an act of lunacy, restores, at least symbolically, the count's reliance on moral principles and offers him an escapist manner of reconciling himself with the new reality: "the best thing I can do is to seek out the ruins of my former home!" (249). The emperor's bust, majestically guarding the road that runs in front of the count's house, is once again resurrected, and not only the count but also the peasants, individuals living in a present without time, start to salute it on their daily travels on the road: "It was as though reverence and recollection also worked on the memorial, and as though every peasant's acknowledgement and every devout Jew's prayer brought the crude work of the young peasant's hand to artistic perfection" (253). And yet, the count receives the news that the newly invested Polish authorities do not want the emperor's bust standing outside of the count's mansion; it represents a threat to the legitimacy of the newly established power. Faced with the incapacity to defend his last symbolic sanctuary, the count decides to dispose of the bust in a highly original manner: instead of getting rid of it, he buries it with the pomp and ceremony due to a monarch. The "funeral," a symbolic act of reconciliation of the world with its past, achieves what history itself was not able to, namely to end the old world in a decent and meaningful way, through the mournful participation of the entire community. After the bust of the emperor is laid in the ground, the count leaves the country forever and retires—symbolically—in southern France. His last reflections, "quoted" by Roth in the form of a figurative testament of the old imperial world, constitute the count's belief that "no human virtue is of enduring worth in this world, save only true piety," which he identifies with the spirit of the old monarchy (257).

Once again, Roth depicts in "The Bust of the Emperor" an imaginary Austrian world defined by the same utopian qualities he uses in the novels: true community, tradition, value hierarchy, and moral inclusiveness. The count and the peasantry, especially the Jewish one, form a true community of spirit based on simple piety and obedience to the paternal authority that the empire represents.[46] The respect for the inherited customs blends with the respect for the feudal offices and symbolical authority that is represented by a strict and formal hierarchy: "The belief in the traditional hierarchy was so powerfully rooted in the soul of Franz Xaver that he loved his Emperor, not for his human qualities, but because of his Imperial traits" (240). The basic rule of mutual acceptance that this world presupposes is emphasized in the peaceful cohabitation of different ethnic groups and religious denominations under the same divine authority of the monarch. This typical conception of ideal belonging, which stresses difference and commonality in the same gesture, is further illustrated in the person of the count, who is a Polish noble of Italian descent whose loyalty lies with the Austrian Crown: "he was a man beyond nationality, and therefore an aristocrat in the true sense" (236).[47]

The assault of modernity on this utopian world is first perceived by Count Morstin as a threat to the moral order of redemption whose guardian he is. As a figure of symbolic authority before the war, he cannot fail to take issue with the spreading of a hostile national ideology that endangers the ethnic harmony of the empire. The separatist and irredentist tendencies of various ethnic groups are qualified by the count as "the precursor to the bestiality" of the interwar years and dismissed as excesses of an evolutionary ideology of frustration and hatred (241). The count's opposition to the march of history is reminiscent of Baron Franz von Trotta's unsympathetic judgment of the nationalists and socialists who disturbed the peace of his provincial department. With the irreversible collapse of the Austrian Empire, Count Morstin cannot reconcile himself with the loss of his world. Because his allegiance to the old order was so complete that even his own ego was subordinated to the duty for his office (following the emperor's own example), he perceives the disappearance of this order as the dissolution of his own identity: "The unnatural excess of world history has also ruined my personal pleasure in what I call home" (244). Loyal to the purely symbolic nature of his office and identity before the war, the count resolves to continue his life as if nothing happened, as if the emperor were still alive and as if history had not started its forward destructive march. His decision is consistent with the incompatibility between the temporality of ritualist tradition and moral inclusion of his own world and that of immoral forgetfulness and exclusion on which the newly established world thrives. In his messianic gesture, the count tries to redeem the objective course of history through its negation, through the activation of a nostalgic reconstruction of the past that, in spite of its rational absurdity, is the only correct ethical decision for a man who cannot compromise his moral convictions: "To the peasants and the Jews of Loptany and environs, Count Morstin seemed not at all ridiculous, but venerable. They venerated his lean, bony frame, his gray hair, his ashen, crumpled face, his eyes, that seemed to be fixed on a limitless distance, and no wonder: they were looking at a lost past" (254).

The melancholy attachment to a reality that is irredeemably lost and the escapist denial of the objective course of history are, however, surpassed through the final gesture of reconciliation that the count undertakes. By deciding to bury the emperor's bust, Count Morstin carries out the work of mourning through which he delivers himself from his traumatic experience. Through this action he acquires redemption's perspective on history, which allows him to contemplate the historical whole with the same kind of active stoicism that Emperor Franz Joseph practices in *The Radetzky March*. The bust's "funeral" is the act of recognition of the old world's demise and a final tribute to its glory and significance. It also indicates Morstin's understanding that while no material opposition can be waged against the objective course of history, a moral one is possible but only from the point of view of an already acquired union of the private mind and the outside world, or from the point of view of redemption. The retirement of the Austrian aristocrat and his final reflections bring evidence to his eventual deliverance from the hopeless course of linear history, which he can now bring to a halt in order to achieve the true messianic interrogation of its moral foundations. In the ending lines, the count gives voice to Roth's conviction that the recourse to history is possible for the present individual only through an act of moral judgment, through the reiteration of a condition that seeks "restoration, reparation, reformation and the recovery of lost harmony" (Löwy 2):

> Faith cannot disappoint us, as it promises us nothing on this earth. The true believer cannot disappoint us, because he seeks no personal advantage. What this means to ordinary people is this: their pursuit of so-called national virtues, which are still more dubious than personal values, is fatuous. That is why I hate nations and nation-states. My former home, the Monarchy, was different, it was a large house with many doors and many rooms for many different kinds of people. This house has been divided, broken up, ruined. (258)

The recasting of the political "national question" in terms of the religious motifs of *vanitatum vanitas* and *fugitas*, which Magris associates with Roth's indebtedness to a Baroque tradition (*Weit von wo* 189), returns to the theological questions of Roth's thinking, to his concern with the problems of sin, atonement, and salvation. This demonstrates that his preoccupation with history and politics stays under the sign of a religious quest for redemption, a quest that in turn is not theological *stricto sensu* but rather moral, general-human, and this-worldly.

Roth's "Austrian" historical-reconstructive literary phase is connected to the early social-critical period through the transfiguration of history according to a soteriological modeling of reality. The early novels bear testimony to a Central European interwar period of social turmoil and hostility that heralds the impending apocalypse and the hopelessness of the individual. The late novels, on the other hand, transcend the horizon of disaster through a critique of linear temporality and "progress" and project the hope for redemption simultaneously into a distant future and into a no longer possible past.[48] The expectation of salvation, refused to the early characters, appears for the late ones in the form of a nostalgic attachment to a reality that acquires shape precisely because it does not relate to the logic of modernity and to the course of linear history. The meaning of this retrospective utopian investment is, however, not historical in the technical sense, for Roth does not aim at the factual reconstruction of the past in the same way in which his fictional descriptions of the interwar period did not attempt to provide a sociological description of his contemporary society either. The "past" functions here in the same way in which "tradition" and "stoicism" functioned in the religious novels, as a moral projection capable of unleashing the potential of redemption.[49] This transfiguration of the meaning of history is, like that of "society" and "community," subordinated to the individual's present need for salvation, for release from the wretched lot in which the impersonal forces of history and his personal hubris have brought him. For this reason, the Austrian imperial past represents in fact the utopian reflex of the need for a redeemed present, for restoring the unity of the private moral mind and the historical world. In this sense, the mythical existence outside of history (the Habsburg past) becomes for Roth the condition for any possible historical existence in the present, confirming Northrop Frye's belief that far from being the absolute opposite of history, the myth "redeems" it:

> Only myth, with its suggestion of an action that can contain the destinies of those who are contemplating it, can provide any hope or support at all. Such myth does not overrule *Weltgeschichte*: by avoiding actual history and its criteria, it sets the historian free to do his own job in his own way. A more traditional language would say that myth *redeems* history: assigns it to its real place in the human panorama. (*Great Code* 50)

Roth's historical fiction, especially the works that reconstruct the late Austrian imperial period, is intrinsically tied into the problematics of his late work in general. In the same manner in which the novels and short stories dealing with the religious, private dimension of redemption offer a positive alternative to a human being who is being incapable of finding one's place in the world or has become victim of a perverted form of moral self-sufficiency, the historical narratives point the way toward the redemption of communities living in political times. The formulation of a space of redemption as a synthetic "third space" between the centrifugal force of individualism and the centripetal one of tradition and between the temporality of existence and the permanence of salvation links the novels of Judaic religious inspiration and the "Austrian" historical novels. This space is the home, albeit imaginary, of the Jew and the Austrian, both forced into homelessness by the implacable forces of history: "In diesem imaginären dritten Raum trifft der Ostjude auf den Altösterreicher Joseph Roth" 'In this imaginary third space, the Eastern Jew meets the Habsburg Austrian Joseph Roth' (Müller-Funk, *Joseph Roth* 196).

The Judaic dimension of Roth's historical fiction becomes clearer when considered in the context of his generation's return to religion in response to the crisis of historicism in the early part of the twentieth century. When in 1910 Rosenzweig was writing that "God must save man not through history, but really as 'God of religion'" and that "the struggle against history in the meaning of the nineteenth century is for us the same as the struggle for religion in the meaning of the twentieth century," he was giving expression to a growing disenchantment with the Hegelian interpretation of history as a teleology of the idea of Spirit (qtd. in Mosès 35). Hegel's historical determinism was perceived by many young Jewish intellectuals as an abandonment of the religious mission of redemption and as the atrophy of the moral relationship between individual and God. History did not need to be abandoned altogether; it simply needed to be reassigned its natural place in the narrative of religious salvation. Only thus would the individual be able to regain control over the workings of history and take responsibility for it. The Jewish people, Rosenzweig believed, had the advantage of their marginal position in relation to history and were able to offer an example to the rest of the world. In analyzing Rosenzweig's *Star of Redemption*, Stéphane Mosès writes:

> Hence, the religious vocation of the Jewish people will be interpreted less as an absence in history than as a distance taken with regard to it, less as a negation of politics than as a *critique of politics*. Its role will not consist, as in Hegel, of putting itself in the service of universal history, but on the contrary, of subjecting each of its elements to an ethical judgement. (44)

By tapping into the same Judaic religious tradition, Roth actively takes on the role of ethical judge of history by putting it on trial. Although this impulse motivates his fictional reconstruction of the Austrian imperial world, it quickly becomes obvious that it is not so much the particular set of events that have led to the collapse of the monarchy that interests him but rather the logic of modernity in general, especially the logic of modern historicism. If the Hegelian historicist paradigm viewed world history as a series of sequences in the implacable development of the idea of reason, then this particular idea of reason was responsible for the collapse of the world, Roth argues. He reconstructs the stations of this movement of the spirit as an intellectual lineage of "decay" that begins with Erasmus of Rotterdam and ends with fascism, as he declares in his 1937 article "Grillparzer": "from Erasmus through Luther, Frederick II, Napoleon, Bismarck, to the clutch of dictators we have today" (*Hotel Years* 244). It is this course of history, the linear, implacable Hegelian "tribunal of the world," that Roth rejects. Instead, he appeals the sentences of this tribunal, as he metaphorically argues, in order to recall all its mistakes and restore justice to those individuals, cultures, ideas, and customs that were much too quickly wiped out. Roth's historical fiction seeks to redeem history not by suspending it but instead by revealing its inner workings, its moral core. This is the essence of the constant awareness of individual responsibility within history and of the reliance on the present as the source of all historical possibilities. The idea that the past has not passed yet and that the future has its roots in the present was popular within the generation of Jewish thinkers of which Roth was part and opened up the way for thinking about the Messiah's arrival within history, for the redemption of the world. In Mosès's words, "the idea inspired by Jewish messianism, proposes a model of history that, after the collapse of the ideologies of progress, gives a new chance for hope by locating utopia in the heart of the present" (14).

Notes

1. While some critics consider Roth's historical fiction a form of historiographical discourse (see Halldén 226; Lukács, "Radetzkymarsch"; Vocelka; Howes; Foster; Tonkin, *Joseph Roth's March*), others object to Roth precisely because of his incapacity to provide a more accurate account of historical reality. For the latter category, see Bronsen, "The Jew in Search of a Fatherland"; Scheible, "Joseph Roths Flucht aus der Geschichte"; Spencer; Reich-Ranicki, *Nachprüfung* 227.
2. A similar interpretation was adopted by Horkheimer and Adorno in their seminal critique of enlightenment modernity, *The Dialectic of Enlightenment*: "The dilemma

that faced us in our work proved to be the first phenomenon for investigation: the self-destruction of the Enlightenment. . . . The notion of this very way of thinking, no less than the actual historic forms—the social institutions—with which it is interwoven, already contains the seed of the reversal universally apparent today. . . . In the enigmatic readiness of the technologically educated masses to fall under the sway of any despotism, in its self-destructive affinity to popular paranoia, and in all uncomprehended absurdity, the weakness of the modern theoretical faculty is apparent" (xiii).

3. The same critique of classical historicism, popular in the interwar period, was embraced by other Jewish Austrian writers, such as Franz Werfel: "According to such theories the history of a people from its rise to its decline follows one single primitive line, determined only by the material forces of earth, soil and necessity. For the spirit there is no room; or rather, alas, it would be apologetically accounted for as the fruit of those material forces" (6).
4. Whether the moral judgment of history has any epistemological value in the historical sciences is an issue hotly debated among historians. John Higham argues for the necessity of historians' moral involvement in the interpretation of the past: "He [the historian] is not a judge of the dead, but rather a participant in their affairs, and their only trustworthy intermediary" (620). Higham's coupling of "causal" and "moral history," whereby the latter provides a better approximation of the former by establishing a relationship to norms in historical interpretation, does not explicitly argue that the purpose of a moral evaluation is to do justice to the past but instead to enhance our capacity of clarifying the moral context in which the event took place. Jörn Rüsen understands the study of history as an evaluation of the past from the point of view of the present. The criteria used in this evaluation are also relevant for the future insofar as the past events took place with a future in mind, so to speak, thus involving the posterity in their significance. By this token, the historian becomes responsible for past, present, and future, while time is addressed as a continuum that combines both the theoretical explanation of the past and its practical evaluation. This conception of history allows the historian to enter into a curative dialogue with the past by shedding light on its obscure, repressed, and muted experiences. Rüsen speaks of "eine heilende oder therapeutische Funktion der Geschichte" 'a healing or therapeutic function of history' in which moral identification brings about a healing of the painful occurrences of the past (57).
5. Hartmut Scheible argues, however, against the identification of a positive utopian dimension in *The Radetzky March*. In his opinion, any Utopia remains an illusion of the grandsons' generation, an unfulfilled fantasy: "Man könnte im 'Radetzkymarsch' die spezifisch österreichische Form einer 'Suche nach der

verlorenen Zeit' sehen; nach der Zeit, die, als Tradition vergangen und gegenwärtig zugleich wäre, frei von den Narben romantisch-ideologischer Entstellungen. Daß es solche Tradition im 'Radetzkymarsch' nicht gibt, nur das Suchen nach ihr, haben die bisherigen Abschnitte dieses Kapitels gezeigt. Geblieben ist als realer Bezugspunkt der rückwärtsgewandten Utopie der Nachkommen einzig der Augenblick, in dem der Held von Solferino dem Kaiser das Leben rettet, nicht einmal dessen gesamte Lebensspanne" 'One could see in *The Radetzky March* the specifically Austrian version of a "search for the lost time"; for the time that would be simultaneously passed and present as tradition, without the scars of romantic-ideological distortions. The previous sections of this chapter have shown that there is no such tradition in the *The Radetzky March*, only the search for it. The real point of reference of the descendants' backward-looking Utopia remains the moment when the hero of Solferino saved the life of the emperor, not even his entire life span' (*Joseph Roth: Mit einem Essay* 96).

6. For Klaus Weissenberger, Roth's *travail de memoire* is directly connected with the Jewish conception of memory as the foundation of moral law: "zwischen dem Erinnern der Geschichte und dem Einhalten der Gesetze eine reziprokes Verhältnis besteht: 'Nur wer den Auszug aus Ägypten nicht vergißt, weiß, daß des Gesetz Freiheit bedeutet, und vermag es zu befolgen'" 'there is a reciprocal relationship between the recollection of history and the observance of the laws: "Only he who does not forget the exodus from Egypt knows that the law signifies freedom, and is able to obey it"' (Jan Assmann qtd. in Weissenberger 60). In this sense, Roth's remembrance of Austria carries with it the sense of restoration that the remembrance of Jerusalem carried during the Babylonian exile (62–63).
7. "This novel, which one would expect to be an apotheosis of the Monarchy, is in reality an epic of decadence which diagnoses the maladies that brought about its demise" (Bronsen, "The Jew in Search of a Fatherland" 59). For Rudolf Koester, *The Radetzky March* is "ein sozialkritisches, manchmal satirisches Epochenportrait" 'a portrait of the times, critical of society, but sometimes also satirical' (64).
8. Georg Lukács appreciated *The Radetzky March*'s capacity to conform to the ideal model of historical novel that he described in the *The Historical Novel*, namely to elevate itself above the singular viewpoint and offer a cohesive, integrated collective sense of historical experience. See Lukács, *The Historical Novel* 282.
9. Paul Hofmann confirms the status-conferring use of "nasal German": "A refined form of Viennese idiom was in use for centuries at the Habsburg court (*Schönbrunnerdeutsch*, the German spoken in Schönbrunn Castle) and was imitated in the palaces of the Vienna nobility and in army officers' mess halls throughout the empire. The Viennese upper middle class, including assimilated Jewish families,

adopted that slightly nasal speech, about halfway between the High German of books and formal oration and the broad dialect of the Viennese populace" (13). An interesting biographical detail, however, is the fact that apparently Roth initially rejected the Viennese dialect in favor of High German. This might have resulted from an attitude of repudiation of Austrian provincialism and identification with Prussian Germanity, although later in his life he advocated an exactly opposite attitude (Bronsen, *Joseph Roth: Eine Biographie* 133).

10. Magris argues that instead of developing throughout history, the story of the Trotta generations is actually a document of immobility. They are incapable of change, being frozen in the mythical act of heroism at Solferino and in the eternity of an empire whose raison d'être belongs to the domain of the divine rather than historical right. This is why the protagonists face the almost tragic condition of not being able to break back into history, except maybe through death (*Weit von wo* 120).
11. Through this imagery of the attachment between the monarch and the "salt of the earth" peasantry, attachment that bypasses the middle-class bourgeois strata, Roth reactivates an older legitimist Habsburg discourse that had been traditionally used to undercut the authority of feudal aristocracy in the newly acquired territories. As Larry Wolff shows, the celebration of the bond between the Austrian monarch and the Ruthenian and Jewish peasants in Galicia was used by Emperor Joseph II as a propaganda instrument in the "invention" of a Habsburg Galicia, purified of its recent Polish historical heritage and feudal institutions: "The Habsburg government supposedly responded to that Galician public and offered a 'recasting' (*Umschmeltzung*) . . . of relations between nobles and peasants. What was being forged, in this metallurgical metaphor, was nothing less than Galicia itself" (825).
12. The figure of Eugene of Savoy is rather controversial for the Pan-German nationalist movement. For Franz Werfel, Eugene represents the symbol of a "made" German and not of a "born" one due to his Italian French roots and Habsburg loyalties. As a consequence, he represents the essence of "Austrianity," which is based on a community of beliefs (much like Roth's view of Austria), not on one of blood: "Prince Eugene is the finest example of what in the monarchy used to be called a '*gelernter Österreicher*.' When one has grasped the idea in all its profundity, one comes to the conclusion that a good Austrian can only be a *gelernter* Austrian, that is to say, made, not born. For to be Austrian means just that: to have got beyond the blood-bound instinctive, the daemonic, to have been remade into the occidental universal human being, in the tradition of the Empire" (Werfel 36).
13. These early articles confirm Józef Wittlin's recollections of young Roth as an intellectual hostile to militarism and the monarchy.

14. For Klaus Westermann, this common moral ground is expressed in Roth's emotional response to the world, in his constant defense of humanity, which takes precedence over any surface ideological contradictions: "Bei allen Gegensätzlichkeiten dieser beiden Standorte gab es doch Gemeinsamkeiten: in beiden Fällen ['Sozialist' und 'Monarchist'] handelte und schrieb Roth eher aus einem Gefühl heraus denn aus ideologischer Überzeugung, ein theoretisches Fundament war nicht vorhanden" 'In spite of all the contrariness of these two positions [socialist and monarchist], there were similarities: in both cases Roth acted and wrote rather from a feeling than from ideological conviction; a theoretical foundation was not present' (214).
15. The question of continuity between the early and late phases of Roth's work has been dealt with by many critics who have emphasized the nonideological, moral nature of Roth's thinking, a nature that escapes easy identifications and categorizations. Hansotto Ausserhofer, drawing on Anton Böhm, writes: "Das gesamte Denken von Joseph Roth beruht auf einer 'moralisch unabänderlichen Ordnung', die eigentlich die 'innere Struktur' seiner Werke bildet. . . . Der Weg von anarchiefreundlichen Sozialisten zum loyalen Legitimisten verläuft demnach bei Roth nicht über viele Erfahrungen und Selbstberichtigungen. Er ist nur eine kurze Spanne, eine spiralförmige Drehung um die eine Achse: Menschheit" 'Joseph Roth's whole thinking rests on a "morally unalterable order" that actually forms the "inner structure" of his works. . . . The path from the anarchy-prone socialist to the loyal legitimist does not run, therefore, through many experiences and self-adjustments. It is only a short span, a spiral rotation around the one axis: mankind' (129).
16. Werfel also identifies the Austrian "over-arching idea" with a transcendent principle of equally religious bearing (16).
17. According to Hans Richard Brittnacher, Roth's preference for certain professions, such as peasant, chestnut salesman, coral merchant, and coachman, has to do with his resistance to the idea of historical change. These professions are honorable precisely because they have a natural "Renitenz gegen den Zugriff der Geschichte" 'refractoriness against the grasp of history' (171). This interpretation is compatible with the concept of a transhistoric "aristocracy of the spirit" that unites people beyond historically determined social divides.
18. Georg Lukács points out in his famous 1939 *Literaturnaja gazeta* article devoted to *The Radetzky March* Roth's "ideologische Schwäche" 'ideological weakness' and that his "Herz ist ja auf der Seite der untergehenden Monarchie" 'heart is on the side of the vanishing monarchy' ("Radetzkymarsch" 148). While Lukács characterizes Roth's ideological attachment to the imperial world as reactionary, Ingeborg Sültemeyer emphasizes the leftist character of his early work (13).

19. Stefan Zweig's memoir of imperial Austria is strikingly similar: "The rhythm of the new speed had not yet carried over from the machines, the automobile, the telephone, the radio, and the airplane, to mankind; time and age had another measure" (25).
20. Stefan Zweig offers a similar portrayal of imperial Austria's immobility: "Everything had its norm, its definite measure and weight. . . . In this vast empire everything stood firmly and immovably in its appointed place, and at its head was the aged emperor" (1–2).
21. Musil reiterates the same idea of lifelessness in his portrait of Emperor Franz Joseph: "In the last decade of his and Kakania's life, younger people who were familiar with the current state of the arts and sciences were sometimes overtaken by doubt whether he existed at all. The number of portraits one saw of him was almost as great as the number of inhabitants of his realms; on his birthday there was as much eating and drinking as on that of the Savior, on the mountains the bonfires blazed, and the voices of millions of people were heard vowing that they loved him like a father. . . . But his popularity and publicity was so over-convincing that it might easily have been the case that believing in his existence was rather like still seeing certain stars although they ceased to exist thousands of years ago" (93).
22. The commitment to the service code (*Dienstpragmatik*), of which Werfel writes in *The Twilight of a World*, constitutes a common motif in Austrian literature, as Heimito von Doderer's novel *Die erleuchteten Fenster* (*The Lighted Windows*) demonstrates. In Doderer's novel, Julius Zihal's series of sensual revelations amount to his liberation from the domineering presence of an internalized service code.
23. Dollenmayer considers the "split" person of the monarch as evidence of the conflict between a real and an imaginary emperor: "Here he emerges as split within himself into a historical and a private persona. Those around him see only the former, while the narrator implicitly celebrates the latter. It is the private Kaiser who is 'true', the public figure who is 'artificial'. The clash of these two constitutes the fictional Franz Joseph of *The Radetzky March*" (307). However, Dollenmayer mistakenly considers that Roth celebrates the private person of the emperor, when he is in fact interested in the mechanism through which the private individual submits his will to the higher calling of the office, of tradition. For this reason, Count Morstin of "The Bust of the Emperor" loves Franz Joseph not because of his personality but because of his office.
24. Alfred Kurer argues that the virtue of loyal and unswerving servitude that Roth underlines in the novel is deeply ingrained in the Austrian literary imagination: "Dienen als Maxime, als Zweck und Erfüllung des Lebens: in ihm manifestiert sich ein Hauptzug österreichischen Wesen, der in unzähligen Werken österreichischer

Autoren relevant wird" 'To serve as a maxim, as a purpose and fulfillment of life: in it manifests itself a main trait of the Austrian essence, which becomes relevant in countless works by Austrian authors' (16).

25. Thomas Düllo traces the origins of Roth's preoccupation with the idea of voluntary vassalage ("der Typus des freien Vasallen") to the beginning of his journalistic career. In a 1924 text devoted to the assassination of Walter Rathenau, Roth writes about the latter's butler as the embodiment of wisdom and self-restraint. Düllo points out that the free vassal represents the ideal expression of the utopian mixture of order and freedom that Roth opposes to the tyranny of historical contingency (224).
26. In the history of Austrian literature from Nestroy to Robert Musil, whose character Leo Fischel, from *The Man without Qualities*, appears as a representative of a petit bourgeois, humanist nineteenth-century cosmopolitan and conservative culture, these qualities have always been associated with a moderate conservatism, Claudio Magris argues (*Weit von wo* 146).
27. The same feeling of ethereality characterizes Werfel's description of the Austrian Empire: "the Empire was dead; it carried on only a deceptive semblance of life" (Werfel 22).
28. Although Jan Schlosser interprets Carl Joseph's alienation as a form of implicit social criticism of the feudal system, Roth is actually more interested in the moral response of the individual faced with complex social and historical situations rather than with the critique of these situations per se.
29. The multigenerational structure of the novel and the contrast between an orderly generation of the fathers and a decadent one of the sons has made some critics draw comparisons with other "family novels." Jacques Le Rider sees similarities to Musil's *The Man without Qualities* ("Arbeit" 22), while Reinhard Baumgart sees in it "den südlichen und ebenbürtigen Pendant zu *Buddenbrooks*" 'the southern and equal counterpart to *Buddenbrooks*' ("Drei Ansichten" 348).
30. This conception of Austria as a conglomerate of nations, a conception opposed to the organicist nationalism of ethnic sovereignty, was widely popular among the Central European Jews who did not want to assimilate into any national group or to follow their own national dream, Zionism. For monarchist authors such as Roth, Werfel, and Zweig but also for socialist politicians such as Otto Bauer, the idea of a multiethnic nation played an important role, whether this was understood in the form of an imperial construct or in that of a federative socialist state: "Österreich ist umzubilden in einen demokratischen Nationalitätenbundesstaat. An Stelle der historischen Kronländer werden national abgegrenzte Selbstverwaltungskörper gebildet. . . . So wird sie [die sozialistische Gesellschaft] die nationalen Gemeinwesen allmählich als autonome Glieder einem großen, neuartigen, internationalen

Gemeinwesen einordnen" 'Austria is to be transformed into a democratic federation of nations. Instead of the historic crownlands, nationally demarcated self-governing bodies are formed. . . . Thus, [the socialist society] gradually integrates the national communities as autonomous members of a great, new, international commonwealth' (Otto Bauer 532–33).

31. Not without irony, Robert Musil credited his quasi-fictional Kakania (a play on the official k.k. or k.u.k.—"kaiserlich und königlich," "imperial and royal"—title of the Dual Monarchy) with the ability of being both conservative and liberal: "By its constitution it was liberal, but its system of government was clerical. The system of government was clerical, but the general attitude to life was liberal" (Musil 33).
32. It is beyond the purview of this study to analyze the complex relationship between Roth's progressive and reactionary discourse and that of the socialist and fascist circles of his time. The delicate balance between the Left and Right political ideologies of the European interwar period, with their distinct goals but often intellectual affinities, makes it a particularly difficult task to assign Roth's highly original political concepts a clear ideological affiliation. Wolf R. Marchand's study *Joseph Roth und völkisch-nationalistische Wertbegriffe* (*Joseph Roth and Ethnic-Nationalist Value Concepts*) is focused precisely on the right-leaning ambiguity of Joseph Roth's political thinking: "Es ging schließlich darum, zu zeigen, daß und wie Roth auf den reaktionären und irrationalen Verfall von Politik und Literatur im nazistisch werdenden Deutschland reagierte, mit einer Entwicklung reagierte, die ihn immer näher an Gedanken und Wertvorstellungen seiner Feinde heranführte" 'Finally, the idea was to show that Roth responded to the reactionary and irrational decay of politics and literature in Nazi Germany and how he responded, with a development that brought him closer and closer to the ideas and values of his enemies' (1).
33. "The irreverent Austrian gave a name to this policy, coining the classic phrase '*fortwursteln*,' a conception allied to the English 'muddling through.' Franz Joseph knew that one single step lay between him and the abyss. But the eighty-year-old man still hoped that he need not take that step. When would it come, the release of death, to free Caesar's soul from the weight of seven decades of cruel responsibility? He would leave the actual end to his successor, that ambiguous, choleric man, whose nostrils twitched with eagerness to take over the long-delayed sovereignty!" (Werfel 26). Robert Musil's concept of "Es ist passiert" (it just sort of happened) satirically conveys the same idea of desubstantialization of reality that characterized the classical Austrian world: "It was a peculiar phrase, not known in this sense to the Germans and without equivalent in other languages, the very breath of it transforming facts and the bludgeonings of fate into something light as eiderdown, as thought itself" (Musil 35).

34. Ulrike Steierwald, who employs Hayden White's terminology, considers Roth's distortion of the historical past an indication of a certain "metahistorical" consciousness, which evinces the textuality of any actual historical account: "Die Wahl eines historischen Themas zielt nicht auf das Wiederfinden einer Vergangenheit, sondern macht durch die offenkundige Transformation von Quellen und historiographischen Studien . . . die Textualität jeder 'Geschichte' transparent" 'The choice of a historical subject does not aim at the recovery of a past, but makes the textuality of any "history" transparent through the obvious transformation of sources and historiographical studies' (149). However, she mistakenly credits Roth with a certain "postmodern" historiographical interpretation when he is in fact interested precisely in the practical, moral character of historical rendition, a reason why the recourse to verifiable historical facts does not concern him.
35. Roth's notion of truth is therefore governed by a practical understanding of verity, by the question concerning the moral implications of the notion of truth. This does not mean that he is a textual relativist, as Steierwald claims—"der Text [kann] nur noch nach der Evidenz seiner Sinnkonstruktion im Rahmen einer vorgegebenen kommunikativen Übereinkunft befragt und bewertet werden" 'the text can only be interrogated and evaluated on the basis of the evidence of its meaning construction within the framework of a given communicative agreement' (155)—but that any interpretation context is relative to a moral truth.
36. Hermann Broch rejected the idealization of the Habsburg world in the interwar literary historical reconstructions as mere "Kitsch" (Steierwald 150). Magris also considers this glorification of the actual harsh social relations in the Dual Monarchy an inversion between reality and fiction, which many Austrian adherents of the "Habsburg myth" supported: "Der Immobilismus wird also mit tiefem Bedeutungsgehalt umkleidet und zu einer Offenbarung höher Weisheit erhoben, während er doch nur eine schmerzliche, von den objektiven Verhältnissen auferlegte Realität war, . . . : so werden Begrenzungen und Fehler zu Vorzügen und Tugenden" 'Immobilism, therefore, is endowed with a profound meaning, and elevated to the status of a revelation of higher wisdom, while it was only a painful reality imposed by objective circumstances, . . . : thus limitations and mistakes are turned into advantages and virtues' (*Der Habsburgische Mythos* 15).
37. Steierwald emphasizes the romantic origins of this philosophy of history. By reminding the reader of Friedrich Schlegel's aphorism "Der Historiker ist ein rückwärts gekehrter Prophet" 'the historian is a backward-looking prophet,' Steierwald argues that the opposition to a historical conception "die die Gegenwart als Schnittpunkt einer durch die Richtung des Fortschritts verbundenen Vergangenheit und Zukunft begreift" 'that understands the present as an intersection of a past and future that

are united by the direction of progress' is rooted in romantic ideology (Steierwald 162).

38. The image of female characters in Roth's work has been addressed by many critics, and although many of them agree on the author's misogyny, others question the validity of such a conclusion. Müller-Funk describes Roth's work as "durch und durch misogyn" 'thoroughly misogynous' (*Joseph Roth* 144), while Dietmar Mehrens talks about the negative influence of the "femmes fatales" over the characters. Similarly, Elke Frietsch argues that Roth associates women's emancipation with social and cultural degeneration, expressed especially in women's art (painting and film), as exemplified by *The Emperor's Tomb* (418). For Helen Chambers, however, women play a dual contradictory role in Roth's work, "both victims and predators" ("Predators or Victims" 127).
39. In the later part of his life, Roth reported about his participation (as a soldier) at the funerals of Emperor Franz Joseph in 1916. This fact is, however, not entirely elucidated, as Roth's military record seems to contradict this claim. Nevertheless, in the 1935 article "In der Kapuzinergruft" 'In the Tomb of the Emperor,' the Austrian author relates this event as evidence of his monarchic attachment: "Wem weinte ich damals nach?—Gewiß dem Kaiser Franz Joseph: aber auch mir selbst, meiner eigenen Kindheit, meiner eigenen Jugend. . . . Damals fühlte ich, daß ich ein Österreicher bin; ein alter Österreicher. Alle Kaiser von Österreich waren meine Kaiser gewesen. Alle Kaiser von Österreich, die noch kommen könnten, werden *meine* Kaiser sein. . . . Deshalb pilgere ich, wenn ich das Glück habe, nach Österreich heimkehren zu können, in die Kapuzinergruft, meinen Kaiser zu begrüßen" 'Whose loss did I bemoan at the time?—Certainly the Emperor Franz Joseph's: but also my own, that of my own childhood, of my own youth. . . . At that time I felt I was an Austrian; a Habsburg Austrian. All the emperors of Austria had been my emperors. All emperors of Austria, who could still come, will be my emperors. . . . Therefore, when I am fortunate enough to be able to return to Austria, I pilgrimage to the Capuchin Crypt (*Kapuzinergruft*) to salute my Emperor' (Roth, *Werke* 3: 672).
40. Alfred Doppler points out that *The Tomb of the Emperor* marks a return to an earlier type of novel construction, both in form and in content: "Aber es ist nicht allein die Form, die er [Roth] wieder aufgreift. Auch die Geisteshaltung des Verlorenseins in der Welt, das Thema der verlorenen Generation werden variiert und bis zur Todesverfallenheit intensiviert" 'But it is not only the form that he [Roth] takes up again. Also, the mind-set of forsakenness in the world and the theme of the lost generation are varied and intensified to the point of morbid fascination' (92).
41. Klaus Bohnen argues that Roth considers the institutions of the Catholic Church, the monarchy, and the Jewish religion from the perspective of their social, cultural,

and political roles, not from that of their actual substance. It is the form of these institutions that is more important than their actual content: "Nicht der Inhalt in ihnen allerdings—weder die sozialen und politischen Fragwürdigkeiten der Monarchie noch die religiösen Anweisungen des Katholizismus oder der jüdischen Religion—stellen diese Ordnung her, sondern allein deren Form als Bollwerk gegen den Zerfall und die daraus folgende Unversöhnlichkeit der Frontenbildung" 'However, it is not the content [of these institutions], neither the social and political dubiousness of the monarchy, nor the religious directives of Catholicism or the Jewish religion that establish this order, but their form as a bulwark against the disintegration and the resulting irreconcilability of factionalism' (64).

42. Similarly, Stefan Zweig has a memory of the serialization of the Austrian archetypes throughout the empire, the reproduction of the same reality throughout a multinational world: "Even today I cannot forget the musty, moldy smell that clung to this house as it did to all official buildings in Austria. We called it the 'treasury' smell" (Zweig 30). Werfel also argues that the face of Emperor Franz Joseph was an emblem of the Austrian world, which explains why it was mechanically reproduced in the hairstyle of many citizens: "The face became a prototype. The streets were full of Franz Josephs; faces familiar and remote, with white beards parted in the middle, were in all government offices. Even porters at the doors of stately palaces wore the mask" (Werfel 22).
43. According to Malachi Hacohen, the theme of Eastern Jewry's loyalty to the Habsburg Crown, often reiterated by Roth, has a historical explanation: "The one-sided love affair that the masses of orthodox Galician *Kaisertreuen* (imperial patriots) had with Franz Josef reflected their recognition of Austro-Hungary as a 'kingdom of grace,' contrasted with the realm of pogroms and 'evil decrees' across the Russian border" (115).
44. Telse Hartmann analyzes in depth the idea of national identity in Roth's fictional and journalistic writings by resorting to the classic theories of nationalism formulated by Benedict Anderson, Eric Hobsbawm, and Ernest Gellner. Hartmann argues that Roth advances the idea of a heterogeneous national identity that resists the uniformity of an abstract concept of nation, uniformity considered indispensable by the theorists mentioned. According to Hartmann, for Roth the national idea is always eroded by hybridization at its margins, which is why drawing national borders will always be imprecise and arbitrary (40). She uses this thesis as evidence of Roth's preference for hybrid, incomplete, and decentered identities, whether personal or collective. However, Hartmann fails to understand that Roth is not simply interested in affirming a fragmentary notion of identity as evidence of the arbitrariness of the modern "grand narratives" of the subject, nation, or class. He

is also keen on demonstrating that this arbitrariness demands our moral responsibility for how we shape our identity. Hartmann's postmodern reading asserts the idea of hybridity as a goal in itself, as the impossibility of the subject's closure, while Roth was interested in it as a means for obtaining a higher form of subjectivity and moral clarity.

45. Klaus Pauli devoted an entire study to the similarities between *The Emperor's Tomb* and *The Silent Prophet*, insisting on the parallel between Franz Ferdinand Trotta and Friedrich Kargan: "Beide Protagonisten wenden sich in einer entscheidenden Phase ihres Lebens auf verschiedene Weise von ihrer Gegenwartszeit ab. Der eine richtet seine Hoffnungen ganz auf eine bessere politische Zukunft—der andere versucht, seine Resignation durch die verklärende Versenkung in die Vergangenheit aufzufangen" 'In different ways, both protagonists abandon their present time in a decisive phase of their lives. One of them aims his hopes at a better political future—the other tries to make up for his resignation through the transfiguring immersion in the past' (23).
46. Roth's paternalistic imagination, credited by Magris with representing the key to the author's work, constantly singles out the destruction of paternal authority in the rapidly modernizing and democratizing Western societies, which is tantamount to the fall into immoral anarchism of individualism. As Roth writes in "Rede über den alten Kaiser," "Welch eine widerliche Ungeduld ist in die Leute gefahren? Weshalb warten sie nicht auf die Entscheidung des Vaters? Der Vater heißt Franz Joseph der Erste" 'What a hideous impatience has gotten into the people? Why do not they wait for the father's decision? The father is called Franz Joseph the First' (*Werke* 3: 939).
47. Zweig also emphasizes the transnational character of Austrian aristocracy as a sign of spiritual community: "At court, among the nobility, and among the people, the German was related in blood to the Slavic, the Hungarian, the Spanish, the Italian, the French, the Flemish" (Zweig 13). For him, the particularity of the Viennese spirit consists precisely in this "meeting of the most heterogeneous elements, and in her spiritual supernationality" (24).
48. Magris also draws an interesting comparison to Jewish utopian thinking by arguing that Bloch built his Utopia in a *Noch-nicht-Sein* of revolutionary nature, whereas Roth built his in a *Nicht-mehr-Zeit* of conservative nature: "Doch Bloch sucht die Heimat in einer zukünftigen Nicht-Zeit, während Roth sie gerade in der Nicht-Zeit der Kindheit sucht, das heißt im hinter uns Liegenden statt im vor uns Liegenden, auf Ithaka wie der homerische Odysseus statt jenseits der Säulen des Herkules wie der dantesche. In diesem Sinn steht sein Konservatismus chassidischer Prägung entschieden gegen jede Form des jüdisch-revolutionären Messianismus" 'However,

Bloch is looking for the homeland in a future nontime, while Roth is looking for it in the nontime of childhood, that is, in what is behind instead of before us, on Ithaca, like the Homeric Odysseus, and not beyond the Pillars of Hercules, as in Dante. In this sense, his Chassidic-inspired conservatism is firmly opposed to any form of Jewish-revolutionary Messianism' (Magris, *Weit von wo* 116). However, Magris does not consider the convergence of the two models in the eternal present of the "now": for Bloch as well as for Roth, the engine of an ontology of not-yet (or no-more) lies in the projective capacity of the present, which melts the future and the past in the same utopian unit. Gershon Shaked also rejects Magris's thesis about Roth's "backward-looking" conservatism, arguing that Roth does not deny the future but instead affirms its problematic nature, a nature that demands moral action from the individuals confronted with it. The problem of Jewish assimilation in the West is one such case (Shaked, "Wie jüdisch" 11).

49. Steinmann sees in this aspect of Roth's literary imagination a reflex of his intellectual and spiritual indebtedness to Hassidism: "Im Gegensatz zu jeder teleologischen Denkbewegung lebt der Chassidismus in einer archaischen Denkwelt: Das Ziel liegt im Ursprung" 'In contrast to any teleological movement of thought, Chasidism lives in an archaic thought-world: the destination is the origin' (*Von der Würde* 23).

Chapter 5

Redemption and Irony: The Case of *The Tale of the 1002nd Night*

A distinct position among Roth's novels is occupied by *The Tale of the 1002nd Night*, first drafted in 1937 but published commercially only posthumously, in 1939, and therefore generally considered Roth's last important work of fiction. Although the *Tale* is usually treated as a historical novel, being often discussed alongside other "Austrian" novels such as *The Radetzky March* and *The Tomb of the Emperor*, there is little in the *Tale* of the way in which history is presented to justify such an association. The distinctive feature of *The Radetzky March*, *The Tomb of the Emperor*, and "The Bust of the Emperor" is the redemptive function of historical reconstruction, the idea that history's injustices could be repaired by a morally invested *travail de mémorie*. Such an intention seems to be absent from the *Tale*, where the world of former Austria-Hungary appears, similarly to Napoleonic France in the novel *The Hundred Days*, as mere background rather than focus. The presence of Austrian nobility, political intrigues, *kaiserlich und königlich* (k.u.k.) institutions and mentalities has led some critics (Sidney Rosenfeld, Alfred Kurer) to compare the *Tale* with distinctly "Austrian" works by Arthur Schnitzler and Hugo von Hofmannsthal, works staged against the same fin de siècle background. The focus on Austria as a historical reality is also highlighted by Irmgard Wirtz, Klaus Zelewitz ("Palmen"), and Wolfgang Müller-Funk ("Nach der 1001. Nacht"), albeit in the case of Müller-Funk it is the ironic, inverted image of Austria that is important. Such associations and interpretations are not irrelevant, but most of them are individually significant in the sense in which certain themes and ideas common to classic Austrian literature reappear in the *Tale* without, however, lending the novel a distinctly "Austrian" character or emphasizing the "Austrian" specificity of these themes and ideas.

But the general difficulty with the *Tale* resides in the fact that it cannot be easily placed into any category of Roth novels. Unlike the novels of religious inspiration, the focus is not on the redemption of the individual through an existential *metanoia,* and unlike the early individualist novels, there is no emphasis on the tragic retreat of the individual from a hostile, inauthentic, and corrupt world. And yet, there are elements from all three categories: there is a disagreement between the individual and the world, there are transgressions and attempts at expiation, and there is also a sense of the clash between transient history and permanent principles. However, these elements do not come together to offer the moral coherence of the other novels, which stay under the sign of the crucial search for redemption. The question of redemption remains somewhat suspended in the *Tale,* even if it surfaces at times without, however, the immediacy with which it appears in the other novels. In spite of all of these ambiguities, the *Tale* offers a refreshing window into some of Roth's persisting themes and dilemmas, delivered with a unique ironic-solemn mixture of detachment and compassion.

The novel begins in nineteenth-century Persia at the court of the shah, whose recent ennui constitutes a source of puzzlement to himself and his subjects. Nothing seems to please him anymore, and his impatience with everyone and everything soon becomes a state issue. His trusted eunuch Patominos seems, however, to comprehend the source of his longing: the shah, a captive of his own self-sufficient comfort and immediate gratifications, unconsciously craves to know the outside world. Once the shah understands the cause of his unhappiness, he decides to leave right away for Vienna, a destination both Western and politically welcoming, given the complex world of nineteenth-century international politics.[1] The complicated preparations necessary for such a trip take place rapidly but without the ruler's knowledge, because a shah cannot be bothered with such trivial matters or be informed that his power is not all-encompassing. Eventually he arrives at his destination, where to his disappointment nothing seems to arouse his interest except the imperial horses, the Lipizzaner, and the Viennese women, whose open Western manners and dress make them enticing to the Oriental eye. Roth plays here with the old motif of the exotic traveler's impressions of Europe, impressions that puzzle the Western audience through their cultural specificity, thus shedding a new light on the relativity of all the things that are taken for granted in Europe. In Montesquieu's *Persian Letters,* the Persian visitor Usbek voices a similar bewilderment at manners and fashions that seem unquestionable to the Parisians.

The shah appears to take a particular interest in a certain Countess W., the wife of an influential count. The shah's demand that the countess be made available to him for the satisfaction of his erotic curiosities produces a great perplexity at the imperial court because of the equal impossibility of satisfying or refusing such a demand. Fortunately, a solution is found by the cavalry captain Baron Taittinger, whose romantic interests once also paused momentarily at the countess. He knows a simple girl named Mizzi Schinagl, a Viennese beauty with whom he was once involved due to her striking similarity to Countess W. It was a simple infatuation, not love, because Taittinger is the kind who is capable of only one type of love, for himself: "He loved only, as per usual, himself" (*Tale* 46). As a result of their affair, Mizzi gave birth to an illegitimate child whom she sent to a foster home. Compromised, she had to give up her engagement to a local barber and, in need of financial support, decided to work in a brothel. Without any qualms, Taittinger arranges for the shah to be secretly taken to the brothel and deceived into thinking that he is having a night of passion with the countess. When the night is over, the shah realizes that the Western world does not have anything special to offer and decides to return home but not before sending Mizzi a pearl necklace of great value as a gift. This fated gift proves, however, to mark the beginning of a chain of events that will bring fortune to some and misfortune to others.

After the shah's departure, the story turns to Mizzi, Taittinger, and their world. Now rich, Mizzi retires from her job but does not relinquish the hope that one day her beloved cavalry captain, Baron Taittinger, will return to her. In the meantime she finds comfort in the company of Franz Lissauer, a small-time crook who takes advantage of her fortune in order to invest in an illegal counterfeit Brussels lace business. When his dealings are revealed, Mizzi loses her money and her freedom, being sentenced to a light prison term. Through an unfortunate set of coincidences, the happy-go-lucky Baron Taittinger, now assigned to a provincial garrison in order to cover up the so-called shah affair, meets Mizzi again, this time in prison: "It was the first time in his life he had felt pity" (121). This feeling of compassion contributes to his increasing discontent with the world around him. He is getting older and, to top it off, goes bankrupt through negligence and naïveté. Trying to keep up the appearance and hoping to regain some admiration, he ill-advisedly allows a tabloid journalist to publish a glamorized version of the shah affair. Once the story becomes public, the influential Count W. arranges for Taittinger's immediate discharge from the army, where he had spent his entire career. Suddenly, Taittinger realizes that the world around him has changed: "All of a sudden, the world seemed a changed place to the Captain of Horse, or, more accurately, it seemed to be beginning to reveal itself to him in its full true ghastliness" (155).

When Mizzi returns from prison she is part of a new circle of plebeian friends, who advise her to exploit her incredible story at a popular freak circus in Prater Park. She even manages to obtain Taittinger's sponsorship to acquire the decor for a theatrical reconstruction of the shah affair, but when the baron sees the reenactment, he is stunned at its vulgarity and decides to have as little to do with Mizzi as possible. Directionless and broke, he seeks a renewed military assignment, in any capacity and anywhere. But his own youthful affair with Mizzi keeps haunting him: their illegitimate son, Xandl, returns from the foster home. An emotionless, crafty, and irresponsible young man, he represents the painful reminder of an emotionless and irresponsible relationship and the distorted image of everything Taittinger imagined his own offspring should be. Trying to rid himself of Xandl, Taittinger offers him some money, which Xandl uses to purchase a gun that he carelessly shoots in public. Once again the press digs behind the story, and Taittinger's name resurfaces at the worst moment possible: the shah is planning a return to Vienna. In order to bury the affair once and for all, the authorities decide to reject Taittinger's request to rejoin the army. Defeated, the baron takes his own life, while Mizzi, having reinvented herself as a circus actress, opens her show to great popular success. The novel ends with the shah's return to Vienna and his conversation with the eunuch Patominos, who reveals to his master the truth about the vanity and transience of all human ambition, or "the characteristic motifs of *memento mori* and *vanitas*" (Heath 330).

"Roth's Satire"

The circular form of the *Tale* emphasizes the motionlessness and permanence of the world, an affirmation of Ecclesiastes' *nihill sub sole novum*. The theme of permanence in change and of the purposelessness of all transformation is consistent with Roth's philosophy of stoicism, a philosophy that brackets the course of events narrated in the story. The *Tale* displays many of the characteristics of a tale, from the Oriental atmosphere conjured up through the title and the opening scenes at the court of the Persian shah to the evocative language and the ritualism of social hierarchies and human interactions. It is the tale of the 1,002nd night, told after all the other Oriental tales of the *1001 Nights* have been told, but it is a deceitful tale because in actuality there is little to be told. In a way, the *Tale* is a pseudotale exactly because there is nothing magic in it; there is no movement, no heroism, and no catharsis. The apparent magic of the Viennese aristocratic world at its golden and sentimental zenith is intentionally contradicted by the spectacle of a base and trivial universe of human desires and actions. The effect is sobering and edifying: there is nothing enchanted, even in a world endowed with all the external and emotional investments of magic. Roth mocks in the story the typical idealization of Habsburg Austria's golden age, of that Viennese "*Gemütlichkeit,*" although his other "Austrian" novels contain instances that partly reenforce the mythology of *felix Austria*. This dissonance sheds a new light on Roth's reconstructions of Austria, which should also be interpreted ironically and not only solemnly. Roth demonstrates through the *Tale* the other side of gravity, the humor of all historical situations and the necessity of always taking such situations with a grain of salt.

Roth's parody of the sentimental folk tale echoes Ödön von Horváth's 1931 satirical play *Geschichten aus dem Wiener Wald* (*Tales from the Vienna Woods*, a direct reference to Johann Strauss the Younger's famous waltz), a mordant caricature of the mythology of Viennese pastoral *Heuriger* and romantic waltzes. But the *Tale* is also similar to Horváth's *Tales* in plot development and the focus on proletarian characters. In both works, a young girl from a Viennese working-class district leaves her plebeian fiancé for a crook who gets her into trouble. In the *Tale,* Mizzi Schinagl leaves the barber Xandl for Franz Lissauer, the shady dealer whose dealings land her in prison. Similarly, Horváth's Marianne, the typical Viennese *Mädel*, leaves the butcher Oskar for the rascal Alfred, who ruins and humiliates her, causing her to end up in prison as well. Mizzi works as a prostitute, while Marianne works as a cabaret dancer who is almost pushed into prostitution. Both women have an illegitimate child who is given away for the sake of convenience, and in both works a puppet maker and a cavalry captain appear. Both captains are typical Viennese *bon viveurs*, proud of their Habsburg world, agreeable but utterly superficial. (Naturally, Roth's Rittmeister Taittinger is the protagonist of the *Tale,* a complex character who is depicted with irony but also with sympathy. By contrast, Horváth's character is minor and presented sarcastically, almost as a caricature.) Both works suggest that the idealization of the Habsburg world, idealization popular at the turn of the twentieth century among the Austrian middle-class strata but dismissed by intellectuals such as Hermann Broch and Karl Kraus as sentimental kitsch, obscures painful but real human experiences that transcend a particular place or time. In this sense, the reality of suffering and the misery and self-destruction of everyday people are more significant than the grand historical narrative of Austria and the Habsburgs, which is often nothing more than a simple adornment, worn proudly by the cavalry officers. In the *Tale*, the eunuch Patominos conveys this truth through his wise conclusion that although things change in space and time, they remain fundamentally the same: "All things change, Sire. . . . And all things remain the same. That's my opinion!" (*Tale* 257).

The *Tale* is to a considerable extent a synthesis of motifs and character types developed by Roth earlier in his fiction. For this reason, Klaus Zelewitz correctly points out that the story is almost an "Intra-Roth-Diskurs" 'Intra-Roth discourse' ("Palmen" 110). There are characters who embody the idea of stoic resignation and wisdom, such as the eunuch Patominos and the officer Zenower, a simple man endowed with common sense and a warm humanity, Taittinger's only genuine friend. Due to their insight into the emptiness of human ambition, they have achieved a position of redeemed harmony with the universe that puts them beyond the tribulations of the other characters. They recall other similar characters in Roth's novels, such as Mendel Singer of *Weights and Measures*, Nathan Kristianpoller of *Tarabas*, and even the emperor Franz Joseph in *The Radetzky March*. There are also characters who typify the very opposite human type, the ambitious, vain, and superficial individual, a product of circumstances and susceptible to the whims of history. Mizzi Schinagl, Franz Lissauer, the journalists, the other plebeian characters, and many others form a kaleidoscope of unstable human personalities, constantly in pursuit of ambitions that ruin them and those around them. In Roth's theological dichotomy redemption/damnation, these characters are condemned to the latter and resemble characters such as the Bernheim brothers of *Right and Left*, Elizabeth Trotta of *The Emperor's Tomb*, and Jenö Lakatos of "The Leviathan." When they do not succumb to their own vanity, these characters tempt others to commit grave sins that destroy their peace of mind and harmony with the world.

Baron Taittinger falls, however, outside of any clear category of characters, although he too combines features associated with various character types. The result is not a composite, artificial personality but is instead a compelling character, consistent and contradictory at the same time. It may even be argued that Roth achieves a peak of psychological complexity through the figure of the cavalry captain Taittinger, who displays the narcissism of an agent Golubtschik, the self-assuredness of a colonel Tarabas, the decorum of a Count Morstin, the naïveté of a Carl Joseph Trotta, the superficial hedonism of a Count Chojnicki (probably not coincidentally, Baron Taittinger shares his name with a famous champagne brand), and the aristocratic hauteur of a Baron Franz von Trotta. Taittinger is the embodiment of a certain type of Habsburg aristocratic officer but one that differs in many ways from Morstin or the Trottas. Although Taittinger shares their feudal-military immobility, mannerisms, and aristocratic sense of social hierarchy, he does not share their Olympian asceticism. To the contrary, he indulges in the self-serving violation of social hierarchies by partaking in the plebeian world of base pleasures and vices but only as long as he can derive a sense of satisfaction from them. When faced with the displeasing aspects of his trespasses, he quickly seeks refuge in his own aristocratic world, proving thus a cowardly inconsistency in behavior. His own characteristic manner of categorizing people in three groups—"first were the 'charmers;' then the 'so-so;' and third and lowest were the 'bores'"—is telling of the expedient and self-centered way in which he interacts with others (*Tale* 28). When he is no longer interested in certain people or situations, he quickly demotes them from "charming" to "boring" or, should his interest suddenly increase, the other way around: "What did he care about Sievering? It was worse than boring: it was 'deadly.' However, a day later, it had become 'charming.'—And that was on account of Mizzi Schinagl" (42).

Baron Taittinger's downfall is due equally to his own failings and to circumstances, a combination of factors favored by Roth in many of his novels. In the *Tale*, the protagonist's poor decisions and character weaknesses enforce the gravity of circumstances that in turn force him into further missteps. The noose of misfortune tightens around Taittinger until it destroys him, which explains why Irmgard Wirtz considers him "ein Verlorener, wie Franz Tunda in der 'Flucht ohne Ende,' Carl Joseph von Trotta im 'Radetzkymarsch' und Franz Ferdinand von Trotta in der 'Kapuzinergruft'" 'a lost one, like Franz Tunda in the *Flight without End*, Carl Joseph von Trotta in *Radetzky March* and Franz Ferdinand von Trotta in *The Emperor's Tomb*' (208). However, Taittinger is different from this gallery of characters insofar as he, and not historical and social forces that transcend his decision power, is the main cause of his own downfall. For this reason, in Klaus Zelewitz's opinion, Taittinger "erweist sich so bei sorgfältigerer Analyse nicht als Vorstufe, sondern als Degeneration des jüngsten Trotta" 'proves himself, upon attentive analysis, to be not a precursor of the young Trotta, but a degenerate version of him' ("Palmen" 115). The baron admits to his errors but only occasionally and without a true attempt at atonement, unlike other Roth characters faced with the reality of their transgressions, such as Tarabas, Golubtschik, and Nissen Piczenik. Shortly before his death Taittinger confesses that "All my life I've behaved like a fool, I can see that now, but it's too late," but he still avoids taking responsibility for his life by hoping for a renewed military appointment that would offer him a predictable and sheltered existence (*Tale* 249). When the appointment fails to materialize, the baron loses any reason to live, taking his own life. This final gesture, which Roth refuses his other major characters, who are either killed or die a natural death or simply disappear into meaninglessness, is another proof of cowardice and evidence for the baron's failed search for redemption.

The baron's existential dependence on a military career is indicative of an underdeveloped personality and of a central fear of individual responsibility. For Roth, individual moral responsibility is the key to finding redemption, regardless of the hostility of historical circumstances. Many of his characters find redemption or a liberating answer to their search in spite of dramatic circumstances, defying enmity or even death and fully assuming responsibility for their actions. The baron's inability to function outside of military life, his inability to grasp the complexity of civilian life, and his evasion of any complications or conflictual relationships are the expression of his moral weakness, a weakness that leads to his eventual downfall: "For the first time in his life, Baron Taittinger was to learn the meaning of the expression 'to take steps.' In the army, you didn't take steps. Everything was done by the book. There were no complications" (*Tale* 116).

The military type that the baron represents might be seen as a commentary on the militarism of the Habsburg monarchy, in which the officers were a privileged and protected caste, but more relevant than the Austrian historical specificity of his case is its general-human dimension. Baron Taittinger recalls Schnitzler's Lieutenant Gustl, the Habsburg officer who hides his worthlessness under the imperial uniform, a uniform that gives him meaning and self-respect, but he is also similar to Dino Buzatti's Lieutenant Drogo of *The Tartar Steppe*, who wastes his life in the military because he refuses to take charge of it. Just like Taittinger, Drogo grows old by putting off a decision that would bring about a change in his life. In the end he is refused the moment of glory he waited for his whole life, dying alone and without purpose. Taittinger's own death is pointless and misunderstood by those around him: when asked why the baron committed suicide, Kalergi, his fellow officer, replies dryly, "I think he lost his way in life. It happens. A man can lose his way!" (251). As is often the case in Roth's novels, the character transcends the sociohistorical dimensions of the narrative backdrop and touches up general-human questions.

And yet, while Taittinger does not achieve redemption in the story, he is not a corrupt soul or a character condemned to objective damnation either. He is not motivated by personal ambition or by excessive vanity, both capital sins in Roth's fictional universe. Instead he is conditioned by habit, by a mentality and social customs that characterize a disappearing world, the world of medieval nobility for whom only the Viennese high society, idealized love, the service code, and horses are of any importance. Everything else is irrelevant or has a purely instrumental value, including people. For Zenower, the baron is a puzzle precisely because he seems to lack any ability to understand human thinking and emotion: "If only he had been exceptionally stupid! Exceptionally wicked! An impassioned gambler or lover! If only he had visibly suffered as a result of being jilted!" (163). The emptiness of the baron's life, his lack of emotions, convictions, and ideas, makes of him, as Reinhard Baumgart points out, "die unheimliche Konstruktion eines leeren Helden" 'the eerie construction of an empty hero' ("Totentanz" 459). Taittinger, the thoroughly mediocre individual, is conditioned by his status and education to act and to relate in ways that alienate him from the rest of society and from himself. This "man without qualities," in his inability to display a personality, is reminiscent of Julius Zihal, the protagonist of Heimito von Doderer's *Die erleuchteten Fenster*, whose typically Habsburg *Dienstpragmatik*, or service code, conditions his entire life, even his most private moments.

In this respect Taittinger shares an important attribute with some of Roth's other Habsburg heroes, the baron Franz von Trotta and the emperor Franz Joseph, who stand out not through their personalities but instead through the intentional suppression of their personalities in favor of their official personas. In *The Radetzky March* and *The Emperor's Tomb*, this characteristic of the feudal service code is presented as further proof of humility, a quality that Roth opposes to the arrogant individualism of modernity. In the *Tale*, the short appearance of Emperor Franz Joseph emphasizes his mediocrity, manifested through his simple Spartan lifestyle, cherished by Roth in some of his nonfictional panegyrics as well, such as the 1939 "Rede über den alten Kaiser." In the novel, the emperor is displeased by the excessive court ceremonies required by the official visit protocol: "Der Kaiser hasste Gastmähler. Er liebte es, rasch zu essen und einfach, wie einer der Gewöhnlichsten seiner Untertanen. Er liebte Suppe, Rundfleisch, Knödel, Apfelkompott. Sein Essen dauerte kaum länger als zehn Minuten. Er liebte ein frisches Krügl Bier, mit recht viel Schaum" 'The Emperor hated banquets. He liked to eat fast and simply, like one of the most common of his subjects. He loved soup, beef, dumplings, apple compote. His meal lasted little more than ten minutes. He loved a fresh mug of beer, with quite a lot of foam' (*Werke* 6: 612).[2]

While not a Spartan, Taittinger is nevertheless similarly molded by his official persona, to the expense of his actual personality. As a consequence, the baron is presented with a considerable degree of sympathy, expressed by Zenower, the character most closely reflecting the auctorial outlook in the novel: "He took the captain as he was, and was fond of him, with his cheery heartlessness, his incapacity to think beyond a couple of thoughts, for which his skull was too roomy, his insignificant love affairs and childish infatuations" (*Tale* 162). But Roth does not limit himself in the *Tale* to the schematic conflict between feudal virtue and modern vice, a conflict that constitutes the core of much of *The Radetzky March*, *The Emperor's Tomb*, and "The Bust of the Emperor." He is interested in the complex processes through which even a virtue, such as submission to the official service code, can become intricately involved with sin. For this reason, "Zenower had no understanding of the machinery that drove a being like the baron to perpetrate such a series of pointless, fatuous, and even self-destructive actions" (162–63). The intricate interlocking of service code, depersonalization, moral paralysis, and historical change constitutes the matrix within which Roth revisits the *locus communis* of the Habsburg myth in order to undermine it and open it to new interpretations.

In Taittinger's case, the intertwining between virtue and sin proves how difficult it is to distinguish between the personal and sociohistorical factors that contribute to the downfall of the individual. On the one hand, his aristocratic and military-Habsburg conditioning is a source of both stoic submission to the service code and lack of personality. On the other hand, the annihilation of his ego leads to a frivolity of behavior that disengages him from the moral connection with the world. It might even be said that Taittinger is amoral rather than immoral. Through the unexpected consequences of his actions, he becomes indirectly responsible for both his own misery and that of those around him. He might see himself as a victim of a conspiracy of circumstances and bad luck—when faced with the gravity of his own indifference and poor decisions, he replies simply "No luck, eh?" (164)—but in fact he bears an individual responsibility. At the same time, although Curt Sanger argues that the decadence present in the novel is that of the characters alone and not of society, the social and historical factors play a role as well (214). Roth is particularly interested in this complex constellation of personal and impersonal factors that lead to the downfall of his heroes and even to that of Austria in the twentieth century.

In a 1939 article titled "The Execution of Austria," Roth argues that Austria has been condemned to disappear not only by external factors but also by its own poor decisions and by its indifference to the rise of modern nationalism. Even as early as the golden era of Franz Joseph's reign the German ethnic component gained precedence over the other nationalities of the empire, sowing the seeds for the future disintegration of Austria. This was not a development from without but instead was "from the hub of an empire," and it happened due to shortsightedness and lethargy (*On the End* 74). The Austrian aristocracy, frivolous, haughty, and "nonchalant," refused to take part in the political developments of the time just because it "was nauseated by politics" and was thus sidelined by the more pragmatic German Junker aristocracy (74). The moral disengagement of Austria's aristocratic leadership from the daily politics of the country at a time of increased democratization led, Roth argues, to the eventual victory of the vulgar political forces, of the nationalists and populists who tore the country asunder. His bitter conclusion is that in order to understand how Austria got where it was in 1939, one has to admit that "historical liability is old. . . . All iniquities are too profound and deeply rooted in the past for our 'sense of the present' to perceive them" (77).[3]

Taittinger in many respects is the typical exponent of this frivolous aristocracy. His indifferent and superior attitude applies not only to his relationship with other people but also to that with politics. For example, he harbors a deep contempt for journalists and for newspapers. As a result he reads only the army's paper, and when forced to come near a stand in order to buy cigarettes, "he had to avert his gaze from the hateful piles of them, with their piercing smell of printer's ink. He didn't exactly know what they contained or what the point of them was" (*Tale* 146). In his trouble-free, orderly, and aristocratic world, only pleasurable and exquisite experiences have any significance: "a good meal, a pleasant drive, an invitation to go shooting, a bottle of champagne, a fortnight's furlough" (235). While the sarcasm of such words contrasts strongly with the admiration for aristocracy that Roth openly displays in his later work, it reminds strikingly of earlier pieces, such as the 1922 article "Der Prinz," in which aristocracy is being lampooned for its easy lifestyle, consisting of nothing more than good food, horse rides, and hunting. In this sense, the *Tale* stands out from Roth's other late novels through its intentional undermining of the conventional image of Habsburg nobility and through its return to motifs and themes developed in Roth's earlier work.

The baron also embodies a type of upper-class romantic libertine and superficial dandy whom other Austrian authors of the time have immortalized in their works. Sidney Rosenfeld compares Tatitinger to Anatol, the protagonist of Arthur Schnitzler's homonymous play and a paragon of fin de siècle narcissistic love, but also with Count Kari Bühl, the main character of Hugo von Hofmannsthal's comedy *Der Schwierige* (*The Difficult Man*), a romantically confused pawn at the mercy of social games and conventions that he cannot grasp (*Understanding* 76). Alfred Kurer sees similarities between the fate of Captain Taittinger and that of the central character of Schnitzler's novella "Spiel im Morgengrauen" ("Night Games"), Lieutenant Wilhelm Kasda, who through ironic twists of fortune has to pay for the mistakes of his youth with his own life (17). The baron is likewise strongly reminiscent of another Schnitzler character, Baron Georg von Wergenthin, a central figure of the novel *Der Weg ins Freie*. Wergenthin is also an empty, self-absorbed, almost unsympathetic nobleman who gets involved with a woman of lower social status, just like Taittinger, but whereas Schnitzler chooses an intelligent and sensitive Jewish woman as the baron's rejected lover, a woman who puts his honor above her own happiness, Roth chooses the vulgar Schinagl for Taittinger, a woman who eventually degrades him and herself. Moreover, Baron von Wergenthin leads a similarly frivolous lifestyle, incapable of any strong commitments or sacrifices, spending his days indulging in his lukewarm hobby of music.

Baron Taittinger displays character traits, social conventions, and mental habits that may be associated with the Austrian and Habsburg aristocratic world at the turn of the twentieth century, but Roth does not intend to make him into a distinctly "Austrian" character. Although his emblematic "charming" manners, nasal way of speaking, and personal aloofness are presented as typically Austrian, the baron transcends the Austrian specificity by illustrating traits and issues associated with the dying aristocracy in the second half of the nineteenth century in general. One is thus easily reminded of the naïveté and interpersonal ineptitude of Dostoyevsky's Prince Myshkin; the hedonism, frivolity, and cynicism of Oscar Wilde's Lord Henry; and the dwindling influence of the noble caste under the increasing influence of liberal-democratic politics as it appears in Tomasi di Lampedusa's *The Leopard*. Furthermore, Taittinger is an illustration of the human failure to take responsibility for one's own actions, a failure that also characterizes other Roth characters regardless of social or ethnic group. In the end, the baron fails due primarily to his individual flaws in conjunction with those of his social class.

Although Roth does not accentuate the political and historical nature of Taittinger's destiny and his world, opting instead for a more balanced perspective that combines personal as well as social factors, some elements pertaining to the political and historical evolution of Austria become apparent throughout the novel. In the beginning, we learn about the peace and stability that governed the world at the time: "Far and wide, the world was deeply, horribly deeply at peace" (138), a leitmotif of the novel. In this "Golden Age of Security," as Stefan Zweig describes it in his memoir, historical events are so rare that the Dual Monarchy's newspapers have to survive on trivial news, something unimaginable from the perspective of Europe in 1937, when the novel was written. And yet in this world of tranquil permanence, the seeds of the future disaster start to bud from the outside but also from the inside. From the outside was the rise of the Prussian power to the north: "A new and still more terrible era was beginning—the Age of Prussia, the age of the Janissaries of Luther and Bismarck" (23). And from the inside were the self-indulgent preoccupation with trivial matters and the generalized boredom brought by stability and prosperity: "Das Problem, an dem

Europa (speziell die k.u.k. Monarchie) leidet ist die Dekadenz durch Langeweile" 'The problem from which Europe (especially the Dual Monarchy) suffers is the decadence caused by boredom' (Oei 177). The *Tale* does not expand on this conjunction of factors, limiting itself to the allusion to its future development. Read in a broader context, however, a context that includes Roth's journalistic and essayistic reflections on the rise of Nazism in Europe, the novel stands out through its somber mood and its anticipation of the disaster looming over Central Europe.

Roth's political and cultural ideas come close in this period to Ortega y Gasset's aristocratic pessimism, especially in regard to the cultural shift produced by the break with tradition. According to Ortega's 1930 *Revolt of the Masses*, the modern "mass-man" has caused this break by taking charge of all the spheres of social life, from education to economy and politics. In the *Tale*, this phenomenon is hinted at as a threat to the political stability of the aristocratic order and to the just hierarchy of values. The proletarian universe of the suburbs, exemplified by Mizzi Schinagl, Josephine Matzner the bordello owner, Leni Kreutzer, and Ignaz Trummer, ironically referred to as "friends from the populace" (230) and by the illegitimate son Xandl, grows in importance throughout the story, moving from the periphery to the center and filling the world of the novel with its increasing demands for visibility, importance, and money. In the end, the baron dies while the proletarian world survives, symbolizing the end of the old world of refined taste and the beginning of a new vulgar era. This new era is not interested in true emotions, real connections, or any social order and is interested only in a society of grotesque spectacle, a spectacle that foreshadows the rise of political demagoguery and social upheaval: "I might be capable," the puppet maker Tino Percoli declares symbolically at the end of the novel, "of making figures that have a heart, conscience, passion, emotion, and decency. But there's no call for that at all in the world. People are only interested in monsters and freaks, so I give them their monsters. Monsters are what they want" (*Tale* 261). The world of these monsters retrospectively anticipates the universe of Roth's early novels, the apocalyptical rule of the "mass-man," and the age of murderous ideologies. Sidney Rosenfeld even sees in Percoli's words "Roth's hopeless protest against the evil of Nazism that Germany now embodied and that threatened to engulf all of Europe" (*Understanding* 97).

The other exponents of the Austrian state, including the secret police, the military establishment, courtiers, and public administration, are presented in the novel in an ambiguous light, in part as the guarantors of institutional continuity, in part as individuals flawed by pettiness and personal ambitions. The secret police force acts unscrupulously but discreetly and ultimately reasonably; the officer corps is undermined by vanity and personal feuds, yet it is the pride of the entire empire; and the well-connected noblemen who occupy important positions in the administration use or abuse these positions for personal reasons, but they are the guardians of good taste, measure, and appropriate decorum. This complex image of Austria, painted in contrasting colors yet with a considerable degree of sympathy and sometimes nostalgia, is appreciated by Ward Powell, who sees in it a "greater perspective and considerably less personal involvement" than in *The Radetzky March* or *The Emperor's Tomb* (200). Irmgard Wirtz considers this image "disillusioned," in contrast to the "rückwärtsgewandte Utopie" 'backward-looking Utopia' typical of the other novels (214). However, while Austria is presented as a political and historical entity in the novel, there is not enough emphasis on it to consider it the novel's main focus. Instead, albeit lively and interestingly depicted, it remains the canvas against which general-human dramas unfold.

The question of redemption constitutes the core of Roth's novels. Refused or granted, beseeched or not, obtained through self-sacrifice or through divine grace, offered to the individual or to an entire epoch, redemption is the center around which everything revolves and toward which everything moves. However, in the *Tale* the question of redemption appears only episodically and in an ironic fashion. Taittinger comes close to personal deliverance when he admits to his errors, but he is too disengaged to assume the full implications of such an admission. In the end, his suicide is a flight from responsibility and an indication of a failed search for redemption. Josephine Matzner, Mizzi's business partner and the plaintiff in the lawsuit against her, is another character who seeks redemption. As a result of the compensation from the lawsuit, she becomes rich but cannot enjoy the money: she feels remorse for having caused Mizzi's incarceration. When Josephine believes that her end is near, she seeks absolution by intending to leave Mizzi all her money after her death. However, when Josephine has a miraculous recovery, she changes her mind. But the recovery is short-lived: she dies the following day while desperately trying to alter her will in Mizzi's favor and thus obtain the much-wanted forgiveness. Not only does Josephne fail in her attempt, but the effect of her exertions is tragic-comic since she tries in vain to buy her own redemption. In contrast to Roth's other novels, in the *Tale* the characters' search for redemption ends in farce.

The *Tale* stands out from the rest of Roth's novels through its compositional diversity and its ironic, farcical tone that is simultaneously detached and involved. In a way, it is a compelling example of what Erica Weitzman calls

"Roth's satire": "an immanent and co-implicated laughter" that relativizes the idea of satire itself (150). The focus is neither the mismatch between individual conscience and the corrupt society, the religious search for deliverance from suffering, nor the redemption of history through morally engaged remembrance. And yet, the novel relies on themes developed in Roth's earlier works, themes woven into a diverse tapestry that manages, however, to maintain its narrative coherence. The theme of the futility of human ambitions is present alongside a distorted, ironic version of *felix Austria*, the motif of the alienated individual is satirized in the person of Baron Taittinger, the idea of penitence is sarcastically conveyed through the characters' ineffective contrition, and the critique of modern democracy is playfully blended with the lampooning of aristocracy. Although anchored in the Austrian society of the late nineteenth century, the *Tale* manages more than other "Austrian" novels to address issues of general-human concern, demonstrating Roth's interest in the problems facing the modern individual in general. In this sense the novel is reminiscent of *Job*, which uses the nineteenth-century Russian Jewish background in order to deal with the dilemmas of modern existence in general.

Notes

1. Klaus Zelewitz points out that the story has a factual correspondent in the visits of the Persian shah Nasir-al-Din to Vienna in 1873 and 1889 ("Palmen" 107).
2. This particular paragraph appears only in the first version from 1937, included in the four-volume edition of collected works edited by Fritz Hackert. The English translation by Michael Hoffmann uses the 1939 edition in which the paragraph is not present.
3. Dietmar Mehrens emphasizes the religious character of the story, demonstrated through the double damnation of the Rittmeister and of the empire: "Beide sind sie als Folge ihres Sündenfalls—und das ist durchaus als religiös zu verstehen—Verlorene. Hierin liegt die ganze Botschaft der 'Geschichte von der 1002. Nacht', in der Roth mit dem Komplex Habsburg und einer religiös motivierten Kritik am sittlichen Zustand seiner Zeit die beiden bestimmenden Themen seines Schaffens zu einem harmonischen Ganzen verwoben hat" 'Both are lost as a result of their capital sin—and this is to be understood in a religious sense. This is the whole message of the *Tale*, in which Roth has interwoven the two defining themes of his work into a harmonious whole: the Habsburg complex and a religiously motivated critique of the moral condition of his time' (331).

Conclusion

Joseph Roth's place in Central European literature is intimately connected with the historical circumstances that shaped the center of Europe in the interwar years of the twentieth century. His work represents a reflection of these circumstances but also an attempt to go beyond them and address problems of general-human validity, such as the role and condition of the individual in modern society and his relationship with his past and his community. This double condition of his work, which is both historical and ahistorical, is not circumstantial. Living in a world in which politics and real history appeared to offer no more than disillusionment and a general feeling of collapse, Roth considered the transgression of reality a necessary condition for offering an actual hope for the individual. However, this flight from history does not simply take on a nostalgic or escapist character but instead reconnects with history on a different, spiritually redeemed, level. It would be equally erroneous to consider Roth's work purely allegorical, hence apolitical, or, to the contrary, highly political and strictly immanent to the historical situation of his time. His fictional world is all about history and politics but a history and a politics of a different kind, one that has been suspended from reality, reconsidered in view of its moral implications, and used as a canvas for the reconstruction of a new reality. For this reason, even if Roth deals with actual historical circumstances (his fictional and nonfictional work alike are rooted in a very acute sense of history), his view on them is always altered by his specific mechanism of perception. Irene Schroeder has therefore credited Roth's literary language with the dual power of reflecting and creating reality through the unification of the moral *Sollen* and the actual *Sein* in a manner reminiscent of the divine logos (28).

Judging the authenticity of his fiction in relation to the real historical events that inspired it is therefore a misunderstanding of his literary imagination and a misinterpretation of his conception of history. Being a realist is for Roth identical with being morally involved in the presentation of reality, even if that means altering it in order to correspond to the moral "truth" of the representation. On the other hand, a purely fictional interpretation of his work ignores the functional, moral (one might even say educational) aspect of his writing, which he always understood as a practical pursuit and not as a lofty, intellectual activity. In a 1935 letter to Stefan Zweig, Roth formulates this practical literary credo in a very original manner: "Writing is a terrestrial thing, and, from a 'metaphysical' vantage point, is in no way different from shoemaking" (*Joseph Roth: A Life* 433). Allegory and realism are not separate categories for Roth, but they merge together at the level of literary imagination through a process that Oei associates with Ernst Cassirer's "symbolische Prägnanz" 'symbolic pregnancy' (43). For this reason, Roth's prose is both a conscious deliverance from the constraints of objective history and a very practical attempt to act upon history through the moral coparticipation of the reader. According to his 1929 article "Es lebe der Dichter!," fiction is a form of "reflection" on observed reality yet is not a bit less real than reality; it is a morally transfigured, upgraded reality (*Werke* 3: 46). This improved form of reality goes beyond the conventional divide separating fact from fiction and reposes the problem of reality from the point of view of authenticity. Thus, the credibility of the literary representation is relative to its degree of aesthetic accomplishment (Weymann 272).

In order to gauge the real dimension of Roth's fictional work, one has to be aware of this specific convergence between allegory and reality that characterizes his writing. Its presence is not arbitrary but instead results from the search for a restored unity of the spiritual and phenomenal world, for a more authentic experience, and ultimately for the redemption of historical existence itself. The realm of redemption represents for Roth not an absolute, static point of reference but rather an experience charged with the values and hopes of historical individuals. It exists through and for them; it changes from generation to generation according to the new challenges brought forth by history, yet it also functions like a living archive of the past. It is the seed of hopefulness that gives confidence to each new individual. For this reason, redemption does not represent for Roth a final posthistorical condition to be achieved or conquered through the apocalyptical eschaton but instead represents a constant desire to redress this world and this time, an aspiration for a reality "still to be evangelized, still valid over the distance, a utopian reality," as Bloch put it in *The Spirit of Utopia* (179). The fact that one cannot obtain a final, absolute deliverance but can only work on redressing what Brod calls the earthly "ignoble misfortune" while hoping for the divine grace that would bring an end to the "noble misfortune" does not constitute a drawback for Roth. It is only a limitation that teaches humility, the right measure, and the adequacy of individual action. As a result, the characters who find redemption in Roth's novels can experience deliverance even if they live in a deficient and hostile environment. In typical Chasidic fashion, they acquire "the mystical redemption of the individual here and now, i.e., redemption not *from*, but *in* exile, or in other words, the destruction of exile by its spiritualization" (Scholem, *The Messianic Idea* 195). This reformed, "neutralized" form of messianism clashes in Roth's novels with the modern world of absolute truths and convictions, generic solutions and unlimited hubris, but also with the world of moral indecisiveness, indifference, and self-sufficiency. The inflexible conviction that redemption can be achieved entirely by history, that only rationality, science and progress, individualism, and the modern national idea can offer the individual the emancipating promise of self-achievement, is as treacherous in Roth's view as the fixation on absolute metaphysical truths and on the inevitability of destiny. On the other hand, excessive moral flexibility, the absence of convictions, and proneness to temptations lead to an equally destructive result and are essentially the opposite of redemption.

Roth describes the search for redemption as a reparatory gesture, as the recovery of a harmony lost through an offsetting of the spiritual balance of existence. When an imbalance is produced either by individual will or through the action of superpersonal historical forces, the effects are immediate—the connections between individual and society, modernity and tradition, and individual consciousness and collective ethos break down. These transgressions against the unity of existence are not conventional offenses against prescribed laws or violations of transcendental commandments but instead are objective disruptions of the human existential condition. In Roth's fiction, the characters who live the predicaments created by these disruptions suffer from a profound existential crisis and struggle to achieve redemption by restoring balance to the universe. However, this balance is precarious: it is not prearranged or assigned by a higher force, neither the expression of individual autonomy nor that of a collective ethos. At the same time, this balance is not a source of comfort, self-sufficiency, or even a guarantee of triumph. In order to achieve stability and actual liberation from their objective suffering, his characters have to assume their imperfect, incomplete existential condition as morally responsible individuals. As a result, Roth's soteriology is based on a moral assumption: it considers that salvation does not come from God or from the individual alone but instead comes from their dialogue, from the convergence between the inexhaustible demand for salvation and the permanent call of history.

Roth's plea for an unconventional yet highly mundane view of redemption, one that does not exclude history but places it at its foundation, is common to other Central European Jewish intellectuals of the first half of the twentieth century. In a more explicit philosophical and political framework, thinkers such as Martin Buber, Karl Mannheim, Ernst Bloch, Franz Rosenzweig, Max Brod, and Walter Benjamin have demonstrated that the condition for breaking away from the crisis ushered in by modernity is to reconsider the original striving for redemption that is planted at the root of our existence. Modernity, they argue, alienated the individual from the messianic hope for salvation that constituted the main support of private and collective existence in the premodern period, a point of view shared also by Roth. By offering a rational explanation of the universe and by placing the individual at the center of the world, modernity metamorphosed the old expectation of salvation into a rational plan of improvement. Instead of projecting his personal hopes and social expectations into a transcendent realm, a realm infused with the magical presence of miraculous phenomena and ancestral, obscure commandments, the modern individual started to plan his existence according to an infallible logic of progress. According to the intellectuals belonging to this generation, this transformation led to a type of social, moral, and political immobility that gave birth to various self-enforcing ideologies of modernity that placed at their center the idea of either free market, of autarkic individualism, the state, or the nation. By rejecting the realm of redemption and the hope for a miraculous transformation of the world, modernity became the prisoner of history and wrongly imagined that its transient state was the completion of the final stage of human development. As a result of this thorough rationalization of all aspects of life, the individual started to feel isolated and controlled, incapable of identifying with the goals set by the state, the law, or the rational ego. It is therefore understandable why at certain moments in history the repressed hope for redemption would erupt with an increased force in the form of revolutions or anarchic movements or of a search for authentic experience. This reaction, they argue, creates more pain than solace but brings evidence that humanity needs a channel for its metaphysical aspirations just as much as it needs history to manifest itself. As a result, the only truly balanced existence is that which harmonizes the antihistorical need for Utopia with the need for history, thus redeeming the unity of the self and the world.

Roth's conception of redemption, like that of Buber, Rosenzweig, Brod, and to a certain extent Bloch, is inspired by a neutralized conception of messianism that is characteristic of Chasidic Judaism. According to this Judaic doctrine, the Messiah's arrival should not be expected beyond history, at the end times. Should this be the case, nothing that takes place in the interregnum of history carries any meaning, and the very laws contained in the Torah would lose all significance. Therefore, the only way to reconcile mundane existence and messianic fervor is to consider that the promise of the Messiah's arrival is itself intimately connected with the historical meaning of the divine laws. Put differently, the Messiah communicates with humanity at every moment of its existence through the latter's capacity of applying the laws and living the spirit of God. Instead of opposing history, the Messiah redeems it, making every moment of existence a reason for moral consideration and celebration of salvation. However, as Gershom Scholem observed, the commonalities between this existentialist Buber-inspired philosophy of redemption and Chasidic Judaism are only partial. In Chasidism, the Messiah's arrival is very real and brings with it the suspension of history and the miraculous transfiguration of existence. For the thinkers of this generation, however, the constantly open-ended nature of individual and social identity is bound to the provision that the final eschaton never happens but instead acts as a constantly withdrawing horizon. In this sense, their conception of redemption is shaped by a secular, philosophical, and modern interpretation of Judaism.

The fact that Roth derived his own conception of redemption from the same Eastern Judaic roots that the other Jewish thinkers of his generation used is indicative of the process of Judaic renaissance that this generation, in contrast to that of their parents, experienced. While educated nineteenth-century Central European Jews entertained the idea that in spite of all difficulties assimilation was possible within the framework of the modern liberal, individualist, and bourgeois state, the early twentieth-century Jewish intelligentsia experienced the sobering effects of the rise of nationalism and anti-Semitism in Central Europe and realized that the dream of assimilation was a devastating deception. Instead of hiding their Jewish identity, these young intellectuals celebrated it and sought modalities of reconnecting with the world of Eastern Judaism, which in their opinion had been spared the destructive influence of modernity and preserved the unadulterated spirit of the early Jews. For Roth as for the entire generation of which he was part, the Jewish identity had a double, ambiguous significance: on the one hand, in its assimilated Western form it represented a symptom of alienation and estrangement that characterized the spirit of rationalist modernity in general; on the other hand, in its unassimilated Eastern form it offered a model of resistance and a blueprint for a revolution of the very way in which the relationship between individual and history, or individual and society, was shaped. Taking their departure point from this idea about Jewish identity, Roth and his contemporaries developed an allegorical view of Jewish identity that had more to do with the political and intellectual dynamics of twentieth-century Central Europe than with the actual life of East European Jews.

Starting from these inauspicious political and historical circumstances, Roth's work reflects on the modern Jewish condition but also on that of humanity in general. The diagnosis of his contemporary Jewish identity crisis is the diagnosis of modernity as a whole, and his celebration of Eastern Jewish spirituality provides a formula for the redemption of humanity in general. Although constantly peering beyond the confines of his own historical times to the perennial questions of belonging, happiness, and redemption, Roth remains, however, indissolubly connected to the Central European world of the 1920s and 1930s, in particular to the circumstances that led to the rise of Nazism in Germany. The tragic destiny of the European Jews, a destiny that Roth anticipated even before his death in 1939, although not to its fullest catastrophic conclusion, casts in retrospect a somber shadow on the idea of redemption as a possibility for a humanity confronted with the unthinkable. The philosophical, moral, and theological implications of the Holocaust for the idea of redemption constitute, however, a set of questions whose complexity goes beyond the purview of the present work.

Concentrically building around the polarity redemption/corruption, Roth's entire work constitutes a unitary fresco that masterfully ties together his reflections on the Central European Jewish identity, his elegy for the Austrian world, his exaltation of the Catholic ethos, and his political pamphlets. The fact that Roth's work is not limited to particular historical circumstances or to strictly parochial problems but that these circumstances and problems are literarily transfigured into a universe of general-human concerns, some of which remain hotly debated even today, such as the modern condition, the relation with tradition and religion, and the moral challenges of history, makes Roth's writings even more interesting and current. The partial failure of the modern, rationalist, and secular paradigm to provide smooth and functional solutions to the crises resulting from the processes of accelerated globalization and mass migration raises once again the issues of tradition, identity, moral responsibility, and religious attachment. In this context, even though in a literary and often allegorical manner, Roth's work might provide significant insights into the complex questions that face the modern individual at a time when the relationships with one's own past and community become relevant again. Roth's constant emphasis on restraint, on moral stoicism, and his advocacy of a moderate form of messianism that does not ignore history but also of a modern historical existence that does not foreclose the relationship with the "Beyond" of tradition and religion is a constant reminder that the human condition is intrinsically incomplete and that no external promise can ever fill out our most constitutive deficiency: the desire to improve, to constantly reconsider our moral existence. The fact that Roth's work provided a valuable source of intellectual stimulation for the Central European intellectuals of the 1970s and 1980s, intellectuals confronted with the existential threats posed by ideological repression and the specter of nuclear warfare, represents evidence of the transhistorical validity of his work and of its potential for inspiring further generations.

Main Directions in the Roth Scholarship: A Brief Chronological Sketch

There exists a rich body of criticism devoted to Roth's work, especially in German but also increasingly in other languages, particularly English, Italian, and French.[1] The translation of his fiction and the recent entry of his work into the public domain (with the passing of the seventy-year mark since the author's death in 1939) have increased the world's exposure to his work as well as scholarly interest in it. It is beyond the purview of this study to offer a comprehensive review of Roth's critical reception, but a general chronological pass in review of the main directions might be useful for readers unfamiliar with the evolution of Roth scholarship.[2] According to Margarete Willerich-Tocha's pioneering reader-response study of Roth's work titled *Rezeption als Gedächtnis: Studien zur Wirkung Joseph Roths* (*Reception as Memory: Studies on the Impact of Joseph Roth's Work*, 1984), there exist three phases in its reception: the first one, contemporary with Roth, until 1939; a second one, until the publication of the first edition of Roth's collected works in 1956; and a third one, inaugurated by the first scholarly study devoted to Roth in 1956, the American W. H. Powell's dissertation "The Problem of Primitivism in the Novels of Joseph Roth" (93). While only the last phase can be declared truly interpretative in a scholarly sense, the first two phases were focused on immediate reception, via the reviews published during Roth's lifetime, and on memorial writing, published shortly after World War II. Interestingly enough, although a popular author before the war, Roth fell into almost complete oblivion after 1940. It is thanks to Roth's closest friends and associates that his memory was resurrected through a series of memoirs and commemorative articles written in order to bear testimony to the extinguished world of the interwar years. These include *Joseph Roth, Leben und Werk: Ein Gedächtnisbuch* (*Joseph Roth, Life and Work: A Memoir*), edited by Hermann Linden (1949), and Hermann Kesten, *Meine Freunde, die Poeten* (1953), but also many articles signed by, among others, Benno Reifenberg, Blanche Gidon, and Irmgard Keun.

Focusing mostly on Roth's scholarly reception, Müller-Funk distinguishes in *Joseph Roth: Besichtigungen eines Werkes* (*Joseph Roth: Surveys of a Work*) three further phases: the early phase, before 1970, focused on Roth the "conservative," legitimist, and "Austro-centric" author; the middle phase, after 1970 and before 1990, characterized by the rediscovery of the left-leaning, "socialist" author, a phase present mostly in Roth's German-language critical reception; and a third phase, post-1990, that offers a postmodern interpretation of Roth's "ambivalence" as a form of "hybridity," "performativity," multiculturalism, and fragmentation, a phase heavily influenced by Anglo-Saxon literary theory. Naturally, these categorizations are partial and do not do justice to the wealth of studies devoted to various aspects of Roth's work, including, among others, his relationship with religion, with the Jewish identity, with modernism, with the East European world, and with exile and "cultural despair." By the same token, they do not account for the many studies that engage in a textual analysis of Roth's style, rhetoric, and narrative technique or for those that compare Roth to other Austrian, German, or Central European authors of the time.

Thus, as Müller-Funk correctly points out, some of the early Roth studies focus on his Austrian and Habsburg nostalgia, such as Claudio Magris's groundbreaking 1963 *Il mito absburgico nella letteratura austriaca moderna* (rendered in German as *Der Habsburgische Mythos in der österreichischen Literatur* [*The Habsburg Myth in the Austrian Literature*]), which sets the tone for Roth's reception as a creator of a "Habsburg myth" in literature, or Alfred Kurer's 1968 dissertation *Joseph Roths 'Radetzkymarsch': Interpretation; Ein Beitrag zum Phänomen des Spätzeitlichen in der österreichischen Literatur* (*Joseph Roth's Radetzky March: Interpretation; A Contribution to the Phenomenon of Recentness in the Austrian Literature*), which further develops the "Austrian" thematic of Roth's work. However, Müller-Funk overlooks the existence of earlier monographs that analyze Roth as an existentialist-pessimist author in the tradition of German modernism. Ward Hughes Powell's 1956 dissertation "The Problem of Primitivism in the Novels of Joseph Roth" proposes an interpretation based on Arthur Lovejoy and George Boas's 1935 concept of "primitivism," which describes a (paradoxically) modern attitude of conscious rejection of modernity and refuge in the past. In a way, Powell's study pioneers an interpretation that will later become popular through the application of the German notion of *Kulturpessimismus* to Roth's work. Rolf Eckart's 1959 dissertation *Die Kommunikationslosigkeit des Menschen im Romanwerk von Joseph Roth* (*The People's Lack of Communication in Joseph Roth's Novels*) offers a detailed study of instances of isolation, alienation, incommunicability, and loneliness in Roth's novels. Looking at the causes of these phenomena, Eckart analyzes not only some sociohistorical factors having to do with modernity and change but also some permanent ones that have to do with individual psychology and human nature. Curt Sanger's 1966 dissertation *The Decadence of Austrian Society in the Novels of Joseph Roth* offers a comparatist interpretation that suggests that Roth partakes in a phenomenon typical in modern German literature—the critique of modern decadence and the consequent adoption of a skeptical view of the future, a phenomenon with origins in Nietzsche's philosophy.

At the same time, the early Roth scholarship, particularly in German, also stays under the sign of a more traditional philological approach, the *textimmanente* interpretation. Peter Wilhelm Jansen's 1958 dissertation "Weltbezug und Erzählhaltung: Eine Untersuchung zum Erzählwek und zur dichterischen Existenz Joseph Roths" ("Worldview and Narrative Mind-Set: An Investigation of Joseph Roth's Literary Existence and Fictional Work") analyzes Roth's fiction as a form of "Autofiktion," or fictionalization of Roth's own empirical self. Hansjürgen Böning's 1968 *Joseph Roths 'Radetzkymarsch': Thematik, Struktur, Sprache* (*Joseph Roth's Radetzky March: Themes, Structure, Language*) offers a comprehensive analysis of Roth's novel *Radetzkymarsch* with a focus on narrative techniques, the structure of the characters, motifs, temporal patterns, and literary tropes. Albrecht Weber's *Joseph Roth: Das falsche Gewicht; Interpretation von Albrecht Weber* (*Joseph Roth: Weights and Measures; Interpretation by Albrecht Weber*), also published in 1968, adopts a similar focus in its treatment of another Roth novel, *Weights and Measures.* Hartmut Scheible's 1971 *Joseph Roth: Mit einem Essay über Gustave Flaubert* analyzes several Roth novels from the point of view of the various narrative techniques employed in order to demonstrate that similar to his literary model Gustave Flaubert, Roth uses language not to reflect reality but instead to create it. Another study published in 1971, Helmut Famira-Parcsetich's *Die Erzählsituation in den Romanen Joseph Roths* (*The Narrative Mode in Joseph Roth's Novels*), analyzes the relations between narrator, author, reader, and fictional world in Roth's novels.

What Müller-Funk identifies as the second phase in Roth criticism, a phase marked by the rediscovery of Roth's early socialist engagement, is triggered in part by the republication, especially in the late 1960s and early 1970s, of Roth's early work. Ingeborg Sültemeyer's 1976 *Das Frühwerk Joseph Roths 1915–1926: Studien u. Texte* (*Joseph Roth's Early Work 1915–1926: Studies and Texts*) pioneers the turn to a lesser-known side of Roth's work. A year later in 1977, Thorsten Juergens published his dissertation *Gesellschaftskritische Aspekte in*

Joseph Roths Romanen (*Sociocritical Aspects in Joseph Roth's Novels*), in which he singles out Roth's social criticism of modern society as the red thread that runs across his entire work. Juergens interprets this criticism of capitalism, bourgeois modernity, inequality, and injustice as the expression of Roth's quest for a more equitable society. Around the same time, interpretations that use the methods of intellectual history and sociology started to become popular. Fritz Hackert's 1967 *Kulturpessimismus und Erzählform: Studien zu Joseph Roths Leben und Werk* (*Kulturpessimismus and Narrative Form: Studies on Joseph Roth's Life and Work*) opens the way for an interpretation of Roth's literary imagination and narrative style as expressions of a pessimistic philosophy of culture that permeated the early twentieth-century German-speaking world. Werner Sieg's 1974 *Zwischen Anarchismus und Fiktion: Eine Untersuchung zum Werk von Joseph Roth* (*Between Anarchism and Fiction: An Investigation of Joseph Roth's Work*) identifies the anarchist thematic as the common ground of Roth's fiction, although as Sieg admits, Roth's own attitude toward anarchism changed over the two decades spanning his work. A similar approach from the perspective of intellectual history is favored by Wolf Marchand, whose 1974 study *Joseph Roth und völkisch-nationalistische Wertbegriffe* (*Joseph Roth and Ethnic-Nationalist Value Concepts*) analyzes the ambiguous ideological overlapping between Roth's critique of modernity and that of his fascist opponents.

A major direction in Roth scholarship, devoted to the Jewish thematic of his work, is opened with the publication of two important monographs in the early 1970s: Hansotto Ausserhofer's 1970 dissertation *Joseph Roth und das Judentum* (*Joseph Roth and Judaism*) and Claudio Magris's 1971 *Lontano da dove: Joseph Roth e la tradizione ebraico-orientale*, translated into German as *Weit von wo: Verlorene Welt des Ostjudentums*. Ausserhofer analyzes Roth's work through the lens of the conflicts between assimilation and nonassimilation, liberalism and orthodoxy, and traditionalism and Zionism, all conflicts exacerbated by the particular situation of the Jews in the late imperial and postimperial Central European world. Magris's study, considered one of the most important monographs devoted to Roth's work, places Roth in the context of East European Jewish literature, with special focus on Yiddish literature. Magris investigates a cluster of problems related to the crisis of the modern Jewish identity but pays particular attention to the tension raised by the simultaneous historical urge to leave the Eastern shtetl and the melancholy that results from this loss. David Bronsen's definitive 1974 Roth biography contributes to the reception of Roth's work as a reflection of his own Jewish dilemmas and struggles in a world caught in the tectonic shift from tradition to modernity. It is also about this time that the themes of "Austrian nostalgia" and Jewish identity become intertwined as part of the same philosophy of tradition, as Magris's study *Lontano da dove* magisterially exemplifies (Willerich-Tocha 112).

The 1980s witnessed a general continuation and expansion of some of the directions developed earlier. Two introductory studies were published in the early 1980s, both titled simply *Joseph Roth* and both offering a primer to readers unfamiliar with Roth's biography and work. The first one, by Helmuth Nürnberger, came out in 1981 (republished later in several editions) and, although sparse in critical commentary, contains a number of useful primary documents, including accounts, anecdotes, and photos of Roth. The second one, by Rudolf Koester, came out in 1982 and provides another general introduction to Roth's life and novelistic work. Géza von Cziffra's memoir *Der heilige Trinker: Erinnerungen an Joseph Roth* appeared a year later, in 1983. The same year, 1983, a new study devoted to Roth's Jewish identity crisis came out, Reiner Frey's *Kein Weg ins Freie: Joseph Roths Amerikabild* (*No Road into the Open: America's Image in Joseph Roth's Work*). Frey approaches the Jewish thematic in Roth's work indirectly, through an interpretation of the literary topos "America" in Roth's fiction and nonfiction. Also published in 1983, Siegfried Müller's *Materialien Joseph Roth: Hiob* (*Supporting Materials Joseph Roth: Job*) provides a set of auxiliary texts and historical presentations intended to help the reader unfamiliar with the background of the novel acquire a basic understanding of the Job motif in the Bible and in literature and of the religious significance of various Jewish holidays and rituals. In 1984 Esther Steinmann published an important study, *Von der Würde des Unscheinbaren: Sinnerfahrung bei Joseph Roth*, that further develops the Jewish thematic along theological lines. Steinmann approaches Roth's fiction from the point of view of a religious, both Judaic and Christian, search for redemption and draws heavily on Roth's own explicit fascination with Chasidism and Catholicism. Margarete Willerich-Tocha's earlier-mentioned study *Rezeption als Gedächtnis: Studien zur Wirkung Joseph Roths* was also released in 1984.

In the same year, 1984, appeared the first Roth monograph published in English, Celine Mathew's *Ambivalence and Irony in the Works of Joseph Roth*.[3] Mathew's study handles stylistic and thematic questions from a sociological-psychological perspective that focuses on the feeling of uncertainty experienced by the modern individual in an age of crumbling hierarchies and ensuing "polyvalence" (*Mehrwertigkeit*). It must be pointed out that the 1980s were a particularly auspicious decade for the Roth readership in English, thanks in part to a renewed interest in fin de siècle Vienna. Carl Schorske's seminal study *Fin-de-siècle Vienna:*

Politics and Culture was published in 1980, and in its wake critics became more and more fascinated by the phenomenon known as "Viennese modernity." The 1984 series of exhibits, concerts, and lectures hosted by the Pompidou Centre in Paris under the title "Vienne 1880–1938: Fin de siècle et modernité" ("Vienna 1880–1938: Fin de Siècle and Modernity") and those at the Vienna Künstlerhaus one year later, in 1985, titled "Traum und Wirklichkeit. Wien 1870–1930" ("Dream and Reality: Vienna 1870–1930") mark the culmination of this rekindled interest. During the 1980s, no less than eight Roth novels were translated into English, some for the first time.

In 1985 a new study was published, Klaus Pauli's *Joseph Roth: "Die Kapuzinergruft" und "Der stumme Prophet"; Untersuchungen zu zwei zeitgeschichtlichen Portraitromanen* (*Joseph Roth: The Emperor's Tomb and the Silent Prophet; Investigations on Two Contemporary Historical Portrait Novels*), a fairly traditional analysis of the characters in two Roth novels, *The Emperor's Tomb* and *The Silent Prophet*. A new chapter in Roth scholarship opened, however, with the publication in 1987 of Klaus Westermann's *Joseph Roth, Journalist: Eine Karriere 1915–1939* (*Joseph Roth, Journalist: A Career 1915–1939*), a comprehensive study of Roth's journalism as an autonomous part of his work. Westermann's study underlines the continuities between Roth's early and late journalistic activity by emphasizing the centrality of his humanism and moral ideas. Westermann's book inspired numerous critics to devote more attention to Roth's journalism during the following decades. Another important comparative study appeared near the end of the decade in 1988 with the publication of Volker Henze's *Jüdischer Kulturpessimismus und das Bild des Alten Österreich im Werk Stefan Zweigs und Joseph Roths* (*Jewish Kulturpessimismus and the Image of Habsburg Austria in the Work of Stefan Zweig and Joseph Roth*). Henze's book reaffirms the interest in questions of sociology and intellectual history in his approach to Roth's work. Henze's reexamination of the notion of *Kulturpessimismus* reopens the debate about Roth's ideological contagions with the German "Conservative Revolution" of the 1920s and 1930s. However, Henze argues, there are historical reasons for the existence of a typically Jewish form of *Kulturpessimismus* that was fueled by the intellectual atmosphere and political hostility of the interwar years. Finally, in 1989 Wolfgang Müller-Funk's collection of articles titled simply *Joseph Roth* (republished in 2012 under the title *Joseph Roth: Besichtigungen eines Werkes* [*Joseph Roth: Surveys of a Work*]) tackles fictional themes such as homelessness, imaginary topography, loneliness, and misogyny but also some of Roth's lesser known nonfiction, including his travels to the Soviet Union.

The 1990s mark, according to Müller-Funk, the passage to a postmodern phase in the interpretation of Roth's work. Müller-Funk's thesis is justified but only to a point. In reality, the directions of research sketched above, including those focused on Austrian history, textual analysis, modernist aesthetics, cultural and intellectual history, and Jewish identity and religion, continue up to this day, while new interpretations rooted in semiotics, cultural anthropology, and gender studies have expanded the exegetic field. Naturally, few if any of the studies analyzed here fall squarely within the described categories, there existing significant crossover and, in the case of the more recent studies, an increasing inclination toward interdisciplinarity.

Roth's Austrian and Habsburg thematic, sidelined for a while, was revisited by scholars in the first decade of the twenty-first century, albeit with a slant toward intellectual history and philosophy. Kati Tonkin's 2008 *Joseph Roth's March into History* reaffirms Georg Lukács's thesis about the authenticity of Roth's historical novels (particularly *The Radeztky March*). According to Tonkin, Roth's novels offer the reader an authentic experience of Austria's historical past due to their emphasis on characters' individual destinies, an emphasis that explains Roth's lack of concern for "scientific" historical reconstructions. Alexander Spieth's 2009 dissertation *Politisch sehn, falsch sehn: Anmerkungen zu Joseph Roths Legitimismus* (*To See Politically Is to See Incorrectly: Observations on Joseph Roth's Legitimism*) interprets Roth's Habsburg legitimism in view of his philosophy of religion and history. Spieth organizes his study around the concept of "verity," which Roth developed during his extended trip to southern France in 1925. Spieth demonstrates that Roth's "verity" is similar to the Pauline notion of "revealed truth," which is a form of internal, moral truth that is simultaneously deeper and more real than empirical truth. Through this understanding of verity, Spieth argues, Roth overhauls the conditions under which truth exists in general, thus resolving the contradiction between his fictional and empirical legitimism. According to Spieth, Roth's Habsburg legitimism should not be interpreted as a strictly political or fictional reality but instead should be interpreted as a combination of both, as a moral-religious truth.

Roth's modernist literary legacy has been further analyzed beyond the 1980s, beginning with Jürgen Heizmann's 1990 *Joseph Roth und die Ästhetik der Neuen Sachlichkeit* (*Joseph Roth and the Aesthetics of New Objectivity*), an important study devoted to the complex relationship between Roth and the modernist aesthetics of the interwar years. Heizmann focuses on the tenuous aesthetics of New Objectivity, an aesthetics that grew out a dialogue with and opposition to other modernist movements, such as expressionism, magic realism, and futurism.

Heizmann demonstrates that Roth was not a New Objectivist author in the strict sense of the word and was more interested in the "cooling down" (*Abkühlung*) of literature in its reflection of reality, a concept better captured by Pierre Bertaux's term "*l'ordre froid*" (Heizmann, *Joseph Roth* 6). Hui-Fang Chiao's 1994 *Eine junge, unglückliche und zukünftige Stadt: Das Berlin der zwanziger Jahre in Joseph Roths Werk* (*A Young, Miserable and Future City: The Berlin of the 1920s in Joseph Roth's Work*) engages with issues of disruption and discontinuity in Roth's representation of the modern urban life of 1920s Berlin. Irene Schroeder's 1998 study of Roth's early prose titled *Experimente des Erzählens: Joseph Roths frühe Prosa 1916–1925* (*Narrative Experiments: Joseph Roth's Early Prose 1916–1925*) offers an investigation of the constantly shifting narrative techniques employed by Roth in order to demonstrate that he promotes a modernist aesthetics of fragmentation and disruption. Jon Hughes's 2006 *Facing Modernity: Fragmentation, Culture, and Identity in Joseph Roth's Writing in the 1920s* is another study of Roth's work in the context of the Weimar Republic's modernism and identity crisis, a period of veritable "epistemological uncertainty" (16). Hughes combines the methods of literary and cultural sociology with postmodern theories of gender and subjectivity, making ample use of concepts drawn from Klaus Theweleit, Peter Sloterdijk, and Michel Foucault.

The genre memoir and biography is equally well represented past 1990 through the posthumous publication of Soma Morgenstern's 1994 *Joseph Roths Flucht und Ende: Erinnerungen*, a book of memoirs written by one of Roth's oldest friends. The same year, 1994, Heinz Lunzer and Victoria Lunzer-Talos published *Joseph Roth: Leben und Werk in Bildern* (*Joseph Roth: Life and Work in Pictures*), a unique collection of photographs, many published for the first time, documenting Roth's places of origin and residence, his geographical and cultural itineraries, and his personal and professional relationships. A new Roth biography came out in 2009 titled simply *Joseph Roth: Eine Biographie*, by Wilhelm von Sternburg. Sternburg offers a valuable reconsideration of Roth's life, seen through the prism of his correspondence and articles. Through its documentary wealth and insightful connections between Roth's life and work, this new biography is a welcome addition to Bronsen's 1974 Roth biography. In 2011 Dennis Marks published *Wandering Jew: The Search for Joseph Roth*, an introductory biography and commentary of some of Roth's fictional works in a historical-geographical context. Marks's book is an attempt to provide, perhaps for the first time, something close to a Roth biography for an English-language readership. In 2014 an interesting fictionalized biography of Roth came out in German, *Ostende: 1936, Sommer der Freundschaft*, translated into English in

2016 as *Ostend: Stefan Zweig, Joseph Roth, and the Summer before the Dark.* In it, Volker Weidermann masterfully interlaces details taken from Roth's correspondence and other biographical accounts into a narrative about the friendship between Roth and Zweig, centered on the time they spent together in Ostend in 1936.

The studies devoted to Roth's Jewish thematic also proliferate after 1990. Two interpretative companions to Roth's novel *Job* were published in 1991 and 1993, both similar in their historical-contextual approach. The first one, *Lektürehilfen Joseph Roth 'Hiob'* (*Reading Guide to Joseph Roth's Job*) by Emil Göggel, is a guide to the specifically Jewish themes and issues dealt with in the novel and is also an attempt to explain these issues in their original historical context. The second one, Hans-Jürgen Blanke's *Joseph Roth: Hiob; Interpretation von Hans-Jürgen Blanke* (*Joseph Roth: Job; Interpretation by Hans-Jürgen Blanke*), is an interpretation of the religious and social issues informing the historical background of the novel. Frank Joachim Eggers's comparative 1996 study *"Ich bin ein Katholik mit jüdischem Gehirn": Modernitätskritik und Religion bei Joseph Roth und Franz Werfel* (*"I Am a Catholic with Jewish Intelligence": The Critique of Modernity and Religion in the Works of Joseph Roth and Franz Werfel*) investigates Roth's ambiguous relationship with his Jewish identity as an expression of his ambiguous relationship with modernity in general. According to Eggers, Roth's criticism of modernity results from a philosophy related to the conservative German *Kulturpessimismus* and defines the nature of his criticism of the Jewish identity in its liberal and assimilated form. In 1999 another Roth monograph was published, Katharina Ochse's *Joseph Roths Auseinandersetzung mit dem Antisemitismus* (*Joseph Roth's Contention with Antisemitism*). Ochse analyzes several Roth novels and some of his nonfiction in order to demonstrate that the most important factor in determining his literary and political evolution was his struggle with widespread European anti-Semitism. Eva Raffel's 2002 comparative study *Vertraute Fremde: Das östliche Judentum im Werk von Joseph Roth und Arnold Zweig* (*Familiar Strangers: Eastern Jews in the Work of Joseph Roth and Arnold Zweig*) engages in a historical-contextual interpretation of Roth's work, limiting itself to reiterating the impossible choice that the Jews of Central and Eastern Europe had to make at the turn of the twentieth century, a choice between exile and oppression. A new interpretation of Roth's novel *Job* was published in 2004, Christine Schmidjell's *Erläuterungen und Dokumente: Joseph Roth; Hiob* (*Commentaries and Documents: Joseph Roth; Job*), a study focused on the historical background of the novel and the conflict of Russian Chasidim with modernity.

Another comparative study, also published in 2004, is Almuth Hammer's *Erwählung erinnern: Literatur als Medium jüdischen Selbstverständnisses; Mit Fallstudien zu Else Lasker-Schüler und Joseph Roth*, a comparison between Lasker-Schüler and Roth with an emphasis on issues of Jewish acculturation and identity crisis. Wolfgang Treitler's 2007 *Zwischen Hiob und Jeremia: Stefan Zweig und Joseph Roth am Ende der Welt* (*Between Job and Jeremiah: Stefan Zweig and Joseph Roth at the End of the World*) is a freely written study that discusses Stefan Zweig's and Joseph Roth's affinities with the biblical figures of Jeremiah and Job, respectively, with the themes of apocalyptic prophecy and individual dialogue with an impenetrable God. Several comparative studies in English, beginning with Malcolm Spencer's 2008 *In the Shadow of Empire: Austrian Experiences of Modernity in the Writings of Musil, Roth, and Bachmann*, continuing with Erica Weitzman's 2015 *Irony's Antics: Walser, Kafka, Roth, and the German Comic Tradition,* and ending with Marjorie Perloff's 2016 *Edge of Irony: Modernism in the Shadow of the Habsburg Empire*, broaden the exposure of the English-speaking audience to Roth's work, although in the case of Spencer and Perloff the only analyzed work is the novel *The Radetzky March*, which is treated in an Austrian context, next to works by Musil, Bachmann, Kraus, Canetti, Celan, and Wittgenstein. Weitzman's study focuses, however, mostly on Roth's early nonfictional writing in an attempt to demonstrate Roth's affinity with an esthetics of irony.

Interpretations with a clearer grounding in postmodern narrative theory began to become popular with the publication in 1994 of Ulrike Steierwald's *Leiden an der Geschichte: Zur Geschichtsauffassung der Moderne in den Texten Joseph Roths* (*To Suffer from History: On the Historical Conception of Modernity in Joseph Roth's Texts*). Steierwald analyzes Roth's historical fiction as an expression of a "metahistorical" consciousness that confirms Hayden White's theory about the narrative "emplotment" of history writing. Irmgard Wirtz's 1997 *Joseph Roth: Fiktionen des Faktischen* (*Joseph Roth: Fictions of the Factual*) continues this argumentative line by drawing on Hayden White and Paul Ricoeur's theory of narrative time in history writing. Wirtz argues that fiction and reality are ambiguously intertwined in Roth's work due to the general interlocking between factuality and fiction in all historical narratives. In 2006 another study based in semiotic theory was published, Telse Hartmann's *Kultur und Identität: Szenarien der Deplatzierung im Werk Joseph Roths* (*Culture and Identity: Scenarios of Displacement in Joseph Roth's Work*). Hartmann uses the semiotic interpretation favored by cultural anthropology in dealing with concepts such as national belonging and ethnic identity. By making use of James

Clifford's notions of hybrid cultural identity as a space between "Deplatzierung und Lokalisierung" 'displacement and localization' (197), Hartmann identifies a fundamental ambiguity in Roth's notion of identity, which is always caught in the tension underlying the opposition between belonging and alienation. Daniel Romuald Bitouh's 2016 *Ästhetik der Marginalität im Werk von Joseph Roth* (*Aesthetics of Marginality in Joseph Roth's Work*) looks at a wider postcolonial context that also includes Roth's connections with Africa and the black identity. Bitouh's theoretical grounding in postcolonial theory and deconstruction is relevant for his preoccupation with concepts such as marginality, the subaltern, and difference in Roth's work.

Several other studies with a more general focus on the philosophical, cultural, and psychological aspects of Roth's work were also published after 1990, although they are a lot harder to categorize due to the interdisciplinary nature of their critical approaches. Thomas Düllo's 1991 *Zufall und Melancholie: Untersuchungen zur Kontingenzsemantik in Texten von Joseph Roth* (*Chance and Melancholy: Investigations on the Semantics of Contingency in Joseph Roth's Texts*) argues that the fear of contingency apparent throughout Roth's work is the result of a crisis resulting from modernity's erosion of hierarchies and stable identities. The characters' search for a "*Kontingenzbewältigung*" 'overcoming of contingency' ends up in the melancholy of loss, Düllo contends, a loss of something idealized in retrospect. Published in 2001, Sebastian Kiefer's *Braver Junge—gefüllt mit Gift: Joseph Roth und die Ambivalenz* (*Good Boy—Filled with Venom: Joseph Roth and the Ambivalence*) argues that ambivalence represents for Roth a complex compensatory mechanism through which life and art complement each other and substitute for each other's inadequacies. Kiefer also considers that this compensatory mechanism has reasons that are equally aesthetic and psychological, being rooted in Roth's artistic creativity and in his hysterical personality. Bernd Oei's 2012 *Joseph Roth: Der verbrannte Himmel; Methaphysik des Zweifels* (*Joseph Roth: The Scorched Sky; A Metaphysics of Doubting*) is a free analysis of Roth's fictional work undertaken through the lenses of various philosophers, such as Ernst Cassirer, Ernst Mach, John Stuart Mill, Karl Jaspers, etc. Oei's central thesis is Roth's preoccupation with the destruction of metaphysics in the modern age through reason and doubt.

Worth noting are also several studies that either continue some earlier trends or stand out as singular creative efforts. In the former category, Dietmar Mehrens's 2000 *Vom göttlichen Auftrag der Literatur: Die Romane Joseph Roths; Ein Kommentar* (*On the Divine Mandate of Literature: Joseph Roth's Novels; A Commentary*) deals with the question of religion in Roth's work and life, arguing that while religion did not play much of a role for Roth in private, his work was strongly influenced by his belief in the divine-creative mandate of literature, an idea that echoes Esther Steinmann's 1984 study. In 2001 an important English-language monograph was published, Sidney Rosenfeld's *Understanding Joseph Roth*, a Roth primer largely for an American audience unfamiliar with Roth's novels and especially with his life. Rosenfeld provides a psychological-historical interpretation of Roth's fictional work as a reflection of the author's own dilemmas and neuroses. His interpretation, similar to Peter Wilhelm Jansen's idea of "Ich-Projektion" 'ego-projection,' reduces, however, Roth's writing to a sort of fictionalization of the author's personal failure to come to terms with his Jewish, East European, and working-class background. In the same historical-biographical vein, Ilse Josepha Lazaroms's 2013 *The Grace of Misery: Joseph Roth and the Politics of Exile, 1919–1939* argues that the experience of exile has allowed Roth to stage himself as a sort of "existential exile" in a variety of political-cultural contexts: the exile from the East, the Jewish exile, the European exile in front of barbarity, etc. In the category of creative efforts, Reinhard Baumgart's 1991 *Auferstehung und Tod des Joseph Roth: Drei Ansichten* (*Resurrection and Death of Joseph Roth: Three Views*) deserves mention as an attempt to use Roth's bio-bibliography as loose material for an original mixture of interpretation and fiction.

While the secondary literature reviewed so far includes some of the most important Roth monographs and comparative studies, the collections of articles devoted to his work deserve mention as well. The fact that the Roth scholarship has progressed a lot is due in significant part to the numerous articles published over the last five decades in various periodicals but also in print collections. Very influential remains one of the earliest of such collections, the 1974 edition of the periodical *Text+Kritik* (*Text + Criticism*), edited by Heinz Ludwig Arnold and devoted entirely to Joseph Roth. Some of the key concepts in the Roth scholarship of the following decades were developed in the articles collected there. Highly important is also a collection edited by David Bronsen a year later in 1975, *Joseph Roth und die Tradition* (*Joseph Roth and Tradition*). Even if not many collections were published in the following decade and a half (a notable exception being Bernd Kraske's 1988 *Joseph Roth: Werk und Wirkung* (*Joseph Roth: His Work and Its Impact*), the 1990s inaugurated a golden age of Roth article collections, caused in significant measure by the increasing number of symposia and conferences devoted to Joseph Roth in the wake of the post–Iron Curtain rediscovery of Central and Eastern Europe: in 1990, Michael Kessler and Fritz Hackert edited *Joseph Roth: Interpretation, Rezeption, Kritik* (*Joseph Roth: Interpretation, Reception, Criticism*); in 1991, Helen Chambers published a collection of articles written both in German and in English, *Co-Existent Contradictions: Joseph Roth in Retrospect*; in 1994, Michael Nüchtern and Ralf Stieber edited *"Die Schwere des Glücks und die Größe der Wunder": Joseph Roth und seine Welt* (*"The Burden of Happiness and the Greatness of the Miracle": Joseph Roth and His World*); in 1996, Alexander Stillmark published *Joseph Roth: Der Sieg über die Zeit; Londoner Symposium* (*Joseph Roth: The Victory over the Time; London Symposium*); and in 1999 appeared Thomas Eicher's *Joseph Roth: Grenzüberscheitungen* (*Joseph Roth: Border Crossings*). This trend has continued into the twenty-first century with Johann Lughofer's *Im Prisma: Joseph Roths Romane* (*In the Prism: Joseph Roth's Novels*), published in 2009; Daniel Keel and Daniel Kampa's *Joseph Roth: Leben und Werk* (*Joseph Roth: Life and Work*), from 2010; Johann Lughofer and Mira Miladinović Zalaznik's *Joseph Roth: Europäisch-jüdischer Schriftsteller und österreichischer Universalist* (*Joseph Roth: European-Jewish Writer and Austrian Universalist*), published in 2011; Wiebke Amthor and Hans R. Brittnacher's 2012 *Joseph Roth—Zur Modernität des melancholischen Blicks* (*Joseph Roth—On the Modernity of the Melancholic Gaze*); and Nora Hoffmann and Natalia Shchyhlevska's 2013 *Joseph Roth als Stilist: Annäherung durch Theorie und Übersetzung* (*Joseph Roth as Stylist: An Approach through Theory and Translation*). This rich body of secondary literature bears evidence to the interpretative curiosity that still surrounds Roth's work and to the diversity of approaches that his work stimulates.

Notes

1. Most Roth monographs in French and Italian have been written over the past twenty-five years, some in dissertation form, others published but not widely available. For this reason, the present study limits itself to mentioning some of these titles. In Italian, aside from Claudio Magris's pioneering study of 1971, dealt with at some length here, several other studies should be mentioned: Maria Sechi's 1994 *Invito alla lettura di Joseph Roth* (*Invitation to Read Joseph Roth*), Mirella Carbone's 2004 *Joseph Roth e il cinema* (*Joseph Roth and the Cinema*), and Marino Freschi's 2013 *Joseph Roth*. In French, aside from an early dissertation, Joseph-Edouard Wagner's 1981 *La pensée de Joseph Roth à travers ses romans, ses articles et ses lettres* (*Interpreting Joseph Roth's Thinking through His Novels, Articles, and Letters*), several other studies should be mentioned: in the 1990s, Gilbert Ravy's *Joseph Roth* and Luc Spielmann's *La Marche de Radetzky de Joseph Roth: Essai d'interprétation* (*The Radetzky March by Joseph Roth: Attempt at an Interpretation*), both from 1990, followed by two dissertations, Jacqueline Bel's 1992 *Péché et rédemption*

ou de l'apaisement du mal d'être: Une approche nouvelle de l'œuvre et de l'écrivain Joseph Roth (*Sin and Redemption or the Appeasement of the Pain of Being: A New Approach to the Work and the Writer Joseph Roth*) and Eveline Demangeon Hey's 1996 *L'errance juive dans l'œuvre de Joseph Roth* (*Jewish Wandering in the Work of Joseph Roth*); in the twenty-first century, Stéphane Pesnel's 2000 *Totalité et fragmentarité dans l'œuvre romanesque de Joseph Roth* (*Totality and Fragmentation in Joseph Roth's Novelistic Work*), Valérie Chevassus-Marchionni's 2002 *Le "roman original" de Joseph Roth: Analyse des stratégies de la création littéraire dans l'œuvre de Joseph Roth* (*Joseph Roth's "Original Novel": Analysis of the Strategies of Literary Creation in the Work of Joseph Roth*), and Véronique Uberall's 2009 dissertation *Joseph Roth, témoin et combattant: Étude de dix-sept nouvelles dans le contexte socio-historique en Autriche et en Allemagne de 1916 à 1939* (*Joseph Roth, Witness and Fighter: A Study of Seventeen Short Stories in the Socio-Historical Context in Austria and Germany from 1916 to 1939*).

2. While the present study relies heavily on secondary literature in German and English, it should be mentioned that a large number of Roth studies written in the two languages could not be reviewed due to the fact that many remain in dissertation format or, if printed, in small runs and are practically accessible only locally. It is the case with such studies as, in English, Peter Winkel's *Thematic and Structural Elements in the Early Novels of Joseph Roth* (1972), Anne Bankowska's *"Wo gibt es Sicherheit?": Aspects of Narration in the Novels of Joseph Roth* (1982), Pamela Saur's "Family Relationships in the Works of Joseph Roth," (University of Iowa 1982), Gail Sarah Jones's *The Attitude of Constancy in the Early Novels of Joseph Roth* (1982), Alison May's *Joseph Roth: Mediator between Eastern European Jewry and the West* (1999), and the comparative investigations by Christoph Prang, *Semiotic Discourses and the Production of Literary Texts: Joseph Roth, Ernst Jünger, Gert Hofmann* (1998) and Nancy Herrigel Eilers *Renderings of the City: Joseph Roth, Siegfried Kracauer and the Literary Reportage of the Weimar Republic* (1999). In German, the list of such studies is even larger and includes, among others, Erika Wegner's 1964 *Die Gestaltung innerer Vorgänge in den Dichtungen Joseph Roths* (*The Configuration of Internal Occurrences in Joseph Roth's Fiction*), Christina Alcantara's 1979 *Das Menschenbild in den Romanen von Joseph Roth* (*The Image of the Human Being in Joseph Roth's Novels*), Myung-Hae Ha's 1993 *Krisenerfahrung und Sehnsucht in den Reisefeuilletons von Joseph Roth* (*The Experience of Crisis and Yearning in Joseph Roth's Travel Columns*), Michael Zimmer's 1998 *Joseph Roth: Hiob; Interpretationen und Materialien* (*Joseph Roth: Job; Interpretation and Supporting Materials*), and Martin Lowsky's 2005 *Erläuterungen zu Joseph Roth: Hiob Roman eines einfachen Mannes* (*Commentaries to Joseph Roth's Job: The Story*

of a Simple Man). The secondary literature reviewed here comprises, however, the "core" Roth scholarship, which is used by most Roth scholars, and a large number of other lesser-known studies. For a comprehensive Roth bibliography up to the year 1995, see Rainer-Joachim Siegel's 1995 *Joseph Roth, Bibliographie.*

3. Mathew's study is, naturally, not the first Roth monograph in English, although it is the first published one. At least five other studies were written in English before 1984, all doctoral dissertations: Ward Hughes Powell's *The Problem of Primitivism in the Novels of Joseph Roth* (1956), Curt Sanger's *The Decadence of Austrian Society in the Novels of Joseph Roth* (1966), Peter Winkel's *Thematic and Structural Elements in the Early Novels of Joseph Roth* (1972), Anne Bankowska's *"Wo gibt es Sicherheit?": Aspects of Narration in the Novels of Joseph Roth* (1982), and Gail Sarah Jones's *The Attitude of Constancy in the Early Novels of Joseph Roth* (1982).

Works Cited

Akrap, Domagoj. *Erich Fromm—ein jüdischer Denker: Jüdisches Erbe, Tradition, Religion* [*Erich Fromm—a Jewish Thinker: Jewish Heritage, Tradition, Religion*]. Wien: Lit Verlag, 2011.

Amthor, Wiebke. "An den Toren Europas: Heterotopie und Passage im Werk Joseph Roths" ["At Europe's Gates: Heterotopia and Passage in Joseph Roth's Work"]. Amthor and Brittnacher 117–38.

Amthor, Wiebke, and Hans R. Brittnacher, eds. *Joseph Roth—Zur Modernität des melancholischen Blicks* [*Joseph Roth—On the Modernity of the Melancholic Gaze*]. Berlin: De Gruyter, 2012. *EBSCOHost*. Web. August 2015.

Arendt, Hannah. "Introduction." *Illuminations*, by Walter Benjamin. Trans. Harry Zohn. London: Fontana, 1992. 7–58.

———. *The Jew as Pariah: Jewish Identity and Politics in the Modern Age*. Ed. Ron H. Feldman. New York: Grove, 1978.

Ausserhofer, Hansotto. "Joseph Roth und das Judentum" ["Joseph Roth and Judaism"]. Diss., Friedrich-Wilhelms-Universität, Bonn, 1970.

Baeck, Leo. *Das Wesen des Judentums* [*The Essence of Judaism*]. 2nd ed. Frankfurt/Main: J. Kauffmann, 1922.

Bailey, Sarah. "Cultural Translation and the Problem of Language: Yiddish in Joseph Roth's *Juden Auf Wanderschaft*." *TRANSIT* 1.1 (2005). http://transit.berkeley.edu/2005/bailey/. Accessed 10 April 2017.

Bauer, Otto. *Die Nationalitätenfrage und die Sozialdemokratie* [*The Question of Nationalities and Social Democracy*]. Ed. Max Adler and Rudolph Hilferding. Wien: Verlag der Wiener Volksbuchhandlung, 1924.

Bauer, Thomas. "Alltag und Persönlichkeit: Joseph Roths Rekonstruktion gesellschaftlicher Konversationsmodelle" ["Everyday Life and Personality: Joseph Roth's Reconstruction of Social Conversational Models"]. Lughofer, *Im Prisma* 441–64.

Baumgart, Reinhard. *Auferstehung und Tod des Joseph Roth: Drei Ansichten* [*Resurrection and Death of Joseph Roth: Three Views*]. München: Carl Hanser, 1991.

———. "Drei Ansichten" [Three Views]. Keel and Kampa 330–51.

———. "Totentanz und Tingeltangel: *Die Geschichte von der 1002. Nacht*" ["Danse Macabre and Vulgar Entertainment: *The Tale of the 1002nd Night*"]. Keel and Kampa 457–64.

Bel, Jacqueline. "Snobisme à l'Est et à l'Ouest: *Die Flucht ohne Ende* de Joseph Roth" ["Snobbery in the East and West: *Flight without End* by Joseph Roth"]. *Germanica* 49 (2011–2012): 95–108.

Benjamin, Walter. *Illuminations.* Trans. Harry Zohn. London: Fontana, 1992.

———. *Reflections.* Trans. Edmund Jephcott. New York: Schocken Books, 1978.

Berlin, Isaiah. "Historical Materialism." *Karl Marx.* Ed. Tom Bottomore. Englewood Cliffs: Prentice Hall, 1973.

Biemann, Asher D. "'Thus Rome Shows Us Our True Place': Reflections on the German Jewish Love for Italy." *German-Jewish Thought between Religion and Politics: Festschrift in Honor of Paul Mendes-Flohr on the Occasion of His Seventieth Birthday.* Ed. Christian Wiese and Martina Urban. Berlin: de Gruyter, 2012. 241–61. *EBSCOHost,* http://eds.b.ebscohost.com/eds/detail/detail?vid=0&sid=9879b83f-afc6-40b6-bb22-a1dc73beb3c3%40sessionmgr102&bdata=JnNpdGU9ZWRzLWxpdmUmc2NvcGU9c2l0ZQ%3d%3d#db=nlebk&AN=448092. Accessed 27 July 2015.

Birk, Matjaž. "Zeitkritische Aspekte im Roman *Die Flucht ohne Ende* (1927)—Einem 'Bericht' von Joseph Roth" ["Facets of Criticism of the Times in the Novel *Flight without End* (1927)—A 'Report' by Joseph Roth"]. *Neophilologus* 80.1 (1996): 111–25.

Blanke, Hans-Jürgen. *Joseph Roth: Hiob; Interpretation von Hans-Jürgen Blanke* [*Joseph Roth: Job; Interpretation by Hans-Jürgen Blanke*]. München: Oldenbourg, 1993.

Bloch, Ernst. *The Spirit of Utopia.* Trans. Anthony A. Nassar. Stanford: Stanford UP, 2000.

Bohnen, Klaus. "Flucht in die 'Heimat': Zu den Erzählungen Joseph Roths" ["Flight in the 'Homeland': On Joseph Roth's Novellas"]. Kraske 53–69.

Boldyrev, Ivan. *Ernst Bloch and His Contemporaries: Locating Utopian Messianism.* London: Bloomsbury, 2014.

Brenner, Michael. *The Renaissance of Jewish Culture in Weimar Germany.* New Haven, CT: Yale UP, 1996.

Brittnacher, Hans Richard. "Von Heimkehrern, Vagabunden und Hochstaplern: Glück und Fluch des improvisierten Lebens bei Joseph Roth" ["Of Returning Veterans, Vagabonds, and Conmen: The Bliss and Curse of Improvised Life in Joseph Roth's Work"]. Amthor and Brittnacher 165–82.

Broch, Hermann. *Hofmannsthal und seine Zeit* [*Hofmannsthal and His Time*]. München: R. Piper & Co., 1964.

Brod, Max. *Im Kampf um das Judentum* [*In the Struggle for Judaism*]. Wien: R. Löwit, 1920.

———. *Paganism, Christianity, Judaism: A Confession of Faith.* Trans. William Wolf. Tuscaloosa: U of Alabama P, 1970. *EBSCOhost,* ezproxy.otterbein.edu/login?url=http://search.ebscohost.com/login.aspx?direct=true&db=nlebk&AN=473548&site=eds-live&scope=site. Accessed 17 August 2017.

Broerman, Bruce M. "Joseph Roth's *Die hundert Tage*: A New Perspective." *Modern Austrian Literature* 11.2 (1978): 35–50.

Bronsen, David. "Das literarische Bild der Auflösung im *Radetzkymarsch*" ["The Literary Picture of Redemption in *Radetzky March*"]. *Jahrbuch der Grillparzer-Gesellschaft* 3–4 (1965): 130–43.

———. "The Jew in Search of a Fatherland: The Relationship of Joseph Roth to the Habsburg Monarchy." *Germanic Review* 54 (1979): 54–61.

———. *Joseph Roth: Eine Biographie* [*Joseph Roth: A Biography*]. Köln: Kiepenheuer & Witsch, 1974.

———, ed. *Joseph Roth und die Tradition* [*Joseph Roth and Tradition*]. Darmstadt: Agora, 1975.

Buber, Martin. *Die Chassidischen Bücher* [*The Chasidic Books*]. Berlin: Schocken, 1927.

———. *I and Thou.* Trans. Walter Kaufmann. New York: Touchstone, 1996.

———. "Introduction." *Tales of the Hasidim,* by Buber, Trans. Olga Marx. New York: Schocken, 1947.

———. *Paths in Utopia.* Trans. R. F. C. Hull. Boston: Beacon, 1958.

———. "Replies to My Critics." *The Philosophy of Martin Buber.* Ed. Paul A. Schilpp and Maurice Friedman. La Salle, IL: Open Court, 1967.

———. "Zion, der Staat und die Menschheit" ["Zion, the State, and Humanity"]. *Der Jude* [*The Jew*] 7 (1916): 425–33.

Butler, G. P. "It's the Bitterness That Counts: Joseph Roth's 'Most Jewish' Novel Reconsidered." *German Life and Letters* 41.3 (1988): 227–34.

Casper, Bernhard. "Responsibility Rescued." Mendes-Flohr, *The Philosophy of Franz Rosenzweig* 89–106.

Chambers, Helen, ed. *Co-Existent Contradictions: Joseph Roth in Retrospect.* Riverside, CA: Ariadne, 1991.

———. "Predators or Victims?—Women in Joseph Roth's Works." Chambers 107–27.

Chertenko, Alexander. "Zufall und Ordnung: Zwei Pole der Moderne in Joseph Roths *Das falsche Gewicht*" ["Chance and Order. Two Poles of Modernity in Joseph Roth's *Weights and Measures*"]. Amthor and Brittnacher 55–68.

Cziffra, Géza von. *Der heilige Trinker: Erinnerungen an Joseph Roth* [*The Holy Drinker: Memories of Joseph Roth*]. Berlin: Berenberg, 2006.

Decloedt, Leopold R. G. "Joseph Roths 'zwiespältige Trauer': Der Franz-Joseph-Mythos im Werke Roths" ["Joseph Roth's 'Ambivalent Grief': The Myth of Franz Joseph in Roth's Works"]. Österreich in Geschichte und Literatur (mit Geographie) [*Austria in History and Literature (with Geography)*] 37.4–5a (1993): 271–78.

Doderer, Heimito von. *Die erleuchteten Fenster: Oder, die Menschwerdung des Amtsrates Julius Zihal* [*The Lighted Windows: Or, the Humanization of the Bureaucrat Julius Zihal*]. München: Biederstein, 1950.

Dollenmayer, David. "History and Fiction: The Kaiser in Joseph Roth's *Radetzkymarsch*." *Modern Language Studies* 16 (1986): 302–10. *JSTOR*, doi: 10.2307/3194910. Accessed 18 May 2015.

Doppler, Alfred. "'Die Kapuzinergruft' von Joseph Roth: Österreich im Bewußtsein von Franz Ferdinand Trotta" ["*The Emperor's Tomb* by Joseph Roth: Austria in the Mind of Franz Ferdinand Trotta"]. Kessler and Hackert 91–99.

Dubbels, Elke. *Figuren des Messianischen in Schriften deutsch-jüdischer Intellektueller, 1900–1933* [*Representations of the Messianic in the Writings of German-Jewish Intellectuals, 1900–1933*]. Berlin: De Gruyter, 2011. *EBSCOHost*. Accessed 21 August 2015.

Düllo, Thomas. *Zufall und Melancholie: Untersuchungen zur Kontingenzsemantik in Texten von Joseph Roth* [*Chance and Melancholy: Investigations on the Semantics of Contingency in Joseph Roth's Texts*]. Münster: LIT Verlag, 1991.

Eckart, Rolf. *Die Kommunikationslosigkeit des Menschen im Romanwerk von Joseph Roth* [*The People's Lack of Communication in Joseph Roth's Novels*]. Diss., Ludwig-Maximilians-Universität München, 1959. München: "Uni"-Druck, 1959.

Eggers, Frank Joachim. *"Ich bin ein Katholik mit jüdischem Gehirn": Modernitätskritik und Religion bei Joseph Roth und Franz Werfel* [*"I Am a Catholic with Jewish Intelligence": The Critique of Modernity and Religion in the Works of Joseph Roth and Franz Werfel*]. Frankfurt/Main: Peter Lang, 1996.

Eicher, Thomas, ed. *Joseph Roth: Grenzüberschreitungen* [*Joseph Roth: Border Crossings*]. Oberhausen: Athena, 1999.

Elias, Norbert. *The Civilizing Process*. Trans. Edmund Jephcott. New York: Urizen, 1978.

Famira-Parcsetich, Helmut. *Die Erzählsituation in den Romanen Joseph Roths* [*The Narrative Mode in Joseph Roth's Novels*]. Bern: Herbert Lang & Cie AG, 1971.

Feher, Ferenc, et al., eds. *Die Seele und das Leben: Studien zum frühen Lukács* [*The Soul and the Life: Studies on the Young Lukács*]. Frankfurt/Main: Suhrkamp, 1977.

Foster, Ian. "Joseph Roth's *Radetzkymarsch* as a Historical Novel." *Travellers in Time and Space: The German Historical Novel*. Ed. Osman Durrani and Julian Preece. Amsterdam: Rodopi, 2001. 357–70.

Frank, Michael. "Objektivität ist Schweinerei" ["Objectivity Is a Mess"]. Keel and Kampa 474–77.

Franzos, Karl Emil. *The Jews of Barnow.* Trans. M. W. Macdowall. New York: Appleton & Co., 1883.

Freud, Sigmund. *The Freud Reader.* Ed. Peter Gay. New York: Norton, 1989.

Frey, Reiner. *Kein Weg ins Freie: Joseph Roths Amerikabild* [*No Road into the Open: America's Image in Joseph Roth's Work*]. Frankfurt/Main: Peter Lang, 1983.

Friedländer, Saul. *Franz Kafka: The Poet of Shame and Guilt.* New Haven, CT: Yale UP, 2013. *EBSCOhost,* ezproxy.otterbein.edu/login?url=http://search.ebscohost.com/login.aspx?direct=true&db=nlebk&AN=568276&site=eds-live&scope=-site. Accessed 17 August 2017.

Frietsch, Elke. "'Kunstgeschmack' und 'Weltuntergang': Die Wiener Werkstätte als Symbol für das Ende der österreichischen Monarchie in Joseph Roths Roman *Die Kapuzinergruft*" ["'Artistic Taste' and 'Apocalypse': Vienna's Workshops as a Symbol for the End of the Austrian Monarchy in Joseph Roth's Novel *The Emperor's Tomb*"]. Lughofer, *Im Prisma* 403–26.

Frye, Northrop. *The Great Code: The Bible and Literature.* San Diego: Harvest, 1982.

———. "Varieties of Literary Utopias." *Daedalus* 94.2 (1965): 323–47.

Garloff, Katja. "Femininity and Assimilatory Desire in Joseph Roth." *MFS Modern Fiction Studies* 51.2 (2005): 354–73. *OhioLINK Electronic Journal Center,* rave.ohiolink.edu/ejournals/article/342526128.

Gelber, Mark H. "*Juden auf Wanderschaft* und die Rhetorik der Ost-West-Debatte im Werk Joseph Roths" ["*Wandering Jews* and the Rhetoric of the East-West Debate in Joseph Roth's Work"]. Kessler and Hackert 127–35.

Gelhard, Dorothee. *Spuren des Sagens: Studien zur jüdischen Hermeneutik in der Literatur* [*Traces of Language: Studies on the Jewish Hermeneutics in Literature*]. Frankfurt/Main: Peter Lang, 2004.

Gelzer, Florian. "Unzuverlässiges Erzählen als Provokation des Lesers in Joseph Roths *Die Flucht ohne Ende: Ein Bericht*" ["Unreliable Narrative as a Provocation of the Reader in Joseph Roth's *Flight without End: A Report*"]. *Modern Austrian Literature* 23.4 (2010): 23–40. *Humanities International Complete,* http://eds.b.ebscohost.com/eds/pdfviewer/pdfviewer?vid=3&sid=98b420d1-cd48-4b4c-a097-3890fabfdf52%40sessionmgr120. Accessed 5 October 2014.

Glatzer, Nahum. "Introduction: A Study of Job." *The Dimensions of Job.* Ed. Nahum Glatzer. New York: Schocken, 1969. 1–48.

Göggel, Emil. *Lektürehilfen Joseph Roth "Hiob"* [*Reading Guide to Joseph Roth's Job*]. Stuttgart: Klett, 1993.

Goldstein, Moritz. "Deutsch-jüdischer Parnass" ["German-Jewish Parnassus"]. *Der Kunstwart* [*The Art Attendant*] 25.2 (1912): 281–94.

Gordimer, Nadine. "Das Labyrinth des Reiches und des Exils" ["The Labyrinth of the Empire and of the Exile"]. Keel and Kampa 279–98.

Habermas, Jürgen. *Philosophical-Political Profiles.* Trans. Frederick G. Lawrence. Cambridge: MIT P, 1983.

Hackert, Fritz. *Kulturpessimismus und Erzählform: Studien zu Joseph Roths Leben und Werk* [*Kulturpessimismus and Narrative Form: Studies on Joseph Roth's Life and Work*]. Bern: Herbert Lang, 1967.

Hacohen, Malachi Haim. "Dilemmas of Cosmopolitanism: Karl Popper, Jewish Identity, and 'Central European Culture.'" *Journal of Modern History* 71.1 (March 1999): 105–49.

Halldén, Eleonora. "Das Phänomen Österreich im Leben und Werk Joseph Roths" ["The Austria-Phenomenon in Joseph Roth's Life and Work"]. *Literatur und Kritik* 104 (1976): 226–38.

Hammer, Almuth. *Erwählung erinnern: Literatur als Medium jüdischen Selbstverständnisses; Mit Fallstudien zu Else Lasker-Schüler und Joseph Roth* [*Remembering Divine Election: Literature as a Medium of Jewish Self-Identity; With Case Studies on Else Lasker-Schüler and Joseph Roth*]. Göttingen: Vandenhoeck & Ruprecht, 2004.

Hartmann, Telse. *Kultur und Identität: Szenarien der Deplatzierung im Werk Joseph Roths* [*Culture and Identity: Scenarios of Displacement in Joseph Roth's Work*]. Tübingen: A. Francke, 2006.

Hartung, Harald. "Ein epischer Gottesbeweis: *Hiob*" ["An Epic Teleological Argument: *Job*"]. Keel and Kampa 424–31.

Heath, John. "The Legacy of the Baroque in the Novels of Joseph Roth." *Forum for Modern Language Studies* 40.3 (July 2004): 329–38. *EJC*, https://journals.ohiolink.edu/pg_99?208867865077491::NO::P99_ENTITY_ID,P99_ENTITY_TYPE:19916756,MAIN_FILE&cs=3Nfc4WXy7GW1IbwkqLHCnj_xQMG-4PbqI7oFQEjkacKSyooh5LdaeBYtzasnnuQ6GmcnOOqehHkz7LFZi-7oyK7A. Accessed 2 February 2015.

Heimerl, Theresia. "'Oberst Nikolaus Tarabas, ein Gast auf dieser Erde': Religiöse Themen und Motive in Joseph Roths Tarabas" ["'Colonel Nikolaus Tarabas, a Guest on this Earth': Religious Themes and Motifs in Joseph Roth's *Tarabas*"]. Lughofer, *Im Prisma* 273–85.

Heizmann, Jürgen. *Joseph Roth und die Ästhetik der Neuen Sachlichkeit* [*Joseph Roth and the Aesthetics of New Objectivity*]. Heidelberg: Mattes, 1990.

———. "Mythen und Masken: Figuren- und Wirklichkeitsgestaltung bei Joseph Roth" ["Myths and Masks: The Composition of Characters and Reality in Joseph Roth's Work"]. Amthor and Brittnacher 185–226.

Heller, Agnes. *A Philosophy of History in Fragments.* Oxford: Blackwell, 1993.

Henze, Volker. *Jüdischer Kulturpessimismus und das Bild des Alten Österreich im Werk Stefan Zweigs und Joseph Roths* [*Jewish Kulturpessimismus and the Image of Habsburg Austria in the Work of Stefan Zweig and Joseph Roth*]. Heidelberg: Carl Winter Universitätsverlag, 1988.

Heuberger, Rachel, and Helga Krohn. *Hinaus aus dem Ghetto . . . Juden in Frankfurt am Main 1800–1950* [*Out of the Ghetto . . . Jews in Frankfurt am Main 1800–1950*]. Frankfurt/Main: Fischer, 1988.

Higham, John. "Beyond Consensus: The Historian as Moral Critic." *American Historical Review* 67 (1962): 609–25.

Hofmann, Paul. *The Viennese: Splendor, Twilight, and Exile.* New York: Doubleday, 1988.

Horch, Hans Otto. "'Im Grunde ist er sehr jüdisch geblieben . . .': Zum Verhältnis von 'Katholizismus' und Judentum bei Joseph Roth" ["'At Bottom, He Remained Very Jewish . . . :' On the Relationship between Catholicism and Judaism in Joseph Roth's Work"]. *Deutsch-jüdische Exil- und Emigrationsliteratur im 20. Jahrhundert* [*German-Jewish Exile and Emigration Literature in the 20th Century*]. Ed. Itta Shedletzky and Hans Otto Horch, Tübingen: Niemeyer, 1993. 205–35.

Horkheimer, Max, and Theodor W. Adorno. *Dialectic of Enlightenment.* Trans. John Cumming. New York: Continuum, 2002.

Horrocks, David. "The Construction of Eastern Jewry in Joseph Roth's *Juden auf Wanderschaft*." *Ghetto Writing: Traditional and Eastern Jewry in German-Jewish Literature from Heine to Hilsenrath.* Ed. Anne Fuchs and Florian Krobb. Columbia, SC: Camden, 1999. 126–39.

———."The Representation of Jews and of Anti-Semitism in Joseph Roth's Early Journalism." *German Life and Letters* 58.2 (April 2005): 141–54. *Wiley Online Library,* doi: 10.1111/j.0016-8777.2005.00310.x. Accessed 29 September 2015.

Horváth, Ödön von. *Geschichten aus dem Wiener Wald: Volksstück in drei Teilen* [*Tales from the Vienna Woods: Folk Play in Three Parts*]. Frankfurt/Main: Suhrkamp, 2001.

Howes, Geoffrey C. "Joseph Roth's *Kapuzinergruft* as a Document of 1938." *Austrian Writers and the Anschluss: Understanding the Past—Overcoming the Past.* Ed. Donald Daviau. Riverside, CA: Ariadne, 1991. 156–67.

Hughes, Jon. *Facing Modernity: Fragmentation, Culture, and Identity in Joseph Roth's Writing in the 1920s.* London: Maney Pub. for the Modern Humanities Research Association and the Institute of Germanic and Romance Studies, University of London, 2006.

———."Violence, Masculinity and Self: Killing in Joseph Roth's 1920s Fiction." *German Life and Letters* 53.2 (April 2000): 216–30. *EJC*, https://journals.ohiolink.edu/pg_99?112380143213460::NO::P99_ENTITY_ID,P99_ENTITY_TYPE:27046036,MAIN_FILE&cs=3ioELu3yAHJ0nQKwUgPT30NASssWd5MlDaPT-XoroFUQwFEC-HKZjigoVkS1HwHz4uq2nEUZFKtUhv5Vmyy9F0w. Accessed 6 October 2015.

Hüppauf, Bernd. "Joseph Roth: *Hiob;* Der Mythos des Skeptikers" ["Joseph Roth: *Job;* The Myth of the Skeptic"]. Kraske 25–51.

Idel, Moshe. *Old Worlds, New Mirrors: On Jewish Mysticism and Twentieth-Century Thought.* Philadelphia: U of Pennsylvania P, 2010.

———. "Rosenzweig and the Kabbalah." Mendes-Flohr, *The Philosophy of Franz Rosenzweig* 162–71.

Jabłkowska, Joanna. "Ein Grab der armen Leute: *Hotel Savoy*—Parabel für das Ende des alten Europa oder Łódź-Roman?" ["A Grave of the Poor: *Hotel Savoy*—Parable for the End of Old Europe or Łódź-Novel?"]. Amthor and Brittnacher 103–16.

Jansen, Peter Wilhelm. "Der autofiktive Ezähler—Roman und Existenz bei Joseph Roth" ["The Autofictional Narrator—Novel and Existence in Joseph Roth's Work"]. Bronsen, *Joseph Roth und die Tradition* [*Joseph Roth and Tradition*] 364–73.

———."In die falsche Revolution geraten" ["Getting into the Wrong Revolution"]. *Frankfurter Hefte* [*Frankfurt Notebooks*] 21.8 (1966): 579–81.

———. "Weltbezug und Erzählhaltung: Eine Untersuchung zum Erzählwerk und zur dichterischen Existenz Joseph Roths" ["Worldview and Narrative Mind-Set: An Investigation of Joseph Roth's Literary Existence and Fictional Work"]. Diss., Universität Freiburg, 1958.

Juergens, Thorsten. *Gesellschaftskritische Aspekte in Joseph Roths Romanen* [*Socio-Critical Aspects in Joseph Roth's Novels*]. Diss., Universität Leiden, 1977. Leiden: Universitaire Pers., 1977.

Kantorowicz, Ernst. *The King's Two Bodies.* Princeton: Princeton UP, 1957.

Keel, Daniel, and Daniel Kampa, eds. *Joseph Roth: Leben und Werk* [*Joseph Roth: Life and Work*]. Zürich: Diogenes, 2010.

Kessler, Michael, and Fritz Hackert, eds. *Joseph Roth: Interpretation, Rezeption, Kritik* [*Joseph Roth: Interpretation, Reception, Criticism*]. Tübingen: Stauffenburg, 1990.

Kesten, Hermann. *Meine Freunde, die Poeten* [*My Friends, the Poets*]. Frankfurt/Main: Fischer, 1970.

Kiefer, Sebastian. *Braver Junge—gefüllt mit Gift: Joseph Roth und die Ambivalenz* [*Good Boy—Filled with Venom: Joseph Roth and the Ambivalence*]. Stuttgart: J. B. Metzler, 2001.

Kilcher, Andreas B. "Die Kalte Ordnung und der Eros des Erzählens: Joseph Roths 'exotische Juden'" ["The New Objectivity and the Eros of Storytelling: Joseph Roth's 'Exotic Jews'"]. *Deutsche Vierteljahrsschrift für Literaturwissenschaft und Geistesgeschichte* [*German Quarterly for Literary Studies and Intellectual History*] 89.2 (June 2015): 265–93. Springer, doi:10.1007/BF03375798.

Kliche, Dieter. "Die Paradoxien des Joseph Roth" ["Joseph Roth's Paradoxes"]. Afterword. *Die Kapuzinergruft: Romane aus der Exilzeit* [*The Emperor's Tomb: Novels from the Time of Exile*], by Joseph Roth. Berlin: Aufbau, 1990. 777–809.

Koester, Rudolf. *Joseph Roth*. Berlin: Colloquium Verlag, 1982.

Konrád, György. *The Invisible Voice: Meditations on Jewish Themes*. Trans. Peter Reich. San Diego: Harcourt, 1999.

Koselleck, Reinhart. *Kritik und Krise: Eine Studie zur Pathogenese der bürgerlichen Welt* [*Critique and Crisis; A Study on the Pathogenesis of the Modern Society*]. Frankfurt/Main: Suhrkamp, 1973.

Kraske, Bernd M., ed. *Joseph Roth: Werk und Wirkung* [*Joseph Roth: His Work and Its Impact*]. Bonn: Bouvier, 1988.

Kraus, Karl. *Die letzten Tage der Menschheit: Tragödie in fünf Akten mit Vorspiel und Epilog* [*The Last Days of Mankind: A Tragedy in Five Acts with Prologue and Epilogue*]. München: Kösel, 1957.

Kundera, Milan. "The Tragedy of Central Europe." *New York Review of Books* 31.7 (26 April 1984): 33–38.

Kurer, Alfred. *Joseph Roths 'Radetzkymarsch': Interpretation; Ein Beitrag zum Phänomen des Spätzeitlichen in der österreichischen Literatur* [*Joseph Roth's Radetzky March: Interpretation; A Contribution to the Phenomenon of Recentness in the Austrian Literature*]. Diss., Universität Zürich, 1968. Zürich: Juris, 1968.

Landauer, Gustav. "Ostjuden und Deutsches Reich" ["Eastern Jews and the German Empire"]. *Der Jude* [*The Jew*] 7 (1916): 433–39.

———. *Werkausgabe: Dichter, Ketzer, Außenseiter* [*Edition of Works: Poet, Heretic, Outsider*]. Ed. Gert Mattenklott and Hanna Delf. Vol. 3. Berlin: Akademie Verlag, 1997.

Lazaroms, Ilse Josepha. "The Double Bind of Self-Narration: Joseph Roth, Jewish Identity and the Undercurrents of European Modernity." *European Review of History* 19.5 (2012): 693–710.

———. *The Grace of Misery: Joseph Roth and the Politics of Exile, 1919–1939*. Leiden: Brill, 2013.

Le Rider, Jacques. "Arbeit am Habsburgischen Mythos: Joseph Roth und Robert Musil im Vergleich" ["Working on the Habsburg Myth: A Comparison between Joseph Roth and Robert Musil"]. Amthor and Brittnacher 19–29.

———. *Modernity and Crises of Identity: Culture and Society in Fin-de-Siècle Vienna*. Trans. Rosemary Morris. New York: Continuum, 1993.

Lessing, Theodor. *Der jüdische Selbsthaß* [*The Jewish Self-Hatred*]. Berlin: Matthes & Seitz, 2004.

Lichtblau, Albert. "Antisemitismus 1900–1938: Phasen, Wahrnehmung und Akkulturationseffekte" ["Antisemitism 1900–1938: Phases, Perception, and Acculturation Effects"]. *Wien und die jüdische Erfahrung 1900–1938: Akkulturation—Antisemitismus-Zionismus* [*Vienna and the Jewish Experience 1900–1938: Acculturation—Antisemitism—Zionism*]. Ed. Frank Stern and Barbara Eichinger. Wien: Böhlau, 2009. 39–58. *Böhlau Verlag*, http://www.boehlau-verlag.com/download/160625/978-3-205-78317-6_OpenAccess.pdf. Accessed 21 August 2015.

Lichtmann, Tamás. "Schein und Wirklichkeit: Illusionen und Erfahrungen im Werk Joseph Roths" ["Appearance and Reality: Illusions and Experiences in Joseph Roth's Work"]. "*Sein und Schein—Traum und Wirklichkeit*": *Zur Poetik österreichischer Schriftsteller/innen im 20. Jahrhundert* ["*Existence and Appearance—Dream and Reality*": *On the Poetics of Austrian Writers in the 20th Century*]. Ed. Herbert Arlt and Manfred Diersch. Frankfurt/Main: Peter Lang, 1994. 40–51.

Liebersohn, Harry. *Fate and Utopia in German Sociology, 1870–1923*. Cambridge: MIT P, 1988.

Linden, Hermann. *Joseph Roth: Leben und Werk; Ein Gedächtnisbuch* [*Joseph Roth: Life and Work; A Memoir*]. Köln: Kiepenheuer, 1949.

———."Tage mit Joseph Roth" ["Days with Joseph Roth"]. Keel and Kampa 95–103.

Loader, Colin. *The Intellectual Development of Karl Mannheim: Culture, Politics, and Planning*. Cambridge: Cambridge UP, 1985.

Löwenthal, Leo. *An Unmastered Past: The Autobiographical Reflections of Leo Löwenthal*. Ed. Martin Jay. Berkeley: U of California P, 1987.

———. *In steter Freundschaft: Leo Löwenthal-Siegfried Kracauer; Briefwechsel 1921–1966* [*In Perpetual Friendship: Leo Löwenthal-Siegfried Kracauer; Correspondence 1921–1966*]. Ed. Peter-Erwin Jansen and Christian Schmidt. Lüneburg: zu Klampen, 2003.

Löwy, Michael. *Redemption and Utopia: Jewish Libertarian Thought in Central Europe*. Trans. Hope Heaney. Stanford: Stanford UP, 1992.

Lughofer, Johann G. "Joseph Roth—Ein Schriftsteller der Hybridität oder der Reinheit von Kulturen?" ["Joseph Roth—A Writer of the Hybridity or the Purity of Cultures?"]. Lughofer and Zalaznik 79–86.

———, ed. *Im Prisma: Joseph Roths Romane* [*In the Prism: Joseph Roth's Novels*]. Wien: Edition Art Science, 2009.

Lughofer, Johann G., and Mira Miladinović Zalaznik, eds. *Joseph Roth: Europäisch-jüdischer Schriftsteller und österreichischer Universalist* [*Joseph Roth: European-Jewish Writer and Austrian Universalist*]. Berlin: De Gruyter, 2011. *EBSCOHost*, http://eds.a.ebscohost.com/eds/detail/detail?vid=0&sid=f-418cb59-e033-4fd4-8b09-f490d510fa10%40sessionmgr4008&bdata=JnNpd-GU9ZWRzLWxpdmUmc2NvcGU9c2l0ZQ%3d%3d#AN=398970&db=nlebk. Accessed July 2015.

Lukács, Georg. *The Historical Novel.* Trans. Hannah Mitchell and Stanley Mitchell. Atlantic Highlands: Humanities, 1978.

———. "Radetzkymarsch." *Kulturpessimismus und Erzählform: Studien zu Joseph Roths Leben und Werk* [*Kulturpessimismus and Narrative Form: Studies on Joseph Roth's Life and Work*], by Fritz Hackert. Bern: Hebert Lang, 1967. 147–52.

Magnou, Jacqueline. "Joseph Roth et la judéité" ["Joseph Roth and Judaism"]. *Religion(s) et littérature en Autriche au xxe siècle* [*Religions and Literature in Austria in the 20th Century*]. Ed. Arlette Camions and Jacques Lajarrige. Bern: Peter Lang, 1997. 47–63.

Magris, Caludio. *Der Habsburgische Mythos in der österreichischen Literatur* [*The Habsburg Myth in the Austrian Literature*]. Trans. Madeline von Pasztory. Salzburg: Otto Müller, 1966.

———. *Weit von wo: Verlorene Welt des Ostjudentums* [*Away from Where: The Lost World of the East European Jews*]. Trans. Jutta Prasse. Wien: Europaverlag, 1971.

Maier, Thomas. "Auf der Suche nach dem verlorenen Maß: Beim Lesen von Joseph Roths Erzählung 'Das falsche Gewicht'" ["On the Search for the Lost Measure: Reading Joseph Roth's Story *Weights and Measures*"]. *Literatur für Leser* 22.1 (1999): 28–41.

Mannheim, Karl. *Ideology and Utopia.* Trans. Louis Wirth and Edward Shils. New York: Harcourt, 1936.

Marchand, Wolf R. *Joseph Roth und völkisch-nationalistische Wertbegriffe* [*Joseph Roth and Ethnic-Nationalist Value Concepts*]. Bonn: Bouvier Herbert Grundmann, 1974.

Mathew, Celine. *Ambivalence and Irony in the Works of Joseph Roth.* Frankfurt/Main: Peter Lang, 1984.

May, Markus. "Joseph Roth und die Zeichen" ["Joseph Roth and the Signs"]. Amthor and Brittnacher 241–56.

Mehrens, Dietmar. *Vom göttlichen Auftrag der Literatur: Die Romane Joseph Roths; Ein Kommentar* [*On the Divine Mandate of Literature: Joseph Roth's Novels; A Commentary*]. Hamburg: Libri BoD, 2000.

Mendes-Flohr, Paul. *Divided Passions: Jewish Intellectuals and the Experience of Modernity.* Detroit: Wayne State UP, 1991.

———. *German Jews: A Dual Identity*. New Haven, CT: Yale UP, 1999. *EBSCOHost*, http://eds.b.ebscohost.com/eds/ebookviewer/ebook/bmxlYmtfXzUzMDE2X19BTg2?sid=65324018-e2b9-4fcc-adf0-b39026010eba@sessionmgr102&vid=0&format=EB&rid=1. Accessed 14 December 2015.

———, ed. *The Philosophy of Franz Rosenzweig*. Hanover: U P of New England, 1988.

———. "'To Brush History against the Grain': The Eschatology of the Frankfurt School and Ernst Bloch." *Journal of the American Academy of Religion* 51.4 (1983): 631–50. *Jstor*, www.jstor.org/stable/1462585.

Miron, Dan. *The Image of the Shtetl and Other Studies of Modern Jewish Literary Imagination*. Syracuse: Syracuse UP, 2000.

Molnar, Thomas. *Utopia: The Perennial Heresy*. New York: Sheed and Ward, 1967.

Morgenstern, Soma. *Joseph Roths Flucht und Ende: Erinnerungen* [*Joseph Roth's Flight and End: Memoirs*]. Lüneburg: zu Klampen, 1994.

Mosès, Stéphane. *The Angel of History: Rosenzweig, Benjamin, Scholem*. Stanford: Stanford UP, 2009.

Mosse, George. *German Jews beyond Judaism*. Cincinnati: Hebrew Union College Press, 1997.

Müller, Klaus-Detlef. "Ein Roman aus der Perspektive des Journalisten: Joseph Roths *Das Spinnennetz*" ["A Novel from the Perspective of the Journalist: Joseph Roth's *The Spider's Web*"]. Lughofer and Zalaznik 207–14.

Müller-Funk, Wolfgang. "Der Antichrist: Joseph Roths Dämonologie der Moderne" ["*The Antichrist:* Joseph Roth's Demonology of Modernity"]. *Literatur und Kritik* [*Literature and Criticism*] 243–244 (April–May 1990): 115–23.

———. *Joseph Roth: Besichtigungen eines Werkes* [*Joseph Roth: Surveys of a Work*]. Wien: Sonderzahl, 2012.

———. "Nach der 1001: Nacht; Überlegungen zur narrativen Logik in Joseph Roths Roman 'Die Geschichte von der 1002. Nacht'" ["After the 1001st Night: Reflections on the Narrative Logic in Joseph Roth's Novel *The Tale of the 1002nd Night*"]. Eicher 119–38.

Münster, Arno. *Utopie, Messianismus und Apokalypse im Frühwerk von Ernst Bloch* [*Utopia, Messianism, and Apocalypse in Ernst Bloch's Early Work*]. Frankfurt/Main: Suhrkamp, 1982.

Musil, Robert. *The Man without Qualities*. Trans. Eithne Wilkins and Ernst Kaiser. New York: Capricorn, 1953.

Niethammer, Lutz. *Posthistoire*. Trans. Patrick Camiller. London: Verso, 1994.

Nietzsche, Friedrich. *The Will to Power*. Trans. Walter Kaufmann and R. J. Hollingdale. New York: Random, 1967.

Nüchtern, Michael, and Ralf Stieber, eds. *"Die Schwere des Glücks und die Größe der Wunder": Joseph Roth und seine Welt* [*"The Burden of Happiness and the Greatness of the Miracle": Joseph Roth and His World*]. Karlsruhe: Verlag Evangelischer Presseverband für Baden, 1994.

Nürnberger, Helmuth. *Joseph Roth: Mit Selbstzeugnissen und Bilddokumenten* [*Joseph Roth: With Personal Testimonials and Visual Documentation*]. 5th ed. Reinbek bei Hamburg: Rowohlt, 1990.

Ochse, Katharina. *Joseph Roths Auseinandersetzung mit dem Antisemitismus* [*Joseph Roth's Contention with Antisemitism*]. Würzburg: Königshausen & Neumann, 1999.

Oei, Bernd. *Joseph Roth: Der verbrannte Himmel; Metaphysik des Zweifels* [*Joseph Roth: The Scorched Sky; A Metaphysics of Doubting*]. Berlin: Lit, 2012.

Oişteanu, Andrei. *Imaginea evreului în cultura română* [*The Image of the Jew in the Romanian Culture*]. Bucuresti: Humanitas, 2001.

Oppenheim, Michael D. *Encounters of Consequence: Jewish Philosophy in the Twentieth Century and Beyond*. Boston: Academic Studies Press, 2009. *EBSCOhost*, http://eds.b.ebscohost.com/eds/ebookviewer/ebook/bmxlYmtfXzQ3OTE5Ml9fQU41?sid=a682ebeb-391c-4fe4-8a24-eb1ed9f18e92@sessionmgr101&vid=0&format=EB&rid=1. Accessed 18 August 2017.

Ortega y Gasset, José. *The Revolt of the Masses*. New York: Norton, 1993.

Pauli, Klaus. *Joseph Roth: "Die Kapuzinergruft" und "Der stumme Prophet": Untersuchungen zu zwei zeitgeschichtlichen Portraitromanen* [*Joseph Roth: The Emperor's Tomb and The Silent Prophet; Investigations on Two Contemporary Historical Portrait Novels*]. Frankfurt/Main: Peter Lang, 1985.

Pfabigan, Alfred. "Der 'Antichrist' als Herr der 'Kalten Ordnung'? Joseph Roths Ambivalenz gegenüber der 'Neuen Sachlichkeit'" ["The 'Antichrist' as Lord of the 'New Objectivity'? Joseph Roth's Ambivalence toward the New Objectivity"]. *Image, Reproduction, Texte/Bild, Abbild, Text*. Ed. Françoise Lartillot and Alfred Pfabigan. Bern: Peter Lang, 2012. 86–106. *EBSCOHost*. Accessed 22 October 2015.

Philippoff, Eva. *Alfred Polgar, ein moralischer Chronist seiner Zeit* [*Alfred Polgar, a Moral Chronicler of His Time*]. München: Minerva, 1980.

Powell, Ward H. "The Problem of Primitivism in the Novels of Joseph Roth." Diss., University of Colorado, 1956.

Rabinbach, Anson. *In the Shadow of Catastrophe: German Intellectuals between Apocalypse and Enlightenment*. Berkeley: U of California P, 1997. *EBSCOHost*, http://eds.b.ebscohost.com/eds/ebookviewer/ebook/bmxlYmtfXzIxMzE4X19BTg2?sid=3a138802-8906-4a14-8e98-acce743455dd@sessionmgr104&vid=7&format=EB&rid=25. Accessed 18 August 2017.

Raffel, Eva. *Vertraute Fremde: Das östliche Judentum im Werk von Joseph Roth und Arnold Zweig* [*Familiar Strangers: Eastern Jews in the Work of Joseph Roth and Arnold Zweig*]. Tübingen: Gunter Narr, 2002.

Reich-Ranicki, Marcel. "Die besten Romane von Joseph Roth" ["Joseph Roth's Best Novels"]. *Frankfurter Allgemeine Sonntagszeitung* [*Frankfurt General Sunday Paper*], 1 July 2005, 22.

———. *Nachprüfung: Aufsätze über deutsche Schriftsteller von gestern* [*Reconsideration: Articles on Yesterday's German Writers*]. München: R. Piper & Co., 1977.

Robertson, Ritchie. "Roth's *Hiob* and the Traditions of Ghetto Fiction." Chambers 185–200.

Rosenfeld, Sidney. "Joseph Roths *Hiob*: Glaube und Heimat im Bild des Raumes" ["Joseph Roth's *Job*: Faith and Homeland in the Representation of Space"]. *Journal of English and Germanic Philology* 66.4 (1967): 489–500.

———. *Understanding Joseph Roth*. Columbia: U of South Carolina P, 2001.

Rosenzweig, Franz. *The Star of Redemption*. Trans. William W. Hallo. New York: Holt, Rinehart and Winston, 1970.

———. *Zeit ists . . . Gedanken über das jüdische Bildungsproblem des Augenblicks* [*It's Time . . . Thoughts on the Current Jewish Education Problem*]. Berlin: Verlag der Neuen Jüdischen Monatshefte, 1918.

Roth, Joseph. *The Antichrist*. Trans. Richard Panchyk. London: Peter Owen, 2010.

———. *Collected Shorter Fiction of Joseph Roth*. Trans. Michael Hofmann. London: Granta, 2001.

———. *Confession of a Murderer: Told in One Night*. Trans. Desmond I. Vesey. London: Chatto & Windus, 1985.

———. *The Emperor's Tomb*. Trans. John Hoare, London: Hogarth, 1984.

———. *Flight without End*. Trans. David le Vay. London: Dent, 1984.

———. *Hotel Savoy*. Trans. John Hoare. Woodstock: Overlook, 1986.

———. *The Hotel Years*. Trans. Michael Hofmann. New York: New Directions Paperbook, 2015.

———. *The Hundred Days*. Trans. Richard Panchyk. New York: New Directions, 2011.

———. *Job: The Story of a Simple Man*. Trans. Dorothy Thompson. London: Hogarth, 1983.

———. *Joseph Roth: A Life in Letters*. Trans. Michael Hofmann. New York: Norton, 2012.

———. *Der Neue Tag: Unbekannte politische Arbeiten 1919 bis 1927, Wien, Berlin, Moskau* [*The New Day: Unknown Political Works 1919 to 1927, Vienna, Berlin, Moscow*]. Ed. Ingeborg Sültemeyer. Köln: Kiepenheuer & Witsch, 1970.

———. *On the End of the World*. Trans. Will Stone. London: Hesperus, 2013.

———. *Perlefter: The Story of a Bourgeois.* Trans. Richard Panchyk. London: Peter Owen, 2013.

———. *The Radetzky March.* Trans. Joachim Neugroschel. Woodstock: Overlook, 1995.

———. *The Rebellion.* Trans. Michael Hofmann. London: Granta, 1999.

———. *Report from a Parisian Paradise: Essays from France 1925–1939.* Trans. Michael Hofmann. New York: Norton, 2004.

———. *Right and Left.* Trans. Michael Hofmann. Woodstock: Overlook, 1992.

———. *The Silent Prophet.* Trans. David Le Vay. London: Peter Owen, 1979.

———. *The Spider's Web.* Trans. John Hoare. Woodstock: Overlook, 1989.

———. *The Tale of the 1002nd Night.* Trans. Michael Hoffmann. New York: St. Martin's, 1998.

———. *Tarabas: A Guest on the Earth.* Trans. Winifred Katzin. Woodstock: Overlook, 2002.

———. *Three Novellas.* Trans. John Hoare. Woodstock: Overlook, 2003.

———. *The Wandering Jews.* Trans. Michael Hofmann. New York: Norton, 2001.

———. *Weights and Measures.* Trans. David Le Vay. London: Peter Owen, 1982.

———. *Werke* [*Works*]. Ed. Klaus Westermann. 6 vols. Köln: Kiepenheuer & Witsch, 1989.

———. *What I Saw: Reports from Berlin 1920–1933.* Trans. Michael Hofmann. New York: Norton, 2004.

———. *Zipper and His Father.* Trans. John Hoare. Woodstock: Overlook, 1989.

Rupnik, Jacques. "Central Europe or Mitteleuropa?" *Daedalus* 119.1 (1990): 249–78. *JSTOR*, http://www.jstor.org/stable/20025291. Accessed 20 June 2012.

Rüsen, Jörn. *Kann gestern besser werden? Essays zum Bedenken der Geschichte* [*Can Yesterday Get Better? Essays on the Consideration of History*]. Berlin: Kadmos, 2003.

Ruyer, Raymond. *L'Utopie et les Utopies* [*Utopia and the Utopists*]. Paris : Presses Universitaires de France, 1950.

Sanger, Curt. "The Decadence of Austrian Society in the Novels of Joseph Roth." Diss., University of Cincinnati, 1966.

Saur, Pamela S. "Joseph Roth's Multicultural Provincialism." *Germanic Notes and Reviews* 35.1 (Spring 2004): 10–24.

Scheible, Hartmut. "Joseph Roths Flucht aus der Geschichte" ["Joseph Roth's Flight from History"]. *Text + Kritik* [*Text + Criticism*], ed. Heinz Ludwig Arnold. München: Richard Boorberg Verlag, 1974. 55–66.

———. *Joseph Roth: Mit einem Essay über Gustave Flaubert* [*Joseph Roth: With an Essay on Gustave Flaubert*]. Stuttgart: W. Kohlhammer, 1971.

Scheichl, Sigurd P. "*Juden auf Wanderschaft*—2009 neu gelesen" ["*Wandering Jews*—Reread in 2009"]. Lughofer and Zalaznik 11–21.

Schlosser, Jan T. "Indentitätsproblematik und Gesellschaftskritik: Zum Solferino-Kapitel in Joseph Roths *Radetzkymarsch*" ["The Identity Problematics and the Critique of Society: On the Soleferino-Chapter in Joseph Roth's *Radetzky March*"]. *Orbis Litterarum* 60.3 (2005): 183–201.

Schlüter, Bastian. "Der Kaiser und das Meer: Ereignis und Dauer im Spätwerk Joseph Roths" ["The Emperor and the Sea: Event and Duration in Joseph Roth's Late Work"]. Amthor and Brittnacher 41–54.

Schmidjell, Christine. *Erläuterungen und Dokumente: Joseph Roth; Hiob* [*Commentaries and Documents: Joseph Roth; Job*]. Stuttgart: Philipp Reclam jun., 2004.

Schmidt-Dengler, Wendelin. "Auf der Wanderschaft: Das Frühwerk Joseph Roths in den Literaturgeschichten" ["On the Move: Joseph Roth's Early Work in the Literary Histories"]. Chambers 15–34.

Schnitzler, Arthur. *Der Weg ins Freie* [*The Road into the Open*]. Berlin: S. Fischer, 1932.

Scholem, Gershom. *The Messianic Idea in Judaism and Other Essays on Jewish Spirituality*. New York: Schocken Books, 1971.

———, ed. *Walter Benjamin/Gershom Scholem Briefwechsel 1933–1940* [*Walter Benjamin/Gershom Scholem Correspondence 1933–1940*]. Frankfurt/Main: Suhrkamp, 1980.

Schorske, Carl E. *Fin-de-siècle Vienna: Politics and Culture*. New York: Vintage, 1981.

Schroeder, Irene. *Experimente des Erzählens: Joseph Roths frühe Prosa 1916–1925* [*Narrative Experiments: Joseph Roth's Early Prose 1916–1925*]. Bern: Peter Lang, 1998.

Schulte, Christoph. "Der Messias der Utopie: Elemente des Messianismus bei einigen modernen jüdischen Linksintellektuellen" ["The Messiah of Utopia: Messianic Elements in the Work of Several Modern Jewish Leftist Intellectuals"]. *Die Wehen des Messias: Zeitenwende in der jüdischen Geschichte* [*Messiah's Travails: A Turning Point in the Jewish History*]. Ed. Eveline Brugger and Martha Keil. Berlin: Philo, 2001.

Schulz, Bruno. *Sanatorium under the Sign of the Hour Glass*. Trans. Celina Wieniewska. New York: Walker, 1978.

Schweikert, Uwe. "'Der rote Joseph' Politik und Feuilleton beim frühen Joseph Roth (1919–1926)" ["'Red Joseph' Politics and Feuilleton in Joseph Roth's Early Works (1919–1926)"]. *Text + Kritik* [*Text + Criticism*]. Ed. Heinz Ludwig Arnold. München: Richard Boorberg Verlag, 1974. 40–55.

Schwienhorst-Schönberger, Ludger. "'Und er ruhte aus von der Schwere des Glücks': Joseph Roths *Hiob* vor dem Hintergrund seiner biblischen Vorbilder" ["'And He Rested from the Burden of His Happiness': Joseph Roth's *Job* against the Background of Its Biblical Models"]. Lughofer, *Im Prisma* 223–36.

Sebald, W. G. *Unheimliche Heimat: Essays zur österreichischen Literatur* [*Uncanny Homeland: Essays on Austrian Literature*]. Frankfurt/Main: Fischer Taschenbuch, 1995.

Shaked, Gershon. "Kulturangst und die Sehnsucht nach dem Tode: Joseph Roths 'Der Leviathan'—Die intertextuelle Mythisierung der Kleinstadtgeschichte" ["Fear of Civilization and the Longing for Death: Joseph Roth's 'Der Leviathan'—The Intertextual Mythicizing of Small Town History"]. Kessler and Hackert 279–98.

———. "Wie jüdisch ist ein jüdisch-deutscher Roman? Über Joseph Roths 'Hiob: Roman eines einfachen Mannes'" ["How Jewish Is a Jewish-German Novel? On Joseph Roth's *Job: The Story of a Simple Man*"]. *Bulletin des Leo Baeck Instituts* [*Bulletin of the Leo Baeck Institute*] 73 (1986): 3–12. *Archive.org*, https://archive.org/stream/bulletindesleoba03leob#page/n761/mode/1up. Accessed 2 March 2015.

Sholem Aleichem. *The Adventures of Menahem-Mendl*. Trans. Tamara Kahana. New York: G. P. Putnam's Sons, 1969.

———. *Adventures of Mottel, the Cantor's Son*. Trans. Tamara Kahana. New York: Collier Books, 1968.

Sieg, Werner. *Zwischen Anarchismus und Fiktion: Eine Untersuchung zum Werk von Joseph Roth* [*Between Anarchism and Fiction: An Investigation of Joseph Roth's Work*]. Bonn: Bouvier Herbert Grundmann, 1974.

Spencer, Malcolm. *In the Shadow of Empire: Austrian Experiences of Modernity in the Writings of Musil, Roth, and Bachmann*. Rochester, NY: Camden, 2008.

Sperber, Manès. *God's Water Carriers*. Trans. Joachim Neugroschel. New York: Holmes & Meier, 1987.

———. "Rebell oder Revolutionär? Zu dem nachgelassenen Roman von Joseph Roth" ["Rebel or Revolutionary? On Joseph Roth's Posthumous Novel"]. *Neues Forum* 13.154 (1966): 625–28.

Spieth, Alexander. *Politisch sehn, falsch sehn: Anmerkungen zu Joseph Roths Legitimismus* [*To See Politically Is to See Incorrectly: Observations on Joseph Roth's Legitimism*] Diss. Universität Tübingen, 2009. Tübingen: Universitätsbibliothek Publikationssystem, 2010. https://publikationen.uni-tuebingen.de/xmlui/handle/10900/46788. Accessed 18 June 2015.

Steierwald, Ulrike. *Leiden an der Geschichte: Zur Geschichtsauffassung der Moderne in den Texten Joseph Roths* [*To Suffer from History: On the Historical Conception of Modernity in Joseph Roth's Texts*]. Würzburg: Königshausen & Neumann, 1994.

Steiner, Carl. "Frankreichbild und Katholizismus bei Joseph Roth" ["The Image of France and Catholicism in Joseph Roth's Work"]. Kraske 89–100.

Steinmann, Esther. "'. . . ein Mann von Ehre, wenn auch ohne Adresse': Zum Ehrbegriff in Joseph Roths 'Legende vom heiligen Trinker'" ["'. . . A Man of Honor, Even If without an Address': On the Concept of Honor in Roth's 'Legend of the Holy Drinker'"]. Nüchtern and Stieber 54–65.

———. *Von der Würde des Unscheinbaren: Sinnerfahrung bei Joseph Roth* [*On the Grandeur of the Inconspicuous: The Experience of Meaning in Joseph Roth's Work*]. Tübingen: Max Niemeyer, 1984.

Stern, Fritz. *The Politics of Cultural Despair: A Study in the Rise of the Germanic Ideology*. New York: Doubleday, 1965.

Sternburg, Wilhelm von. *Joseph Roth: Eine Biographie* [*Joseph Roth: A Biography*]. Köln: Kiepenheuer & Witsch, 2009.

Stillmark, Alexander, ed. *Joseph Roth: Der Sieg über die Zeit; Londoner Symposium* [*Joseph Roth: The Victory over the Time; London Symposium*]. Stuttgart: Heinz, 1996.

———. "Die Literarische Beichte: Joseph Roth und Dostojewskij" ["The Literary Confession: Joseph Roth and Dostoyevsky"]. Stillmark 62–78.

Sültemeyer, Ingeborg. *Das Frühwerk Joseph Roths 1915–1926: Studien u. Texte* [*Joseph Roth's Early Work 1915–1926: Studies and Texts*]. Wien: Herder, 1976.

Timms, Edward. "Joseph Roths Antisemitismuskritik und die jüdische Identitätsproblematik" ["Joseph Roth's Critique of Antisemitism and the Jewish Identity Problematics"]. Stillmark 18–30.

Tonkin, Kati. "A Parable of Germany: History, Anti-Semitism, and Redemption in Joseph Roth's *Tarabas: Ein Gast auf dieser Erde*." *Journal of European Studies* 43.2 (2013): 154–66.

———. *Joseph Roth's March into History*. Rochester, NY: Camden House, 2008.

Tönnies, Ferdinand. *Community and Society*. Trans. Charles P. Loomis. East Lansing: Michigan State UP, 1957.

Treitler, Wolfgang. *Zwischen Hiob und Jeremia: Stefan Zweig und Joseph Roth am Ende der Welt* [*Between Job and Jeremiah: Stefan Zweig and Joseph Roth at the End of the World*]. Frankfurt/Main: Peter Lang, 2007.

Trommler, Frank. "Roth und die Neue Sachlichkeit" ["Roth and the New Objectivity"]. Bronsen, *Joseph Roth und die Tradition* [*Joseph Roth and Tradition*] 276–304.

Vocelka, Karl. "*Die Kapuzinergruft*: Ein Spiegel der Geschichte des frühen 20. Jahrhunderts?" ["*The Emperor's Tomb*: A Mirror of the History of the Early 20th Century?"] Lughofer, *Im Prisma* 427–37.

Vom Hofe, Gerhard. "'Reigen aus Mühsal' und 'Schwere des Glücks': Joseph Roths Hiob Deutung" ["'Ronde of Hardship' and 'Burden of Happiness': Joseph Roth's Interpretation of *Job*"]. Nüchtern and Stieber 66–91.

Von der Lühe, Irmela. "Zur Anthropologie der Kälte im Romanwerk Joseph Roths" ["On the Anthropology of Coldness in Joseph Roth's Novelistic Work"]. Amthor and Brittnacher 29–40.

Weber, Albrecht. *Joseph Roth: Das falsche Gewicht; Interpretation von Albrecht Weber* [*Joseph Roth: Weights and Measures; Interpretation by Albrecht Weber*]. München: Oldenbourg, 1968.

Weber, Max. *Economy and Society*. Trans. Ephraim Fischoff. 2 vols. Berkley: U of California P, 1978.

Weissenberger, Klaus. "Joseph Roths Präzisierung seiner dichterischen Intention im Exil" ["Joseph Roth's Clarification of His Literary Intentions in Exile"]. *Vier große galizische Erzähler im Exil: W. H. Katz, Soma Morgenstern, Manès Sperber und Joseph Roth* [*Four Great Galician Storytellers in Exile: W. H. Katz, Some Morgenstern, Manès Sperber und Joseph Roth*], Ed. Robert G. Weigel. Frankfurt/Main: Peter Lang, 2005. 53–73.

Weitzman, Erica. *Irony's Antics*. Evanston, IL: Northwest UP, 2015.

Werfel, Franz. *Twilight of a World*. Trans. H. T. Lowe-Porter. New York: Viking, 1937.

Westermann, Klaus. *Joseph Roth, Journalist: Eine Karriere 1915–1939* [*Joseph Roth, Journalist: A Career 1915–1939*]. Bonn: Bouvier, 1987.

Weymann, Ulrike. "Epische Objektivität: Zur Romanästhetik Joseph Roths in den 1920er Jahren" ["Epic Objectivity: On Joseph Roth's Aesthetics of the Novel in the 1920s"]. Amthor and Brittnacher 257–72.

Wild, Reiner. "Beobachtet oder gedichtet? Joseph Roths Roman *Die Flucht ohne Ende*" ["Observed or Composed? Joseph Roth's Novel *Flight without End*"]. *Neue Sachlichkeit im Roman: Neue Interpretationen zum Roman der Weimarer Republik* [*New Objectivity in the Novel: New Interpretations on the Weimar Republic Novel*]. Ed. Sabina Becker and Christoph Weiss. Stuttgart: Metzler, 1995.

Willerich-Tocha, Margarete. *Rezeption als Gedächtnis: Studien zur Wirkung Joseph Roths* [*Reception as Memory: Studies on the Impact of Joseph Roth's Work*]. Frankfurt/Main: Peter Lang, 1984.

Winiwarter, Verena, and Helmut Haberl. "Verlorene an der Peripherie: Eine humanökologische Betrachtung von Joseph Roths Roman *Das falsche Gewicht*" ["Lost in the Periphery: A Human-Ecological Consideration of Joseph Roth's Novel *Weights and Measures*"]. Lughofer, *Im Prisma* 388–99.

Wirthensohn, Andreas. "Die 'Skepsis der metaphysischen Weisheit' als Programm: Das Fragment *Der stumme Prophet* im Lichte von Joseph Roths Romanpoetik" ["The

'Skepticism of Metaphysical Wisdom' as Platform: The Fragment *The Silent Prophet* in the Light of Joseph Roth's Poetics of the Novel"]. *Deutsche Vierteljahrsschrift* [*German Quarterly*] 72.2 (1998): 268–315.

Wirtz, Irmgard. *Joseph Roth: Fiktionen des Faktischen* [*Joseph Roth: Fictions of the Factual*]. Berlin: Erich Schmidt, 1997.

Wittlin, Józef. "Erinnerungen an Joseph Roth" ["Memories of Joseph Roth"]. Bronsen, *Joseph Roth und die Tradition* [*Joseph Roth and Tradition*] 17–26.

Wolff, Larry. "Inventing Galicia: Messianic Josephinism and the Recasting of Partitioned Poland." *Slavic Review* 63.4 (Winter 2004): 818–40. *JSTOR*, doi:10.2307/1520422. Accessed 12 May 2015.

Wörschnig, Martha. "Die rückwärts gewandte Utopie" ["The Backward-Looking Utopia"]. *Text + Kritik* [*Text + Criticism*]. Ed. Heinz Ludwig Arnold. München: Richard Boorberg, 1974. 90–101.

Yerushalmi, Yosef H. *Zakhor: Jewish History and Jewish Memory*. Seattle: U of Washington P, 1996.

Zelewitz, Klaus. "Palmen von Friedhof: Roths 'Geschichte von der 1002. Nacht'" ["Palm Trees from the Cemetery: Roth's *Tale of the 1002nd Night*"]. Eicher 105–17.

———. "Zur Dialektik des insistierenden Dementis: Joseph Roth und der Zionismus" ["On the Dialectics of the Insistent Denial: Joseph Roth and Zionism"]. Lughofer and Zalaznik 39–44.

Zweig, Arnold. "Das Mittel des Geistes" ["The Agency of the Spirit"]. *Der Jude* [*The Jew*] 1 (1916): 52–53.

———. *Ritualmord in Ungarn: Jüdische Tragödie in fünf Aufzügen* [*Ritual Murder in Hungary: Jewish Tragedy in Five Acts*]. Berlin: Hyperionverlag, 1914.

Zweig, Stefan. *The World of Yesterday*. New York: Viking, 1943.

Index